D0880908

BARREL OF A GUN

BARREL OF A GUN

A WAR CORRESPONDENT'S MISSPENT MOMENTS IN COMBAT

AL J. VENTER

CASEMATE

Philadelphia & Newbury

Published in the United States of America in 2010 by
Casemate Publishers
1016 Warrior Road, Drexel Hill, PA 19026

and in the United Kingdom by
Casemate Publishers
17 Cheap Street, Newbury, Berkshire, RG14 5DD

ISBN 978-1-935149-25-5

Cataloging-in-publication data is available from the Library of
Congress and from the British Library (LCCN: 2010930564).

Printed and bound in the United States of America.

10 9 8 7 6 5 4 3 2 1

For a complete list of Casemate titles, please contact

United States of America:
Casemate Publishers
Telephone (610) 853-9131, Fax (610) 853-9146
E-mail: casemate@casematepublishing.com
Website: www.casematepublishing.com

United Kingdom:
Casemate Publishers
Telephone (01635) 231091, Fax (01635) 41619
E-mail: casemate-uk@casematepublishing.co.uk
Website: www.casematepublishing.co.uk

Mixed Sources
Product group from well-managed
forests and other controlled sources
www.fsc.org Cert no. SW-COC-002283
© 1996 Forest Stewardship Council
FSC

Contents

For the two women in my life, Madelon and Marilyn, without whom this book would never have happened.

I began my history at the very outbreak of the war,
in the belief that it was going to be a great war . . .
Thucydides

Anybody who believes that the pen is mightier than the sword
hasn't spent time in Somalia, or in Beirut in its bloody heyday.
Or even Baghdad or Afghanistan's Helmand Province in more
recent times.
Al J. Venter

The best of military professionals thrive on what is unambiguously termed 'the incontrovertible system of the seven Ps': Prior
Planning and Preparation Prevents Piss Poor Performance.
Andy McNab in *Seven Troop*

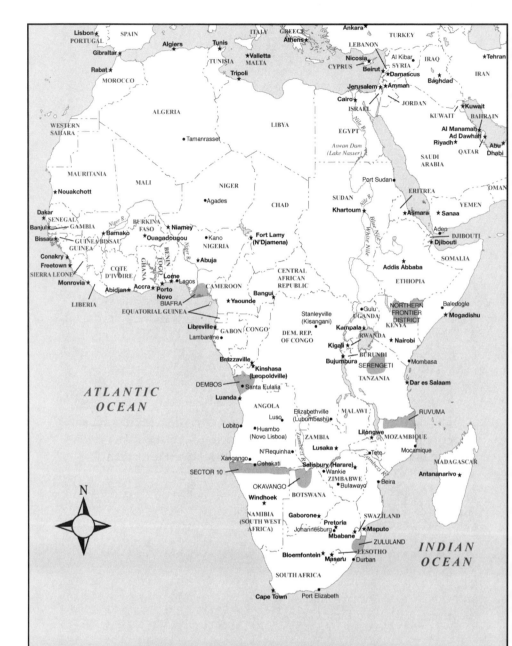

Africa & the Middle East

★	CAPITAL CITY
•	OTHER SETTLEMENTS
—·—·—	INTERNATIONAL BORDER
---------	DISPUTED BORDER

Parallel scale at 0° 0°

0   1000 Miles

0   1000 KM

The Dubious Life of a War Correspondent

It wasn't all guts and 'derring-do', but it was certainly fun while it lasted. As John Miller, one of the better-known Fleet Street foreign correspondents, was heard to comment from his almost permanent seat at the bar of the Royal Cape Golf Club, 'this is actually a hell of a lot better than working . . .'

DANGER IS A MARVELOUS TONIC once you accept your limitations; the trick, I imagine, is to know how far you can push the envelope. Unfortunately, the lady doesn't always smile and I've lost a few friends over the years, some of them professional news gatherers who were simply doing their job.

In my case, I'm only alive because I'm the original coward. When the shooting starts I get my head down. Damon Runyan had it about right when he said something about life being a case of six-to-five against . . .

Not so with some of my colleagues. The tally of those who went to what British journalist Jim Penrith likes to call 'that great scriptorium in the sky' includes Mohammed Amin who died brutally in an Ethiopian Airlines passenger jet that had been hijacked by zealots and came down in the sea alongside a tourist beach in the Indian Ocean Comoros Archipelago; Ken Oosterbroek, 'accidentally' shot by soldiers of the old apartheid regime in South Africa; George De'Ath, with whom I covered Israel, South Lebanon and Beirut and whose death also raised questions; and the incomparably romantic Nicholas Della Casa, who was killed in the aftermath of the First Gulf War by his Kurdish guide.

Let us not forget Danny Pearl and Michael Kelly, both more associates than friends, with whom I exchanged notes. The film *A Mighty Heart* – about Danny's murder in Karachi by Islamic fanatics – was a good rendition of what took place. It also serves to underscore some of the issues that correspondents face in these countries: different mindsets, different norms as well as seemingly irreconcilable cultures. More often than not these disparities come along with diverse home-grown values. Kipling reminded us of these alienable differences a long time ago when he wrote: 'East is east and west is west . . . '

Before Oosterbroek and Pearl there was Priya Ramrakha, another East African colleague with whom I shared a few events in West Africa's Biafra, and, a while before that, George Clay, who was shot in the head while accompanying one of 'Mad' Mike Hoare's mercenary columns in the approaches to Stanleyville in the Congo – known today as Kisangani. George and former British Army colonel, Hoare, that indomitable unconventional tactician who headed up 5 Commando in the Congo, became quite good friends. That happened despite the fact that this military maverick – who not long afterwards went on to launch an aborted attempt to unseat the legal government of the Seychelles – had a strong aversion to members of the Fourth Estate.

Years later, Miguel Gilmoreno arrived on the scene, in this case, Sierra Leone. He gave up everything as a Barcelona-trained lawyer to follow the action and worked as a cameraman for Associated Television News. He died in the same West African ambush as Kurt Schork, a former Rhodes Scholar who was at Oxford with Bill Clinton.

I am aware that the kind of work that journalists do today is often dangerous. It sometimes feels like death follows in your footsteps, or perhaps it could be said that we are following in the wake of the Reaper! Either way, you sometimes see things that you would afterwards not like to recall.

I know that I've been instrumental in the deaths of two young men, one of whom, a young Lebanese combatant by the name of Christian, has his tragic story detailed later in this book. Indirectly, the tally is three, if you count former British television personality Nicholas Della Casa, who would probably still be alive if I hadn't hired him early in his career as an apprentice sound man.

Tall, good-looking and insouciant, this young Englishman, who had served in the British Army, was the definitive man about town. As the saying goes, he could charm any bird out of a tree. One of the women who moved about in our circle, and with whom Nicholas briefly shared a relationship, made the comment that his eyes were set in the kind of face that drew attention when entering a room for the first time. They were alternately fierce and vacant, depending on what took his fancy.

Nick was a most intriguing character. After he'd gone, the circumstances surrounding his death acquired the kind of cult status that centres more on legends than on facts, not all of them substantiated. In an alluring way, Nick was also a bit of shit who, like Denys Finch Hatton of *Out of Africa*, allowed his derring-do reputation to make his fecklessness into something of an art form. One of his friends ended up in a Botswana prison because of a reckless action that might ultimately have had far more serious consequences.[1] There has even been a book written about him.

Distinctly of upper class British, Italian aristocratic and Argentinean stock, he was fluent in half a dozen languages. Small wonder, then, that it didn't take him long to come to the attention of the Secret Intelligence Service, and probably several other intelligence organizations as well.

Illegitimi non carborundum, he would comment with nonchalant indifference when things got tough, which was often enough when we worked in Africa: don't let the bastards get you down.

Nicholas' CV included a spell with a Special Forces unit about which he was always vague. He'd opted out and gone on to fight as a mercenary in the Rhodesian Army – again, it is said, under British auspices. That was followed by time spent in several other Third World conflicts including a period with Renamo rebels, eager to displace the government in Mozambique. The first time his mother phoned me she had a desperate request for help in getting him out of that country after he had been arrested by the rebels. They had accused him of being a spy. One of the men who came to his rescue was former CIA operative Bob MacKenzie, who was later to die brutally in Sierra Leone.[2]

Before all that took place, I'd given Nicholas his first job as an assistant on a television shoot in Senegal. He loved it enough to go on doing that sort of thing for the rest of his short life, until he, his lovely wife Rosanna and her brother Charles Maxwell were shot and killed. All three disappeared following a dispute about wages with their Kurdish guide. The SAS was eventually tasked with the search, because, as tradition allows, the regiment looks after its own. The bodies of the two men were found buried under an open fire pit. However, Rosanna's body was never found.

So, while I was not directly implicated in those grisly deeds, the odds are good that Nicholas would still be alive had he not been delegated to assist cameraman Henry Bautista, another resolute character out of the recent past who went on to make a name for himself with CBS in the United States. However, I digress.

The first of the young men to die – because I was there at the time – was a guerrilla who had been fighting South African occupying forces in

Looking over the shoulder of the 'tech' onboard a South African Air Force Alouette helicopter gunship deep inside Angola. (Author's collection)

Southern Angola. I'd been on board one of the South African Air Force (SAAF) helicopter gunships after the Battle of Cuamato, the kind of cut-and-thrust operation that delineated much of a conflict that would occasionally go conventional.

What was evident the first morning of the battle was the volume of Soviet-supplied anti-aircraft firepower that the Angolans were able to hurl at circling South African Alouettes. With a number of Cuban regulars in their ranks, the Angolans fired salvoes that accounted for several lives, all lost during the ground attack on what was termed an 'enemy' military base.

Initially, the South Africans had hit a fairly large military concentration in some pretty ragged bush country near the Angolan hamlet of Cuamato. They were in search of insurgents, I was told. However, the intelligence boffins were wrong, and instead the heavily fortified encampment belonged to FAPLA, the Angolan Army. Its presence in this desolate open country that the Portuguese, centuries before, had dubbed *Terras do fim Mundo* – Land at the End of the Earth – was perfectly legitimate.

The battle lasted for two days. For my part, it included a series of

12

infantry assaults through Angolan Army trench lines, with the rest of the time spent in helicopters looking for what some of the aviators like to call 'targets of opportunity'.

One of the pilots with whom I flew was Heinz Katzke, an easygoing professional who seemed to enjoy any challenge while at the controls of a gunship. If he could manage it, I suggested, I'd like to get my hands on a bayonet, preferably for a Kalashnikov.

'No problem', was his reply. 'Let's see if we can find you one', and off we went. A short time later, we spotted the body of an Angolan soldier lying kind of half-secreted under a tree, his AK at an odd angle across his knees. We were aware that these troops all carried bayonets, though in Africa they were rarely attached to the barrel. Most were tied to their webbing, prominently displayed, almost like a badge of courage.

'Looks like he's not going to need his AK any time soon', said Heinz half jokingly as he lost altitude and went into the hover. 'Or his bayonet', the gunner behind us added with a chuckle.

We were still at about 300 feet when Heinz decided to bring the chopper down onto an open clearing in the bush a short distance from our man. Over the mike – to which all three of us on board were connected – he told the gunner that he would put down about 20 paces from the body. 'I'm taking her down just south of that large tree to the south', he said pointing.

'Roger' was the reply. By then the gunner was already unstrapping himself. There was no question of telling headquarters what we were doing because it was illegal. Instead, Heinz just went in: it was that kind of war.

Once on the ground, the helicopter's gunner – a sergeant who was normally crouched across a 20mm cannon protruding from the portside hatch – undid his last safety belt, took off his helmet, grabbed his issue carbine and sprinted towards the 'gook'.

He was perhaps two or three yards from the Angolan when the 'dead man' suddenly sat up, took hold of his AK and lowered the barrel, but he wasn't quick enough. The gunner killed the combatant with a short burst of automatic fire. Wasting little time, he turned over the body, ran his hands over the now-dead man's uniform and, having found the blade, sprinted back towards the helicopter. Perhaps 30 seconds later, we were back in the air. Nobody said a word while we soared back up to operational height and I was able to check my newfound trophy in its red-baked Bakelite sheath.

About then the gunner came through on the mike. 'He wasn't wounded, Captain . . . very far from dead, in fact', he told Heinz Katzke. 'How do you know?'

'Patted him down, Sir . . . there were no other wounds on him. He was playing possum . . . probably would have made a run for it as soon as the sky was clear.'

A silence followed, none of us knowing what to say . . .

'Well' said the captain after a little while, motioning with his left hand in my direction, 'at least you got your bayonet . . . and what's another dead fucker between friends?'

'But just don't tell the colonel about it when we get back . . . '

As Chris Munnion, the former *Daily Telegraph* correspondent in Africa, says in *Banana Sunday*, the effort was heroic.[3] Some of the yarns that surfaced are legend, and so are a few of the hangovers! As Chris comments, in inimitable Munnion style, rarely was there a life lost. These scribes 'rushed about from riot to revolt, from the back-and-beyond to the front, from palaces to prison cells to telegraph, telex, phone, pigeon post and the use of many other ingenious ways to get the unfolding story of Imperial Retreat back to their newspapers'. They seemed to do so with impunity.

The old order of those days – the 1960s and the 1970s – has long since gone. It's been replaced by much distress and violence. Indeed, things are much worse now than during earlier decades. Then the international community wasn't only genuinely interested in what was happening in Black Africa, but Europe and the Americas were directly engaged. They trusted the new black leaders of Africa, people like Nkrumah, Tubman, Hastings Banda, Jomo Kenyatta, Julius Nyerere the Tanzanian President, Sir Abubakar Tafewa Balewa and Modiba Keita of Mali, which in almost all cases was a bad mistake.

Now, well into the new millennium, the game has changed once more. The Cold War is over and there is no need to gratify the demands of some psychotic tyrant because if you didn't help him the Soviets would (though that, too, could quickly change if Beijing becomes too pervasive). Few cared if deaths in Rwanda were measured in thousands or, in reality, in hundreds of thousands. It's all old-hat, or in the minds of some, it should be, though recent events in Darfur have rekindled that nightmare.

Instead, today's headlines are more concerned with shrinking budgets, the latest goings-on in the White House, chaos on the outskirts of Kandahar or possibly some obscure outbreak of violence south of the Urals or a Moscow suicide bombing. If Africa does get a mention, it's usually because some company's commercial or mining interests are at stake. Sadly, Africa has reverted to darkness and cold night.

However, from a sufficient distance, African troubles do have their comic side. It can sometimes be quite amusing as cultures clash and egos need to be nursed. The illustrious former *Newsweek* and London *Daily Mail* correspondent Peter Younghusband has captured much of what happened over three or four decades of reporting on the continent in a book recently published in Cape Town, titled, appropriately, *Every Meal a Banquet, Every Night a Honeymoon.*[4]

An uproarious read, it puts much of what happened in Africa yesterday thoroughly in context.

Some of the stories that emerged over the years had more sinister implications. This became apparent as the Congolese war spread eastwards towards the Ugandan and Rwandan borders and then south to Katanga (now Shaba Province). By then a mercenary army had been raised, commanded by the same Mike Hoare with whom George Clay went into battle before he was killed. Moise Tshombe, meanwhile, had declared Katanga independent and overnight Hoare, the ultimate mercenary, changed sides.

The UN intervened and another civil war followed. However, these were real wars and a lot of real people, innocent or otherwise, were being slaughtered.

Because of faulty or inadequate phone and telex links with the world outside, most of the hacks worked from the Edinburgh Hotel in Kitwe, a modest mining town in Zambia then listed on the map as Northern Rhodesia. It was part of the Central African Federation, a British political invention that, as might have been expected, failed after only a few years.

The border between Northern Rhodesia and the Congo at the time was patrolled by the Federal Army, a very professional, little military force that operated in a typically British fashion. All the African countries in the region except the Congo (Zaire) and Angola (which was Portuguese) were still British territories and Whitehall's influence was manifest. Here an event, or rather a series of events, took place which will be remembered long after we are all gone.

Peter Younghusband and his *Daily Express* colleague John Monks were involved. Since I had commissioned Chris Munnion to write his book and sent him around the world in a bid to capture some of this history while I was still into publishing, I'll repeat what he told me on his return.

Apparently, Younghusband and Monks were relaxing in Kitwe one evening, having just returned to file their copy to London from Elizabethville, the Katangese capital (Lubumbashi, today). They were approached by a mild-mannered American who introduced himself as Weldon Wallace of *The Baltimore Sun*. Wallace was that newspaper's distinguished music critic and he had been covering the opera season in Milan when the Katanga crisis erupted.

'My newspaper noticed that I was the man nearest the spot and asked me to pop down here to cover the story', Wallace explained to Younghusband. 'I have actually never been to Africa before so I wonder if I could possibly get a lift with you to Elizabethville?' The two old hands pointed out the difficulties of getting through the roadblocks and explained that as he, Weldon Wallace, had an American passport, the Katangese might easily pick on him as his government was involved with the hated United Nations, then occupying parts of Katanga.

'We felt a bit guilty about this, especially as he was such a nice guy', Monks said afterwards, 'but it really was becoming a hairy run and we knew that having a stranger with an American passport could easily put us all at risk'.

Wallace appreciated their point. Unbeknown to Monks and Younghusband, he'd earlier sought out two other newly arrived journalists, Arthur Bonner, a fellow American, of CBS as well as Lionel Fleming of the BBC, who travelled on an Irish passport. All three journalists agreed to drive to Katanga together the following day.

Weldon Wallace had heard mention that Africans across the border were starving and he'd thoughtfully loaded his hired car with cans of dried milk and sacks of flour. 'I thought if I distributed food to refugees, it would generate a spirit of goodwill and enable us to pass through to Elizabethville', he said at the time. He was soon to learn that there was precious little goodwill left in Central Africa.

The three men set off early, quickly negotiated the Northern Rhodesian border post and drove down the hill to the Katangese frontier a mile beyond. It was still early morning, but the Katangese troops lounging around the border post were drunk and high on pot. They could scarcely believe their eyes when three white men emerged from the

16

car cheerfully waving their passports – two American and one Irish. As the cry went up 'Americans! Irish! UN spies . . . kill them . . . kill them!' the three realized their error and tried to get back to the car. They were beaten and dragged at gunpoint to a fetid shack about 100 yards away while other troops cheerfully ransacked the car and began bayoneting the bags of flour in the trunk.

The shack to which the three scribes were shepherded had a floor of compacted cow dung and a tin roof.

Wallace: 'It was hot and very smelly but that was the least of our problems. We were being slapped, beaten and jabbed with rifles. As the man who appeared to be the sergeant screamed threats and insults at us, hands reached out and grabbed our wallets and watches.'

Through a window, Wallace saw a large white man approaching. It was a guardian angel in the unlikely form of Peter Younghusband. 'When he saw what was going on, an expression of astonishment crossed his face. He inclined his head in acknowledgement of our plight. My hopes rose.'

Monks and Younghusband had set out for the border shortly after Wallace and friends. At the Northern Rhodesian border post they had exchanged pleasantries with a Federal Army officer, a major whom Monks, then based in Rhodesia, had known for some time. They were told that two Americans and an Irishman had just gone through. With mounting concern the pair approached the Katangese border.

'The first thing we noticed was this great cloud of flour hanging in the air. The troops were fighting over the spoils from our colleagues' car', Younghusband remembers. 'It was an amazing sight. There were these crazed black men reeling around covered in white flour, their eyeballs rolling. We realized something pretty nasty was going on. A Katangese immigration official indicated that three white spies had been "taken for execution".' Monks and Younghusband made a swift decision. Younghusband would try to do what he could to calm the situation which by then was totally out of control, while Monks would dash back to the Northern Rhodesian border post to summon help from Federal troops.

'Bigfoot' Younghusband strolled as casually as he could towards the shack where he heard sounds of another commotion. He glimpsed the terrified face of Weldon Wallace through the window and made his way to the door.

'I burst in and, trying to sound authoritative, I bellowed in French:

'Stop this immediately! These men are famous journalists who have come to see President Tshombe.' I was armed with nothing more useful than a Katangese press card which I brandished wildly. It didn't work.'

The Katangese officer, his face contorted in fury, stepped towards the big guy, knocked the press card out his hand and hollered 'Spies, spies . . . you are all spies.' With that he slapped Younghusband across the face.

'I was transformed from a liberal to an Afrikaner nationalist in 30 seconds flat', Peter recalled with wry humor.

There was nothing funny about his situation at the time, however. He was pushed onto the floor with the other three. To his horror, one soldier dragged a Bren gun into the open door of the hut, spread-eagled himself behind it and pointed it at the hostages, for that was what they'd become. The others, meanwhile, kept ranting with a chant of 'Kill them . . . kill them'. The Bren gunner suddenly rolled over onto his back and started to laugh.

'I sensed they were waiting for somebody', said Younghusband. 'So I urged the others to try not to show their fear . . . if they see it or smell it, it makes them worse, which was much more easily said than done.'

The Katangese immigration officer suddenly appeared in the doorway and spoke to the soldier in charge. He pointed at Younghusband and said he knew him as a British journalist. Peter was ordered to his feet and told to get back to the other side of the border. Wallace, Bonner and Fleming were then dragged out of the shack and bundled into a vehicle that took them several miles down the road, where the car swung off into a clearing in the bush. Wallace took up the story.

'The soldiers crowded around. They tore off our jackets and ordered us to remove the rest of our clothing. One of them said they did not want our clothes to show bullet holes . . . I was convinced this was the end. We were going to be executed there in the bush.' The half-naked trio was then pushed into a line. Once again the soldiers cocked their rifles.

Back at the border post, Younghusband found John Monks with some Federal troops in armoured cars. The friendly major was talking urgently into a field radio. Monks had got through to his old friend, Sir Roy Welensky, the Federal Prime Minister, who ordered his troops to do everything possible to rescue the journalists. The troops then drove to the Katangese border post where the major was now trying to reach his opposite number in the Gendarmerie on the radio. He succeeded.

A senior Katangese officer raced to the scene just in time to prevent what would almost certainly have been the execution of the three men. They were given back their clothes, shoved back in the car and handed over at the border post. Bonner and Fleming were shaken but unhurt. Weldon Wallace also had no injuries but was white and shaking and clearly in shock.

Monks and Younghusband rushed him back to Kitwe and summoned a doctor from the nearby copper mine.

'Weldon was put straight to bed and heavily sedated', Monks said. 'Just before he went under, he kept muttering that he had to write a story for his newspaper. He had to file, were his words. We told him not to worry, which was when he went into a deep sleep.'

The two men sat down at a typewriter and, under Wallace's name, composed a dramatic first-person account of what had happened. 'My American passport nearly cost me my life yesterday . . .' it started, and went on in punchy Fleet Street style. They then cabled it to *The Baltimore Sun* which ran it prominently with Weldon's by-line and his picture under the banner headline 'A Captive of Wild Katangan Troops'.

By the time the newspaper's music critic came to in Kitwe's Edinburgh Hotel, there was a pile of cables from his editors as well as his proprietor congratulating him on his escape and his story. They advised him too that he was being nominated for a Pulitzer Prize for 'a story written under great pressure'.

Poor Weldon was totally bewildered. 'But I didn't write anything . . . what are they talking about?'Monks and Younghusband tried to tell him that he'd dictated his account to them before he was sedated, but he was not convinced.

Younghusband told me: 'He went straight back to the US and we had a long letter of thanks from him. However, he said that, under the circumstances, he could not possibly accept a Pulitzer nomination . . . a pity because that's the closest we ever came to winning a prize.'

Monks' hometown newspaper, the *Melbourne Herald*, meanwhile, ran the story of his exploits under the memorable headline 'Australian Reporter Saves Three from Natives'.

Considering the risks of covering the African beat, I reckon I must have been pretty lucky over the years. Apart from some scrapes and being left half-deaf from a series of blasts while covering the Angolan War, I have been fortunate to have survived a career that spans more than four decades in the field, though I'd like to think that it's not over yet.

I use the word 'survive' lightly, as there is something inexplicable about emerging on the other side alive and with all your bits and pieces intact. People talk about a sixth sense, a kind of warning of danger. My theory revolves around a seventh, eighth or even a ninth sense, 'every cell inside you crying out to live, just live!' as it was graphically described by Arkady Babchenko, a brilliant young Russian writer when he talks about his experiences in Chechnya in *One Soldier's War in Chechnya*.[5]

Throughout it all, I have been doing what I loved best, be it going into Beirut with the Israel Defence Forces (IDF) during the 1980s Israeli invasion of Lebanon; covering the war in El Salvador with a group of American mercs; or, during the Balkan War, flying in a Joint-STARS operation with the United States Air Force over Kosovo. I didn't regard any of it as inordinately demanding at the time, though it obviously was, because I earned a good living from the proceeds.

Nor was it a chore to traipse around some of the African and Middle Eastern conflicts that I'd chosen, or been chosen, to cover. It was the same when I joined the Police Air Wing, a paramilitary helicopter unit in South Africa, in the winter of 2006 for a combined three-week ground and air operation that resulted in the destruction of about 20 tons of marijuana in what was once known as Zululand.

Before that, I went into Angola with South African units on long-range penetration strikes. During 'Op Daisy' a week-long onslaught deep into Angola, I was embedded with an attack force that involved Ratel infantry fighting vehicles from 61 Mech. 'Op Daisy' was hardly a success, and we were mightily intimidated by the way the enemy deployed anti-tank mines. I was on the turret of one of the Infantry Fighting Vehicles (IFVs) when we triggered a TM-57: my only injury was a broken arm, and though I was choppered out to have it set, I was back again by nightfall.

It was also in Angola in 1980 that I went into combat with 1 Parachute Battalion, and, as mentioned earlier, while with the unit, attacked what we thought was a rebel SWAPO base at Cuamato. With Charlie Company (79/81), we were dropped straight into the bush from a string of Puma helicopters and it didn't take us long to realize that the enemy was all over the place, many of them armed with RPG-7s. Most of the youngsters around me were still in their teens and they fought with a kind of dedicated resolve that astonished us older guys.

South Lebanese M113 armoured personnel carriers – American made and supplied, mainly to Christian forces in Lebanon – were very much in evidence in the areas adjacent to the Israeli border. (Author's collection)

Close to me in that attack was one of the war dogs of his time, a young Lieutenant Johan Blaauw, who led from the front throughout. I was with him when he used a grenade to flush a bunch of the enemy from a bunker that had been used for storing fuel. Johan was lucky to have survived the back-blast, which left him with his face and uniform seared and almost no hair on his head.

Also involved in that attack was that incorrigible British mercenary, Peter MacAleese, who later went on to fight in Columbia's drug wars. He'd gone straight in with us from the helicopter and was the first to tackle an enemy soldier whom he'd spotted targeting our approach with a rocket-propelled grenade.

We eventually took the base, but elements of the parachute battalion suffered fatalities, including Leon 'Chunky' Truter, a youngster who took a shard of steel in the brain after an enemy mortar landed in the middle of his squad. It was a lucky shot for the enemy and it did serious damage.

I was there when – after a spell of going in and out of consciousness – 'Chunky' breathed his last. Afterwards I visited his mother in Cape Town to tell her that just before he died, he'd quietly called for her. I heard afterwards that she never got over his death.

As Charlie Company section leader Manie Troskie recalled afterwards, 'Chunky's' death had an effect on these youngsters and I was to see some of it myself from up close. If they had any reservations about warfare before, a kind of primitive hatred emerged. Overnight, these adolescents became focused, their instincts atavistic, brutish and elemental and beyond the comprehension of most ordinary folk. But then, that's the way it is with all wars, which was why Charlie Company went in the next day and thought nothing about killing as many of the enemy as they encountered in an engagement that lasted several hours.

'We had a score to settle', said Manie at the 30th anniversary of the Cuamato attack at a resort outside Bloemfontein. 'And let me tell you,' he said in Afrikaans, '*ons het daardie donders goed gebliksem*', which loosely translates into 'we fucked them up good and proper'.

What remains vivid was the counter-attack that came after we'd bedded down later that night: salvoes of Soviet 122mm Katyusha rockets forced us to scamper into a row of trenches that had been vacated by Angolan troops earlier in the day. I deal with another aspect of that attack later in the book.

Curiously, a lot of what took place when I found myself in Africa and the Middle East might be summarized as events that 'just kind of happened'.

I'd initially qualified as a Fellow of the Institute of Chartered Shipbrokers at the Baltic Exchange in London and though the British capital never bored me, being office-bound and stuck in a tedious, unimaginative routine certainly did. The overcrowded, often stifling

In Angola's flat, arid hinterland that Lisbon had long ago called *Terras do Fim Mundo* – Land at the End of the Earth – the troops used whatever high point was available to observe the activities of the other side. (Author's collection)

22

Underground was a nightmare, which was why I ended up in Nigeria. Bit of a contradiction in terms, I suppose, but at least things were happening in West Africa.

By the time I got to Lagos, I'd barely missed the first army mutiny, but there was plenty more action before the second putsch took place in July 1966 and still more coups, mutinies and revolutions have taken place since then. Suddenly, I was thrust into the kind of African upheaval that had become commonplace in Africa and has never quite let up since.

My office was at Lagos Airport, where there was constant movement to London, New York and Johannesburg. I could easily get my stories and photographs out without drawing attention to my actions by using 'pigeons', otherwise known as obliging third parties. I'd approach boarding passengers in the departure lounge at Lagos' Ikeja Airport, these days officially referred to as Murtala Mohammed International Airport, and ask them to take an envelope or two out of the country, which is unheard of today.

I sent scores of news reports out of Nigeria that way. What was curious was that during the year that I reported locally, not one of my typed reports or any of the rolls of film that accompanied them went missing. There was no fax or e-mail, or even computers as we know them today, but such were the good old days.

The truth is that while I'd never trained as a journalist, I was 'telling it like it was'. Moreover, it was great fun, tweaking the system, as it were.

The Nigerian government prohibited journalists from entering the country and like it or not, I was the only scribe around. My first editor, Wilf Nussey – who headed up the Argus Africa News Service – was heard to comment that some of my dispatches read like letters home.

It took time to assimilate the elements of good journalism, but there were competent people out there helping me – professionals like Younghusband, the late, great, always irascible Johnny Johnson, as well as Jim Penrith and Henry Reuter, both men then working out of Nairobi. Also, I was getting good money for my efforts and it wasn't long before I discovered that this was a great way to earn a living. It was certainly a good deal better than any office job.

I was even fortunate enough to go to Lambarene in faraway Gabon to meet Dr Albert Schweitzer. That was an assignment for United Press International (UPI) and came as a prelude to his 90th birthday. I still have the old man's photo, affectionately inscribed and framed, which he gave to me the day I left his jungle hospital.

If a little dark at times, it was all adventure. To me, distant destinations, shadowy airports, raids in the small hours and so on became integral to a way of life that offered many opportunities.

Much of what I did in those distant days got me into trouble, especially in places like the Cazombo Panhandle in Angola, the mountains around Morozan in Central America, as well as Gaza and Damascus (which to the consternation of the *Moukhamarat*, the Syrian security police, I visited without an appropriate visa because I'd gone in unheralded, as a bona fide tourist).

Once I went down the Nile from Khartoum to Cairo by road, lake steamer across the great Aswan, and in the latter stages, by *felucca* sailing boat and finally by rail.

The author during one of his first sweeps through West Africa as an aspiring journalist: it was taken at the home of a Peace Corps volunteer in Conakry, Guinea, a few weeks before the death of Winston Churchill in 1965. (Author's Collection)

Then came the Niger Delta, where I was rocketed by Biafran Minicon trainers that had been converted into fighter aircraft in 1969, which was followed by intermittent visits to the always-majestic Zambezi Valley in Mozambique. Beautiful it certainly is, but the valley is stiflingly unhealthy during the Southern Hemisphere summer. I contracted cerebral malaria while on an assignment to one of the abandoned Portuguese Air Force bases in Mozambique after Lisbon had capitulated in Africa. It got so bad that I collapsed while having lunch, in what was then still called Salisbury, with P. K. (Pieter) van der Bijl, the Rhodesian defence minister. That evening, my condition deteriorated and my family was called to my bedside in the Andrew Fleming Hospital. To some of the doctors who were treating me, it seemed like I wasn't going to make it. Obviously I did, but I still go down with the shakes from time to time.

Nigeria originally shaped it all for me, when I was there a few years before the start of the civil war. It was the one country in Africa where reality was often filtered through the hazy lens of patriotism.

I arrived in Lagos in early 1966 with Tony Cusack, a friend from Liverpool, and afterwards he accompanied me overland down the west coast of Africa to Johannesburg. Along the way we were faced with another conflict that few people had heard of and even fewer remember today: the colonial struggle in Angola.

The Portuguese had been in Africa for five centuries and suddenly in 1960, their rule was being disputed by a group of revolutionaries in the bush. Imperial traditions that went way back suddenly began to crumble. There were plenty of people who wanted to know about that war too, so I obliged, which was where my first book was written. I rather wish it wasn't, because it was so terribly bad!

It was in Angola, almost overnight, that I learnt to use a camera because I had to. I was suddenly in business as a photo-journalist with wars all over the place: in Mozambique, Arab–Israeli clashes, Rhodesia, the Sudan, Ethiopia, Biafra and elsewhere. Journalists were in demand in these Third World outposts, especially those who were prepared to take the occasional risk: the rest of the gang was doing something similar in Vietnam . . .

I met plenty of others involved in the same sort of thing. As might have been expected, I'd meanwhile added a few of strings to my bow, which included NBC Radio News in New York, the BBC, as well as Interavia in Geneva, a connection that eventually opened doors for me with Britain's Jane's Information Group.

There were many good friends made along the way, including Alan Pizzey, who later headed the CBS Rome office (we became mortar and machine-gun targets one quiet afternoon in Luanda) and my old pal Younghusband along with the equally intrepid John Monks of the *Daily Express*, to whom I owe a measure of thanks for handing me that Cape Town string. There was also Angus McDermid, the BBC World Service's longest-serving Africa correspondent, at whose feet I sat, listened, learnt and took a few knocks when I didn't do the job as I should have.

Then there was Frederick Forsyth, with whom I shared a few exploits in Biafra prior to his returning to London at the end of that dreadful internecine struggle to write his epic, *Day of the Jackal*.

Not very long afterwards, Chris Munnion appeared on the Southern African scene. He wrote the book *Banana Sunday* for the publishing house I subsequently founded. It was a curious title, but it had a legacy: journalists in those days would slug their copy both with the day on which it was written and where they were at. One of Chris' reports was dispatched to London's *Daily Telegraph* late on a Sunday afternoon from the Congolese port of Banana.

Chris' book – soon to be updated and reissued under the title *Deadline Africa* – is arguably one of the best from those of us 'Old Africa Hands' who worked this difficult continent and covered so many of its foibles and little-understood idiosyncrasies. It's way up there with David Lamb's *The Africans* and Ed Behr's classic *Anyone Here Been Raped and Speaks English?*

There were many others, including *Newsweek*'s Holger 'Captain Wilderness' Jensen who was probably the single 'most wounded' journalist in the South East Asian wars: his tally was something like 14 injuries and counting. I also worked for a while with Peter Hawthorne of *Time* magazine. That project involved a book that chronicled Dr Christian Barnard's first human heart transplant at Cape Town's Groote Schuur Hospital.

Of course, there was Mohammed Amin, who honed my journalistic skills, if only because this man – who routinely worked a 15-hour day, and often started at three in the morning – was committed to the profession like no other person I've ever met. Amin perfected his craft to the extent that before he was killed, he earned more in a year than most of us scribes took home in a decade.

He topped that by being awarded accolades from just about

everywhere, accepting them from presidents, regents, princes, prime ministers, the famous and the celebrated. In his office he had framed portraits of himself with President Reagan, Henry Kissinger, Princess Di, Queen Elizabeth, Margaret Thatcher, Kofi Annan and even one with the Pope, which says a lot for this devout Muslim.

Amin was remarkably blessed. For a start, he was exceptionally 'Africa-wise', more than any other journalist I know. He was arrested many times, once by the Soviets in Zanzibar when that country teetered towards anarchy. He spent a while in jail and came out alive when there were others dying in their thousands. Above all, he understood the continent, especially its vagaries and its often-dangerous pitfalls.

He was also a master of survival, though at high personal cost. He limped most of his adult life because of shrapnel that he took in his leg from a Legionnaire's grenade in Djibouti. Then there was the arm that he lost in Ethiopia, blown away in the explosion of an ammunition dump in Addis Ababa in 1992. That was the same blast that killed his sound man, who had been standing beside him. Amin had qualified fairly early on in life as a pilot, but he took so many chances that I flew with him only once.

He was flying when he was killed, this time onboard an Ethiopian Airlines passenger jet that had been hijacked by a group of Islamic zealots after it had taken off from Addis Ababa, which was more than a little ironic since my old pal was himself of Islamic persuasion. The hijackers ordered the captain to fly the plane to the Comoros Archipelago, off the east coast of Africa. Though he warned that they didn't have enough fuel for that kind of distance, they stuck a gun to his head and asked him whether he wanted to die then or later.

The crash was captured on film, purely by chance, by a tourist on the beach alongside where the passenger plane came down. The footage became one of those real-life sequences you regularly see on The Discovery Channel. The Boeing came in low, its left wing clipped the water, after which it immediately broke up. That film is arguably the most complete real-life passenger jet disaster caught on camera.

Word had it that Amin went down fighting, and those of us who knew him accepted that he could be as cocky as he was sometimes brash, both fine qualities for a news-gatherer. Though handicapped with his artificial arm, Amin didn't sit back in his seat and wait for the inevitable. After trying to reason with the hijackers, he ended up grappling with them when it became clear that if somebody didn't do something, everybody would be doomed.

While a number of passengers survived, he didn't.

In due course, doing my own thing as a newsman, I was also to learn something about Africa. I discovered how to become, if not familiar with, then comprehending of some of the continent's convoluted conflicts and politics, were that ever possible.

When I was offered an irregular job as Africa and Middle East correspondent for *International Defence Review*, then a multi-language magazine published monthly in Geneva (it only became part of Jane's Information Group some years later) it was a step up. To do the job properly, I needed to know and understand my subject. Also, I had to learn fast.

At a glance, I needed to be able to identify an RPD 7.62mm light machine-gun and not confuse it with the RPK (same calibre, later vintage). Much of this is esoteric and to those not involved with the military, more than a little confusing. Africa, and the Arab nations – as well as the rest of the Middle East – offered rich opportunities, and obviously the Cold War helped.

Being a freelance, I've always liked to work on my own. For a start, it was easier to get into a revolution, a political upheaval or even a war if one didn't have a 'label'. I wasn't publicly linked either to Fleet Street or to the American media, though I did a lot of work for both. That included an extremely well-paid film project on the war in Afghanistan funded by a large government organization in Langley, Virginia.

This project involved a lot of young people who have since gone on to make worthwhile careers for themselves, including: Tim Lambon, today deputy news editor on BBC's Channel 4; Paul Moorcraft who went on to write a string of his own war books; John Rubython who was murdered some years ago by an intruder in his Cape Town home (John covered Kandahar and its environs); the incorrigible New Zealander Mark Stucke, who today runs a major film company in London; Chris Everson, who made enough of a fortune as a cameraman for American networks while covering conflicts in Africa and the Middle East to buy himself a wine farm in South Africa; and then, the irrepressible Nicholas Della Casa.

How this all came about is an interesting tale. I was approached by a group of Americans – they called themselves an independent-minded group – to do a one-hour documentary that would commemorate the fifth anniversary of the Soviet invasion of Afghanistan early in 1985.

The war had been going on a while, and wasn't all that well reported so, basically, the idea was sound. Things dragged on a bit after a couple of visits to the States and it stayed that way until I pointed out that if they wanted the film made in time, my guys would have to go in and return before one of Afghanistan's horrific winters set in. That gave us a window of only several months.

By May 1985, I'd discovered the true identity of my backers and when I asked them why they didn't use their own people for this kind of work, they replied that Congress prohibited the CIA from employing American working journalists for what was tantamount to intelligence work.

From there on I was fast-tracked through a rigorous vetting process, most of which had already been quietly achieved *in loco*: Langley knew everything about me, including where I lived, details about my home in Noordhoek in the Cape Peninsula, my family, my circle of friends and the fact that I liked to travel first class whenever I ventured abroad.

By then Washington had started to pick up the tabs and since I was commuting to the United States and back on an almost monthly basis, they were prepared to settle for Business Class, but I held out for more. That meant that since I always routed my journeys through London, a reasonable add-on allowed me to fly Concorde, courtesy of the American taxpayer.

Once the formalities had been completed, which included a lie detector test in a hotel room at Tyson's Corner on the outskirts of the US capital, we were ready to move. I'd already been told that since I was a British citizen, Langley would, as a matter of course, advise the British establishment that it was hiring one of their citizens for a 'project', which meant that I probably had another file opened in my name at Vauxhall Cross.

At the end of all that, I sent three crews into Afghanistan to make the hour-long film. The same team went twice out of Peshawar, from where they travelled by truck across the Himalayas and then set out on foot in a circular route around Kabul, filming as they went. John Rubython took his team out of Qetta into an area around Kandahar. Paul Moorcraft captures some of the trip admirably in a book he subsequently wrote about those experiences, though it wasn't until years later that he and the others discovered the identity of their actual paymaster.

A quarter of a million dollars for a three or four month job in the 1980s wasn't bad going, especially as it was tax free . . .

Most of the time, when doing the customary journalistic work for which I quickly acquired a taste, I'd go in, do the necessary and get out fast.

There were places that I'd covered and couldn't get back into again, often for a long time after my reports had appeared in print. I never returned to Zaire after I was jailed for espionage in Lubumbashi and I don't much wish to either. In my mind the place had long ago been relegated to the status of *anus mundi*: I'm not alone among my colleagues for thinking so and since that experience is dealt with in Chapters 19 to 22, you can judge for yourself.

Sometimes we journalists found ourselves in situations that we'd rather had not happened. Simon Dring, whom I met on his first foreign assignment in Nigeria, was wounded by a landmine in Cyprus. Lord Richard Cecil, another old friend and a veteran of numerous exploits with the SAS in Northern Ireland, was shot and killed in the Rhodesian war, as was his fellow countryman, André Dennison. Like Chris Munnion, Richard Cecil been writing for the *Telegraph*.

Al Venter (second on the left) and some members of his team whom he sent into Afghanistan to make a documentary that covered the fifth anniversary of the Soviet invasion. To his right is cameraman Chris Everson and on the far right is British academic-turned-war-correspondent Dr Paul Moorcraft. None of them knew at the time that the CIA was picking up the tab. (Author's collection)

There have been others, but the majority survived, though quite a few succumbed to that perennial disability among those who called themselves foreign correspondents and which we sometimes prefer not to recognize as cirrhosis of the liver. It's an occupational disease among journalists everywhere.

Then there was the occasional broken nose from a bar-room brawl or an over-enthusiastic *policier* trying to establish whether some of us were secret agents. Most of the time we'd be dealing with officials whose very mién would suppurate malice, almost like some people like to project authority. This was a perennial issue in Third World Countries, Africa especially.

With the publication of documents from the KGB archives, after the old Soviet Union had been relegated to history, it now transpires that a few of my former colleagues were doing a bit of moonlighting for some of these communist states. A very prominent British journalist was found to have been on the payroll of PIDE, the Portuguese secret police, for many years. We'd all been taught that journalists simply don't do that kind of thing, but some did, and my own ties to the CIA don't count because until the Berlin Wall came down, they were the 'good guys'. A few of these spooks were flushed out in subsequent Eastern Bloc disclosures, their careers left in tatters.

Looking back, I reckon it was all rather a gas. I was mortared, rocketed, blown-up by mines, nearly killed in a trench line assault in Angola, robbed, beaten and arrested. I was shot at and, more than once – particularly in Lebanon – targeted by snipers.

Once, back home in Johannesburg, I was stabbed, breaking an arm in the process. As the attacker lunged, I hurled myself backwards to avoid becoming a statistic. It was close, because the woolen pullover I'd been wearing had a six-inch slit along the lower part of my chest. To cut through knitted-wear, the blade must have been razor sharp.

I realized soon enough that it was never difficult to get arrested, in Africa especially, and more recently in some parts of Asia and the Middle East. We tended to be in the wrong place at the wrong time, especially if we'd just arrived in somewhere that had declared war on the country which we'd just left. Things could be both confused and confusing.

Christopher Dickey, Paris bureau chief for *Newsweek,* phrased it best when he commented in a book review for *The New York Times* that correspondents were not oracles. But, he declared – and herein lies the rub – 'they're on the ground'.

Beirut during the Lebanese Civil War of the 1970s and 1980s was fraught with uncertainties. Both sides quickly became masters of urban guerrilla warfare and deployed snipers from most vantage points. (Author's collection)

I quote further:

When wars and massacres loom on the horizon, they see what's happening. They have the ability to tell the world; and they do, for the most part, in measured, reasonable terms. And then – nothing. The deluge comes. It is worse even than they expected; more brutal than they could dream, so that afterward their reasoned moderation feels like cowardice, and 'professionalism' and 'balance' seem like euphemisms for self-serving ambivalence. Most become cynics. Some are drunks. And when they do go home, making excuses to themselves, some of them write fiction.

Dickey, always the master of the understatement, encapsulates it well.

There were other times when circumstances would remind me of Elspeth Huxley's incisive comment about the continent. She famously miswrote that 'Africa is a cruel country; it takes your heart and grinds it into powdered stone — and no one minds.'

I suppose it was to be expected that I should eventually turn to television reportage. From 1980 on, I made almost 100 documentaries on more than 30 countries in Africa, the Middle East and Asia, as well as South and Central America. It was good while it lasted, but I moved on when the politics linked to the film industry started to get to me. As I was to discover, making television documentaries is one of the toughest regimens around.

One notable experience was filming in Rio's slums, or as they are known in Brazil, *favelas*. The Brazilians with whom I came into contact said that either I or Alwyn Kumst, my cameraman for that venture, would be killed. We'd be 'iced' by what they referred to as 'some of the most brutal criminals on God's earth'. It never happened, even though we went in every day for weeks: the wretched people with whom we dealt were among the most helpful I'd encountered anywhere and, let's face it, they didn't need to help us: we didn't even speak their language.

Since then, I watched that remarkable movie *Cidade de Deus* (City of God), and our detractors may have been right. But those *favela* folk, pathetically distressed, destitute and still living today in some of the worst ghettos on any continent, knew exactly what we were doing. They actually helped us with our movie, aware, that by our actions we were for the underdog.

It was Brazil's state security apparatus that eventually came down on us and we had to up sticks and get out fast. However, I had my film, shot by Alwyn Kumst on miniscule 100ft rolls of 16mm film using a hand-held Arri. He has since gone on to make a name for himself in Canada's film industry.

That documentary was followed by *Aids: The African Connection*, which made the shortlist in the documentary section for the Pink Magnolia Awards at one of Shanghai's film festivals. Then came the documentary that I produced on the Afghan War: the one that commemorated the fifth anniversary of the Soviet invasion.

My final documentary film, sponsored in part by Washington's Howard University and flighted on PBS in the United States, covered the fall of Idi Amin and the last days of the Ugandan Civil War. It was called *Africa's Killing Fields* and what a tragedy that debacle eventually turned into: the absurd brutality of a maniac, all those lives lost . . . I deal with that period as well within these covers.

After all the adventure, there came a time when I needed to break free from an existence – for that was what it really was – that allowed precious little time for my family. I was always on the road, or in the air. My lovely wife Madelon, in all those years, was all but a single parent and my children grew up without me. As it was, I hardly ever spent quality time with the two younger ones.

What finally forced change was my last visit to Gulu in Northern Uganda. Even now that part of Central Africa is being primed for rebellion from Southern Sudan. I went in there with a television crew from *Antenne Deux* after my own cameraman refused to leave his hotel room in Kampala. He and his girlfriend – who was doing sound – said the north of the country was too dangerous, though that's why I hired them as a team, dammit!

They were right, of course. We had to leave Gulu in a hurry because filming had been forbidden by the local military commander, but we went ahead anyway, rather pointedly and dangerously ignoring his order. Clearly, if we hadn't left as soon as the camera stopped rolling, we'd have been arrested and who knows what would have happened? One of the sequences captured during that assignment was of the Gulu town jail: there was blood dripping down the wall from between the bars.

Just as we were leaving Gulu, word arrived of a rebel force approaching from the south. We could hear the firing and were left with only two options: hit the trail or get ourselves arrested by the Ugandan Army.

They shot at us all right; but we got safely to the cheering mob at the edge of the next town. They'd heard the gunfire and spotted us hurtling down the only road, through the kind of undulating bush that you find throughout much of Northern Uganda. Meanwhile, I was huddled on the floor at the back of the vehicle, as if that would have been protection against RPG rocket fire . . .

Although the 10 or 12 minutes it took to cross Injun Country seems like aeons, I realized that if any of us had taken a hit that day, it would still have been a six-hour drive to Kampala to get help. After years of misrule, we could hardly count on what was left of medical services in the Ugandan capital, even if we could have found a doctor. In any event, Aids was rampant and we had been warned that the country's blood supply was contaminated. None of us would have survived a gut wound.

At that point, I decided that Uganda should be my last war. However, since then, because I've needed to fill gaps, I've covered a few more. The death of Bob MacKenzie in Sierra Leone – my compadre from guerrilla fighting in El Salvador, Vietnam and Rhodesia – took me back there in 1995. I also ended up going into Hizbollah country in South Lebanon after the spate of bombings in Israel in March 1996, and that, too, fringed on the cathartic. And then, for *Jane's Defence Weekly*, I spent a while with Hizbollah in Beirut.

War in the Balkans and then Sierra Leone again in 2000, followed. In West Africa, I mingled with a variety of regular and unconventional forces. As well as Neall Ellis and his helicopter gunship team, there were a handful of SAS operatives as well as a squad of Royal Marines and a Parachute Regiment detachment that were active on the outskirts of Freetown. The two British regular units worked the periphery of Lungi International Airport and it wasn't long before the rebel force was bloodied. British media spoke about a handful of rebels killed in a series of contacts: in fact, the number was in the hundreds.

There were quite a few South Africans within those British ranks, as there are today with the British Army in Afghanistan, and it was nice to make contact so far from home.

When talking about life as a war correspondent, the last word should go to Lord Deedes, Bill to his friends and an erstwhile member of that illustrious and civilized Old School of Journalism that seems to have passed the modern generation by. Bill died in the summer of 2007 and it says much that at the age of 93, he was still writing. He ran his column in the *Daily*

Telegraph to the end. In fact, he was still working a few weeks before he died.

As a reporter for the *Morning Post*, young William Deedes covered the 1930s Abyssinian campaign that Evelyn Waugh captured so exuberantly in his book *Scoop*. Those who have read it can't fail to detect the unmistakable link between Bill and the principal character, but as Waugh subsequently commented, 'that's all part of the game'.

'Journalists do not make good historians,' the venerable Lord Deedes wrote in the introduction to a book put out some years ago.[6] The old warrior went on: 'They like to deal in bright colors, and much of history is grey', which is true.

As for me, I don't profess to write history, but, as people like to say, 'I was there'. What's more, it was interesting, it was colourful and it was exciting.

Let those be my reasons.

AL J. VENTER
Cape Town, July 2010

With time, the conflicts in Africa became more sophisticated and white mercenaries were brought in to fight the wars of some of the black states. Both Angola and Sierra Leone – states combating years of rebel insurrection – eventually bought Soviet-era Mi-24 helicopter gunships to successfully quell insurgencies. Many of these gunships were flown by South African Air Force veterans of their own border wars. (Author's collection)

CHAPTER ONE

Getting to a Lebanon at War

The war in Lebanon began in Beirut in 1975 after the forerunner of the Lebanese Force Command – a staunchly Christian group of militants – attacked a Palestinian militia group. A succession of horrors, rather than any kind of organized military campaign, followed and soon enveloped the country in the kind of disaster that the Middle East had never experienced before.

THERE HAS BEEN MUCH BLOODLETTING in the Middle East over the ages, the chronicles tell us. But nothing like this had ever happened before, not on this enormous scale of bloody retribution and bombardment. In Lebanon in the 1970s and 1980s the killings were often accomplished with a kind of barbaric intensity that was almost apocalyptic.

First there were the Black Saturday massacres at the eastern end of Beirut's Ring Road in December 1975. Four Christians were found murdered in a car at the head office of an electricity company. Bashir Gemayel, one of the most popular Christian leaders to emerge in the war – and a brilliant tactician to boot – was as ruthless as he was tough. He ordered his Phalangists to kill 40 Muslims in reprisal.

The first large group of Muslims to arrive at a Christian roadblock – some of them on an afternoon outing with their wives and children – were targeted. The Islamic community retaliated and hundreds more innocent people were killed. Within days, these irregular, sporadic outbreaks resulted in a massive wave of reciprocal killings on both sides. It didn't take long for Lebanon to be plunged into a civil war. As somebody said at the time, this corner of the Levant typified the old homily that it is easy enough to start a war, but sheer bloody hell to bring it to an end.

Killings intensified still further and the conflict see-sawed back and forth. With time, a few significant differences with conflagrations elsewhere emerged. Many more women and children were being murdered than fighting men, underscoring the perception in certain circles that traditionally the Lebanese have a predilection for soft targets.

Also, it didn't take long for torture to become the norm. There were instances of victims not having been shot outright, but subjected to unspeakable acts of cruelty. Some innocents had their eyes gouged out before a *coup de grace* was delivered. In the end, there wasn't a single family, Muslim or Christian, that hadn't been affected by the carnage.

These days, those few Lebanese who might be prepared to discuss their woes will talk guardedly about the events of 1976. To some it might have happened yesterday. Robert Fisk, then of the London *Times*, described it as 'a kind of catharsis for the Lebanese . . . who have long understood the way in which these dreadful events should be interpreted'.

He went on to say that in Lebanon during those extreme times, 'victories were the result of courage, of patriotism, of revolutionary conviction. Defeats were always caused by the plot; the *mo'amera* . . . a conspiracy of treachery in which a foreign hand – Syrian, Palestinian, Israeli, American, French, Libyan, Iranian – was always involved.'

In his book on Lebanon, *Pity the Nation: Lebanon at War*,[1] Fisk – no apologist for either the Lebanese Christians or the Israelis – makes a reasonable attempt to explain the origins of this conflict. What he concludes is as relevant to what is going on in Lebanon in the 21st century as it was 30 years ago.

The causes of conflict go back centuries, Fisk suggests, but the consequences of Christian Maronites (who owe their name to a 5th-century Christian recluse from Syria) unwisely associating themselves with the Frankish crusaders are still visible.

With the defeat of European Christendom, the Maronites too retreated, up into the mountains of northern Lebanon, where their towns and villages still stand, wedged between great ravines, clinging to icy plateaus of the Mount Lebanon range. Under assault by Muslim Arabs, they found that these pinnacles provided their only protection and they clung on there, up amid the remains of the ancient cedar forests. They were a pragmatic, brave, distrustful people who learned that responsibility for their continued existence lay exclusively in their own hands, that their ultimate fate depended solely upon their own determination and resources. It was a characteristic that they were to share with all the minorities of Lebanon; and later with the Israelis.

Certainly Robert Fisk has the measure of these issues.

Ultimately, strife between Christian and Muslim, when it came, was both prolonged and bloody. The history of Lebanon is full of disasters in which the casualties are numbered in tens of thousands. There was the Christian–Druze war of 1860, which left at least 15,000 dead. Some historians say it was more than 20,000 and the final tally depended rather on who was doing the counting; if anyone bothered. This butchery was serious enough to result in French troops being brought in to protect the Christians.

History repeated itself when the Americans arrived a century later. US Marines landed in Beirut for the first time in 1958 at the behest of the Christian President Camille Chamoun. That happened because the threat from Islam had become still graver after Nasser's strident call for what he termed an 'Arab revival'. That event took place a few years before Britain and France made their half-cocked attempt to invade the Canal Zone.

By the 1970s, for reporters trying to write about the war, there was only one safe way for a Westerner to enter Lebanon once Beirut International Airport had been closed by the machinations of Muslim fundamentalists and that was by sea.

We could, of course, drive in through Damascus and Syria, but that still meant an overland haul through the Beka'a Valley, across the Litani and over the Shouff. It also meant being stopped at perhaps 30 roadblocks by the PLO, Amal, Shi'ite freebooters, local warlords, ideologues or another anti-Western group. Most liked to brandish their AKs in our faces as they plundered baggage for booty and occasionally arrested somebody for no evident reason.

There was always more than a whiff of danger. Some of us ended up feeling very uneasy, especially if we'd spent time in one of the Christian enclaves. An Israeli stamp in a passport meant certain arrest and that could be followed by a death warrant. As subsequent events showed, being a journalist counted for nothing; in fact you avoided that marque if you could.

In theory, it was possible to enter Lebanon through Israeli lines in the south, but that was difficult and only possible with connections in Jerusalem. I went through the Good Fence on numerous occasions on assignments with the South Lebanese Army (SLA) at the time of Sa'ad Haddad and afterwards, once, with my wife Madelon. We were shuttled across by the enigmatic journalist-appointed-colonel Yoram

The author spent a lot of time in Beirut with the Israeli Army during the course of 1982. The events then taking place shaped much of what subsequently happened in this troubled land. This photo shows him with a small IDF column near Beirut Airport, an area that later became notorious for the number of snipers around. (Author's collection)

Hamizrachi, who originally created the SLA.

Once the Israeli invasion force had pulled back from Beirut, I was allowed by the spokesman for the Israel Defense Forces (IDF) to go with my cameraman, George De'Ath, in and out to Naqoura, the United Nations Interim Force in Lebanon (UNIFIL) headquarters, while making a documentary film there.

It was always hairy on that coastal road north of Nahariya. Hizbollah was active in the region, only in those days the movement called itself the Pasdaran, the name by which they are officially known in Iran. Pasadran, it should be remembered, has always been a close affiliate of the Islamic Revolutionary Guards Corps or, as it is referred to in the media, the IRGC.[2]

Although we were moving between one UN camp and another, there were some lonely stretches of road in-between. The only unit that ever offered us an escort of sorts was the Ghanaians, and half of them were smashed, high on either alcohol or Ganga or possibly both. Their

In Lebanon, snipers were a far more serious problem than the mines. Both sides had numerous snipers who were as professional as those in any regular army. Christian forces used a variety of American weapons, including specially adapted M16s. (Author's collection)

infantry fighting vehicles were comforting, though, filthy as they were.

In the end, most of us were routed into Lebanon through Cyprus. Cut off from the outside world, there were ships leaving the ports of Larnaca and Limassol almost daily.

Quite a few scribblers would land at the Christian port of Jounieh and later, a regular ferry plied the route. Those intent on covering the war from the Islamic side of the front would try to go in through Beirut harbour, then still under Muslim control. If that wasn't possible, they would land at Jounieh and most times the Christians wouldn't stop them from crossing the Green Line – an avenue of sepulchral ruins that stretched from the water's edge near the port all the way through Chiyah, Galerie Semaan, Quadi Dbaa and on into the foothills of the Shouff – in the heart of this all-but-devastated Middle East conurbation.

It was a lot more difficult the other way round; then all sorts of questions would be asked, with some scribes even arrested for 'wanting to go over to the enemy'. In fact, all they'd hoped to do was go home, since most of the ferries used the Christian sector of the city for berthing.

Twice, getting to Beirut, we were transported by the last word in luxury, high-speed motor launches that completed the 120-odd miles in three or four hours – once through an Allied warship blockade. On that occasion, French, British and American helicopters hovered overhead and took photographs while our craft raced for the mainland.

Somewhere in Washington, Paris and London – and probably Moscow as well – there are pictures of me standing on a polished deck in T-shirt and shorts, trying very much to look the part of a tourist out on a casual jaunt. It didn't work. We all knew that our passports were carefully scrutinized on the Larnaca dockside by intelligence people who specialized in such things before they were handed back to us with perfunctory smiles.

On two occasions I was accompanied by several South African Special Forces operatives. By then, Pretoria was pretty sure that the country would soon have to deal with the same kind of urban guerrilla issues then faced by Lebanon and they were eager to acquire the know-how. In exchange, the South Africans offered training facilities for Christian military recruits and medical assistance for their more seriously wounded. F. W. de Klerk, the newly elected President of South Africa, circumvented that eventuality by releasing Nelson Mandela.

Those were curious times. On these VIP visits we were grandly accommodated and feasted, though I never did get accustomed to eating raw sheep brains and pig liver or taking five spoonfuls of sugar in my coffee.

Lebanese hospitality could be hard on the constitution. Apart from the food – which, at best, was dodgy because the war meant there were no kind of health controls – once a bottle of whisky had been cracked it had to be quaffed and that led to some prodigious hangovers.

I took my still adolescent son, Albert, to this country once for a summary lesson of what happens when religious or tribal factions go berserk. His reaction was interesting because none of it made sense. Also, it was dangerous; we were sniped at on the Green Line one morning and he had at least one near miss. On these tours my minders seldom let me out of their sight, and on that trip they had an additional responsibility: my son.

Their close protection caused some difficulty on my last trip to Jounieh in the ferry, which left Larnaca at last light and arrived in Lebanon at dawn. I was given a cabin and a key. However, having travelled for two days from Islamabad via London to get to Cyprus – I'd seen off a film crew that I'd tasked with circumventing Kabul during the early stages of the Soviet invasion – I left the belly-dancers in the saloon about midnight. For once, I told my minder, I could find my own way to my cabin. Anyway, he was interested in the dancers.

It could be that I had had too many gin and tonics, but I soon found myself way down at one of the lower levels of the ship and in a cabin with the same number as on my key. It wasn't my original cabin because my luggage wasn't there, but it was late and I was bushed. Anyway, the key worked, a bunk beckoned and I was out the moment my head touched the pillow. I didn't know until later that, somehow, I'd found my way into the crew's quarters.

Of course, when they checked my original cabin some time after midnight, I wasn't there. In fact, I wasn't anywhere. All eight of our bodyguards spent the next three hours searching. They went through every corner of the ship, except, of course, where the crew were billeted. At some stage very early in the morning, they concluded that I'd either been murdered or had fallen overboard, which was when they woke the captain and ordered him to put about to look for me.

The exchange apparently went something like this:

Minder: 'He's gone. We must go back and look for him.'

Captain: 'That is difficult. We have to keep to our schedule. Anyway, how do you know he isn't with some woman in her cabin?'

Minder: 'We've checked. There are only so many women travelling alone . . . he's not with any of them.'

Captain: 'Well then, how do you know he isn't with some man? Do you know his preferences?'

They left it at that.

I surfaced several hours later when I had to get to the heads in a hurry. When I emerged onto the passenger deck, there was one-armed Claude, the man responsible for keeping me alive, sitting with his head in his hand. He was convinced I'd been murdered. When I walked up the stairs to where he was sitting, he looked up, blinked, looked hard again and finally smiled. With that he got up and kissed me on both cheeks, which was when I realized that the Lebanese can be pretty effusive in a crisis.

To get to East Beirut at the time of the fighting in Sodico in 1981, I had to use whatever contacts I could get. I had been in touch with some

Christian contacts in Cyprus on my way back to London from Israel after having been with Sa'ad Haddad's people in South Lebanon. One of them gave me the name of someone with 'contacts' in Limassol. And what a peculiar set of connections they were.

The man's one claim to fame was that he owned a Ford Thunderbird and spent hours each night cruising around looking for girls. Also, I was regarded as little more than a meal ticket. His name was Habib and I only found out later that he was a con artist of repute.

In great detail, I explained to this devious bastard what I needed. I had to get 'to your own people' in Beirut, the Christians. Many boats from Limassol went to Jounieh, I said, stating the obvious. Could he get me onto one?

My sole criterion, I stressed, was that the boat should have a Christian skipper and, if possible, a Christian crew. I had no particular wish to make any kind of close acquaintance with the hot end of the Jihad.

The matter of hostages had not yet arisen; it would be a while yet before people like the journalists Terry Anderson and John McCarthy or Bill Buckley and Peter Kilburn, the librarian at the American University in Beirut (both of whom died in detention), were taken by the militias. Others, like the American priest Father Lawrence Jenco, would soon be kidnapped and held under appalling conditions.

'My dear friend', suggested Habib, putting his arm around my shoulders, 'there is no problem. I find you very good boat.' That, in itself, sounded ominous. He was confident that the entire exercise would probably be only fractionally more difficult than buying a beer. It would cost me $300 down, he said, half up-front. I didn't argue, though I never found out how much Habib kept back for himself.

I waited three days. Then one evening, I was taken through the harbour gate at Limassol to board the archetypal rust bucket, the motor vessel *Ali*, a couple of hundred tons of badly eroded steel held precariously together by huge dollops of red lead paint on the superstructure. I discovered later that the *Ali* was 29 years old and was capable of seven knots with a following wind. I was also distressed to find that she was Syrian; her port of registration, painted in faded white letters on the stern, was Latakia.

Habib reassured me. 'They're good people. Just remember, not all Syrians are crazy . . . only some of them. I wouldn't send you into danger, now would I?' I wasn't convinced, but I also knew that I couldn't hang about the Cyprus waterfront indefinitely. Perhaps it would be alright, I persuaded myself.

It wasn't. About an hour after we left I asked Captain Mahmoud how long it would take us to get to Jounieh.

'Jounieh?' he said. '*Jounieh*!' he shouted. 'Who tell you we go to Jounieh? *We go Beirut!*' I was being delivered into the hands of zealots, and with all the Israeli stamps in my passport, I was sure they would be very pleased to see me.

Captain Mahmoud, a tubby, curly haired little Syrian, watched me carefully as he spoke and was suspicious from the start. Who the hell was I, anyway? And why was I going to Lebanon? I cursed Habib. The situation wasn't only invidious, it was bare-back dangerous.

My friends tell me that when things get uncomfortable I have a talent for ingratiation. It's a blessed quality that has its advantages. More to the point, it is also probably why I'm still alive.

On the *Ali* that night, I knew that if I put one foot wrong, the Syrian crew would most certainly deliver me to Damascus. They would do so even if they just thought I was up to no good. All Westerners were assumed to be foreign agents in the Levant in those days and in some parts, they still are.

I took the initiative and made it quite plain that I was a *sahafi*, a reporter. I said I had heard about the atrocities committed by the *Kata-ib*, the Christian Phalangists and I wanted to see these monsters for myself. I showed Captain Mahmoud my *Daily Express* press card and he appeared satisfied. For the moment, anyway.

The voyage should have taken a day. Because of bad weather, it took more than two. In that time the crafty little Arab captain questioned me often, and he could be subtle. What did I think of President Assad? Had I ever been to Israel? Was I a Jew? Did I believe all that rubbish about the Nazis killing Jews? I lied with accomplished fluency.

As vessels go, the motor vessel *Ali* had little to recommend it. This small ship – more like a boat, really – had originally been built by the Germans for the Baltic trade. Its most elegant quality was its porcelain ashtray with the word 'Dunhill' that appeared in prominent letters on all four sides. Obviously stolen, it was proudly displayed in a salon that had been stained by generations of mariners sloshing their soup about.

For the two days at sea I kept to the saloon, the only place where I could get my head down. I ignored the dirty plastic wallpaper, the buckled ceiling and unswept floor. A page of the Koran was prominently displayed above the fridge, stuck onto the bulkhead with cello-tape. The captain's hookah stood in a corner. As a good Muslim he refused the whisky I proffered, though he made up for it by coughing his way almost ritually through wads of tobacco at all hours.

The 'usual offices' on board were austere. There were two heads; the Western one didn't work and the other was the ubiquitous Oriental hole in the deck over which you squatted, in the company of swarms of green flies that delight in Middle Eastern latrines. We ate in common out of an unwashed aluminum pot, with our hands and a spoon. I hoped that the others were scrupulous in their observation of the usual Muslim ablutionary injunctions.

The boat was carrying earth-moving equipment for the 'rehabilitation' of Beirut; the war would end in a month or two, Captain Mahmoud told me confidently, adding that the dreaded Christians were being pummelled so badly by the Muslims that they were about to surrender *en bloc*. I didn't argue.

The day-to-day duties on board were the responsibility of the captain and an engineer, a little Syrian who spent most of his time down below in the engine-room. There were five other crew members.

We broke down twice. The crew – two Syrians, an evil-looking Egyptian and two Lebanese boys who lounged about the saloon and with whom I communicated in sign language – were a disparate lot. Looking back, I am pretty sure that if Captain Mahmoud had not had a firm hand on his men like the Turk he was, they would have considered my Nikons as well as my money belt as their rightful perks. I felt utterly alone.

We eventually arrived at Beirut and even with the war going on, I was pleased because the place had a seductive charm about it. Kim Philby regarded Beirut as the most beautiful city in the world. Now the blackened shell of the tall Holiday Inn in the western part dominated the skyline and could be clearly seen from where we lay. We'd anchored in the roadstead for the night because Captain Mahmoud didn't want to go in until daylight; he feared we might be mortared. 'The *Kata'ib*', he said. 'Murderers!'

Getting ashore the next morning was not easy. Captain Mahmoud prepared to go to the port offices as soon as we docked. He said that I should go with him to show my passport. I had a bellyache, I replied. Would he mind if I rested a while?

The options open to me were limited as I observed the harbour surrounds very carefully from the gangplank. How to get to the

The Soviet RPG-7 was the weapon of choice among many combatants on both sides
of Beirut's Green Line. (Author's collection)

Christian quarter past the harbour authorities and others who would want to know what I was doing there without a visa? There was also the stamp showing that I had been in Tel Aviv the week before.

I spoke to a couple of dock workers and they asked me if I was an American. I answered no, definitely not! They were sceptical and for the moment left it at that. Then an official came on board, but he had worry beads in his hand and I didn't risk telling him anything. I only found out later that the beads are as common among Christians as among Muslims.

At about eleven that morning a taxi deposited a passenger at a ship farther along the quay. When the driver had turned his car around I stopped him. Was he going into town?

'Sure,' he said in American English. Where did I want to go? I looked for any indication that he might be a Christian. There was: a St Christopher badge among the artificial fur on the dashboard.

'You Christian?'

'Yes, I am' he answered, his eyes narrowing. He looked at me, now also suspicious. 'Why you want to know?'

'Just curious. Can you wait while I get my bags?'

When I got back in his cab I took my life in my hands and asked him whether he could get me through port control without having to show my passport. 'I want to get to the offices of the Lebanese Force Command', I told him quietly, and for once I was deadly earnest.

It was a gamble, of course, but I had no alternative. I explained what I was trying to do. I was a journalist and a Christian. I wanted to report on the war from his side.

'You sit in front here with me,' he said quietly. With that he got out, put my bags in the trunk and came back with a dirty old cap which he told me to wear. 'You are my brother. I talk when we go through checkpoint.'

Three minutes later Michael Chamoun (who became a good friend until he was killed in a mortar attack on a crossroads in Bourj Hammoud three years later) dropped me off at the offices of the Lebanese Force Command. It was a fine old two-storey building about 500 yards from the entrance to the port and it had taken a battering.

I tipped Mike $20 US which, for a freelancer in those days, was a lot of money.

CHAPTER TWO

Death of a Young Man

Like Nicholas Della Casa and the Angolan soldier killed after we decided to take his bayonet, I also felt indirectly responsible for the death of a yong soldier in Beirut. I never did get anything but his first name and that was Christian. He died under very different circumstances from the other two, after we'd spent almost a week together along that city's embattled Green Line. In the brief period that we operated together, we'd got to know each other quite well, which happens often enough in wartime.

CHRISTIAN WAS BARELY 21 YEARS old and had returned to Beirut after several years of studying science at the Sorbonne in Paris. He'd come back to 'fight for something in which I truly believe', he told me, implacable in his determination to make some kind of impact against an enemy whom he would refer to as 'fucking barbarians'.

His job, while I remained on assignment in Lebanon, was to act not only as a military escort, but also as my general factotum. Duties included protecting and feeding me, as well as finding us a place to put our heads down after dark. It was a thankless, unforgiving task in a society where any contact with a foreigner is regarded with distrust. Together, to his credit, we overcame a labyrinth of obstacles.

His name, in itself, was a declaration of sorts in a country where religious divisions have given rise to 14 centuries of conflict, and to my eternal regret, his death was pointless, utterly so. I would have liked to have said as much when I met his mother afterwards, but it would have been inappropriate: he was her only child and his death was not only unnecessary, it should never have happened.

Christian did a sterling job as guide, facilitator, interpreter and friend. We operated under deplorable conditions and nothing was easy. He had been detailed to accompany me as my 'minder' by Max Geahel, the undisputed head of the Lebanese Force Command's G-5 office. Simply put, you couldn't get into this war with the Christians unless

G-5 – Max's press-cum-security office – gave the nod.

Interestingly, Max was another of those characters who emerged prominently as the war progressed. American author Jim Morris, who followed me into Lebanon afterwards, described him in one of his reports as 'the mad monk with the thousand yard stare'. It was Max who told Christian that whatever happened, he wanted me back at headquarters when I'd completed my tour of duty.

'And I want him alive!'

The war that raged around us in the early 1980s eventually caused Lebanon to transmogrify. It went from the most ordered society in the region to the most violent and chaotic the world has experienced in the past few centuries

For many years, once hostilities had started, the country remained an anarchist's fantasy. Murder was the norm and the word compassion wasn't part of its lexicon. By the time all this madness had ended, there were about 100 different militias, each with its quota of zealots – some Christian, the majority staunchly fundamentalist Islamic.

Apart from Amal, Hizbollah, the Christians and the Druze communities – together with perhaps a handful of other political or factional groupings – very few of the rest maintained even a semblance of order. Within their ranks, only the most powerful individuals ruled, and they did so absolutely and without compromise. Foot soldiers were expected to do their bidding and if they didn't, they were killed.

It is one of the oldest axioms, dating back to before the time of Caesar, that in a prolonged struggle, you eventually become like your enemy. So it was in Lebanon. With both Christian and Muslim, the crust of ideology made an honest reckoning in this singularly violent society uncommonly difficult.

At first glance, this was a nation that had lost all reason. The journey from progression all the way through to mindless mayhem had been swift, with huge numbers of people killed. Now and again, entire towns, settlements and ghettos – some Christian, others Muslim – were wiped off the map. Sabra and Shatilla (both Islamic) were among them. There was a Christian town south of Beirut where it was estimated that between 10,000 and 12,000 people – men, women and children – were systematically slaughtered one morning in the early days of the struggle. Things went on to deteriorate to the point where there were people in the streets of Beirut, Sidon, Tripoli and elsewhere slaughtering each another with the kind of ferocity that has recently surfaced even more mindlessly – be that even possible – in Iraq and Afghanistan.

The battle in which young Christian died extended over a 20-mile radius. Still worse, both he and I, together with two more of his colleagues had – truth be told – actually been responsible for the bloody sequence of events that had begun a few hours before his death, ultimately causing Beirut's Green Line to erupt along its length. It was a most horrific experience.

It started on the night of Saturday, 21 May 1981. Some Syrian soldiers had been killed by the Christian Lebanese Force Command following a surprise attack that had been launched – at a whim, mark you – by none other than Christian and his two compadres. Clearly, the trio could never have envisaged the terrible consequences that were to follow. How were they to know that in a single rocket strike, they would end up killing half a dozen Syrian troops hunkered down on a first-floor balcony on the Green Line?

In any event, I was the media guy they were trying to impress and if nothing else, they were appallingly successful.

Christian forces in Lebanon sported a variety of American-built vehicles, such as these M113 armoured personnel carriers. They performed well among the rolling hills of South Lebanon. (Author's collection)

It was the classic, after-dark kind of operation that involved us quietly penetrating towards the edge of the defensive perimeter along the Green Line. Our mission, with almost no planning in place – usually a recipe for disaster – was to hit hard at a previously selected target and quickly withdraw. The entire operation would last perhaps ten minutes; a tidy, surgical rocket strike within the close confines of some of the tall buildings that fringed Christian defences.

The attack, when it happened, went off like clockwork. Together our little party had finished the six-pack that I'd brought off the boat, which was when Christian turned to me.

'I've got something for you', he had said. 'Our guys have got word of a Syrian lookout post. It was abandoned before, but been manned again. As the crow flies it can't be more than 100 yards or so from here . . . right on the Line. It's a bastard of a position . . . caused us a lot of trouble in the past couple of months.' The question he posed was whether I wanted to go in with his team and knock it out?

'When?' I asked.

'When we're finished here . . . in a few minutes' he replied, smiling. Always game for the unexpected, I acquiesced.

With that we dipped our unleavened pitta bread into the communal bowl of hummus soured with lemon juice, just as the Lebanese like it, and shortly afterwards four of us set off through the pitch-black warren of fortifications that had been strengthened by Christian's people a few years before. One of the soldiers of the Lebanese Force Command who knew the building had been detached from his unit and led the way.

I was aware that our immediate problem was going through a warren of black tunnels with only a torch to guide us. This was risky because the week before a Palestinian commando group had managed to penetrate that self-same structure. They'd used grappling irons and ropes to climb up to a balcony on the second floor and once there, set up an ambush in the dark. When one of the other side's patrols came by, they attacked.

'They killed one . . . two more wounded. So tonight we're going to settle that score', Christian had called quietly over his shoulder as he headed for the rear exit of the makeshift restaurant where we'd all come together.

It took a while to get to our objective. Slowly, deliberately, we felt and prodded our way along innumerable corridors and stairwells. The

Member of one of the Christian militias armed with an LMG on patrol along
Beirut's Green Line. (Author's collection)

place was musty, almost stifling. Finally, we reached a balcony that
obliquely overlooked the Syrian position.

Indeed, it was a novel experience. I was able to observe from up close
that much of the Christian side of the Green Line was only a few paces
from similar Syrian and Palestinian positions. In fact, as subsequent
visitors pointed out, the two armies could have thrown stones at each
other had they chosen to do so. Christian had already cursorily
explained that we were heading for a position that had been used as an
observation post several times in the past.

'We'll see them from there', he stated, adding that the enemy
wouldn't be more than 50 yards away. Like the others, I'd already
blackened my face and taken off the white T-shirt I'd been wearing. In
its place, I was handed a camo jacket.

The Lebanese were armed with the usual array of infantry section
weapons, with one difference. We had with us a Yugoslav 64mm M80
LAW rocket-launcher, nothing big, but with a three-pound, high-
explosive warhead that promised results.

After carefully examining his options, Christian told us in whispers
that we'd hit them at an angle of about 45 degrees. Having been

involved in similar attacks in the past, he understood the implications. But first we'd have to prepare ourselves, he warned.

' . . . mustn't show our faces . . . night-vision equipment. The Syrians have the best infra-red goggles . . . Soviet', he'd ruminated earlier. If they spotted anything amiss, they'd let fly.

The idea was that two of us would launch the attack from the balcony. The other two would take up defensive positions behind and inside the building 'in case we get a visitor or three'. I'd been told that I would stand immediately to Christian's left, since the rear had to be perfectly clear of all obstructions; a five-yard tongue of flame would shoot out from the back of the launcher and incinerate everything in its path. It would also sear the walls of the room behind us. There were no windows to concern us they had long since been blown away.

'I'll give the signal . . . you cover your ears . . . the blast is deafening . . . like a bomb going off.' It was interesting that he didn't bother to protect his own hearing.

Then, almost like he'd done this sort of thing every week, Christian popped his head over the parapet to judge angle and distance. That much done, he took cover again. With a jerk of the head he invited me to have a look. 'Be quick . . . you never know . . .'

The Syrian strongpoint was on a balcony very much like our own, but on the other side of the road. I was sure that they anticipated nothing so I took a little longer than I'd intended. I could spot a dim light, possibly 50 or 60 yards away, and I could hear Arab music, probably Radio Damascus and barely audible. The troops on the other side were talking in quiet tones, oblivious of being scrutinized.

'How many?' I asked.

'About six, perhaps more. If we're lucky we'll get them all', were his final words on the subject.

Two minutes later Christian fired the LAW and we didn't chose to hang about to admire our handiwork. The explosion, so close to where I was huddled on the far side of the balcony, was thumping, even through my cupped hands. For a second or two it lit up the entire street outside. The job completed, we ducked back through a wall of smoke into the corridors behind us even before the echoes had stopped reverberating. We heard screams but there was nothing retaliatory. Nobody even fired a shot.

Moments later, an almost palpable wall of silence enveloped the place. Once back at the little restaurant, we stayed a short while to

The inappropriately named 'Green Line' stretched through the length of Beirut and the only 'green' to be found was the slime that collected in festering pools in hollows and shell holes between the structures. Opposing forces were often 'just across the road' and within a whisper of each other. It was in a such a position that our attack on the Syrian observation post took place. (Author's collection).

report to the officer in charge, had a quick coffee and then headed outside for one of the mortar-spotting posts at Sodico, half-a-mile up the Line.

Christian then said something that was to echo in my mind for a long time afterwards: 'Enemy reaction is always in direct proportion to the amount of damage you cause.' It made sense.

Once the job was over and obviously successful, Christian and his buddies were warmly congratulated by the officer in charge. My regret at the time was that there hadn't been enough light to take photographs.

Clearly, everybody was ebullient about the outcome. We'd gone in, struck at a specific strongpoint and successfully extricated ourselves. We were also aware – judging by the screams that followed the attack – that there had been casualties. In the ten seconds or so that we listened for a reaction after the attack, there was no mistaking the cries of the wounded.

To Christian and his friends it mattered little that they had taken lives. As they were always telling me, they hated Muslims. Their rancour came from somewhere deep inside, the same kind of venom that Jews and Palestinian Arabs hold for one another just across the southern border.

Questioned about the unmitigated bile for his adversaries the previous day, Christian told me that there could never be any possibility of compromise. 'Not with those savages', were his words.

It took the Syrians a while to react. By now we'd reached a tall, partly finished skyscraper that was being used by the Lebanese Force Command to observe both their own targets as well the placement of hostile mortars firing from across the Line.

The building overlooked the battleground for miles along that ruinous border. After reporting in, we took an old builder's lift up to the 17th floor, little more than a metal frame and open on three sides of four. I couldn't help but get the impression that the other side might have been watching our progress, but it was quite dark and the lights of Beirut opened up before us as we ascended.

Getting to the top was an eerie experience and something I'll always remember. The upper half of the building had only a central reinforced concrete core that was completely exposed since just the lower ten floors had walls. What this improvised eagle's lair did provide was a splendid view of what was happening in much of the city below. Beirut lay spread-eagled like a giant illuminated carpet: so much for blackout procedures . . .

From 200 yards up, Beirut looked different from any other city that I'd visited. Paris at night from the top of the Eiffel Tower is ablaze, as is Manhattan. In Beirut, by contrast, the illuminations were intermittent, as if some parts of the city had no electric power, which they probably didn't. Smoke hung in patches in a few of the distant valleys, while half-a-dozen ships lay at anchor well away from the coast, their navigation beams hardly visible. Like mariners everywhere, they were the most cautious of the lot.

Christian pointed out where we'd just emerged from, the entire suburb having taken on a subdued, cloudy hue, with parts almost entirely in darkness. There were enemy dead out there somewhere, I couldn't help thinking: more mothers' sons.

Then, as if by unified command, the entire front erupted, almost like a succession of explosions at a firework display. We were suddenly enveloped in a thousand blasts, with guns firing everywhere. It was a spectacle that stunned, a *son et lumiere* that reeked of cordite. A great series of cannonades came from dozens of different positions and all we could do on our lofty pinnacle was watch and pray and hope to hell that nobody turned their muzzles in our direction.

Katyushas screamed past to the left and then again towards the right. A shower of ZSU shells – clustered in a huge ball of fire about 100 yards across – hurtled past almost within touching distance from where we crouched. How else to describe it but as horrific? If the gunner had aimed half a degree to the left, it would have all been over.

The ZSU, like anti-personnel mines being deployed in the hills around Beirut, were constant subjects for discussion among Christian forces at the time. Both were new innovations in the war and were making sometimes horrific inroads into their defences. The multi-barrelled ZSU had the additional distinction of being one of the most destructive weapons devised by man, It has since become the ultimate killing machine in scores of wars across the globe, Iraq and Afghanistan included.

Originally of Soviet origin – with four barrels and a liquid cooling system to allow for sustained fire – there were few Syrian strongpoints in Beirut that didn't have them, each one capable of pushing out 4,000 rounds of high-explosive ordnance a minute.

It is worth mentioning that the first time I heard a ZSU deployed in anger – in bursts of about two or three seconds at a time – it sounded like a bulldozer revving its engines.

Add to that, clusters of rockets exploding way out towards the Christian sectors of the city, and still more missiles which roared into the hills behind us and in the direction of Jounieh. Somewhere near the foothills to our left, artillery batteries of the Lebanese Force Command responded.

Meanwhile, mortar teams deployed by the Christian forces below had opened up, with Jamal, a slight man with three days' beard growth, providing the sector with coordinates over his radio. A veteran of eight years of war and the commander of the observation post on which we were precariously perched, he was apparently brilliant at what he did.

How did he distinguish between his own and enemy fire? Long experience, was his retort. Anyway, he seemed to have no difficulty.

More Katyushas and more ZSU salvoes from across the Line followed, each time a little closer. We had to be hit sooner or later, and I said so. At about this point, I'd seen enough and, being no hero, suggested to Christian that we go down. I suddenly felt quite vulnerable.

A loud crack on the floor below, which was only half-finished, shook the structure around us. Probably a rocket-grenade, Jamal reckoned. If so, he added, we were up shit creek because somebody was aiming straight up at us. Even I knew that RPGs aren't fired at random; you select your target, you aim and you fire.

The prospect of our Muslim opponents using night-vision equipment suddenly entered the equation. Another blast rocked our landing, and then one more. From the corner of my eye as I crouched low, I spotted Christian moving backwards towards the incomplete elevator shaft in all probability, looking for more adequate cover.

What happened next was anyone's guess, except that another huge explosion shook our ledge. One of our mortar-spotters threw himself headlong away from the narrow parapet on which he'd been standing while I quickly got down low behind a narrow ledge.

Then there was another blast, followed by a scream. It was Christian, his cry unmistakable over the echoes of mortar and machine-gun clatter. It came just as Jamal was telling the rest of his men to get themselves down to ground level and to use the stairs, not the elevator.

It didn't register at the time, but I was told afterwards that Christian screamed again before he hit the bottom of the shaft. A thud followed, which never penetrated to our level because of the noise.

After that, only the sounds of intermittent firing reached us, together with the rattle of artillery from across the way as the firing picked up again. The young man's shriek of terror had been heard by some of the Phalangist soldiers manning guns and mortars on the ground way below us and Jamal was already on his radio talking to them.

We didn't know immediately what had happened. Only later did we work out that when the last shell rocked us, Christian had probably taken a big step backwards, into the unguarded elevator shaft. The young man dropped into a chasm of nothingness as he plummeted down the same shaft we'd earlier used to get to the mortar spotting position on the roof. We all had our theories about the accident, for that is what it was; he wasn't hit either by a bullet or by shrapnel. At the same time, he must have been conscious until he hit bottom.

The shock of losing one of your own in such an unusually tragic manner was unsettling, and it stayed that way for a long time afterwards. In fact, it was much worse than taking a hit. All that I could think of just then was that if I hadn't been there, he'd probably not have been on top of that derelict half-finished building at Sodico. Had I not come to Lebanon, the youthful Christian would probably still be alive.

When they lifted him out of the pit at the bottom of the shaft – cumbersome, and unwieldy – they had to manoeuvre it so as to pull his torso out through a narrow opening, which was difficult in such a confined space. Anybody who has manhandled a lifeless body will understand the meaning of 'dead weight'.

I'd already made my way down all 17 floors by then and stood by as they extricated Christian's body, the men working carefully, almost gently at the task in hand. The back of his head had touched his heels at one point and it seemed as if his vertebrae had turned to paste. One of his eyes had been forced out by the impact and it was hideous. Those impressions and the scream that followed his toppling will remain with me for the rest of my life.

When it was learnt that Christian was dead, Rocky, the commander of the mortar post, decided that if it was anybody's fault it was mine. I was the only stranger there. Christian had been escorting me. Ergo, I must be an enemy agent and, therefore, I had hurled him down the elevator shaft!

Rocky was actually on his way up the stairs as we were heading down. We met halfway and though I didn't yet know it, he was set on throwing me to my death. A big, powerful man with wrap-around combat boots and a 9mm pistol in a shoulder holster, he could easily have done so.

'If you had resisted I would have shot you', he said seriously when we had a drink at a little bistro within sight of that same building at Sodico a year later. He had menacing dark eyes but he was a good man to have at your back if there was trouble. I'd brought him one of Richard Davis' Second Chance body armour vests.

Rocky: 'I was actually stopped from killing you by Jamal coming down those stairs with you', he told me. 'I asked him why you were still alive. It took him a minute or two to convince me that the moment Christian stepped backwards, you were already taking cover behind the same ledge as he was. If you'd headed down those stairs alone, we wouldn't be having this drink tonight.'

I knew nothing of all this at the time because I can only manage the most cursory Arabic.

For 36 hours or more, the Christian-dominated Lebanese Force Command and Muslim soldiers did battle. They lobbed everything they had at one another: infantry, artillery, missiles and mortar bombs, together with the full gambit of light and heavy machine-gun fire. Those close enough to enemy lines even lobbed the occasional grenade.

It was absurd enough for Soviet TM-57 anti-tank landmines to be laid by one side or the other on the concrete of what remained of some of Beirut's super-highways; huge, 12-kilogram circular objects that you had to be blind to miss.

Heavy DShKA machine-guns that more recently have been much in evidence in places like Georgia, and Grozny thundered into our defences. Nor could you miss volleys of Katyusha 122mm rockets that screamed over the rooftops. These emanated from what we later discovered were banks of Russian BM-21 rocket launchers that had been clandestinely ferried into the city at night by the Syrians.

My friend Christian wasn't the only one to die during those two terrible days. Many more people were ripped apart in bursts from ZSU four-barrelled guns. Fusillades of 23mm shells slammed into houses, blocks of apartments, villages, hospitals and schools. Carnage took place simultaneously on both sides of the line.

During much of the Lebanese war, this kind of exchange would be sporadic. Only occasionally did it result in a total, all-out effort. When it did, opposing sides would launch full-scale, all-or-nothing attacks, with men and machines manning successive lines of steel that ringed the city. Only when you examine some of the photographs taken at the time is it possible to grasp the horror of these appalling battles that sometimes went on for days.

I spent the night in the darkest, deepest basement garage at Sodico and was thankful for it because from then on, there were shells pouring down on our positions at ground level. Stalingrad, I imagined, must have been something like this. For hours the Syrians seemed to concentrate on our building, as if they knew that it was us who had started the crap. A few dozen Soviet 240mm mortars – fearsome, weighty bombs that they are – rocked the building all the way to its core. Every time one of them struck, shards of plaster, paint and dust would rain down on us. Sleep was out of the question, though I did fall into an uneasy doze for a few hours as Rocky's men on the floors above retaliated. It seemed absurd, was one of the thoughts constantly going through my mind. Firing at what? Empty spaces in looming canyons of fire.

Apart from Christian, there had been a handful of casualties on our side and only one more death: one of the irregulars had caught some shrapnel in his throat. As jagged and sharp as a carving blade, nobody was even aware that he'd been hit till morning; he'd silently choked to death in his own blood. When they discovered his body, it was in a half-crouched position on a landing in one of the stairwells into which he had crawled.

A few of the men and one of the female radio operators were slightly hurt by blast, one of them with a flesh wound in the butt. The Lebanese nurses who shared our ordeal dealt with them.

Dawn came slowly. The image of Christian's broken body was still before me and it must have showed, for an officer of the Lebanese Force Command came and sat on my stretcher. He told me to get a grip on myself. 'There's nothing anybody could have done,' he said. It's the price we all pay for this war . . . what those people do to us. What we do to them . . .'

Almost half-heartedly he cursed his Crusader forefathers for not doing a more efficient job a millennium before. Then he stood up and smiled because he too realized that he was a product, if not of that epoch, then of this one, which was equally savage.

He suggested I get something to eat. They'd got a makeshift canteen at the end of the garage, he said. But hummus and tahini at six in the morning wasn't on my agenda. A bit later, perhaps, because there was nothing else, if you didn't count the cucumber salad.

A short while later, at about ten that morning, we heard bells. They echoed across a city of empty, pock-marked passageways and tall buildings that had been mutilated by war. Though the setting was vastly different, it sounded much as it does along Columbus Avenue when the bells of New York's St Patrick's Cathedral ring out early on a Sunday morning. These peals came from an adjacent Maronite church that Christian and I had passed on the way to Sodico. They were for my dead buddy.

'They're burying the young man' said the officer who'd spoken to me earlier. He made the sign of the cross, kissing his thumb as he completed his devotion. Apparently the boy's parents were there, even though the fighting went on. They'd been called in the night and, as a precaution, had been escorted to wait in the church in the early hours. Fluent in Arabic, French and English, fit and strong for his years and an outstanding shot with an M16, young Christian was also some mother's son.

His parents buried his body before it was cold; such was the custom both in that war and elsewhere in the Arab world. As somebody explained, the dead putrefy quickly and Beirut that summer was steaming.

These were things that simply had to be done in wartime, 'a precaution', said another before he went off to comfort a young soldier sobbing alone in a corner. It was one of Christian's schoolboy friends.

Jacques Tabet, an old friend from many visits to Beirut, fetched me from Sodico about noon in an almost derelict VW Beetle. He arrived at high speed and we left with as much urgency as before. I was struck by the crazy look in his eyes and that worried me, though in retrospect his concerns were justified. Alone, he had driven through one of the toughest urban battles to hit Beirut for a while.

'Let's go', he said brusquely, 'you can't spend the whole fucking war here.' He had his own way of expressing himself and was invariably impatient to get an unpleasant job done. Just then the firing intensified: they must have spotted him racing along the Line.

'You're joking', was my reply. 'We're not going into *that*?'

Even though there was still some heavy mortar fire coming in, he insisted that we move. I was happy to wait in the basement until it eased a little, I told him. Give it an hour, was my suggestion.

A strange conglomeration of weapons converged on Lebanon as the war progressed: these ranged from Steyr Mannlicher sniping rifles from Austria (bought by Iran, purportedly for that country's Olympic team and handed to Hizbollah), to Chinese recoilless rifles, Soviet Katyusha rocket batteries and many more. This jeep with its American recoilless rifle was fielded by the Christian Lebanese Force Command. (Author's collection)

'No. it's not going to get any better . . . You must come! We've got something else for you', was his retort. That said, he walked briskly towards the car without even checking whether I was following. Jacques obviously hadn't time for patter and I acquiesced by squeezing myself into the front seat alongside him. There were no other passengers.

Jacques didn't hesitate a moment and shot out of the Sodico building like a man possessed. As with much else that had taken place in the past few hours, it was an unusual experience roaring out of that basement and on reflection afterwards, I realized that it was probably the single most dangerous journey of my life. We were the only car on the road and suddenly we seemed to attract an awful lot of attention.

Jacques swerved, criss-crossed a dozen highways, ducked under bridges and zigzagged in an ongoing effort to confuse those who were targeting us from across the Line. Because we were moving fast, we probably didn't present an easy target, even though there were chunks of brick and mortar constantly falling onto the road around us. There was no missing the unceremonious pasting as we passed. The Beetle was compact and presented a low profile . . . for once, comfortably so.

The time that it took us to get away from the Line was the longest couple of minutes ever. Meanwhile, attrition of another kind had begun as both sides opened up again.

CHAPTER THREE

Levantine Woes

'Now I watch from another continent, but I find those same emotions resurfacing. The conspiracies, the car-bombs, the threatening rhetoric and political deadlock are all eerily familiar. The actors are like shadows from a long gone past. They are more grey perhaps – those who have avoided assassination. But the cast in Lebanon's tragedy has changed little in two decades. Then, as now, a presidential election is the setting, and the struggle where religion and clan play the main roles threatens to set Lebanon back 20 years.'

16 November, 2007: Octavia Nasr, CNN's senior editor for Arab affairs, on how little had changed in Lebanon's political hierarchy since the 1980s.

BEIRUT, THEY USED TO SAY when I first came ashore from Cyprus in the early 1980s, was a city of shattered facades, bad dreams and few prospects. To this newcomer, it was impossible not to perceive a fundamental, visceral antipathy towards peace, which is how it often is when people are trying to kill each other.

The war had been going on a while. Dawn was greeted each day by the unholy trinity of Israeli reconnaissance planes in the sky, mortar bombs exploding at intersections and muezzin calls from the minarets in the foothills of the Shouff. All that and more car-bombs than you could care to count, along with roadblocks on the outskirts manned by factions that were almost exclusively Islamic and at war with one another and anybody else who came into contention. Anarchy ruled.

In its day, Beirut had been among the wealthiest and most delightful of cities; 'Pearl of the Mediterranean', aficionados would call it. With its boutiques that rivalled those of the Avenue Montaigne, it had the best on offer from the world's capitals including its own up-market versions of Harrods and Bloomingdales, chic cafes and the finest patisseries east of Lyon. It had long ago put Cairo to shame as the finest city in the Islamic world. Still more important, Beirut was the hub of the oil-rich Arab banking world.

By the time I got there, few vestiges of that old exuberance remained. Half the population had fled and the other half was fighting a rear-guard action that was hopeless. The future, one sensed, was a narrow tympan of confidence so easily shattered by daily bombardments that sometimes resembled earlier European wars. Still, the people who stayed could only hope for better because for the majority, there was simply no other option.

Also, this was Beirut, their beloved Beirut. Public buildings and private houses that sometimes gave the city a look of Tuscany or Provence were still there; at least those hadn't been destroyed, although just about all had been hideously disfigured by gunfire. Their occupants – the ones with the money – were long gone. Others had retreated to high ground outside town, especially those with children.

While war waged, there were stark contrasts. There were many Christians around who were extremely well off, many having made

A scene of destruction along Beirut's Green Line. We were not to know it then, but this kind of warfare was subsequently to repeat itself in a spate of other wars that ranged through the Balkans, Chechnya and Iraq, as well as in parts of the African continent. (Author's collection)

fortunes in West Africa's diamond fields. In contrast, to the west of the Green Line – the 'World of the Mullah' as some liked to call it, and still do – there were warrens of poverty where people with nothing to lose but their faith gathered in semi-permanent camps. They did so amid a stench and pestilential filth that was utterly unforgiving.

Some of the most radical Muslim or Palestinian fighters came from there. When they joined one or other faction, they might have been given a bit of cash, perhaps enough to keep their families alive or they would simply take what they needed from travellers like us at roadblocks. For these journeys, I used my second British passport because it had no Israeli stamps in it.

The Islamic rebellion had its start in a string of festering slums south of Beirut, including those at Sabra, Bourj al Barajneh and Chatila. Almost all were as fetid as anything I'd seen in Lagos, Accra or Luanda after the Portuguese had been evicted; cesspits that had become home to millions. Journalists came and went and reported what they saw, but let's face it, they really couldn't even begin to relate to the squalor because none had ever experienced it for themselves.

One American journalist, having been taken around a camp near Sidon, said in a report home that he thought it 'quaint'. Commonly described as 'refugee camps', these dreadfully impoverished ghettos underscored the oldest of axioms: poverty and conflict tend to spawn euphemisms that are rarely appropriate.

In fact, the Muslims in those days didn't hold any kind of a monopoly either in misery or poverty, and a generation later almost nothing has changed. The truth is that Christians living near the Green Line in the 1980s hardly suffered any less than their former Islamic neighbors, gathered together as they both were in clusters and little more than a holler away from each other.

As some of us were to discover later, those stuck (or abandoned) there had neither the means nor the will to leave. Why should they? They'd been there all their lives. In any event, the majority were too old or too sick to go anywhere.

The churches helped of course, almost all of them Maronite, that staunch and uncompromising Eastern following that embraced Constantine and forsook Rome, even though Catholicism has persisted, always a powerful presence among Christians in the Levant.

It was the Maronites who were able to breach the gap and provide the adhesive that kept Lebanon cobbled together for a thousand years. They were still doing it in 1980 and they're at it again as we reach into the second decade of the new millenium. With that fair sprinkling of Catholics, they do what they've always done, quietly and without bother. Remember, these Christians had been fighting for survival even before the first of the Crusaders arrived. They espoused a fundamental credo that encapsulated the oldest communal philosophy of all: one for all and all for one . . .

With time, even that touchstone became flawed. More recently it has been viciously exploited by Syrian leaders who have expansionist dreams and created schisms within the Lebanese Christian community. The Franjieh crowd who travelled on the ferry with me from Larnaca to Jounieh were among these dissidents. With all the assassinations that followed over the years, there were wounds generated that will probably never be healed.

The last President, another old friend, General Emile Lahoud – whom I got to know in the days when he was still Lebanon's army chief – seemed to have become used to taking his orders from Damascus, which was a pity because I regarded him an as enterprising fellow. He even brought the civil war to a halt, something I covered in some detail for Washington's *Middle East Policy*.[1]

In the hours I spent at the building that housed the Lebanese Force Command near Beirut harbour after I'd come off the motor vessel *Ali* from Cyprus, I was asked scores of questions by a succession of officials. They had good reason to be suspicious. Why should anybody who had not been specially sent to Beirut by a news agency or network wish to come to such a dangerous place? Didn't I know that I might get killed?

I showed them some of the tracts that I'd written on other wars, but it was my books that probably won the day. Also, they could have checked with their friends, the Zionists (I'd been there often enough in recent years), and no doubt they did.

I knew that there were good links between the Lebanese Force Command supremo, the youthful, ever-charismatic Bashir Gemayel, and Jerusalem. Even after he'd been assassinated, again with Syrian collusion, the Jewish State continued to cooperate with the Christian Forces. Many of the weapons used by his Lebanese Force Command troops came from the south by sea, usually at night. A common enemy explained this apparently unnatural alliance: the enemy of my enemy . . .

Gemayel was always cautious of Israeli motives. He was wary, as his spokespeople would indelicately phrase it, of getting into bed with the Jews. That could also have been because there was a link between the Phalanghists and the Iraqis. Some of the weapons then reaching the Christians had been sent by Saddam Hussein in a complex attempt to weaken relations between the Iranians and Arab fundamentalists who were then supporting another group of Islamic zealots.

It was certainly a hotchpotch of ideologies, all of them convoluted and more times than not, conflicting. By then almost the entire Arab world, in one way or another, had been dragged into the fray, even the Saudis.

There were also strange little groups of European radicals from France, Germany, Italy, Ireland and elsewhere working closely with the PLO. Meanwhile, Americans trained Christian soldiers in close combat. Lurking everywhere, we all knew, was Shin Bet, whose influence extended northwards throughout Lebanon, though we would never know who their agents were.

The plot was murky, and to us relative innocents, impenetrable.

Buildings sometimes had their foundations blown out from under them. However, life in Beirut tended to go on, down to a small bunch of flowers among the mayhem on the balcony. (Author's collection)

Moving about Beirut in the ensuing weeks and on later visits, I was amazed at the ability of the people to endure.

Every basement had become a home. Beds and tables were placed so that at least two walls separated any occupants from the outside; the first, it was hoped, would absorb major impact. For years these people had been subjected to bombings, rockets, mortars and artillery barrages that sometimes lasted for days. There was no point in talking about 'getting used' to such things. Nobody could.

At the time of my first visit, the war was into its sixth year. Already more than 10,000 Christians were dead. The casualties on the Muslim side of the Line, partly as a result of Israeli attrition and from actions of the Lebanese Force Command – and, to a much lesser extent from Sa'ad Haddad's South Lebanese Army – were almost ten times that number.

Even so, there were diversions to relieve the stress: parties up the coast at Byblos – beyond the range of the guns and the Katyushas. There were picnics in the mountains, regular events when the fighting and the weather conspired to lift. As were fishing in the sea (guarded by patrol boats) and the endless 15-course dinners that are always a feature on the Lebanese social calendar. Christian radio stations helped relieve the tension, mostly in French, and invariably hip. Some of their DJs were easily as good as their counterparts in Brussels or Cannes.

Listening to a French-speaking announcer in some lonely post at Kfarchima or in the mountains overlooking the city, you might have forgotten that you were on the fringe of what was then one of the most dangerous conflicts east of Algeria. For all this, it was astonishingly easy in those days to become a cipher on a clipboard. Each day, between 18 to 25 people died violently in the Christian sector alone, most from random artillery and mortar fire from Syrian and Muslim militia and PLO positions across the way.

The usual tactic was to hit East Beirut during the morning or evening rush-hour. Since the town had been carefully mapped years before, even the Syrians possessed reliable charts and they were able to drop a bomb within a yard or two of any street corner. Some intersections would be teaming with traffic when the mortars arrived and the carnage could be terrible.

You could never know when a single bomb or a cluster would drop silently out of the sky, four, five, even six at a time. Once the first one struck, we'd all watch carefully to see in which direction the rest of the pattern went. Each mortar bomb would land a few yards from the one before it and sometimes a pattern of explosions would 'walk' in a straight line for as much as 150 yards or more. It all depended on whether the base-plate had been set on hard ground: the softer the surface, the more expansive the spread.

On my third morning in Beirut I was invited to lunch by some G-5 friends of Fadi Hayek and Jacques Tabet. There was a cafe three blocks away, well sandbagged and accessible only through a narrow, reinforced entrance. Steel plates hung over the door and offered good protection.

We'd finished lunch and were ambling back to the office. There was no need for caution because there were buildings on all sides and we were at least a mile from the front. Suddenly the first mortar bomb exploded in the road about 200 yards ahead. Moments later there was another, 20 yards closer than the last. By now we were in full gallop for a large entrance to a building nearby; any opening would do. A stone doorway which gaped immediately ahead was just fine.

We reached it with about a second to spare before the last bomb exploded in a shower of fragments outside. None of us was hurt, but our ears rang for days and a shard of jagged steel about five inches long ricocheted off one of the eaves to land with a loud clink at my feet. That chunk of metal remained on my desk for years, even though it was always an unfriendly reminder.

What was sobering was the realization that in full flight a piece of shrapnel that size can sever a man's arm, or his neck. More worrying, there had been five journalists killed and a dozen wounded in that phase of the Lebanese conflict.

As with all wars, there were escapes aplenty, some that we still marvel about when some of the old hands get together for a couple of a drinks. A French television crew was filming in downtown Beirut close to the Green Line when a Russian 82mm mortar bomb hit the curb immediately alongside the cameraman. Fortunately, it landed in the gutter and the raised curb absorbed most of the shrapnel, if not a large portion of the blast. When I examined the place afterwards, I was astonished that the man was still alive. As it was, he was spattered by bomb fragments down the length of his body.

He was flown out the next evening; the airport was then still open.

Afterwards, I saw an Arriflex 16mm camera at the offices of Gamma in Paris. It had a hole in it, with a sniper's bullet neatly lodged where the magazine had been clipped onto the body. The trajectory had been straight in line with the side of the cameraman's head when it struck and

Graffiti commemorating the deaths of about 100 innocent civilians killed in an
Israeli artillery strike in the South Lebanese town of Qana. This kind of mindless
brutality on the part of the Jewish State – it was not an accident since several salvos
were fired – polarized passions in the region even further, were that possible.
(Author's collection)

clearly the marksmanship was outstanding. But it didn't kill the man:
apart from a big bruise above his ear, he was unhurt.

While in Beirut, I spent a lot of time in an apartment near the headquarters of Fadi Hayek's G-5.

Always a gracious host, his hospitality in this strange and dangerous
land was not only welcome but essential, because most of us were broke.
Short on ceremony, Fadi was a convivial entertainer who could drag a
bottle of Château Lafite-Rothschild out of somebody's cellar in an
instant and like a prestidigitator of old, produce the best pate de foie
gras from what passed as the local gourmet store.

Living in Fadi's shadow, as it were, served two purposes. He could
keep an eye on us, ostensibly friends of the Christian Forces but who
could just as easily have been enemy. Also, by then all Christian hotels
in East Beirut had become targets for a proliferating number of car-
bombers. With so much activity, their job was easy.[2]

Not long before I arrived, Jihad bombers had destroyed the US Marine barracks at Beirut Airport. Only years afterwards we were to discover that this was one of the first acts of a new brand of Islamism that called itself Hizbollah, the same Pasdaran who, by then, had entrenched themselves in South Lebanon and whom I encountered while moving about from the UN Headquarters base at Naqoura.

The Hizbollah, or Pasdaran, strike on the airport base was uncompromisingly brutal. More than 300 American servicemen were killed in that attack, and it was followed soon after by two suicide bombs, one at the entrance of the American Embassy that killed many of the top CIA officers in the Middle East, who were at a conference at the time. The other hit the French diplomatic mission, a few streets down. After the Israeli invasion, similar tactics were used in the destruction of an IDF military headquarters in Tyre, in the south of the country.

At about that time, another, less conventional type of fighter started to arrive in Lebanon. Mostly of European extraction, with quite a few

The UN base at Naqoura in South Lebanon is the largest UN military establishment in the world, yet its role throughout decades of fighting in the Levant has been divisive: the Israelis have repeatedly invaded their northern neighbour, usually brushing aside UN forces as if they didn't exist. For its part, Hizbollah, while offering customary lip service, is today equally dismissive of the so-called UN peace-keeping role in the Middle East. (Author's collection)

Germans in their ranks, these radicals were sharpshooters, the majority extremely well trained. From what I gathered, quite a few had psychopathic tendencies, which might have been expected since their role was to target purposely those less fortunate than the rest. The poor souls who came into their sights included the old, the very young and, in particular, people who had been incapacitated. Those in wheelchairs and the decrepit appeared to attract inordinate attention.

Snipers of all nationalities were active until the end, but the average journalist seemed to take little interest in these actions, though this was clearly an issue tailor-made for the front page. Why? Because this was an extremely delicate subject, they were told in the kind of language that allowed no room for debate. More than one hack in the Commodore Hotel got a friendly nudge whenever the topic was raised: sniping wasn't a good story, he or she'd be told. And of course they'd agree . . .

Nonetheless, the subject was in everybody's face. A French-woman was killed by an Amal sniper in a boulevard not long after she had disembarked in Beirut harbour, intending to walk into town. It was a senseless murder, because she was clearly a foreigner and there was nothing to be lost in letting them retrieve her body afterwards. Instead, she lay there for days. Anybody who tried to get near her remains became fair game. The French Embassy protested, but Amal wasn't listening.

The almost blanket silence in the Western press about sniping was peculiar, since these marksmen accounted for substantial numbers of casualties. The gunmen were all around us on both sides of the Line and, as a result, we'd never hang around in exposed places.

Sniping went on through every ceasefire except the very last one, which ended the war. The Muslim rate for a kill during the early and middle 1980s, whether man, woman or child, old or young was about $250. The Christians, in contrast, regarded it as part of their war effort and their soldiers charged nothing because they were getting at the hated enemy.

Many of the Jihad fighters used Soviet Simonov rifles with telescopic sights. There were also Russian Dragunovs; a more refined variant of the AK, though nowhere nearly so accurate for sniping as the rifles made by McMillan or the Springfield Armory MIA National Match.

Then the Syrians got hold of large numbers of Austrian Steyr-Mannlichers, prized hunting weapons and the finest and most accurate in their day. The end-user certificates stated that they were for the Syrian Army Sniping Team, all 300. We all decided that it was curious that nobody in Vienna seemed to notice the quantity, and there is little doubt that despite subsequent protestations, the authorities were aware that many German and Austrian weapons were finding their way into Arab countries at the time.

Bob Brown, owner and publisher of *Soldier of Fortune* magazine, sent in his own teams of sniping specialists, always embedded with Christian forces. One of his reporters had indicated this gap to special forces and Bob filled it, as he had done in El Salvador, Rhodesia and elsewhere. Soon we had people like Peter Kolkalis and Phil Foley teaching Christian lads the sniper's intricacies of minute-of-angle and windage. Bob MacKenzie, with whom I afterwards covered the war in El Salvador (see chapters 7 to 9), was also there for a while.

More Americans entered Lebanon to help the Christian side after Jim Morris, good friend, author, university lecturer and journalist spent time with the Lebanese Force Command. He was freelancing and his reports were widely published in the United States.

The acquisition of more sophisticated types of weaponry was always a problem for the Christian forces. Some came by sea to Jounieh harbour from Haifa. Still more were acquired in France at hefty premiums and would arrive in packing cases marked as machine parts. The Phalanghists captured a lot of materiél early in the war, but they constantly needed to build up reserves in readiness for any big push by the Muslims. In that they succeeded, but Bashir Gemayel also took the precaution of establishing a number of central depots in caves in the mountains of the interior.

The Christians also manufactured their own ammunition, grenades and mortar bombs and made a very efficient 7.62mm rimmed explosive bullet of their own. Then, astutely, they built a bazooka based on the French Sneb 68mm air-to-ground rocket, which worked well in a ground-support role. The tube was made of unpainted aluminium and it astonished a lot of us that they never bothered to camouflage the device, because it must have glinted in the moonlight.

Fadi's people always had their own way of doing things. It was the kind of enterprise that had enabled his people to survive centuries of invasion, subjugation and persecution and, on the face it, the Christians seemed to manage pretty well considering that they were both outnumbered and outgunned. 'But never outmanoeuvred', one of their officers stressed at one of the few press conferences conducted at Hadace while I was there.

By 1981, the Syrians had moved large numbers of men and

equipment into the Lebanon. They also had irregular 'volunteers' who, over the years, had been infiltrated into the ranks of the various Muslim factions. This was done more to keep some kind of control over a situation that was volatile and which tended to resist any kind of overall authority, than to provide additional manpower. There were then in Lebanon 35,000 regular Syrian soldiers, eight batteries of 'Special Forces' each consisting of 5,000 men and another 5,000 *Moukhamarat* or secret police, who were working clandestinely in civilian clothing. This force was already many times what the Christians could field even in a concerted effort.

The Syrian forces were supported by several hundred tanks, mostly not-so-old Soviet T-55s (excellent for close-quarter work) which were deployed round Zahle, an isolated mountain enclave in the east that was completely surrounded. This hardware was backed by armoured personnel carriers (APCs) – including several hundred BTR-152s and 40 or so BM-21s, mounted with batteries of 40-salvo Katyusha rockets. It was a formidable arsenal and to many of us, it all seemed unstoppable. But again, with good tactical Israeli counter-measures, the Christians seemed to manage.

Additionally, the Syrians spent millions of dollars a week on ammunition, much of it arriving from Russia as part of the Kremlin's Middle East programme of destabilization.

Syrian anti-aircraft guns, to which they added the full range of surface-to-air missiles (SAMs) fielded by the Soviets, were no less impressive. Most deployed around Beirut were specifically reserved for Israeli Air Force reconnaissance flights and we'd spot their white plumes rising in the sky from time to time, even though hits were scarce.

In the end, for all this hardware, Lebanon's conflict was very much a People's War. Every civilian in East Beirut or across the way in Jounieh, in or out of uniform, was a soldier, and that included the majority of young women of military age. I rarely met one who wasn't carrying at least one concealed weapon: a revolver or a pistol. Among the men, one in five or six would have a grenade in his pocket.

American revolvers were the most popular: mostly Smith & Wesson, Ruger or Colt, usually in .357 Magnum calibre. Dirty Harry's .44 Mag was regarded as excessive. 'Overkill', Fadi called it. My own preference for the .45 Colt auto was dismissed with contempt, probably because it was American (weren't they almost all?). Consequently, the 9mm Parabellum quickly became the in-thing among the younger set. They discussed ballistics like today's crowd talk Lady Gaga or Beyoncé.

Certainly, the greatest advantage that the Christians had over their adversaries was a single command structure. In this respect the Lebanese Force Command was run like a regular army. At the same time, it seemed that apart from the wherewithal that was being used to fight this war, all things American and Jewish were despised with a passion that us transients found disquieting.

It was almost like biting the hand . . .

There was another, softer side to the conflict that seemed almost incongruous under the circumstances. While the war raged, people seemed to get on with their lives.

Take Jacques Aboul, who owned the excellent patisserie that was popular with all who lived in the Beirut suburb of Hadace. Hadace was both an expansive and expensive place before the war and was home to many wealthy Lebanese expatriates who had second and third homes on other continents. It lay to the east of the airport, a little above the American university, and was highlighted by a big sign that read: 'Ville de Hadace'. Its quarter-of-a-million inhabitants were a fair sample of Lebanese Christians: tradesmen, doctors, artisans, electricians, architects, bankers and politicians.

The common language of the more-educated classes, apart from Arabic, was French. Those who left the country usually found a niche for themselves in France or in the French-speaking African colonies, where the Lebanese tend to monopolize business even today. Quite a number emigrated to the United States, where the more industrious prospered and continue to do so.

Aboul's shop stayed open almost throughout the war. Just before I arrived, he'd stocked his shelves with good things: the best imported whisky and gin, Swiss chocolate, some excellent French cheeses, South American coffee and other delicacies from abroad. Then it was hit by a mortar bomb and the boards and sandbags went up again. It was like a game, Aboul would comment sourly when we talked about it in good English. 'A very expensive game . . .'

Aboul was introduced as a Christian Lebanese who had accumulated a fortune in Paris and was now losing it. So why did he return?

'Why do any of us come back? Ask any of these people here; they're all good people, informed people. They could go abroad tomorrow. But we stay. It's our country. It's the land, the heritage of our children . . .'

As with many Israelis, the Lebanese – like my friend Aboul – really believed that there was only one country on earth worth a dime. In Aboul's view, the war would soon end, though he never counted on the tenacity of the Syrians, who needed to dominate that part of the Middle East for the sake of their own partially landlocked security. The Syrians remained the dominant force in Lebanon for a long time after the civil war ended, but in the end because Damascus overplayed its hand in murdering prominent Lebanese who opposed their presence, even their forces had to go home.

My destination in Hadace was the command post of 'Sheikh' Tony Karam, a fifth-year medical student who'd spent as many years fighting for the ideals in which he passionately believed. I was taken there by Claude, also from G-5, the one-armed leader of a commando platoon who was one of my bodyguards on board the ferry from Larnaca.

Karam's headquarters was protected by two solid reinforced concrete structures and, as he explained in an early briefing, it dominated much of the fighting.

Like most other commands along the Line, Karam's front was divided into sections of about 400 yards each, with small groups of soldiers given responsibility for particular areas, which were usually close to where they lived.

How many men in his command? 'That's a secret', he replied with his customary demeanour. 'You ask a stupid question and you get a stupid answer', he would joke moments later.

Weapons? Also secret, he averred, though I could make my own assessment simply by moving along the lines, which was easier said than done because of PLO or Jihadi snipers. They're pretty good, Karam warned.

When the Christians acquired some French infra-red image-intensifiers, Karam's sharpshooters took the initiative. It was hard going nevertheless, he admitted, as most of these specialists seemed to work from isolated observation-posts among tall buildings and always from high ground.

'The problem is that the enemy knows roughly from where we operate, just as we're aware of their deployment. So, if one of my men is preparing to use his weapon, he can't loiter long in front of that little hole from where he pokes out his barrel . . . some of their snipers could hit a cigar box at 500 or 600 yards' he told me. Christian marksmen sometimes spent hours after dark on rooftops looking for vantage points from which to hit the enemy at first light.

'Sheikh' Karam (he preferred the appellation *le Chef*) had a reputation for employing unusual methods, like bomb detectors, at his control points and pulling a vehicle off the road into an open basement and making the driver open everything – including removing the tyres – while his own men watched from a distance.

An agreeable adjunct to his command was a squad of sloe-eyed beauties, quite a few of whom were still in their teens or early twenties, who made themselves useful in all sorts of ways, such as in logistics and supplies. Others monitored Syrian radio traffic. Their presence was a tonic to the men. Those of us who have spent any time in the Eastern Mediterranean know how stunningly attractive many of these young women are. Trouble is, they know it too . . .

A year or two later, the Lebanese Force Command began training women for combat. At that stage, females were regarded as strictly rear-echelon personnel. Some of the girls in uniform enjoyed sporting an AK in town, particularly after dark, and they looked appealing in an androgynous sort of way in their American olive-drab fatigues and boots. We'd long ago been warned not to take liberties with any of them.

'Look, but don't touch' was the rule, and even then you didn't make a meal of anybody with your eyes. A well-known foreign correspondent, an Irishman, was found dead with a knife in his back in a Beirut apartment after a bit of hanky-panky with a married Lebanese woman.

The fighting in Hadace was not nearly as intense as in sectors closer to the downtown high-rise areas. Unlike the enemy – billeted in places to which they had been drafted and often bought in from the mountains of the north or from Sidon or Tyre to

Female soldiers, while rarely used in combatant roles in Lebanon, provided valuable service on both sides of the Green Line. While playing key roles in communications, administration, intelligence and in caring for the wounded, they were not averse to handling weapons when critical circumstances demanded it of them. (Author's collection)

the south – Karam's men had intimate knowledge of their own backyard. Most had played there as kids.

Every narrow passage between buildings, each little path that allowed access to the front as well as the buildings that surrounded them, all had their uses. Though the *Chef* wouldn't comment, we were made aware that his people were able to infiltrate Syrian and Palestinian lines, if not at will, then often enough to make things difficult for the other side. Their local knowledge made them accurate scouts, always on the lookout for something new to put their minds to.

One of these opportunities was exploited while I was with Karam's people. A bulldozer was heard each evening working on Syrian defences a few hundred yards beyond Christian lines. Then, one night, three men with two RPG-7 rocket-launchers slipped out a little after midnight. They were back an hour later, the driver of the bulldozer dead. The Syrians retaliated with heavy stuff, but the intruders were already underground.

As with most unconventional struggles, urban guerrilla warfare in Beirut was an extremely difficult option, but it was vital if the Christians were to hold their own in the ever-vacillating climate of war. It was almost impossible to reconnoitre enemy positions in streets where look-outs could see any kind of movement at a glance and usually for some distance. Also, as we were already aware, their night-vision goggles were Soviet, third or fourth generation and the best.

What was taking place behind those rows of buildings? No one knew until it happened. The Muslims would collect their forces along a street on the Line. The Christians would be aware of these concentrations because the rate of fire would pick up and there would be movement. Meanwhile, they would move up more of their own men to bolster defences.

The other side, in turn, would pre-empt, this time en masse, sometimes catching the Christian forces unprepared. Such attacks would take place in great force, perhaps across half a mile of battlefront, and would sometimes concentrate on what might have been perceived as lightly defended positions. Many penetrations were made in this manner. Gemayel's people used the tactic to good advantage too, but their options were constrained because his people didn't have any kind of depth in numbers.

When buildings had to be cleared in close fighting, the combat became a horror of confusion and high casualties. Most of the time the light was bad, and fighting sometimes took place in the dark. Both sides would accidentally shoot their own people, and since this kind of thing could not be planned beforehand, the Christians tended to leave their fighters to their own devices. The Islamic Jihad was less flexible because they just targeted everything that moved.

As Rocky – the Sodico commander – had originally suggested: 'If you're somewhere where the lighting is low or there's none at all – and you know that the fellow in your sights might be one of your own – you shoot him in the legs. *Just in case!*'

Karam was one of the Christian fighters recruited into the ranks of what began as an irregular guerrilla force at the beginning of hostilities. Those were early tit-for-tat days, one strike answered by another, invariably in retaliation for events that had taken place perhaps hours, or days before. As the war progressed, the conflict became more convention-al, but throughout the conflict, his job was to hold the line, even against the tanks.

He once rolled barrels of fuel down a hill into an attacking force and exploded them with tracers. They were never attacked from that position again.

Ranks within Lebanese Force Command seemed to be vague. They existed, of course, and there was clearly an established order, but it wasn't anything definitive, in part because the enemy would target anybody who looked like being in authority. More significantly, there was no formal flummery, no standing on dignity or ceremony. The bottom line was to stay alive. Obviously, that applied to us scribes as well.

Similarly, there were no concessions. Prisoners of war were often kept alive no longer than was needed to extract information, though in later years both sides classically used prisoners as bargaining chips, in clear contravention of the Geneva Conventions. It was a war in which both sides made their own rules.

One of Karam's men captured by the Syrians had his arms and legs cut off by a surgeon in the enemy camp. After his eyes had been gouged out, he was left in the open under the muzzles of snipers. They waited for the Christians to try to bring him in. *Le Chef* himself had to fire the fatal bullet. It would have been impossible to get him out without taking losses, he explained, but he refused to be drawn further on the subject, except that it would have been inhuman to keep the man alive.

Karam had spent four years at university with the fellow and the catastrophe had a lasting effect. He made it his business to kill the customary three or four Syrians every week, using – in preference to standard-issue army rifles that came from the Israelis – a Brno .30-06 hunting rifle with a ten-power Leupold sight. His ammunition was Winchester 180-grain soft-point.

Essentially, the Lebanese Force Command was a group of civilians drawn into the fight by force of circumstance. When the fighting was over, or when there was a lull, they went back to their jobs or their studies.

Anybody who could use a gun was a soldier. Even non-combatants helped the cause by packing food, preparing dressings or priming ammunition, old men and women alike.

One young zealot who'd turned 22 while I was there fought on with one eye; he had lost the other in an RPG-rocket attack. An unusually talented individual, he had studied classical guitar under the Armenian master Joseph Ichkhanian. During the war he was to become an expert with the weapon that had cost him so dearly.

Another young Phalangist officer with whom I spent a little time was a third-year engineering student. He fought on despite the loss of a leg below the knee, his perseverance generating much respect among his pals. His closest friend was a student of mathematics. There was also a dental student, a cabinet-maker who specialized in Louis XIV reproductions, as well as two lawyers. All were tough, aggressive fighters, who with time became experienced and battle-wise. Few were hotheads who were likely to get themselves killed or maimed.

Had these people been serving in any regular army, they would have been characterized as model combatants who took few chances, though obviously, there were times – sometimes every other day – when they'd have to put their lives on the line. If they needed to enter a particularly dangerous area, they'd go in only after a careful reconnaissance, and then crouched low and at the double. When there was shelling, nobody exposed himself if it wasn't essential.

As the war went on, accommodation for the media covering the east side of the Line became difficult. G-5 couldn't support us indefinitely.

I usually stayed in the Christian Quarter or up the coast in Jounieh. Quite often, because it was safer, I'd head for Byblos, a delightful little harbour that dated from Phoenician times and lay roughly 15 miles as the bird flies from Beirut's always-delightful Cornice. I liked it because it was well away from the carnage, but then Byblos was also far away from it all and that sometimes meant being out of touch. Then I would seek other options and occasionally I was led across the Line.

The Commodore Hotel was not one of my favourites because I had to pass through Muslim lines to get there. However, it was a necessary stage in any journalist's itinerary in that part of the world. We all billeted there at some time or another.

I got to know Fuad Saleh, the manager during the Israeli invasion of 1982. When I wasn't staying at one of the Israeli Army headquarters in a big villa in Baabda, George De'Ath and I would go down to the Commodore, usually by taxi. It was there that we missed a Christian car-bomb by minutes. We'd been seeing a friend at another hotel in West Beirut and hadn't been out of the building for about an hour before it went up in a huge column of smoke and debris. The entire facade came down and a lot of people were killed.

At the time we were being hosted by the Israeli command and were sleeping on the balcony of the Baabda HQ. We'd hardly bedded down for the night when we heard the blast and got up to view the fire. It didn't particularly bother our Jewish hosts overmuch because it had all taken place in the Islamic half of the city. George and I counted ourselves lucky.

The Commodore was also bombed, but in spite of omnipresent danger, the place was invariably a hive of activity. In February 1987 it became the target of rival squads of Druze and Shi'ite militants who fought for control of the building with tanks and rockets. The Druze took the honours; as they usually did when they made up their minds to strike at a specific target, customarily displaying a level of aggression seldom seen outside the Middle East.

I was to see a lot of Druze combatants during the course of the war but never tangled, officially or otherwise, with them: they made no secret of their loathing for us 'journalist scum'.

To my mind, the Druze were the toughest, the most dedicated of the combatants in Lebanon. They had to be because their numbers were limited and it said much that they never took prisoners, Christian, Israeli or Muslim.

In many respects the old Commodore was different from any other hotel I'd frequented over the years. It was shabby and run-down, yet as comfortable as a pair of old slippers. The ebb and flow of events in the Middle East could be gauged by the number of foreign correspondents packed into the round bar any evening.

There we would find a rare diplomat priming journalists and vice versa, UN 'peacekeeping' soldiers on leave – usually talking amazingly tough – and, of course, the usual spooks, professional murderers and friendly ladies. It was a congenial watering-hole and I often wonder what happened to Younnis and Mohammed who served behind the bar.

Signing in at the Commodore was a ritual. 'Sniper side or car-bomb side?' the clerks would ask new arrivals, usually nervous at the prospect of possibly coming under fire. Yet, once through those doors, you felt strangely comfortable, even safe. From the top of the Commodore we could sometimes watch the nightly display of Christian tracers.

John Kifner of *The New York Times* describes a night after the American Embassy had been blown up for the second time by a suicide truck bomber.

'Suddenly the windows around the bar shook and then dissolved as Shi'ite fundamentalists bombed nearby bars and bingo parlors. Thirty journalists dived onto the floor in a heap. Their glasses were placed neatly around the circular bar and not a drop spilled.'

'Oh,' someone said, 'it's not going to be one of those nights!'

One of the bitter-sweet gratifications of any experience in wartime is that one can look back dispassionately on events that at the time seemed to be extraordinary or, as Wordsworth succinctly phrased it, 'emotions recollected in tranquility'.

Obviously, a great deal has changed in Lebanon over the years and it continues to do so. For a while peace seemed to have arrived in this troubled land, but it has been deceptive because Hizbollah, now legalized and with seats in Parliament, was waging its own little war along the length of the Israeli border. Then, in the summer of 2006, the IDF invaded again and its warplanes destroyed much of South Beirut, including almost all the suburbs occupied by Shi'ites.

Israel was forced back behind its own lines once more and things went back to normal: more rockets into Galilee, more IDF commando probes, but nothing on the scale of before.

There is still the occasional explosive charge laid and some very prominent people – mainly Christians – continue to be murdered. Syria, as always, stays menacing. The old President Hafez al-Assad is long gone, his place taken by Bashar, who we'd all hoped would be a moderating alternative. How wrong we were.

Bashar Assad had been working as a dentist in London when he was called to take over in Syria. Because of the number of assassinations since orchestrated by his security people – including another old friend,

During the course of the civil war, Beirut took a monumental plastering from both sides over many years. Nothing was left intact. However, once the fighting had ended, reconstruction started almost immediately and these scenes in downtown Beirut are no more. (Author's collection)

Prime Minister Rafic Hariri (who'd actually bought my son's 100,000-acre hunting concession along the Kafue River in Zambia) – that brutal tyrant is now vilified by almost all the people of Lebanon, Muslims as well as Christians. Though curiously, hardly ever by anyone linked to Hizbollah . . .

Looking back, only now can one appreciate how Lebanon's children must have suffered in that war. Children in the Levant tend to be spoilt and pampered anyway; and all the more because of the war. They were seldom visible except when things were safe, usually only fleetingly.

During hostilities, an entire generation of Lebanese children seemed to live in bunkers, parking garages and basements: catacombs, as it were. There were subterranean playgrounds with swings, sandpits, jungle-gyms and games. Naturally the kids almost all looked pale, except those in the mountains or at school. Of course they pined for sun and air, and came out whenever they could, but as soon as a social pattern of sorts became evident, the other side would hurl mortars.

We see it often enough on TV these days: dying or mangled children being taken to hospitals in Chechnya, Afghanistan, Pakistan, Darfur and

Iraq especially, all corners of the world where Islamic zealots remain active. For those who have experienced it from up close, this is not something you can get used to. Certainly, normal people can't.

Those of us who recorded these events, in script or on TV, were outsiders. Very few of us had emotional ties with the Lebanon. Most of us tried to preserve a degree of objectivity, but it was impossible to be dispassionate amid the horrors of such sights and sounds, especially once you got to know the people hosting you and could see and understand their problems first hand.

The children who suffered the worst were those in the dreadful camps to which Palestinian refugees had been consigned. One camp I visited in Tyre defies description. There was no running water and nothing that even resembled a bathroom like you and I regularly visit. Children were playing in their own excrement. These were lost souls, abandoned by the world, even today. We seldom see that side of things in Western television reports.

It was a child who left me with one of my most memorable moments of this war. I'd been staying with a family in the foothills above Beirut and we were woken up by the wails of half a dozen Katyusha rockets that screamed over our heads as we lay in our beds. If you were awake, you heard them coming and for a second or two your heart would stop. As they shot past, you knew you could breathe again. Moments later explosions higher up the Shouff told all.

Then your thoughts would turn to those who had taken incoming who were possibly wounded or burnt alive . . . or had been killed outright. And when you heard ambulances in the distance, you just knew there had been casualties. It happened almost every night and clearly, it could have been us at the receiving end.

At breakfast one morning, one of the children mentioned the rockets that had gone over the house the previous night. The father translated what the little girl said:

'The most beautiful sound in the world', were her words.

'What sound is that?' I asked.

'Screaming rockets . . . when they go right over our house and we know we're safe.'

In Lebanon, who could argue?

CHAPTER FOUR

Lagos and an Army Mutiny

Like the earliest of loves, coming under fire that first time, if
not sacrosanct, leaves its mark. Rubbing shoulders with the
Reaper is unforgettable, a milestone of sorts. The fact is, I've
yet to meet anyone who simply sails through combat: I've
always found the experience unsettling. My so-called baptism
of fire came in Nigeria in the mid 1960s and the events that
took place remain etched in my mind as if it were a week ago.
But first, I need to set the scene . . .

VERY EARLY ON IN MY career, Nigeria became something of a turning
point. I'd worked and studied in London, got myself professionally
qualified and after a year or two in the big city, I started hankering after
what the media disparagingly referred to as the 'Dark Continent'.

London was fine, for a while at least, but after all that crush and bother,
unabated noise and unwashed masses, this wild soul hankered after places
that might offer some kind of challenge. I actually started to miss Africa
and the quietude of the bush. Also, I needed action, lots of it. More
importantly, I knew exactly where to find it: back in Africa, of course.

'Untamed' is how the travel magazines of the day would refer to the
vast landmass to the south of Europe and in a sense they were right. In
their own manner – clichéd and often repetitive – Hollywood and
Hemingway had entrenched a bit of that mystique as well as some of the
more glamorous aspects of a continent that was as uncertain of its future
as mysterious. With books such as *The Snows of Kilimanjaro* and
Robert Ruark's *Uhuru* as well as films like *King Solomon's Mines* and
Where No Vultures Fly, they did a good job of creating the kind of
mystique, particularly about East Africa, that appealed to the younger
generation. Elspeth Huxley and Karen Blixen had originally set the
scene: those who came later followed a well-travelled road.

Almost overnight, there was a casual Western drift towards Africa
involving young people intent on uncovering some of these 'New
Frontiers' for themselves. They would hang about The Thorn Tree in the

forecourt of Nairobi's New Stanley Hotel, or drink endless Tuskers on the verandah of the old Norfolk Hotel, all the while talking about their experiences, which they would embellish once they returned home. President Kennedy's newly created Peace Corps was an integral part of it.

Meanwhile, the euphoria of new-found independence and charismatic and well-educated black leaders all had a hand in igniting some of the emerging torches of egalitarianism, almost like the Free Slavers of previous centuries. Sadly, it wasn't long before some of this enthusiasm was tempered by a series of military mutinies and violence, much it coupled to corruption on an almost biblical scale. We were to learn soon enough that on the African continent, all these upheavals were extensions of the same equation: power and money in the hands of the few. It is also fair to say that black people had no monopoly in this truck: they'd already been well-tutored in the wiles of making a fast buck by their friends in Europe and America. For all this, I was still keen to go back. In fact, the more I heard the more eager was I to have a look for myself.

That was about the time that I returned to Britain from South Africa. In theory, I could have flown directly to London again, but instead, I decided to hitchhike. In practice, a white man in undeveloped countries doesn't cadge lifts from poor people. Instead, he pays.

Though it took me four hard months, the trip was remarkable, if only because I survived an escalating guerrilla war in Portuguese Angola. That liberation struggle was my first real taste of things military and I found it both unusual and exciting. I was also to take one of the last flights out of Luanda to Pointe Noire in Congo Brazzaville, at that stage in a de facto state of war with Lisbon.

I even managed to cadge a lift on a ship from Pointe Noire to Port Gentil in Gabon, from where I travelled two days upriver on an open boat to Lambarene in a quest to meet the great Dr Albert Schweitzer.

Prior to that escapade, these were only places on the map in my mind, but they had always caught my interest. While at boarding school, I'd spent many hours pouring over maps – Papua New Guinea, the Okavango Swamps, Niger's Delta, the Mississippi and the rest. One day, I swore, I'd visit them all. To some extent, I eventually did.

In the course of that trans-Africa expedition, for that was what it was, I went down with malaria several times, travelled overland and totally alone for lengthy stretches through the wilds of Liberia and spent a while in Dakar in Senegal, which was idyllic because it was almost like being on the Mediterranean coast in France, except that almost all the faces were black and this was the Atlantic. From Dakar I got a lift on an old oil-service tug to the Canary Islands.

Of all the countries along the way, I found Nigeria the most intriguing. It had become independent just five years before and it was possible to go anywhere you liked in complete safety. Equally, you didn't have the level of criminality for which the country has since become notorious nor anything like the number of murders that now take place. Though some of this mayhem may since have been limited by the combined efforts of both the army and the police, it is only recently that people were still being murdered for the Nikes on their feet, sometimes on the way into town from the airport.

During that first 1960s visit I managed to explore almost the full extent of Africa's most populous state and I loved it. I adored the people and their disjointed, garish, cacophonic cities. Even the food appealed: plantain, gari and fu fu, which was sometimes so hot it could sear leather.

Moving overland in Peugeot taxis (or the more cumbersome, cut-price mammy wagons – trucks with seats on the back and with something of a roof for cover), it took me about a month to cross from the Cameroon Republic to what was then known as Dahomey (Benin today). Along the way, I found a Nigeria that was a very different kind of country before a series of army mutinies and civil wars ripped it apart and moulded it into the crooked, inefficient and brutal catastrophe it has since become.

I would have liked to make even better acquaintance with the place, but I had to get back to Britain, if only to put bread on the table. If I was ever to come back, I told myself, I would need the cash to do so.

I spent five or six months establishing a daily shipping service between Tilbury and Calais. The ship was called *The Londoner* and we offered return fares to Paris for less than six pounds. It was owned by that imperturbable Swede Sten Olsson who established Stena Line – now run by his son – that still plies many British ferry routes.

Having accomplished that much, I hung around the Moorgate offices of one of the subsidiaries of the shipbrokers Clarksons while waiting for the next project, but it never arrived. There were lots of promises: a Chinese trade show when Beijing was still Peking (getting a visa was almost like winning the lottery), Angola's Cassinga iron ore project and others. Angola offered promise, but then the project was

Nigeria was a happy place to start with: then came the bloodletting. Tony Cusack from Liverpool (left), shown in a Yoruba costume, and the author (on the right) quickly slotted into the routine at John Holt Shipping Services in Lagos. The Nigerian Army mutiny changed all that. (Author's collection)

stymied by a guerrilla insurrection. Though I was given a couple of raises while I waited, nothing caught my fancy and frankly, I was bored.

Finally, in the summer of 1965, I applied for a shipping job in Nigeria. In fact, I wrote three letters for three different positions in that country and got back firm offers from them all.

I took the one offered by John Holt Shipping Services in Lagos, in part because it enjoyed the illustrious title of Export Shipping Manager. The job came with an apartment, my own personal steward – his name was David and he was there solely to attend to my personal needs – a new blue Ford Corsair and an office at the country's principal commercial airport at Ikeja on the northern outskirts of this great rambunctious metropolis that, like Cairo, was as noisy and dirty then as it is today.

I arrived in Nigeria with bags and baggage as well as Tony Cusack in tow, the same individual with whom I was afterwards to travel through Spanish Guinea (Equatorial Guinea today), the Cameroons, both Congos and Angola.

There were problems almost from the moment the plane landed in Lagos. The first Nigerian Army mutiny had taken place weeks before, during which a number of prominent Nigerian politicians and Islamic religious leaders were murdered by recalcitrant southerners, most of them Christians. Sadly, the country never recovered from those early strikes; over subsequent years, a three-year civil war and half-a-dozen more military revolts followed; a million people were to die as a consequence.

The Nigeria of January 1966 was a very different place from the one that I had left the year before. Tribal enmities that had been kept firmly under control by the exiguous British administration were now becoming a serious political factor.

Some junior Ibo army officers with a few Yorubas of the Western Region assassinated the most prominent Northern and Western political figures as well as some Nigerian household names like Sir Ahmadu Bello, the Hausa-Fulani Premier of the Northern Region. Also murdered were Chief Akintola, Premier of the Western Region, and two Federal ministers, Sir Abubakar Tafawa Balewa and Chief Festus Okotie-Eboh.

Though the names of these victims might stare at you out of the history books, they, in their day, were the leading lights of the African independence movement. Their efforts – and those of others like Nelson Mandela, Mzee Kenyatta and Angola's Agostinho Neto – eventually freed the continent from many of its colonial constraints, even if it did involve bloodshed along the way.

Consequently, in Nigeria – as anybody with realism will tell you – if you wanted a civil war, all you had to do was to start killing prominent political (or tribal) entities, and that, basically, was what took place.

The murders that wiped out some of Nigeria's most senior political leaders shocked the Federation as no other acts of violence had done since independence, irrespective of the fact that by then there had already been thousands of innocents slaughtered in factional violence. Also, there had been two Northern religious leaders murdered in their own homes in particularly brutal circumstances. All this was a serious business, and certainly not helped by being viewed as something distinctly tribal, a filthy word in Nigeria at the time.

The Ibos of the South-East (they're listed as Igbo in today's reference books, a strident community that had always caused much resentment in the North) were suddenly cast as dangerous enemies of Islam.

During Nigeria's 'Imperial Period', the Northern Region in particular, was largely left to govern itself, a legacy of what in its day was termed Lord Lugard's 'Indirect Rule'. The Islamic faith was held in great respect and the British never meddled with it. That the Ibos, of all people, should perpetrate such violent acts was insufferable to Muslim people everywhere, but in those days it took them a little longer to react. The subsequent coup was to cost these Christian Southerners dear.

Islam, we all know, is a deeply conservative religion. In Nigeria it enjoyed a certain respect not always then seen elsewhere in Africa. However, even then Muslims were not all that happy with what was referred to as 'progressive' American norms, especially with regard to sex. More importantly, the education of people from Nigeria's North was almost exclusively Koranic; they were to that extent 'backward' by the criteria of the Western world.

The Ibos, in contrast – a bush and village people – had no such comprehensive Arabic culture as the North had enjoyed for more than a dozen centuries. Originally animists who worshipped the spirits of their forefathers, they took readily to the sort of education offered by Christian mission schools. It may have been limited, but at least it turned the Ibo people into employable clerks and government servants. As such they spread all over Northern Nigeria; the Muslim people, by contrast, offered little in the way of competition.

Instead, the majority of people of Islamic faith had to stand by and watch while good steady jobs were filled by these detestable aliens. They were taking the bread out of their childrens' mouths, was the universal complaint in places that were mainly north of the great Niger River. The not unnatural result was a series of outbursts and quasi-massacres in the *Sabon Gari* (the Stranger's Quarter) of the old walled cities of Kano, Zaria and Katsina. So far this was a sociological matter rather than anything political.

Then came independence, that blessed word, after which oil was discovered on the coast of the Eastern region. Looking back, it seems almost to have been a curse. Most of all, it made the Ibos greedy. Hitherto the majority of Easterners had been quite content with their place in the Federation. It brought them many benefits. Now that they found themselves standing on top of mind-bending potential riches, their avarice was aroused.

At the time of independence, only about 15 per cent of the officer corps in the Nigerian Army came from the North and the West. Most of those who replaced former white officers were Ibo. To avoid friction between the three regions, it was now determined that the army should be recruited by quota: 50 per cent from the North and a quarter each from the Ibo East and the Yoruba West.

However, by 1965 – five years after much-vaunted independence, it was Ibo officers who filled nearly half of the places at Sandhurst offered to Nigeria by Britain. Once again the Easterners were showing that they were pushier than all the rest, and in so doing, they became all the more despised. The fact that they seemed to be taking over the whole Federal Army was regarded by some Nigerians as positively dangerous.

In the event, the officers responsible for the first military insurrection disclaimed any tribal motive. All they wished to do, they said, was to get rid of corruption in government, which even a fool could see was rampant. Only the armed forces could be trusted, was the word in many barracks.

Most Nigerians were less convinced, especially after an Ibo became head of the new government after the coup. This man was Major General Johnson Aguiyi-Ironsi the former General Officer Commanding, or GOC. He declared that he had nothing to do with the revolt, but his protests were heard with scepticism and for good reason.

Most of those who had taken part in the murders were plainly Ibos or other Easterners. It was there for everyone to see. The majority of those killed belonged to other tribes. What that first coup did arouse was an overall fear of Ibo dominance in the northern and western parts of Nigeria. Aguiyi-Ironsi consequently found himself presiding over an increasingly tense and volatile country as it teetered towards more violence, which was roughly when I stepped off the plane at Lagos.

Those who have studied subsequent developments in Nigeria tell us that the Northerners began to prepare a military counter-coup the morning after the murders of their leaders. In May 1966, five months later, Hausas and Fulanis set upon any Ibo they encountered who was living in the North. This action was to become an extremely violent and bloody pogrom in which these Eastern Nigerians were specifically targeted.

Nobody was spared: the sick, the lame and the old – together with women and children – were slaughtered in their thousands. If you were Ibo and the mob got you, you were dead.

I travelled a great deal in Nigeria in the months after my arrival: among other cities, to Kano, Kaduna, Maiduguri and Gusau in the North and Port Harcourt, Calabar as well as Onitsha – that great Ibo city on the east bank of the Niger – which became a focal point in the civil war. Everywhere there was tension. In the *Sabon Gari* in Kano I saw places that had been gutted and plundered, stalls burnt, the owners dead or gone.

'If the Ibo comes back again, we shall kill him too', said one old

Refugees from a succession of internecine slaughters throughout Northern Nigeria streamed back into Eastern Nigeria in their hundreds of thousands. (Author's collection)

Hausa. He had been among those who had instigated the riots.

No town or village in the North was spared. There were many Ibo dead. A hundred thousand were hacked to death with cutlasses or set on fire. Most abandoned all their possessions. The survivors fled back to their traditional homes in Eastern Nigeria.

The Premier of the Eastern Region, General Odumegwu Ojukwu, whom I'd met before the war, watched these events with dismay. He voiced his fears aloud. The North was systematically trying to kill off his people, he proclaimed over the radio. If the killings did not stop, the Eastern Region would have to take 'appropriate action', were his words.

The idea of secession was already being discussed in Enugu and Onitsha. The new-found oil resources in the East, it was generally agreed, would give the Ibos the economic power to secede from the Nigerian Federation and we know now that the Easterners had already begun to buy weapons from Europe.

More importantly, they were no longer the Eastern Region of the Federation of Nigeria: they were already a nominally independent 'Biafra'.

Then it happened as we knew it would, though most of us got the timing wrong.

Suddenly, on the morning of 19 July 1966, on my way to work, I found myself in the middle of what – less than an hour before – had been an extremely tough battle for Lagos' Ikeja Airport (today Murtala Mohammed). Dozens died, almost all of them soldiers.

I had just turned off the main road to the airport when I saw bodies strewn all over the place, along the kerb, with more in adjacent fields where they'd been cut down by automatic fire as they tried to flee. British-built Ferret armoured cars, Nigerian Army troop-carriers and civilian vehicles, some burning, some capsized, lay in disarray.

I'd made a terrible mistake by turning off the main road. Suddenly I found myself directly in the line of fire, though the shooting by then had stopped.

Of course, I could have turned round, but that might have drawn attention to my presence, and possibly worse, as not any one of the soldiers across the way would have missed my car turning into that critical airport road in the first place. Consequently, I did the only thing I could: I drove slowly and deliberately ahead, straight towards the airport, just as I had done every morning since I had been in the country.

In spite of the carnage – and you couldn't miss it because some of the wounded were still crying out and many of the vehicles were ablaze – I acted like all this was a familiar occurrence. My radio was on, my elbow rested on the open window – no air conditioning in those days – and I tapped on the wheel in time to a high-life tune. I twisted my face into what I hoped would be interpreted as a smile and drove straight on. What else to do?

Then, quite unexpectedly, for I hadn't seen another soul, there were troops ahead. Half a dozen Nigerian soldiers lay prostrate on the ground behind their weapons and from what I could detect, they were very much alive. There were several heavy machine-guns on either side of the road and while I had no idea of type or calibre, it all looked pretty formidable. Worse, I still had to get past them before I could turn in towards the airport.

'Good morning, gentlemen', I called loudly as I pulled abreast but not stopping. 'Everything OK?' I waved, still smiling. There wasn't a murmur from any of them. This was as surly and grim-faced a bunch of fighters as any I've seen.

I suppose they must have been nonplussed by the sudden appearance of this lunatic white guy driving right through what a short while before had been a killing ground. Also, I'm certain that my presence didn't fall within the scope of what must have been very specific instructions: kill anybody who attempts to approach the airport.

I'd been aware, of course, that there had been plenty of killings and murders during the troubles in the months after I had arrived in Nigeria. But this seemed to be a regular pitched battle and these young soldiers – many of them not yet out of their teens – had been responsible. It says a good deal that they let me pass.

Meanwhile, my office in Apapa – John Holt Shipping Services – had been told by my steward David that I'd gone to work that morning. They said later that they'd tried to warn me, but the telephone lines were cut and it took a while to establish whether my body was among the 20-odd civilian people killed in the ambush on the Ikeja Road. Only one of the dead was an expatriate, a Lebanese businessman.

I took no such chance on my return that evening. This time I asked for permission to go back through army lines and got it. The officer in charge, a Hausa who had been to Sandhurst and loved it, took me to the main road himself. As we drove, windows down again, he spoke fondly of the rugby he'd watched at Twickenham. It was like that in Africa in the old days.

By the time we traversed that same stretch of road at about five o'clock that afternoon, all traces of the earlier carnage had been removed. Everything once more seemed peaceful. It would have been

Ikeja Airport, the main hub that served Lagos – and since renamed Murtala Mohammed International Airport – was both a civil and a military aviation facility. This photo, taken from the author's office, shows some of the Nigerian Air Force helicopters and fighters lined up outside the hangers which were supposed to house them, but never did. (Author's collection)

hard to believe that Nigerian soldiers were at that moment slaughtering every Ibo in the country who had not fled. There are occasions in Nigeria when things can be deceptive. The Pax Britannica on that day was only a memory and, sadly, Africa was its old self again.

The expatriate community, of which I had become a member in Lagos, was a mixed bunch. Many were there because they couldn't succeed elsewhere. So soon after independence it was still essentially a colonial and a racially stratified society.

Nigerian businessmen, by and large, were well aware of the shortcomings of these white folk who came out to the West Coast, usually on two- or three-year contracts. Some of these misfits – many in pretty easy jobs – were referred to deprecatingly as 'white trash', and looking back, I suppose quite a few were.

The interests of a lot of them rarely extended beyond cheap Nigerian gin and an endless array of dusky floozies. The man who ran one of John Holt's motor vehicle divisions, for instance, was said to be a con artist from London. He was quite candid, after a few drinks, that he was into as many fiddles that he could manage, solely to set himself up comfortably back in the old country. My old boss, Harry Whittaker, had been in Nigeria for so long he'd gone bush: Harry kept a voodoo shrine in the front room of his Apapa home, to which, it was said, he made offerings.

While the majority of my colleagues were from the United Kingdom, there was a fair sprinkling of Australians, Canadians and other European nationals. There was even a South African technician at Ikeja Airport who was doing specialized work. The Nigerians let him stay, though there was no other contact with the 'racist south'.

Our status quo was dictated strictly by the given or implied terms of our contracts. Certainly, the 'tween-ranks' pecking order was maintained by a system that smacked of militarism, a tradition that went back a century or more, not only on Africa's West Coast but in some of the other far-flung outposts of what had once been Empire. Officers simply did not mix with those from lower ranks.

For all that it was a good life. Accommodation – according to your status – came as part of the deal that you were offered before you left Britain, which was always referred to as 'home' and never as England, Scotland or Wales.

Higher echelons got houses. Those pathetic creatures lower-down the scale, like me, were given apartments. All were rent free and included a steward, like my own David, an Ibo. A manager could have three or four if he had children or entertained a lot. Many did.

There was a complicated array of perks. For those who qualified, there were one or two or even more free flights home each year. Also, if you were lucky, the firm paid for the education of your children at public schools in Britain. Their travels – two or three times a year between Heathrow and Lagos, Kano or one of the eastern 'stations' – was also part of the deal.

The big expatriate event of each week in Lagos, Kano, Port Harcourt and elsewhere was the Sunday curry lunch at the Apapa club. It was a grand, boozy affair to which few locals were ever invited. In the old days the clubs had been fairly vigorously segregated along racial lines and little had changed by 1965. There was nothing defined, no by-laws stipulating that blacks were not welcome, it was simply the accepted thing. Nigerians had their own clubs anyway, it was argued with some conviction by the Brits.

That changed quickly once the military took over. It had to. When a Nigerian soldier arrived at the Apapa Club and ordered a Star beer or a Guinness, the man was served with a smile. Because he was armed and we weren't, he was rarely asked to pay. Word quickly got around the barracks.

There were other distractions. The most important of these centred on the fact that in these outlying posts in the former colonies, there were few eligible females from back home. Those that there were, invariably had jobs in the embassies, high commissions, a variety of UN bodies or with various aid or religious missions. Quite a few were American Peace Corps volunteers or from its British counterpart, Voluntary Service Overseas (VSO).

Of course, there were many married women and if you were 'lucky' you hit a homer. However, in a small, thoroughly integrated social environment like Lagos, such liaisons rarely lasted long before people started to talk. Indeed, it was difficult to maintain any kind of a secret life in those stifling communities: each one of us was under some kind of surveillance, if not from our bosses then from the government. As a result you either cooled it or you were sent 'home' in disgrace.

There were any number of local girls, but in those days it wasn't done to be seen with a black lady on your arm, and almost never at the club. Upcountry, yes, but not in your parlour, as the locals would quaintly phrase it.

These things were happening, naturally, but always well away from expatriate residential areas and anyway most of my associates didn't advertise their predilection for 'something local'. That came later in the evening at any one of hundreds of little open-air clubs along Ikorodu Road, Yaba and Ebute-Metta, or on Victoria Island. Those who did get involved were discreet; Britain had only recently emerged from an age when black people were regarded as inferior. Some of my colleagues had married black women and weren't any the worse off for it, though their children suffered because, as unsavory a reality as it is, people of mixed blood in Africa are more often than not discriminated against by both black and white.

It was to the Apapa Club that I went on the morning after my escape at Ikeja. I needed to talk to some of my colleagues, and with battles still ranging on the outskirts of Lagos, it seemed the only secure place to go. Obviously, nothing like that had ever happened before: the January revolt was a Wednesday afternoon exercise in the West Country by comparison.

More ominous in the latest uprising was the fact that the Nigerian Army was everywhere. The British High Commission and other diplomatic missions encouraged us to keep a low profile. Those not at work gathered at their respective clubs and compared notes. The stories seemed to improve with telling as the beer flowed.

By lunch on that first day, I'd decided to check things out for myself. Wilf Nussey of the Argus Africa New Service in Johannesburg had been calling and he wanted to know what was happening. Because I didn't have easy access to Ikeja, I wasn't able to file in my usual manner, having already written my first few reports assessing the deteriorating political situation in the country. Reuters, the BBC and the other news agencies based in Nigeria did their own thing and I was still very much the backroom boy. For the moment, that suited me. Nobody draws attention to themselves in the middle of an African revolt.

Discussing the situation with my friends at the club, I decided that since the largest naval base in the country lay adjacent to Apapa Docks, I could possibly learn something by heading out there. Why not? Ex-navy myself, I'd always regarded sailors as a cut above the rest. After all, the Nigerian Navy was regarded as the most disciplined and best-ordered of the Nigerian forces.

Since Apapa was home turf while in Nigeria, I had a rough idea of how to get to the base, even though the roads in the area were a mess. They'd been laid over what had once been a swamp and followed no set pattern or grid. After a couple of wrong turns in my car, I eventually came to a road that led directly to the Apapa strongpoint: it lay dead ahead, about 1,000 feet away, its steel gates shut and its twin towers, one on either side, manned. That alone should have stopped me cold because it already started to look ominous. I'd halted my car at the head of the road, unsure of what to do next. Another mistake.

While mulling over what to do, a siren sounded. The base gates suddenly swung open and a squad of about a dozen troops – all of them armed – rushed out. An officer appeared and shouted loudly in my direction: 'You there! Come here now or we shoot! Now!'

I hesitated. Then a shot rang out. It was the officer, pistol in hand walking down the road towards me, his firearm was pointed in my direction.

That decided it. I drove slowly ahead and once more tried the 'pasted smile and elbow out the window' routine that had worked on the Ikeja road a day before. However, this time it was a little more difficult because the Nigerian had made up his mind that I was up to no good.

Instead of accepting that I – a lone civilian in a sedan – was in the process of complying with his order, the officer started flaying his arms. He shouted that I should hurry up. I could see by the two-and-a-half gold bars on his tropical whites that he was a lieutenant commander. At that point he was already ahead of his men, still wildly waving his pistol in the air. 'Come!' he shrieked.

What next? I couldn't make a run for it because the road in the final approaches to the naval base was too narrow for me to turn quickly around. Anyway, by now he was just ahead of me.

Perhaps 150 feet short of the gate, which had machine-gun emplacements on either side, I pulled up. The senior man was directly ahead of me mouthing incomprehensibly. To my surprise, he was actually foaming at the mouth and had a crazed look in his eyes. This guy was high.

'What you want? *What you want here?*' he screamed, his voice rising an octave each time he called. Obviously, I was terrified, though I dared not show it. The rest of the troops around this crazy man surrounded my car, most of them also under the influence. There were rifles pointed at my head. Several more muzzles were pressed against my body. With my windows open, I was easy meat.

'Get out!' was the next command. I quickly complied and turned to place my hands on the roof of the vehicle, just as I'd seen them do in the movies. I suddenly believed that I really might be killed. The word was out at the club that the expatriate community in Nigeria had already taken six or eight casualties, most of them fatalities.

'Lykes Lines . . .' I said loudly, 'the American shipping company . . . Lykes Lines!' I had seen the offices of the shipping line on an adjacent road as I approached the base and so had he, I surmised, since the building was in clear sight. It was obviously a ploy and just then, my only real option.

The officer stepped back a pace, possibly surprised at the mention of the word 'American', though he clearly didn't have a clue what I was talking about.

'Lykes Lines. The American shipping line', I said again. I tried to point, but he knocked my arm down. The befuddled officer shook his head. He lowered his gun and moved forward until his face was directly in front of mine. The man smelt like a drunk.

'You say *what?*' he demanded. 'What has America got to do with you on this road?' was his next question.

My mention of the nearby shipping offices must have had some kind of impact, especially since it was impossible to ignore the Lykes Lines' building because it was prominently situated to the left of the road. Even by Lagos standards, this was an imposing structure. At another level, it was also no secret that Washington hadn't exactly looked kindly on the antics of General Aguiyi-Ironsi and his Ibo goons. In fact, the State Department had been vocal about it. The Nigerian press reported most of the events of the first coup because they were allowed to do so, all of which would have been something with which this Nigerian naval officer – drunk or not – would have been familiar.

'What you mean? Lykes Lines? What do you mean?' The man was shouting again, this time into my face, spittle and all. Then, brandishing his pistol, he forced me back into my vehicle.

'Stay there! You stay where you are! Do you hear, you English piece of shit?' were his words, guttural and crude. I offered no argument. It's not only in Africa that you don't try to reason with a man who holds a gun to your head!

Then, in a more direct approach, I mentioned the American shipping line once more and again pointed towards the company's building across the way. The Nigerian officer turned and looked in that direction. By now all the soldiers around me were gesticulating, shouting, stamping their feet and waving their rifles in the air. That followed after one of them had screamed: 'Kill him! Kill dat bastard! He not supposed to be here!'

Another man, holding a submachine-gun, stuck the muzzle in my ear and demanded to know why I was spying?

'Who you spy for?' he shouted. It was all so fucking predictable, I thought, and thoroughly intimidating.

Looking back, I'm now aware that none of it had the ingredients of ever being re-enacted, simply because it was too bizarre. It was all so loud and repetitive, which suggested that there'd never be any possibility of reasoning with these people. Once they had made up their minds, they went for it. Being a lone white man in a black man's country didn't ease matters.

Also, I was totally unprepared for what was happening on that lonely stretch of road in Apapa. I was aware, too, that if I hadn't kept my head, I could have been shot and chances were good that there would never be any questions asked. What was I doing on that lonely road close to a strategic naval base a day after an army putsch anyway?

By their actions some of these cretins really appeared to believe that I was up to no good. A mercenary, perhaps? The papers were full of stories of white 'War Dogs' murdering black people, as had recently taken place in the Congo. Such injustices were alive in the minds of most Africans, especially some of the sensational newspaper reports that detailed events that surrounded Colonel 'Mad' Mike Hoare's 5 Commando and Stanleyville's Simba rebels. A lot of Africans had been killed by Hoare's 5 Commando and there were Nigerians who believed that the same could happen in their country. The anti-European paranoia that swept across independent Africa must have played its part in what was taking place in Lagos that day.

There was a solution of sorts, I suppose, but it took a while, and I expect that my apparent off-hand, friendly nonchalance helped. Any other approach, any kind of belligerence or animosity – or panic, possibly – would almost certainly have lead to disaster. By this time I'd mentioned the name Lykes Lines possibly 20 times. I'd also become quite vocal in my protestations, even though I smiled throughout, and the officer eventually put his hands in the air to silence his men.

'Get back . . . get back' he shouted at them. 'You!' he pointed at me. 'You get out of the car!' I complied without protest.

I stood beside the sedan again with my hands in the air. Then, for the first time, I saw that both automatic weapons on the turrets besides the main gate had been pointing directly at me while this dim-witted spectacle had been going on. The only comfort I might have had was that if they had actually opened fire, they'd probably have killed us all.

Having achieved a modicum of order, the officer slowly lowered his gun. He then stepped back a pace or two and in an effort to assert authority, astonished me further by quietly asking: 'Now, you tell me, exactly, what is your business?' I knew I had little time. Because the man was drunk, his attention span was likely to waver. Already his bloodshot eyes were darting this way and that.

In as few words as possible I explained that Lykes Lines was an American company. Its ships called regularly at Lagos. One of their vessels was arriving soon and I needed to get some papers to clear my goods, I lied, at which point I indicated towards some John Holt shipping documents which I had on my back seat. I had taken the more important papers from my office at Ikeja the day before, just in case.

The officer looked me over carefully once more, obviously undecided. He then peered in through the rear window and with his free hand, turned over the pile of papers. What he saw seemed to placate him, but that didn't prevent his going through the rigmarole again.

It took at least 15 more minutes of talk and banter to finally get the lieutenant commander to accept my story, if not for its veracity, then for the sake of saving face. Even then he did so grudgingly. I knew that my smile and nonchalance helped and that I needed to convince him that I really was not a threat to the security of the nation. Ultimately I succeeded. But just!

Finally, he allowed me to turn my car around. I did so, very slowly and deliberately, all the while in the shadow of the turrets above. Meanwhile, his men kept their rifles pointed in my direction, as I could see through my rear-view mirror until I had turned the corner at the far end of the driveway. God, was I glad to get away!

When I told them what had happened at the club, some of the more experienced old Coasters agreed that I had been lucky, extraordinarily so, said one of them. Several Apapa residents had been threatened by troops in the dock area earlier that day, he revealed. One was wounded by rifle fire, for no other reason, apparently, than because he was there.

'The same old story', said some of them: 'wrong place at the wrong time.'

Domestic scene at Ikeja Airport after the coup d'état. British-built Ferret armoured cars of the Nigerian Army patrolled the area and would not hesitate to shoot at anything considered suspicious. I managed to quickly slot into the routine by not asking too many questions. Consequently, I was rarely hassled by the troops manning airport strongpoints. (Author's collection)

In retrospect, I simply had to accept that things like that happened from time to time in Nigeria. Judging by what is going on in the oil-rich Niger Delta today, not a lot has changed in the Armpit of Africa and it has been going on for almost half a century.

All of us were a lot more cautious afterwards. My steward David kept me informed of what was happening. He had his own grapevine and some of the details that emerged were spot-on, down to where the next anti-Eastern attacks would take place and yesterday's casualty figures. Young Ibo males, he told me, were being pressured to return home. The idea was for them to undergo military training, even though the Biafran War would still be a year in coming.

With the assassination of General Ironsi in the July coup, his place as national leader was taken by a 30-year-old Army Chief of Staff, Lieutenant Colonel (later General) Yakubu Gowon, possibly one of the most amiable of all Nigeria's post-independence leaders. 'Jack' – as we got to know him – Gowon was the original 'Mister Nice Guy'. Uncharacteristically (for a Nigerian) he was short on either pretension or pomp and believed implicitly in the direct approach. His only flaw – if it was one – was that he was a Christian in a Nigeria dominated by an Islamic North.

Gowon was the son of an evangelist from the Plateau area of the Middle Belt. He was overthrown five years after the end of the so-called War of National Unity (as the Biafran War was euphemistically phrased by Nigeria's military leaders) and went back to university in Britain.

I continued to travel throughout the country during the course of my last months in Apapa and a good deal of my time was spent in the East with my John Holt assistant, Silas Anusiem, another Ibo.

A quiet, reflective individual who viewed developments with alarm, Silas nurtured some excellent connections within the government in Lagos.[1] His leaks were always accurate and I invariably appeared to be ahead of the pack when it came to the kind of projections I used in my articles about the future of the country. I was grateful for his help.

Then came an incident that might have had severe repercussions had things gone awry. I was asked by friends in South Africa to help them 'secure a contract'. Someone was tendering for a construction deal in Lagos harbour; a multi-million dollar project, I was told. Because South Africans were banned from any commercial contact with just about all of Black Africa, the scheme would have a British identity and be handled offshore from an office in the Bahamas. To do so, they said, they would require a set of naval charts of Lagos harbour. That included the entire port area, as well as Apapa.

I wasn't to know it yet, but should this request have been intercepted by Nigerian intelligence, my actions would almost certainly have been construed as hostile. Why else would anybody need detailed drawings of Nigeria's biggest maritime facility? Overnight I'd become a spy, though I was never paid a penny.

It was an odd request that had come through the post. I was to send the charts to the Naval Attaché, Commander (later Rear-Admiral) 'Solly' Kramer, at the South African Embassy in London. I had served briefly under Kramer in Simonstown while he'd been skipper of one of South Africa's former Royal Navy frigates, the SAS *Good Hope*.

In Cape Town, after I'd left the navy, I'd met Kramer socially through an old friend of the family, Commander Joe Gower, a former Royal Navy submariner and at that stage head of Naval Intelligence. Joe and his wife Elizabeth – they had a beautiful home in Constantia – were good friends.

Of course, I should have put together all the pieces, but I didn't. It was years before I was to discover that the charts were intended to be used in an attack on Soviet and East European ships in Lagos harbour during the Biafran War, which was then slowly gathering its own momentum. Most Soviet ships entering Nigerian waters over the next few years were loaded with weapons for the Nigerian war effort against

Lieutenant Colonel Ojukwu's breakaway state.

Apparently, the South Africans had plans to use limpet mines against these vessels as they lay alongside the quays in the port and the charts I acquired were a vital part of their planning. Also involved were two other good friends of mine, Colonel Jan Breytenbach, one of the founders of South Africa's crack Reconnaissance Commando, and an old diving buddy 'Woody' Woodburn. Admiral Woodburn was later to become head of the South African Navy.

The original idea had been to take a demolition team close to the Nigerian coast in one of South Africa's small French-built Daphne-class submarines. At the last moment, Woody told me years later, the attack was called off.

That was why, in all innocence, I'd asked Silas Anusiem to buy the charts from the government office responsible for such things in Lagos. As a consequence, I'm aware now that had things gone wrong, we might both have been arrested on espionage charges, something that would have proved difficult to counter when there was a revolution brewing. In the heady political climate that preceded the war, we might even have been executed for treason. There was reason enough; the charts were invaluable. Others were shot for much less once hostilities started.

But Silas – with his remarkable network of contacts – was forewarned. Halfway though one of our trips to Onitsha, the biggest city in Nigeria's East, he turned to me in the car:

'Those charts, Al. Where are they now?' I sensed there was more to come.

'Why?' I asked, no longer above suspicion.

'Because questions have been asked.' My Ibo associate was well aware of my South African connections. He'd been grilled by the Nigerian Special Branch. I knew too that my Apapa apartment had been searched once or twice while I was away on trips. David had told me.

I explained to Silas exactly what I had done and also the reason why. Silas paled perceptibly. Give him his dues, he never said a word. Nor did he ever raise the issue again.

Silas Anusiem had told me once before that he had a brother in the higher echelons of the Nigerian Navy who served at Naval Headquarters in Lagos. I have no doubt that it was left to him to sort matters out.

It would seem that once again, the lady smiled.

It was with Silas Anusiem that I had my last adventure of any consequence in Nigeria, at least before I returned to cover the Biafran War on the 'other' side. It was during a long road journey through the Eastern Region, which was always a very different experience from the rest of the country.

I'd always enjoyed covering the East before the war. The people there were friendly and certainly much chirpier than the rest. There was always something going on, a High Life session or a feast with palm wine by the calabash-full. Also, you got things done among the Ibos: they were always willing to help and though it cost some, you didn't mind sticking your hand in your pocket for good work done.

In Lagos, in contrast, the lifestyle was a perpetual round of haggling, delays, cancelled appointments and very little achieved without 'dash', the universal system of crossing palms with silver, or – increasingly – with large denomination Naira banknotes.

Our route this time took us across the Niger River at Onitsha and then on towards Owerri and Port Harcourt, both critical points in the war to come. We were on the second day out and so far it had been an uneventful journey. Then we reached the small town of Nsokpo about a dozen miles or so from Port Harcourt. Quite unexpectedly we came upon a crowd, several thousand strong. This mob had totally blocked the road ahead and what appeared to be an angry, ugly melee had developed.

Silas suggested I park next to the road and wait for him; he'd go and see what was happening.

Shortly after I'd pulled up, I spotted several youngsters throwing stones at cars that arrived along the same road that we'd just used. Being white, they ignored me: it was the Nigerian fat cats they were after. Most of these people turned around and roared off. Then an army truck with about a dozen soldiers on board came hurtling down the same road towards us at speed. The mob surged towards them in a fury of roars and obscenities and the driver made the mistake of stopping. This was clearly a very angry group of dissidents as they converged on the troops, a frightening, shrieking black mass. I thought I knew Africa, but I'd never seen anything like this. The corporal in charge put his truck into reverse and in double quick time pulled back a third of a mile or so before turning around and moving off.

There was no question that the mood had become menacing, which was when I turned my car around and also moved back down the road a short distance. I was afraid that the situation would get worse.

I waited half an hour; then an hour, but still no Silas. By now I was worried. Also, I was hungry. We'd been on the road for half the day and hadn't stopped once.

So why not take a photograph? I thought. There was obviously a reason for the troubles and who knows, there might be a story there somewhere. Certainly, Nussey would use it. So I pulled my camera out and, for good effect, climbed onto the roof of my car. I was just starting to focus when a couple of young men near to me noticed the camera.

'No *pitcha*!' they shouted, their arms raised high above their heads.

More of the men around them heard their cries and turned towards me. Soon there were dozens of people screaming. Fists in the air, they bellowed: 'No pitcha! *You no takka pitcha*!' It was fundamental Pidgin English and the message was clear.

I smiled, waved and went on with what I was doing. By now I was attracting an awful lot of attention. At that point there were two or three hundred people very vocally focused on what I was doing. Perhaps 30 seconds later it had become a thousand. Or it could have been five times that because I wasn't counting. Except that there was an ocean of black faces in front of me and there wasn't one among them who wasn't incensed by the presence of this stupid foreigner taking pictures.

Who was this white man who had so rudely intruded on the ground where some of their folk had been gunned down earlier in the day? That I'd wanted to take photos compounded the issue. For such is the volatility of Africa at a time of crisis.

Just then this massive surge was heading straight at me. The cry '*No pitcha*' had become a roar. Some of the youngsters alongside started to rock the car. Hell, this was serious!

I'd already jumped to the ground, just before the first wave of protestors got to me. I tried to say something to those nearest me but was completely drowned out by their screams. It was useless: a lone voice against thousands. What had started as a few calls to desist, had become hysteria.

I must have saved my life by jumping into the car at about the same time as those closest to me started to beat on my windscreen and roof with their fists. By now the mob was shouting at me in their own language and I understood none of it. If I didn't get away, and fast, they'd haul me out, drag me away and who knows what would happen then? There was no way that I would be able to reason with this rabble.

In a single, fluid motion that comes with practice, I started the engine and at the same moment, released my brakes. A split second before, I'd shifted the car into gear. It all happened in a blink and a screech of rubber. Some of the mob was ahead by now, but I went right through the crowd without touching any of them. That was the moment, I knew, that if I had to run over any of them to get clear, I would do so. I was 100 feet down the road before the first rock hit my back window, shattering it.

It is notable that my car had been giving trouble on the trip up. Once or twice I'd had difficulty starting it, usually in the mornings when Silas had to push. Had I stalled then, I would most certainly have been killed. The mob was berserk, totally out of control.

As it happened, the car took in a flash. I heard later that with me gone, they then turned on some more soldiers who had just arrived.

Silas joined me later in Port Harcourt. We'd agreed that we would be staying at the Cedar Palace and that should we become separated, he'd find me there. He did so some time before midnight that evening.

What had happened, he told me later, was that the army had apparently shot a group of striking students at Nsokpo earlier in the day.

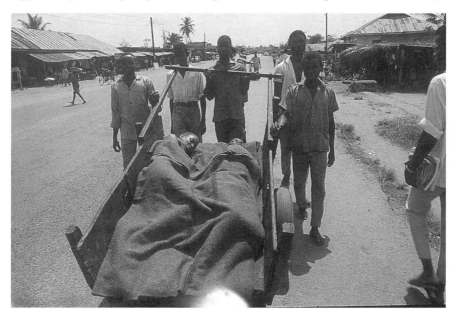

Wounded soldiers being carted off to hospital by an 'ambulance' in Eastern Nigeria. They were the lucky ones . . . (Author's collection)

A riot had developed. More soldiers arrived and more people were killed.

Then the mob cornered some troops. Though the army held its own for a while, every one of them was overpowered, disarmed and killed. The slaughter developed into a ritual; limb by limb these poor souls were ripped apart and the corpses burnt. It didn't help that most of the troops involved in this fracas were Northerners. By the time we'd arrived, the mob was already out of control.

Certainly, said Silas later, if my car had stalled, I wouldn't have survived. The mob was frenzied and conditions stayed that way until the first Nigerian Army armoured car arrived and more live ammunition was used, though details of that action were never made public.

Nor was I able to discover how many people were killed that violent afternoon. It must have been a hefty tally because at that stage the Hausas were intent on making a dramatic example of Southerners who voiced dissent. People would be pulled off the roads by troops and simply disappear.

None of it ever appeared in the Nigerian press.

Many lives were lost in Nigeria in 1966 for no apparent reason and not all the victims were Ibo.

There was never anyone who would or could do anything about it. We, the public, only heard rumours, which were often exaggerated. The reason was simple: the moment the military took power they occupied the editorial offices of all the country's newspapers. They already controlled all the radio stations.

Rumour then feasted on its own excesses and that didn't help either.

CHAPTER FIVE

Biafra: The Build-Up

It's a truism that for those in the West with expanding commu-
nications, the world has shrunk. For Africa, it has grown
immeasurably . . .

AS WITH IRAQ, ALMOST 40 years later, oil in the mid 1960s lay at the core of Nigeria's problems. Huge deposits of fossil fuels had been discovered along the coast of the Eastern Region, or Biafra, as it was known for the short time that it existed.

Even today there is much squabbling about exactly who owns what. At one stage in the early 2000s, Nigeria and the Cameroon Republic almost went to war over the disputed Bakassi Peninsula: nobody even knew it existed until oil was discovered there. Until then, Bakassi might have been a new brand of toothpaste.

There was more sabre-rattling over what constituted the offshore rights of Equatorial Guinea – formerly Spanish Guinea – and, more recently, a botched South African mercenary attempt to oust the President of that island government, one of the most brutal and corrupt countries on the globe. Oil motivated that lunacy as well . . .

Four decades earlier, it was oil that made the Ibos greedy because they wanted all the black stuff for themselves. Certainly, they didn't need what they termed the 'Backward North' to enjoy any of it: all the oil under the ground was rightfully theirs was it not? Therefore, ran the argument, which was quite public, let's keep it for ourselves. Goodbye Nigerian Federation!

It was about then that quite a few developed nations – Britain, America and Russia in particular – began to look seriously at the military options involved. It seemed clear that Nigeria was heading for civil war. Nevertheless, it was a complicated issue. Internecine strife – as we have seen more recently in places such as Chechnya, Kashmir, Sri Lanka, Iraq, Afghanistan, Lebanon and elsewhere – usually is.

Meanwhile, I'd settled into my new job in Lagos and there had been some interesting developments following the army mutiny that had almost claimed my life. I stayed on at Ikeja during this period, running the military gauntlet each day until I was on first name terms with most of the senior Nigerian Army and Air Force officers there.

From my office at the airport, despite being open to large numbers of commercial airlines, including the old Pan American Airways (the company ran a regular service between New York and Johannesburg), I could see that the government was starting an arms build-up of its own in anticipation of an Ibo secession. The first evidence of this was the arrival, in full Nigerian Air Force livery, of a squadron of Czechoslovakian Delphin trainer/fighter jets. Some of these trim little aircraft were parked outside my office.

Everybody was delighted. At last, the Federal government was showing a bit of muscle! For the first month these brand new warplanes were almost mollycoddled. Each morning they were carefully washed down and polished. Come the end of the day, someone would emerge from the hangars and close the cockpits. It was all meticulously done.

A squadron or two of Czechoslovakian Delphin jet trainers/fighters was bought by the Federal government for service against the 'Dissident East'. They were parked outside my office and for the first few months kept in tip-top condition. Afterwards nobody even bothered to close their cockpit canopies when it rained and it wasn't long before they became inoperable. (Photo courtesy of Michael Draper, author of *Shadows: Airlift and Airwar in Biafra and Nigeria, 1967–1970*)

Additional canvas covers would be spread over the planes so that nothing would be damaged if it rained. By the second month, the covers had disappeared. Weeks later nobody even bothered about rain, or whether the cockpits were open or closed to the weather.

Obviously the Delphins weren't operational for very long thereafter, which was when Lagos started shopping around and eventually bought Soviet MiG-17 fighters.

Meanwhile, as part of my job, I continued to travel. Most of all, I enjoyed heading out towards the East, near the Cameroon frontier. Though unsettled because of the refugee problem – a million Ibos had been forced to return to their roots because they were being slaughtered elsewhere – this was still the most ordered part of the country.

When I had first entered Nigeria – impecunious and overland from the Cameroon Republic the year before – I'd managed to visit the delightful little port of Calabar that nestles like a cherub at the head of a river inlet in the extreme east of the country. It was a tropical hideaway from all the country's travails and I made friends with a group of British and American volunteers. Also a charming place was Jos, a big area in the interior with its tin mines and strange, primitive tribes who wanted only to be left alone.

The North was pleasant enough, at least when there weren't people slitting each other's throats. Anyway, whites were regarded as very much apart from that kind of violence. Then things started to get nasty and one couldn't escape the tension.

Meanwhile, the military governor of the Eastern Region, Lieutenant Colonel (later General) Ojukwu, watched all these events with dismay. The son of a wealthy Ibo businessman and an Oxford graduate (see Chapter 6), he was outspoken about the long-term consequences of these killings. The nation was being irrevocably split, he warned. War might follow, if only because the minority that was being persecuted simply had to do something to survive.

The idea of seceding from the Nigerian Federation was already a hot issue in Enugu, Port Harcourt and Onitsha. Among the arguments that Ojukwu and his people liked to use, was that the boundaries of the country had been arbitrarily drawn by the British colonial government a century before.[1] Consequently, they were of little use now, they maintained.

Of course, by then, matters relating to oil had become a very substantial issue. The new-found oil deposits, it was agreed, would give the Ibo Nation (it had been the Ibo 'people' before) the economic power to go it alone.

We were aware that Ojukwu had already sent his emissaries abroad to acquire what weapons they could from Europe. The word that came back was that some of his requests were being met, with France and several Eastern European countries willing to sell arms for cash. It was all over-the-counter stuff, and the problem was getting it back to Ojukwu's already-embattled enclave.

At about this point, things moved quickly. Violence in the Northern reaches continued, with killings in the Yoruba-dominated West abating markedly over the months that followed. No fools, the Yoruba were already well aware that this was a North–South thing, with the preponderant Islamic militants in the North doing what they could to cripple the largely Christian Eastern Nigeria.

Indirectly, that led to questions being asked in Lagos and Ibadan and they went something like this: once the Ibos and the East have been dealt with, are we likely to be next? The phrase 'Islamic Jihad' was being bandied about as if this threat was already a reality.

Undeterred, the Eastern Region was soon to be declared. The Republic of Biafra it was called, and its symbol was the rising sun again a black backdrop. Then, as some of us knew it would, came the counter-revolution launched by the Nigeria's Islamic north, though most of us got the timing wrong. Worse, with my offices at the airport, I seemed to be in the middle of it.

At that early stage, there was very little known about the man who had taken over after Nigeria's second military coup.

General Yakubu Gowon was a quiet-spoken Christian soldier who originally came from a small northern tribe, the Angas. Though he had a minor role in the July 1966 counter-coup, he emerged as a compromise head of the new government.

Frederick Forsyth remembers him emerging out of the gathering chaos as the mild-mannered adjutant of the Nigerian Army. He was the typical young Nigerian officer. More important, he wasn't Muslim. Being, as it was termed, 'Middle Belt' – neither from the North nor the South – he couldn't be tarred with a brush of being an Ibo. In fact, recalls Forsyth, he suited everybody.

As far as the coup leaders were concerned, their attitude was that 'we can run the country behind this man'. So too with Sir David Hunt, the British High Commissioner: Gowon was the perfect choice.

Sir David was a traditionalist, and liked the fact that Gowon would snap to attention whenever the British High Commissioner walked in . . . that pleased the old Brit. In contrast, there were those among us who regarded the Nigerian military leader as an overgrown boy scout.

In contrast, Sir David's relations with Lieutenant Colonel Ojukwu were 'frosty', recalls Forsyth:

The British High Commissioner, very much a product of the old British colonial establishment, viewed black people in 'their proper place'. Certainly, Ojukwu didn't fit into that mould: he was the product of a British public school education and could actually be regarded as a black Englishman. He'd been to Oxford, played a good game of rugby, his father had been knighted by the King and was a self-made millionaire . . . this was a man of substance.

Ojukwu, recalls Forsyth:

regarded Sir David Hunt with the direst suspicion, well-merited as it eventually turned out. From the outset the British High Commissioner detested the Ibo military leader and the sentiment was thoroughly reciprocated.

On Hunt's part, there were two reasons. Unlike Ojukwu, Hunt was not public school, despite a brilliant classical brain demonstrated at Oxford. But he *was* a simply crushing snob and covert racist. Two, he divorced his wife and married Rio Myriantusi, the favourite niece of the mega-rich, Lebanese-Greek Nigerian-based tycoon A.G. Leventis . . . and what complicated matters here was that she had been Emeka's [Ojukwu's] girlfriend, with the younger man vastly better endowed!

A career army officer, Yakubu Gowon was very different, though he was also a contemporary of the rebel leader Ojukwu. The two men actually served in the same units on occasion and knew and understood each other's foibles, which could have been one of the reasons why the Biafran leader believed that he could pull off his wager to withdraw from the Nigerian Federation and go it alone, much as Rhodesia had successfully done just a few years before.

Indeed, the two men were very different. Gowon wasn't one for publicity: in fact, says Forsyth, it took him an age to get his first interview with a man whom he always found extremely reserved and quiet-spoken.

Never recalcitrant, he was reticent to talk about his own life and though he could have claimed one of the presidential palaces as his own, he never did. None of his successors wasted any time in moving into the biggest and most lavish palaces on hand, most times with excessive brass and hoopla. Gowon preferred to stay on in the barracks with his family, in part, it has been said, because the presence of his own soldiers offered better protection.

Eschewing limelight and controversy, General Gowon was different

Conditions in the east of the country were difficult from the start. Biafran troops had to manage with improvised training and instruction, which often involved no weapons at all because everything available had been shifted to the frontlines. (Author's collection)

in other respects as well. The media made a thing about his having been trained in England at the Royal Military Academy, Sandhurst, as well as in Ghana. The truth, says Forsyth, 'is that while it sounds like the full three-year permanent commission background, it was actually a three-month summer course which Commonwealth officers literally couldn't fail'. Gowon did get involved in two tours of duty with the Nigerian Army during the Congo's upheavals and, by all accounts, did a sterling job in putting down uprisings in the interior.

When the Biafran War ended, it was General Yakubu Gowon who initiated the remarkable reconciliation that took place between the victors and the vanquished, in itself an astonishing gesture because it avoided still more unnecessary bloodshed. That this happened at a time when the Nigerian military clamoured to bring the entire Biafran command and their supporters to trial, made his efforts even more commendable.

There were those who wanted them all executed. The fact that Gowon managed to sidestep this bristling, emotional matter underscores the measure of his resolve. After all, his opponents argued, hundreds of thousands of their own peoples' lives had been lost in what they regarded a senseless war.

Gowon had a ruthless (and some say, a pragmatic) side to him that went unheralded. He was the first African leader to hire foreign pilots to fight his war: first Egyptians to fly his MiG-17s and then a batch of South African and British mercenaries who eventually played a seminal role in turning the war around. He was also powerfully opposed to any direct humanitarian aid going into Biafra without the aircraft first landing at Nigerian airports to be checked. As a consequence, he was implacably opposed to organizations like Oxfam and Joint Church Aid, which flew their planes into Biafra from the offshore Portuguese island colony of Sao Tomé and from Libreville in Gabon.

In the political climate in an unstable Nigeria that was both unpredictable and volatile, General Gowon simply couldn't last. On a diplomatic mission to Uganda in July 1975, the army deposed him.

Forsyth commented that:

Both the harsh and the gentle side of Gowon were deceptive because he was throughout like a glove puppet; either of the Fulani/Hausa zealots like Murtala Mohammed or of British advisors who might spot a brilliant opportunity for hood PR.

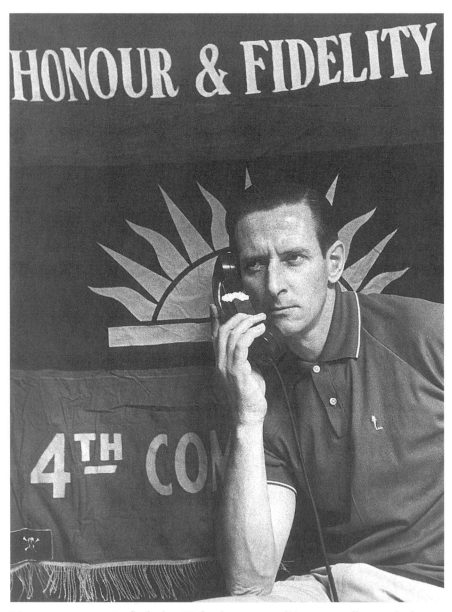

Not many mercenaries flocked to Biafra, because conditions generally were bad. Taffy Williams, a South African Welshman, shown with the Biafran flag behind him, was one of the few. Another was Rolf Steiner, who liked to draw attention to himself in front of his troops by firing his pistol in the air. He was eventually removed from the country in shackles. (Author's collection)

Visiting correspondents and residents like Angus McDermid were constantly briefed by the High Commissioner, almost as if he were in total charge in all matters. In fact Hunt wasn't: he constantly deferred to his British and Northern advisors.

Before the war started there was one crucial effort to prevent conflict at Aburi. It was staged by the British High Commissioner before David Hunt and Sir Francis Coming-Bruce (aka to the hack community as 'Cunning Brute'). All the parties involved were represented, with the idea of finding a compromise settlement and heading off secession and a Nigerian civil war.

Forsyth comments:

Ojukwu turned up at Aburi wholly focused and minutely briefed. While he ran rings around the poor, floundering Gowon, the deal was nevertheless signed to general jubilation and relief. But Lagos had made concessions that some of the country's leaders didn't like. For instance, the East was allowed to retain federal taxes to cope with her almost two million penniless refugees who had fled the North and the West with only the clothes on their backs, leaving behind 30,000 dead and bringing with them the same number of machete-mutilated victims.

Back in Lagos afterwards, the Northerners exploded and denounced it all as a charade. The British briefed the Press that Ojukwu had taken gross advantage of the not-too-bright Gowon [who could have brought a team of scholars, but chose to negotiate alone]. Lagos then reneged on every point that had earlier been agreed to at Aburi.

Ironically, accused by Sir David Hunt of being a dictator, Ojukwu was the only one of the two who bowed to the will of his people. The Nigerian attitude, as we have seen, was 'good riddance' . . . until London pointed out exactly where the oil lay.

The war that everybody regarded as inevitable became a reality when the secessionist West African state of Biafra unilaterally declared itself independent from Nigeria in May 1967. The split came months after I left Lagos, when tens of thousands of Ibo people in the Northern Region were massacred. Perhaps a million more fled southwards to Eastern-dominated areas. In turn, huge numbers of non-Ibos were expelled from the East.

While hostilities started well enough, with the secessionists marching half-way across the country to take Benin and much of the central regions, the Biafran Army was hesitant to continue on to Lagos. It was Ojukwu's worst mistake of the war. The city was wide open and government forces – though not in disarray – were on the back foot and unable to respond to this brilliant Biafran initiative.

Then came betrayal. Ojukwu himself today admits that the role played by Colonel Victor Banjo – a non-Ibo, but one of his senior planners – had a significant effect on the outcome of that early, extremely critical phase. His forces were never supposed to have taken the mid-west city of Benin. They wasted weeks and a lot of lives in doing so. Then Banjo clandestinely made contact with Federal Army officers in Lagos. It didn't work, because Banjo was unmasked, court-martialed and shot.

As Frederick Forsyth wrote – he spent a lot of time in Biafra and wrote a classic book on the war *Biafra Story: The Making of an African Legend* – 'it was also clear that the Nigerian Army was a rabble, a shambles from beginning to end'.

Government forces did get their act together after a while, in part because either they did so or went down. Lagos' forces then proceeded to blockade all eastern ports in the hands of Ojukwu's troops and within months the conflict had degenerated into one of the most brutal tit-for-tat wars of attrition that Africa had seen in post-colonial times.

Fighting everywhere was both ferocious and confused. Towns changed hands, sometimes three or four times in as many months. Eventually, the preponderance of Federal power prevailed and the Biafrans were pushed back, first from the coast and finally into several loosely linked enclaves in the heavily forested interior. Government atrocities at the hands of what had become a Northern-dominated, mainly Islamic force soon convinced the rebel nation that secession from the Federation was no longer the principal issue. Rather, it had become a battle for survival.

One of the reasons why the Biafrans were initially so successful was that only a small percentage of the officer corps came from the North and the West at the time of Nigeria's independence from Britain in 1960. Most of those who replaced white officers were of Ibo extraction.

As war gathered pace during the latter part of 1967, I was determined to get back to West Africa and cover it. My sojourn in Lagos had provided me with some valuable connections. Since Vietnam tended to hog the headlines (and most of the more experienced foreign correspondents) there weren't too many scribes either eager, or willing, to go into a conflict that, from abroad, looked only a step removed from disaster.

Because of censorship on both sides of the front, nobody got the entire picture right. The reason was basic: one of the first measures taken by both the Biafran and the Federal government was to hire a succession of crack European PR companies to push their military claims, most of them inflated. There were some battles that took place that – if you had to judge by respective PR reports – might have happened on different continents. One of the consequences was that just about everything about the war, from start to finish, was clouded by fogs of duplicity and equivocation.

Still a cub reporter – and an untrained one at that – I thought I knew better. After all, I'd seen developments from the inside. I'd been living there from the start, right at the core of it. I also knew that if Biafra came into being, the resolve of these persecuted people wouldn't make for an easy pushover. Of course, it didn't happen like that.

Biafra at that stage was recognized by only four countries, and then only circumspectly. Tanzania, with a revolutionary cauldron brewing along its borders in neighbouring Mozambique – then still ruled from Lisbon – was one of them. For all that, though, there was a Biafran diplomatic legation in Dar es Salaam.

I decided early on that I'd get myself to Nairobi, make my way by road to Dar es Salaam and with my *Daily Express* press card in hand, bang on the door of the Biafran Embassy. While it took time for the West Africans to check my bona fides, a visa eventually came through, delivered to the office of my foreign editor in Fleet Street. It was sent to me in South Africa and from there I headed for what antiquarian maps have always displayed as the Bight of Benin.

In theory, I expect I could have covered the war from the Nigerian side, but things there were ultra-difficult at the time. For a start, the media was suspect. Individual Nigerian commanders weren't shy to show their displeasure if somebody reported something contrary to the official line.

One senior Nigerian Army officer, Colonel Benjamin 'Black Scorpion' Adekunle, commander of Nigeria's 3rd Marine Commando Division, was a psychopathic bully who was quite happy to shoot his own men if he thought he needed to make an example. He did so once in the presence of foreign journalists and dared them to file their stories. Adekunle often blasted off about the kind of journalism then coming out of West Africa, blaming his nation's woes on the CIA, Westminster, the Pope and who knows who else.

It was even worse if the object of his venom happened to be white. Europeans were responsible for all of the ills of Africa, he would proclaim. He was much more rancorous when he was drunk.

Mike Williamson, in *A Measure of Danger*, mentions a dinner at which Adekunle drew a pistol and pointed it, in turn, at each of the journalists at the table. Eventually he pressed it against Williamson's temple and pulled the trigger. It went click. Black joke from the Black Scorpion, as somebody commented.

With all this in mind, I didn't really want to cover the war from the Federal side. In any event, the Biafran effort had much more appeal in the eyes of this eager youngster. I'd be going in by air and from accounts already published, you didn't have to go looking for action because the Nigerian Air Force – with mercenaries flying their aircraft – provided it every day of the week, Sundays included.

But first, how to get there? I could enter the beleaguered state from one of three places: Lisbon, which had regular flights to the island of Sao Tomé, from where there were nightly, mainly Church Aid, relief flights across the Nigerian coast into Biafra. However, that would have meant starting off in Portugal and I didn't feel like doubling back to Europe just then. Also, it was expensive.

The only viable alternative was Gabon, another of the four countries that had recognized Ojukwu's cause. Trouble was, most flights into the rebel territory out of Libreville were military, which meant getting to the war on an aircraft loaded with ammunition, artillery shells and a variety of explosives that the rebels needed to enhance their fortunes.

I was candid when I spoke to the Biafran press officer in Dar es Salaam. 'Put me on one of the relief planes carrying food or whatever. I'll give the military flights a miss for now.' He could only smile, well aware that even that had become dangerous after one of the British mercenaries flying a Nigerian Air Force MiG-17 shot down an International Red Cross flight loaded with baby food.

Having covered a story in the Ivory Coast for a European magazine, I found myself in Ghana shortly afterwards. From there I reviewed my options. For a start, money was tight and I had to budget carefully. I knew that I could only afford perhaps one flight and that I would have to make the best of that.

As I had decided early on that Gabon was my best option, I now had the problem of getting there from Ghana. Any flight between Accra and Libreville, the Gabonese capital, would have meant changing planes at Lagos. I hesitated for several reasons, not least that having worked at Ikeja International Airport for six months, everybody knew me by my first name. Embarrassing questions might have been asked.

Also, because I had lived in the country, the Nigerians would have been interested to learn what it was that had brought me back to West Africa at a time of war. They were familiar with what I had done before and, anyway, people involved in shipping don't go traipsing about Africa without good reason. I could probably have talked my way out of that one, but I didn't relish the hassle. Who knew where it could lead?

By then, we all knew, mercenaries had already become an issue. Lagos had Egyptian and South African pilots while Biafra had started recruiting British, South African and French mercs, among them Bob Denard. I might have been mistaken for one, particularly since I was headed for Gabon.

So instead of going by air, I did the next best thing. I made for Tema docks, Ghana's biggest port where, for a few days, I shopped around. I eventually found what I wanted: a cargo ship that would take me to Cameroon, to the immediate east of Nigeria. My saviour was the Norwegian-registered 12,000-ton freighter *Titania*.

No, the captain assured me, there would be no layovers in Nigerian ports. Yes, he said, he was going to Douala. Problem solved. We discussed a price and ten minutes later, over a couple of glasses of aquavit, we had a deal. I knew that I could fly from Douala to Libreville, the capital of Gabon.

What I hadn't factored was that cargo ships all over the world are subject to the prerequisites of their owners. If there's a cargo waiting to be picked up along the way and there's financial return in doing so, the master will get his orders. So too, with the *Titania*.

We'd barely slipped moorings at Tema when he called me to the bridge. There was a change of plan, he said. The ship was going into a Nigerian port after all. Some oil drilling equipment had to be hauled out of the Niger Delta port of Warri. But first, he said, there would be a stop in Lagos.

As expected, I was closely questioned about the reasons for my visit to Nigeria when the *Titania* berthed at Apapa Docks. My name was on file and so was the fact – very clearly imprinted in my passport – that I'd been in South Africa a short while before. That half-hour was gruelling and uncertain, but eventually the man – clearly linked to one of the Nigerian intelligence offices – let me continue my journey.

When I disembarked at Douala, my troubles started afresh, largely over what was termed the *mercenaire* issue.

Many of those who have travelled the West African coast refer to Douala – in the middle of hundreds of square miles of swamp – as the original 'Armpit of Africa'. It is hot and clammy, with mushrooms often sprouting on the carpets of your hotel.

The colonizing Germans, no doubt, had good reasons for settling at the estuary of one of the unhealthiest rivers in Africa, although they've always escaped me. Victoria – the British-controlled enclave along the western fringe of the Cameroon, lying at the foot of the great Mount Cameroon – is a much more appealing setting. Also it's healthier.

At Douala, in contrast, the river is nearly always shrouded in a tropical mist after dark and the mosquitoes are legion. There was an appalling number of deaths among the colonists in the early years, with most dying of yellow fever.

Travellers arriving at Douala these days are still greeted by that same almost impenetrable swamp. An aircraft flying to Europe from Johannesburg in the 1960s crashed immediately after take-off with more than a hundred passengers and crew on board. Although it went down almost within sight of the airport, it took French Army and Navy rescue teams three days to reach the wreckage, though one must ask the obvious: were there no helicopters? Nobody survived and the word went out that crocodiles feasted on the bodies, which was perhaps just as well in that heat, though that was something you could hardly convey to the families.

History repeated itself when a Kenya Airways Boeing jet crashed after take-off from Douala in May 2007. Again there were more than a hundred people onboard, all of them killed and once more, it took days for the authorities – this time working with helicopters – to discover the site of the wreck. As with the crash more than 40 years earlier, it came down just a short distance from the airport . . .

After leaving the *Titania*, my intention was to fly to Libreville from Douala and make contact with the Biafran Embassy there. From Gabon, hopefully, I'd be able to hitch a lift on a plane to Uli, Biafra's main runway in the jungle, which after dark was lit by paraffin wicks set in jam jars. Because of a powerful Nigerian Air Force presence, we could only go in at night. That part of my trip, I knew, had been arranged two months prior by Ibezim Chukwumerije at the Office of the Biafran Special Representative in Dar es Salaam.

I had no difficulties in Douala, except that I was kept for an hour by an officious immigration officer who quizzed me repeatedly about my intentions.

'You're not going into Biafra?' he asked in good English. He looked hard at me and it didn't help that I was sweating in his airless office above the harbour.

'Not at all, Sir, I'm going south.'

'Strange that you should come through here, through Douala,' was

Hardly an inspiring picture of Biafran troops in training. The country was starving and so were these soldiers: it took four of them to move the kind of ammunition box a reasonably fit man could handle on his own. (Author's collection)

his comment. Because the man was obviously suspicious, I said something about preferring sea to air travel. In fact, I had served in the navy and liked ships, were my words.

I was only to discover later, that a couple of weeks before, two young Americans had arrived in Douala, very much as I had, though they'd flown in directly from New York. They'd heard about the plight of Biafra and their motive was strictly humanitarian, as they confessed 'to offer help to the starving millions'. At least that's what they told an immigration official at Douala Airport, perhaps even the same official who grilled me.

When things started to get tough, one of them pointed to the fact that newspapers all over the world had made it known that Biafra needed medical help. These two youngsters were obviously sincere do-gooders.

In their case, however, simply mentioning their intention of going to the rebel state set off a chain of events that they could never have foreseen. First they were arrested. Then, for several days they were inter-rogated and savagely beaten. The *Agence Camerounaise de la Presse* declared that they were mercenaries, but that was after they had been taken to hospital and the American Embassy in Yaounde had delivered a protest note.

The youngsters were nothing of the sort, of course. Both could show that they had solid medical backgrounds; both believed that they had a role to play in a country at war.

The two young men were flown out as soon as the American Consul in Douala could get them released and he had to do so against hefty guarantees. One of them spent months in hospital after he got back home.

CHAPTER SIX

Survival in a West African Conflict

This author reckons he's the only journalist to have been
rocketed by the aircraft of both sides of an African war, the
first time, when two rebel Swedish-built MFI-9B 'Minicons' hit
the *Titania,* the merchant ship on which he was travelling.
That attack came while it lay moored at Nigeria's Warri
harbour. Later – while reporting from inside Biafra – he came
under fire from Nigerian Air Force MiG-17s that were flown
by South African and British mercenary pilots.[1]

EVERY WAR HAS A 'PERSONALITY' of its own. It's mostly idiosyncratic,
like the Taliban or a recalcitrant Arab government in Khartoum
overseeing developments in Darfur.

One needs to understand the vagaries of combat and the circumstances in which particular wars are fought in order to write about them.
That applies as much to Iraq, Vietnam, Lebanon, the ongoing
insurgency in the Philippines or Israel's Yom Kippur War as it does to
what is going on in Afghanistan today, whether it be along the Tora Bora
or in the plains beyond Kandahar.

Likewise, in Somalia in the early 1990s, where the majority of
journalists lived in town, I made vigorous efforts to stay on base because
I felt more comfortable with good security. Those away from the
military were on extra alert when gangs of local youths got busy,
especially when stoned on *Qat.*[2]

Most had been influenced by Islamic fundamentalists who had been
coming across the Red Sea by dhow from Yemen. They have been doing
so in increasing numbers and continue to arrive as I write. What we
observe going on in that sad country today is nothing short of a totali-
tarian disaster.

As far as the Jihadis were concerned, the 'bad guys' in their sights
included us media folk, who were almost exclusively Western anyway.
That we had some females in our ranks only accentuated the issue.

Such influences tend to have a profound effect on what some

journalists report, especially if they are made aware that they might become a target if they stayed critical of a so-called 'popular' cause. We saw that kind of undercurrent taking place in Beirut, especially on the Muslim side of the Green Line.

The same holds for Sudan today. If you highlight government mismanagement in Darfur – and to be fair, it is impossible not to implicate Khartoum in what is going on there – chances are that you'll find yourself on an aircraft home.

Biafra was different. You simply couldn't help but relate to the proverbial underdog. In a sense, this was a colonial war. The only difference from other African conflicts (Darfur excepted) was that the 'imperialists' involved were black. The devil in disguise there was the Nigerian government itself.

Each one of us was aware that the Ibo leader had tried to break free from Federal Nigeria after tens of thousands of Easterners had been massacred by Muslims. Men, women, the frail, the old, the lame and the halt, as well as children of all ages were targeted. Nothing mattered as long as there were Ibos murdered.

Ultimately, as we have already seen, it was the discovery of oil in the Eastern Region that caused the Biafrans to cut that sacrosanct umbilical cord that incontrovertibly linked their part of the country to Lagos. However, made the break, options were severely limited. It was a decision fraught with imponderables, because self-styled Biafra had neither the men nor the resources to succeed, nor at very least did the rebel state enjoy the support of any of the Great Powers, a *sine qua non* in this kind of adventure.

Inevitably, in today's difficult world just about everything hinges on politics. You can get away with most things if you have the clandestine support of Beijing or Moscow (as with Zimbabwe, North Korea and Iran). But if, like Biafra, you have nothing to offer or even something useful like a port, or a strategic asset (Egypt at the head of the Red Sea and Suez, Guinea-Conakry with a major port on Africa's Atlantic coast and Mozambique, straddling a large swathe on the Indian Ocean), your cause is a non-starter.

The Ibos had oil, granted, but anybody who wanted to get at it would have had to go through Nigeria anyway.

Nigeria was another matter altogether. The Biafran War, for all its disjointed priorities and mismatched participants, was a near-run thing, especially at its start. In the three years that it lasted, there were severe

The miniscule Biafran Air Force had a few successes, including attacks on several Nigerian installations. One of these targeted a Nigerian Air Force base in the Mid-West, where an Illyushin-28 (pictured here), originally flown by Egyptian pilots, was destroyed on the ground. (Photo courtesy of Michael Draper, author of *Shadows: Airlift and Airwar in Biafra and Nigeria, 1967–1970*)

casualties on both sides, with almost a million people dead by the time the guns stopped firing. Tragically, only a tiny proportion of those who did the actual fighting were killed. Most of the casualties were children, the majority of whom starved to death. Biafra was the first of the more recent Third World wars to claim an inordinate number of war victims.

It was in Biafra that I made my first acquaintance with a remarkable young Englishman who was quadrilingual in English, French, German and Spanish, and who had flown de Havilland Vampire jets for the Royal Air Force in the days when military conscription was still obligatory in Britain.

Freddie to us all, then and now – or more formally, Frederick Forsyth – had worked for Reuters in Paris and Berlin before accepting a job with the BBC and heading out to West Africa, where he became a friend and confidante of the rebel leader Lieutenant Colonel Ojukwu. This enthusiastic young Brit eventually became so close to the rebel hierarchy that he was actually attached to the main Biafran invasion army that struck out in force in a lightning raid to capture Lagos, then the Federal capital. The fact that he'd fallen out with his bosses in London because of their partisan approach to the crisis, which ignored the slaughter of the innocents, had a good deal to do with it. He deplored British support for a government that had caused so many innocent deaths. In the end, he resigned from the BBC but stayed on in the disputed rebel enclave to work as a freelance.

Had the Biafrans succeeded in their attempts at secession, Forsyth has always said, Nigeria would probably have another name today. But they didn't, because of Colonel Victor Banjo's betrayal. Freddie also maintains that there were also other factors that contributed.

The experience of Biafran troops' almost taking Lagos, the country's biggest city, as Forsyth will tell you, taught Nigeria a lesson. Once the Biafrans had pulled back to their own lines, the Nigerian government completely changed its military policy. To bring the recalcitrant Biafra to heel, Lagos needed tens of thousands of soldiers and there was no option but to 'to recruit, recruit and recruit'. As Forsyth explains, 'within almost no time at all, the Nigerian government increased its army up from the original 6,000 to something like 150,000'.

The newcomers came from all over. The Nigerian authorities used the prisons, such as Lagos' awful Kiri Kiri Prison, which was nearly emptied of every thug, gangster and killer. Murderers were summarily released and put into uniform. Then the recruiters virtually emptied Lagos University. They grabbed every student they could find, gave him a rifle, and, as was the case in Angola 30 years later, all these young men were turned around and transported to the front. There was never any question of training this new group of improvised soldiers.

It was about then that the prospect of Nigerian oil supplies entered the picture. Suddenly there were those who became aware that if Biafra were to succeed in pulling away from the Nigerian Federation, Nigeria's oil supplies to Britain and America might be disrupted. London panicked when it realized that perhaps this civil war thing was not going to be quite as simple as Whitehall had originally said it would.

The man who made all this disruption happen – and who was to become a close friend and confidante of Forsyth – was the self-appointed Biafran leader Ojukwu, the son of Sir Louis Odumegwu Ojukwu, a transport tycoon and one of the first native multi-millionaires of Nigeria.

The old man had originally started out as a typical West African working-class man with one truck. From there, he built up an entire pan-national transport chain and made a fortune during World War II in his not altogether altruistic bid to help the British war effort. He was eventually knighted for services to the Empire.

His son, also Odumegwu, who must have been born round 1933, was sent to Epson College, one of the best fee-paying schools in England. From there he went up to Lincoln College, Oxford, one of the world's oldest academic institutions, with its 15th-century façade, its medieval hall, a 17th-century chapel and its famous baroque library. Forsyth states:

He ended up playing rugby for the college, so in a sense, young Odumegwu was one of those very Anglicized young Africans that the British were seeking to turn out, right across all the old Dominions, Africa, especially.

He returned to Africa and was expected to take over the reins of his father's commercial empire. Instead, Ojukwu decided to join the Nigerian Army and that surprised everybody at the time because they presumed he would just live the life of a young hyper-privileged Nigerian.

In terms of education and culture, there was just nobody that could begin to match him. The Nigerian military establishment in those days was commanded by a Scot, Brigadier or Major General, Mackenzie, I think his name was. He was supported by a number of British officers, so it was all the chaps together.

Ojukwu, by now a subaltern, rose rapidly through the ranks. Then came the 1960s and independence and he progressed even further, followed in 1966 by the first army mutiny that January.

According to Forsyth, there were not only Ibo officers involved in the putsch. There were even a few Northerners.

The Ibos, we know, were the driving force, the motivators. But there were other officers as well and the revolution's orientation was much more left wing than tribal. Many of these young officers had returned from training in Europe with very distinct radical or egalitarian sentiments. I wouldn't say Marxist, but it could be viewed as close to the Marxist or Leninist view of life. These people were idealists for a better world. One and all they abhorred the nepotism and corruption then rampant throughout Nigeria.

With that, the chaos started. Every single minister, in the wake of the killings, literally disappeared: 'gone for bush', as they used to say, or vaporized into the jungle.

As with more recent African conflicts – Sierra Leone and Liberia included – few prisoners were ever taken in the Nigerian Civil War. Those held, even for brief periods, were displayed solely for propaganda purposes. POW camps, as such, didn't exist. In any event, the Biafrans had neither the means nor the ability to feed anyone but their own.

We were all aware that Federal forces would murder any of the enemy they captured. In fact, the vast majority of those taken by the Nigerian Army were lucky to survive much longer than a few hours of hard interrogation. There were exceptions, but only when scribes were around.

Journalists saw it all in a curious light. As 'guests' – on both sides – they made the best of brief, distorted and slanted handouts, erratic and sometimes dangerous transport (especially in the air) and a frontline that could waver by as much as three, and once or twice 20, miles overnight. Never mind vile accommodation – or no accommodation at all – and food that never warranted close inspection. Most of the journalists took their own food and nobody entered the country without a wide range of antibiotics.

There were often scarcely veiled threats of expulsion if you got the

Biafran air raid drills. These were hardly worth doing because the soldiers didn't have the ammunition to retaliate when strafed. (Author's collection)

story wrong. You'd get a friendly visit from an official and get the message. You saved the juicer bits for after you'd left the country.

Intimidation – as with Beirut at its worst – was routine. If you followed the Biafran line while in Lagos, you were kicked out unless you had first-class contacts within the Federal government, as was the case the BBC's Angus McDermid when he first reported on the Ibo secession.

Conflict in Nigeria had as much to do with the people as with the money to fund the fighting. With a population of about 60 million (double that today) the Federal government had a distinct preponderance where numbers were concerned – and naturally, as much hardware as Britain and Russia could sell to them because Lagos usually paid in cash. That was a good deal more than Biafra could muster, even had it had the funds.

While Federal forces had their 'hero', the psychopath Colonel Adekunle, Biafran Colonel J.O. 'Hannibal' Achuzia – who commanded the Biafran Red Commando strike force, one of the best unconventional units of the war – was a totally different kind of person.

Achuzia had fought in Korea as a soldier in the British Army and at one stage was taken prisoner and tortured by the Chinese. He applied much that he'd learnt abroad to his own tactics in Biafra and sometimes sent his men on long-range raids. In one attack, his men caught more than a hundred Nigerian Army trucks in an ambush. Munitions and equipment not destroyed were later put to good use by his own forces.

Towards the end of the war, Colonel Achuzia was ordered to take his force south. It was a last, desperate attempt to stem a Federal advance from the town of Aba across the Imo River. Since his forces were outnumbered ten-, sometimes twenty-, to-one, and his men were often down to a couple of rounds of ammunition each, with no artillery support, it was hopeless.

A charming, perspicacious man, Joe Achuzia was married to an English woman and was very much the antithesis of the dreaded Adekunle. Like the urbane former Federal Supreme Court Judge, Sir Louis Mbanefo, and the Biafran Chief of Staff, Major General Philip Effiong – another product of Sandhurst – he was a gentleman of great dignity. In that respect the Biafrans were streets ahead of their former comrades-in-arms. Many Federal officers we met were boorish in manner and uncooperative in their dealings with us and in this regard Frederick Forsyth was spot-on. They despised and often ridiculed us scribes. How different the Biafrans.

Early on the morning of my arrival at Uli, I was taken to State House at Ihiala where I was to have my passport examined.

The grey-brick building was well camouflaged from the air with palm fronds spread over the roof. The Biafrans wanted to confirm that I was who I said I was. The suspicion of infiltrating Federal Nigerian agents had become an obsession. Also, the stamp 'Enugu Airport – Biafra' looked incongruous in my passport considering that the former capital of the Eastern Region had fallen to Federal troops more than a year before and lay a week's march up the road, were that possible.

There I met Brigadier Okorafor of the Overseas Press Service. He was responsible for 'processing' those like me who had entered the rebel territory overnight; 'putting you through your paces' he liked to call it. Some reporters were spared the routine, such as those, like Forsyth, who were there by special request of H.E., that is, His Excellency Odumegwu Ojukwu.

The brigadier, a distinguished-looking former diplomat, welcomed me warmly. 'You obviously haven't had breakfast; please join me.'

The meal was revolting. He apologized and said it was the best he could offer under the circumstances. Anyway, gari is an acquired taste, especially when smothered in eye-watering pepper: I usually gave it a miss, even while I was living in Lagos before the war. The bread was half sawdust, but it was all part of the daily fare. At least the tea was Earl Grey.

'If you'd come last week', said the brigadier, 'I would have offered you an egg. We get three a month. Ours arrived last week. Sorry about that.' He was contrite.

My host himself ate as if we were at the Savoy Grill. I could have done with a steak, but by then meat was equally scarce in Biafra and what there was, usually enjoyed a dubious provenance. Every cat and dog in the country had long since gone. Rats – especially West Africa's huge cane rats – were a rare delicacy and made for a feast when caught or shot. Not bad as meat dishes go, I'd savoured some earlier in Togo where it came with a spinach and hot pepper sauce.

At Ihiala, I also met another of the stalwarts who had led the country into war after some of his family had been wiped out in faction killings in Kaduna in the Northern Region. This was Major G.C. Akabogil, a former high-school principal, then the security officer at Uli Airport. Genial but tough; 'G.C.' scrutinised all new arrivals.

He quoted Virgil like an Oxford don as he compared the war to the Roman rebellion against the cruel Etruscan king Mezentius. The analogy was good, he thought, because Yakubu Gowon, the Nigerian military leader, in the guise of Mezentius, would ultimately be vanquished, even if it had to be with foreign help. With his excellent English he sounded rather like a black version of Richard Burton.

Until I had travelled from Ihiala to Owerri – which was to be my base while I was there – I had no idea how badly the war had been going for Ojukwu's people. The Biafran High Command consisted of optimists who constantly spoke of victory. They continued to do so to the very end, even though the Feds were banging on their back and front doors, and as Forsyth once quipped, 'trying to climb in through their windows as well'.

The country was desperately short of food, other than starch, and it showed. At the airport it took four men to lift a single ammunition case that I could have handled on my own with ease.

It was the same in the towns. The people were listless and debilitated, their eyes sunk deep into their heads and their pathetic arms and legs displayed little of the kind of muscle that the average Nigerian these days is proud to display when the opportunity allows.

It was worse for the kids. Every child that hadn't been placed in one of the scores of camps that were dotted about the territory was swollen-bellied. Most had distinct white patches in their hair, the most visible evidence of kwashiorkor, a disease which is caused by starvation.

'Thank God all the children haven't yet been sent off into bush. They're our most effective air raid early warning system', said one old man. I hadn't been in Owerri for an hour before the first MiG-17 streaked across the sky, its arrival preceded by long, loud whistles. Like domestic pet dogs – if there had been any – the children could hear the whine of jet engines long before we could. At their signals we scuttled into improvised underground bunkers.

The walls of the one that I ducked into were crumbling and I could see sky through the roof. 'Why didn't they finish the job?' I asked my escort, Emeka Nwofor, formerly a teacher. His sister was at Kilometre Onze in Gabon looking after Biafran orphans. 'Because we haven't got the energy to do it', he admitted. 'The men take it easy when they aren't working or fighting. We have to conserve what little strength we have. If I want it mended, I must do it myself.' It was hardly a matter for debate.

At Owerri I was unceremoniously installed in a caravan, the same standard box-on-wheels commonly used all over Nigeria before the war. This one was barely habitable. There was a latrine pit at the back, and for a shower I used a bucket under the palms. Anywhere else in Africa, it might have made for a pleasant safari camp.

Several more caravans were clustered together in the shade of some big trees. The exposed sides were also camouflaged with palm fronds, elephant grass and bushes.

My nearest neighbour was the Italian photographer, Romano Cagnoli, who – like the Cockney lensman Don McCullin – seemed to have taken up permanent residence in the country. Between them they were responsible for many of the colour spreads of wounded, dying and emaciated Biafran children that appeared in *Life*, the London *Sunday Times* colour supplement, *Paris Match, Bunte* and others on all five continents. The Biafrans made good use of the stuff, as images of dying children stabbed at the conscience of the West. Europe was responsible, not Africa, they said and gradually people started to listen.

Mohammed Amin repeated the process not long afterwards by bringing back the first alarming scenes of millions of starving civilians in Ethiopia. That set in train the largest international aid programme ever, of which Somalia – and the war in Africa's Horn that followed – was an offshoot. Amin garnered a decoration from the Queen in the process.

In Biafra, in contrast, General Ojukwu was effectively helped in his campaign by the public relations firm Markpress of Geneva. The company thoroughly vetted everybody who wanted to go into Biafra, and again, the paranoia with Federal agents was palpable.

Cagnoli and the rest of the bunch of news gatherers into which I was thrust at Owerri lived pretty well. They'd brought with them all the booze they needed and trunkloads of food. I'd been led to believe in Libreville that we would be catered for while we were there; since we weren't, I all but starved during my entire stay. I should have known better because pictures of the breakaway state's starving children were in every newspaper in the West. Certainly, the Biafran representative in Gabon failed to warn me that his government not only wouldn't, but, more to the point couldn't, feed me.

So, while at Owerri, I was almost entirely dependent on Cagnoli's goodwill and let's face it, he could only help so much. Nobody was sure how long they'd be around or how long the war would last and they weren't taking any chances.

I ended up famished, and it made for a novel, if disagreeable experience. Everybody has fasted for a day or two and generally speaking, you're that much the better for it. However, when it goes on

OFFICE OF THE SPECIAL REPRESENTATIVE OF THE REPUBLIC OF BIAFRA

Telephone 67829

Telegram: BIAFRAN.

Our Reference BGD/SEC/16/71 .

Your Reference ....

10 Hill Road,

Oyster Bay,

P.O. Box 2431,

Dar es Salaam

CONFIDENTIAL

20th September, 1969.

Mr. Al J. Venter,
c/o Foreign Editor,
Mr. Jag Nicoil,
"Daily Express",
Fleet Street,
London, E.C. 4.

Dear Sir,

                    Visit to Biafra.

        With reference to your application to visit Biafra, we
wish to inform you that approval has now been given for you
to enter Biafra through Sao Tome. You should make your
arrangement direct with the Joint Church Aid for your flight
into our country.

2.   May I remind you that your stay in Biafra cannot exceed
seven days and as you will be catered for by the Biafra
Overseas Press Services while you are there, you will be
required to pay 35 U.S. Dollars per diem for the duration of
your stay. This must be paid in U.S. dollars.

3.   Please find attached hereto, a letter of introduction
which will facilitate your entry into Biafra. Your photograph
should be affixed to the letter.

4.   Kindly acknowledge the receipt of this letter.

                    Yours faithfully,

                    (Ibezim Chukwumerije),
                for Biafra Special Representative,
                    (EAST & CENTRAL AFRICA).

The author went on assignment to Biafra for the London *Daily Express*, having first
called at the country's 'embassy' in Dar es Salaam to obtain clearance. He eventually
flew into Uli 'Airport' from Libreville in Gabon. His clearance document specified
entry from the Portuguese island of Sao Tomé, but he pushed his luck in Libreville,
in mainland Gabon instead, and succeeded. (Author's collection)

for a week or ten days, it starts to get to you. Life becomes difficult. I could hardly complain because the Biafrans had been hungry for two years.

By the time I got back to Nairobi I couldn't stop eating. I also found it difficult to stop hurling myself to the ground each time a car backfired. I was bomb-happy for a while afterwards.

It was the little everyday things about life in a country at war that astonished those of us who visited Biafra for the first time.

We discovered an inordinate will to survive, which was natural enough, except that the odds were powerfully stacked against Ojukwu's people. I saw conditions at fairly close quarters, since my escort Emeka and I went just about everywhere on foot. Cars or pick-ups were a luxury reserved for longer trips.

The Biafran social code was enforced with the rigour of an Amish settlement in the MidWest. Civil and criminal courts were held from Monday to Friday in all big towns. The Biafran Supreme Court of Appeal sat in session in Owerri when it was in rebel hands or in Umuahia when it wasn't. Colonial traditions were strictly observed: wigs and robes for all senior members of the bar, which was absurd in that climate; such flummeries still persist in most of the former British territories, although wigs are no longer worn in British courts. The prisons had not been abolished either. Inmates could be seen in working parties under guard on the last day of the war.

Ojukwu printed his own money, now of good value among collectors. The notes, gaudy and in every colour of the spectrum, were professionally printed in Europe. A planeload of it disappeared on the way back from Switzerland. Biafra also had its own coins, stamps and postal orders. In spite of restrictions necessitated by conflict and a breakdown in communications, Biafran welfare officers continued to pay pensions to war widows until the end and postal deliveries always remained efficient, even after hostilities ended.

When an area had to be evacuated – as in the case of Owerri before its recapture (following the fall of Umuahia to the east) – the first to be moved were the wounded and civil prisoners, the latter carrying litters or supplies. Likewise, entire hospitals disappeared into the bush. Former inmates of mental institutions had long since been released to fend for themselves in the jungle and by all accounts, they seemed to manage.

Medicines, or rather the lack of them, were a constant problem.

Whatever drugs were brought into the country went straight into the tummies of hundreds of thousands of sick and starving children. Adults, civilians and combatants had to make do with bush remedies and potions. Witchdoctors thrived.

I spent many a night at the French Red Cross Hospital in Owerri watching the forerunners of *Médecins Sans Frontiéres* (Doctors Without Borders) treating the wounded. There were no formalities and I could walk into the operating theatre at will, with or without a mask over my mouth and nose. Operations were carried out without anaesthetics because there were none. Only the officiating surgeon and his theatre sister wore surgical gowns. The rest of us were in our everyday gear. There was no sterilization, not even scrubbing soap.

The wounded were brought in from the various fronts at night in mammy-wagons, the universal means of transport in West Africa. During the day there was very little movement on the roads, as MiGs

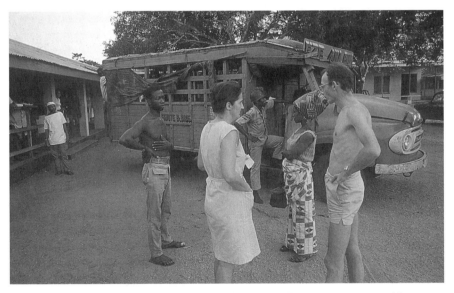

The wounded were brought back from the front, usually at sunset (to avoid being strafed by MiGs), in the backs of so-called 'mammy wagons', one of which can be seen in the background. These were used as improvised ambulances. The expatriate medical staff that dealt with casualties (foreground) was mainly French and forerunners of *Médecins Sans Frontiéres*. Because there were few dressings, and as one exclaimed, 'no anesthetics, no antibiotics, no nothing', the survival rate was pathetic. (Author's collection)

fighters were an omnipresent threat, as I discovered for myself a few times. The wounded had to wait for nightfall before they could be moved and for those with gut wounds, the delay could be serious; septicaemia is fatal in about six hours if not treated.

In every mammy-wagon that arrived in Owerri with its 25-odd casualties, three or four of the wounded were already dead.

'We have to work fast when the first ambulance gets here', said one of the French doctors who'd volunteered to come to Biafra to gain trauma surgery experience.

The wounded, some walking, others supported, as well as a few on makeshift bamboo litters, were taken to an 'emergency station', usually an empty room lit by paraffin lamps. The worst cases would be separated from the others and the young doctors would go to work, often through the night. It was harrowing.

By nightfall some of the patients would have gangrene, which sets in very soon in the heat and humidity of tropical Africa. At Owerri arms and legs were hacked off without ceremony. A piece of wood would be thrust between the victim's teeth, several soldiers would hold him down and the doctor would get to work with a saw.

'What else can we do?' said Dr Michel Fontainebleau. 'If we didn't amputate the limb, he'd be dead by morning.'

Bullet holes in the chest, unless a vital organ had been pierced, were simple by comparison. Many bullets of large calibre – such as the NATO 7.62mm – passed straight through the body. The holes were washed out with disinfectant, usually with a narrow garden hose.

I'd watch these dedicated young Frenchmen plunging steel rods tipped with a length of lint into a bullet hole in the chest and push it through to the other side. It was like cleaning a rifle. While most amputees would scream, none of the soldiers given the rod treatment so much as whimpered.

I never found out what proportion of casualties survived, but it must have been a fair number. The Biafrans I discovered, famished or not, were a remarkably tough bunch. They rarely complained and, let's face it, their fortitude was exemplary to us Western softies.

The nightly flights into Biafra, which concentrated mainly on the needs of the children and the military, could hardly have been expected to supply the demands of four million people cut off from the world outside. As a result, prices in Biafra were the highest in Africa.

A meal of roots at the Progress Hotel in Owerri, for example, cost the equivalent of two dollars, an ounce of meat was as much again. Salt for this meal would be priced one Biafran pound or two US dollars, all of which we had to exchange on our arrival at Uli for foreign currencies, at par with sterling at pre-secession rates. By the end of the war, inflation was rising at several hundred per cent a month.

The cost of 'non-essential' goods was greater. A single cigarette in the last two months cost ten Biafran shillings, roughly a dollar. So did a cup of tea with goat's milk. What sugar there was mostly went to mission hospitals, where it was used as a substitute for glucose intended for starving children.

Petrol (as they still called it) was a strategic material and not sold on the open market, although a gallon of gas could be bought easily enough on the black market for $30 or $40, although only in American dollars. A pair of men's flannels cost $20, a shirt sometimes as much as $50. Second-hand clothes were barely any cheaper and it puts things in perspective when you realize that 40 years ago, that was a lot of money!

I was soon confronted by inflation. After breakfast on my first morning at State House, I was told to wait because there was no transport, something I soon got used to. The morning newspaper arrived: a single folded sheet of school exercise paper that, I was assured, had a circulation that ran well into four figures. I was charged a dollar.

'It's the only paper we've left', said the youthful editor of *Jet,* the Biafran daily; 'but it gives us what we need: objective news of the outside world'. Anything from Federal Nigeria was tainted. *Propaganda!*

The news was printed in bright red ink, which looked like a compound of shoe polish and ochre and probably was: they certainly didn't have money to spare for the real thing. That particular issue of 4 November 1969 celebrated Ojukwu's 36th birthday. Half-page adver-tisements on the crammed sheet had been taken by two expatriate companies that had formerly traded in the Eastern Region: the United Africa Company (Unilever) and the African Continental Bank.

A two-column advertisement on the last page of *Jet* urged subscribers to book in time for their Christmas cards and New Year greetings.

All foreign companies that formerly operated in Eastern Nigeria were now managed by their Ibo staff and though little happened – for instance at the local office of Caterpillar, or Bata shoes – many were surprised after the war ended to find that nearly every branch office had kept up-to-date books.

In spite of some lighter moments, the grim reality of conflict was omnipresent. Cripples were everywhere and there were many. Young boys, some barely into their teens, hobbled legless on crutches. Anywhere else they'd have been in an institution, or being prepared for prosthetics. Only the very worst cases could be dealt with at Red Cross and government clinics.

I came across several groups of shell-shocked youngsters, and these were experiences that remained fixed in my mind for many years. Huddled in small groups almost like zombies, they communicated with grunts and gestures in an absent-minded sort of way. Most were tended by some older person until they recovered. Quite a few got better and some were even posted back to their units. Quite a number, one of the Red Cross people told me, never would.

Decades later, some of these poor souls are still afflicted.

Major General Phillip Effiong, the Biafran Chief of General Staff, hosted us several times at his improvised headquarters in the jungle. Because of constantly changing front lines, we met him at a different location each time having, along the way, run the gauntlet of being strafed by Nigerian Air Force MiG-17s flown by Ares Klootwyk and his bunch of British and South African mercenary pilots. (Author's collection)

It was at the headquarters of 44-year-old Major General Philip Effiong – the Biafran Chief of Staff and a Sandhurst-trained veteran of two Nigerian operations in the Congo – that most strategy in this war was planned. It was a sandbagged and well-camouflaged camp on the outskirts of Owerri (it would have made a marvellous film set).

My visit there promised to be an experience and we went by car. Because of the MiGs, each of us carefully observed his quarter of the horizon as we drove. I sat behind the driver, so my responsibility was rear quadrant, on my side of the vehicle. The system worked well because the Biafrans had become pretty adroit at recognizing distant dots in the sky. We weren't bothered on that trip.

The road to General Effiong's camp was littered with the ruins of previous battles and obviously the area had seen some pretty intense fighting. Bridges had been destroyed and the burnt-out hulks of a number of armoured cars were scattered along the verge. As at Uli, the foliage of palms and tall trees had been stripped clean by God knows how many shells and mortar-bombs fired by two opposing armies. The bare stumps reminded me of photos that one of my grandfathers had shown me of Delville Wood in World War I.

Near the camp there was a petrol tanker that had been strafed from the air. A line of bullet holes ran its length. Farther on, there was a large road-safety poster also riddled: a legacy of the pre-war days. 'Better be late than *the* late', it proclaimed. The driver chortled as we passed.

From the road it was impossible to see the camp until we reached the gates of the Biafran Army base. Suddenly, the car turned into a wide clearing lined with palms and guarded by a machine-gun turret. Everybody saluted as we passed. For all they knew it might have been Ojukwu himself. He travelled about unannounced and seldom used the same vehicle two days running. Now and again he turned up where he was least expected.

Discipline was strict: all the men wore freshly washed khaki and officers' uniforms were starched.

General Effiong, showing none of the egotism that some of us had found on the Federal side, walked at a brisk pace to greet us, his swagger-stick comfortably under one arm; a black Englishman, complete with tailor-made uniform. With his trademark smile, he greeted us kindly. We'd risked our lives by coming into Biafra, and he was honoured, he said, his English like something out of the Old Country. His adjutant, a captain, looked us over carefully. We were unarmed, but if there were to be any trouble, this young officer would be ready for it.

It seemed difficult to believe that people like Effiong and Adekunle had actually served and trained together in the Nigerian Army during the pre-secession era. Indeed, the two men were as unlike as their respective armies.

What was his worst difficulty? I asked of the general. 'Air power', he affirmed. Federal air-strikes both at the front and behind the lines had created havoc, he admitted. He said he always knew when the next Nigerian offensive was coming.

'They like to soften the place up for a few days with air-strikes. How can our men hold their own against modern jet fighters armed with Russian and British weapons?' he queried.

'Still, we've survived against great odds for two-and-a-half years, so we can't be doing too badly.'

And manpower? How was he coping? 'Not so simple', he answered. Speaking from behind a heavy mahogany desk with a little Biafran flag dominating one of the corners, he pointed at a large map studded with coloured pins behind him.

'Biafra is divided into 20 provinces. The central government in Owerri levies men on a quota system, even in those parts overrun by the Feds. It's easy to bring groups of civilians through the lines for training', he explained. Lagos was asleep when it came to controlling movement, he reckoned, though he did admit to a serious shortage of young men. 'So we've just got to make do with what we've got' he declared.

'Before the war started, we had the highest literacy rate in Africa. That means we've never been short of men of officer calibre. They lead every attack, just like the Israelis, from the front . . . most effective way, but we've lost many of our best men as a result.' We could all faintly hear the rumble of artillery. It couldn't have been that far away.

What about prisoners of war? Yes, his people took prisoners and held them, was all he was prepared to say before he changed the subject. Later, one of his officers told me that the Biafrans would have taken larger numbers of POWs, but that the Federals shot their wounded whenever they were in the retreat.

'A nation of over 60 million can easily afford that sort of thing', was his parting comment.

It was hard to grasp, as the war continued, that Biafra was completely surrounded by the enemy. At best, 200 tons of ammunition was being brought in by air at night. Whenever Uli was knocked out, and it happened routinely, there would be nothing coming in for days. And that was all they had to keep a couple of hundred thousand Federal Nigerians at bay.

Also, throughout hostilities the casualty rate rose steadily. It puzzled us all, considering that this was a strictly African war, how the Biafrans were able to hold out so long? There were several reasons.

Biafra's ability to survive, it was agreed afterwards by those of us who were able to observe conditions from up front, was due largely to the remarkable competence of the ordinary Biafran. This was – and still is – a community that is able to improvise, plan for the unexpected and take the initiative. Their adversaries, often disparagingly, call them the Jews of Africa and of course they're right. Ibos like to roll up their sleeves and get things done.

Also, Ibos make money; they work and succeed where others fail. Like the Luo in Kenya and the Mandingo of Guinea, they are sometimes thoroughly disliked by less pushy tribes, much like American Southerners are wary of New Yorkers. It's a patchy analogy, but you get the picture. In that regard (with notable exceptions) they are consequently very different when compared to the average Yoruba, Hausa or Fulani. Success, as they say, breeds distrust.

What I do know is that with time, I became friendly with many Ibos, and any day of the week I'd put my life in their hands.

We, who favoured the Ibos, also shared somewhat in their unpopularity. Frederick Forsyth resigned his job at the BBC not because he was vociferously committed to the Biafran cause, but because the British Broadcasting Corporation ended up being partisan in a conflict where, in keeping with a tradition that went back to its first days on the air, it should have shown impartiality. It was all oil politics, we knew, and in the end it made a difference.

Richard Hall, one of the most experienced Africa hands, was greatly taken by this rebel community. Dick, as we all knew him, was the co-founder and editor of Zambia's *Central Africa Mail* and no newcomer to this volatile continent. His comments about Biafran people are instructive. He described them in the *Sunday Times* of London at the time as:

a people I respect and like [who] are threatened with persecution and death. I cannot therefore pretend to be impartial. But Biafra is more than a human tragedy: it is the first place I've been to in Africa where the Africans themselves are truly in charge . . . where there is a sense of nationhood . . . free from the African vices of graft, superstition and ignorance.

It had suddenly become a furious debate.

Some of the best stories to come out of Biafra were not so much about the war as the ability of the Biafrans to do their own thing. Certainly, they were ingenious.

We could walk through any Biafran town, even at the end, and discover that life continued as if nothing were happening. Shops were open, though their stock was exiguous, post offices were selling stamps and money orders and, with fair warning, you could even buy foreign exchange in the banks, although you had to have a very good reason.

There were dozens of home industries repairing or recycling old things or making new ones: iron bedsteads, car engines rebored on makeshift lathes, stoves and, of course, there were the market mammies at their stalls. The army took most of what was left after a proportion had been set aside for the children, so their offerings were meagre.

That was what you were allowed to see and obviously, there was much else besides. Behind the towns, in forest and bush clearings, hundreds of factories turned out all sorts of things, such as boots for soldiers and ammunition. Emeka took me on guided tours through some of them.

In a factory near Umuahia, engineers were making – or rather recycling – motor parts for an otherwise ageing fleet of army trucks, mostly mammy-wagons that had been seized. Brake-linings, I was told, were among the items on the urgent list, which was one of the reasons why some were modified from crashed aircraft parts at Uli.

There were jungle workshops making uniforms. Since there was no cloth, long lines of women were busy making a rough substitute from bark. It was not the best or most supple of materials and was probably tough on the skin, but it was better than nothing. The army needed boots and since there was no leather, they added chemicals to raw rubber latex and made a strong and pliable material for the uppers. The soles were made from old tyres.

They refined their own oil in cooking-pot refineries, rather like illicit Arkansas gin stills. Up to the end they produced enough fuel to keep several hundred vehicles running.

To me just then, the most interesting aspect of this remarkable ability to continue fighting was the varied array of home-made weapons. These included hand-grenades – almost like the German potato-mashers of the two great wars and known locally as the Giraffe – and a primitive rocket with a range of about five miles. There were also anti-personnel mines, and what was probably the most destructive improvised explosive device of all, developed long before the Iraqi IED became ubiquitous. This one was known to us all as the Ojukwu Bucket. In simple terms, it employed the same principle as the American claymore.

It was said that a series of Ojukwu Buckets detonated electrically once killed a couple of hundred Federal troops in convoy. They knocked out Nigerian Army armoured cars so effectively that for some time the Federal forces stopped using their Ferrets in the jungle.

The 'bucket' was also used at Uli. Aircraft of the Federal Air Force regularly bombed and strafed the landing-strip during daylight hours, swooping low across it. The devices were placed at various points along the runway and were detonated when a jet passed over. We learnt afterwards that some mercenary pilots in the NAF had a few close calls. Ares Klootwyk, a South African gun-for-hire who had flown as a mercenary in the Congo, told me: 'On two occasions the blast caught me unawares and my MiG nearly flipped. But the MiG-17 is a strong machine. Had it been a prop-engine, with less speed, they'd have got me.'

Not surprisingly, towards the end, a certain amount of lawlessness became manifest within Biafran ranks. This was particularly evident on the fringes of the fighting. Reports emerged of soldiers waylaying trucks and stealing food intended for children. Others took provisions from aircraft off-loading in the dark. Those caught were hauled off into the nearby bushes and shot.

There were many deserters. Because of the ever-changing military situation, there was nobody to stop them, not that anybody had the energy to do so, anyway. Entire units were sometimes caught on the wrong side of the front when a Federal attack closed its pincers. The fact is, everybody was starving, not only the children. Soldiers sometimes drove refugees out of their camps and seized their stores.

To be fair, such reports were not as commonplace as they might have been. There was certainly far less lawlessness on the Biafran side than among the Feds. When a Nigerian Army rabble went berserk and started killing, looting and raping, there was little their officers could – or would – do.

It says much for President Gowon's command at the end of the war in January 1970 that he managed to hold his Federal forces in check. Had he not done so, a lot of old scores would have been settled. Slaughter might have become the norm, because the Biafrans, by then, were hardly able to defend themselves, never mind retaliate. But then that's another amiable Nigerian trait; they can be enemies one day and friends the next. A few years later, travelling through the Eastern Region, it was as though there'd never been a war.

One of the first of the journalists into the ravaged east after it had all ended was Colin Legum, another old pal from my days as a scribe. He went to the army barracks in Onitsha, that huge Ibo city on the Niger that I so often visited while I lived in West Africa.

'There in the officers' mess', he wrote, 'were the Biafran officers and the Federal officers drinking beer together as though it was the end of a cricket match. They'd fought very sternly and they were now chums again, as they'd been chums before.'

The end, when it came, was mercifully quick. Once Biafran lines had broken, Federal forces overran all that was left of the rebel territory in a day. So much effort, so many dead, and let's face it, how many people these days have even heard the name 'Biafra'?

CHAPTER SEVEN

A Dirty Distant War: El Salvador

El Salvador is a small, Central American country bordered by Honduras, Guatemala and the Pacific Ocean. In recent years, it has been plagued by violence and poverty due to over-population and class struggles. The conflict between the rich and the poor of the country has existed for more than a century and while the military struggle has ended, disparities remain.

I WENT TO WAR IN El Salvador with former Vietnam War veteran Bob MacKenzie, a good choice because Bob had originally been a captain in the Rhodesian SAS. He managed that achievement despite having a crook arm from a war wound that got him invalided out of the United States Army. Some years later he fought with Renamo guerrillas in Mozambique. Bob had also worked as a mercenary in the Balkans, where he trained Serbs in the esoterics of insurgency warfare.

This always-smiling, unflappable American freebooter – by then a colonel – went on to become the first white officer for many decades to head a West African fighting group. In a remote area adjacent to the Malal Hills in Sierra Leone, he was killed and eaten by savages, who ambushed the pathetic bunch of bush warriors he'd been trying to mould into something of an effective fighting force. In the Central American guerrilla war, however, he was the unit's star.

The conflict in El Salvador was a very different conflagration from most other insurgent struggles. There were several reasons, the first being that both the Soviet Union and Cuba had a marked influence on its outcome. As might have been expected, Washington backed the non-communist side, not only politically but with men, machines, hardware and whatever else was needed to keep San Salvador, the country's capital, from becoming a Comintern clone.

A lot of people died in the terrible conflict that totally ravaged this tiny Central American state, but in the end, with solid US and Latin American support, a peace of sorts was negotiated. Against all odds, it survived the strains of some of the most convoluted and conflicting Cold

War interests in the hemisphere. Critics called it a loveless, arranged marriage, but in the end, it worked. At least the shooting stopped and more recently El Salvador sent 11,000 of its troops to fight in Iraq. Not bad for a country of only eight million people.

The country's civil war took an atrocious toll, not only in lives, but also on an economy that was stripped of just about everything. After almost a decade of fighting, there were about 75,000 people dead and several million exiles, more than a million of them in the United States.

Looking back, it would seem that El Salvador had always laboured under a tyranny of sorts. By the time we got there, the country reflected hope and desperation in equal parts, always a recipe for revolt. Its real misfortune – like that of Nicaragua next door – was to become a pawn on the great international chess board.

In Central America, it all began as a domestic quarrel. In 1980 a group of landowners and coffee traders in El Salvador launched a military coup. They were supported by the police, the judiciary and obviously, the military. The reason for the putsch was a wish to perpetuate the old system that kept the establishment rich and the rest of the people on the breadline.

As one paper phrased it at the time, 'those sweaty, growling masses who opposed the plotters – including many churchmen – were murdered, exiled or driven into rebellion'. Small wonder then that the Russians and their Cuban surrogate friends – quite justifiably in hindsight – armed the oppressed and took over the revolution, for that was what it was.

Such was the leaden symmetry of the Cold War that that old warrior-leader Ronald Reagan chose El Salvador as the place to 'draw the line'. He was doing so, he said at the time, 'against communist encroachment in the Americas'.

With the benefit of hindsight, he probably did the right thing. In the end, however, it cost the US taxpayer six billion dollars, not much by today's standards when the American taxpayer doles out hundreds of times as much in Iraq, but in those not-so-long-ago times, it was a sizeable sum.

Washington's tactics in El Salvador included a grand strategy to sap rebel support by fostering democracy, land reform and civil rights. To some extent these moves, while moderating the homicidal propensities of the army, didn't altogether stop them. The Rand Corporation, in a

The El Salvador Army was mainly conscript and composed largely of young indigent peasant who had more in common with the guerrillas than a corrupt government. It was American training of men like this that eventually turned the tide. (Author's collection)

report to the US Department of Defense, calculated that in 1981 alone, the army and its agents murdered 10,000 people. The new dispensation that followed – a truce of sorts between the government and the guerrillas, almost a decade later – was effective enough to reduce that figure to roughly a hundred-a-year, though for a long time there were bloody incidents in and around the city after dark.

In so many different ways, the civil war in El Salvador resembled a hundred civil wars before. It was mostly the unarmed, the dispossessed and the despised civilian mass that were at the receiving end. They suffered first from a succession of corrupt and brutal governments and later from a guerrilla force that began with laudable intentions, but which ultimately became no less murderous and oppressive.

To the grandly named Farabundo National Liberation Front (FMLN) you were either for the revolution or against it. There was nothing in between. 'No greys', as one American adviser tried to explain to me after a bibulous diplomatic function in the capital.

The war in El Salvador made one lasting impression on this observer; nowhere else had I seen so many young men who had been crippled by landmines. Even the guerrilla struggles in Rhodesia and Angola were nowhere near as bad. Yet few of the correspondents ever mentioned that dark aspect of the war when they left this Central American crucible of violence; it was almost as if those casualties did not exist.

In retrospect, they were there for all to see. In every military base I visited, there were young men who had lost a foot or a leg, and sometimes more. They hobbled about with a crutch or a stick – it was a sad spectacle.

In El Salvador, the prosthetically endowed were a rarity. There was simply no money for such extravagance. Most of the national budget was devoured by hostilities that not only started at the edge of the country's biggest city but, with assassinations of prominent people, also sometimes inside it. It was a tragic business when you observed it from nearby.

My lasting conclusion was that if ever there was a case against any mother sending her son to fight for a foreign cause, right or wrong, this was it. The war, it seemed, was pointless. Yet ideologies (strange that they seem so facile now) played a powerful role. Not everybody recalls that the Cold War was a cauldron bubbling over an open fire pit less than a generation ago.

The mines that crippled the majority of these men were small anti-personnel bombs, or 'APs' in the terminology, usually buried a few inches into the dirt near a path or stream that might be frequented by the enemy. Many were little, round PMN-2s, which weighed a few ounces and could fit comfortably in the palm of a man's hand; they were invariably made in Russia or somewhere east of the Elbe.

'Black Widows' they were called in Vietnam, though widow-makers would have been more appropriate.

Then came the TMA-3 or TM-57 anti-tank mines (the former Yugoslav, the latter Soviet). These were bigger, heavier and more difficult to hump in any kind of significant number across mountains, but the guerrillas managed it and the devices took a steady toll. These days insurgent movements prefer the anti-personnel version of the bomb: you can get more of them into the ground, cover a greater area and achieve more widespread devastation.

The conventional wisdom about such things in this kind of insurgency is that it is better to maim your enemy than kill him. A wounded comrade needs three or four others to tend to his needs and, quite often, haul him out of the combat zone: that means more manpower tied down when soldiers in the field might have been fighting. Nor is that the end of it, because still more effort, time and money must be spent treating this casualty; all this is solid revolutionary economics.

Sadly, as we now know, anti-personnel mines eventually caused many times the number of casualties among civilians than they did among the troops in this Central American state, just as they've done in dozens of African conflicts. Children were the worst affected. They were everywhere in this war and were thus far more likely to trigger a mine. It was a process to be repeated in Afghanistan when the Soviets were there.

However, in all the time of the conflict, I read no more than a handful of articles on the effects of mines in the American press which makes one think that if Princess Diana had been around a little earlier, things might have been different. The landmine threat was all but ignored by the correspondents of the *Washington Post*, Britain's *Guardian* or *Time* and *Newsweek*. One needs to question why this was so.

In the eyes of some American and European reporters, the guerrillas – or 'Gs' in local lingo – could do nothing wrong. They were the good guys. Good guys just didn't lay mines, was the thrust of it.

I had long intended to go to El Salvador. The only man that I knew who could get me and my cameraman, Alwyn Kumst, into that war was Lieutenant Colonel Robert K. Brown, owner and publisher of *Soldier of Fortune* magazine which the *New York Times* in February 1996 said had 'carved out and dominated a unique editorial niche' for itself over the past few decades. It wasn't called 'The Journal of Professional Adventurers' for nothing.

Sensing opportunity, I had taken Brown on his first African safari in

Rhodesia some 20 years before to cover that conflict. To get into Central America, I called in a favour.

My first stop was at the offices of the magazine on Arapahoe Avenue in Boulder, Colorado where I found an entrance with a small sign:

Stop before entering: Fill out a card saying where you want your body shipped otherwise it will be used for scientific purposes.

Brown's office was part of the image, the bravado. There were photographs on just about every wall, even in the toilet, of foreign legionnaires, of Bob Brown with South-East Asia's Montagnards, Bob Brown in Colombia (or was it Peru?), Bob Brown in Rhodesia and,

Lieutenant Colonel Robert K. Brown (seated on the right) – Bob to his friends – took a group of us into the war in El Salvador. Pictured here at one of the army bases in the interior with the author is former US Marine underwater demolition specialist John Donovan (on the left). Peering over our shoulders (top right) is Bob MacKenzie, who went on to become the first white man to command the Sierra Leonean Army after rebels had invaded most of the country. MacKenzie was killed and eaten by said West African rebels shortly afterwards. (Author's collection)

among scores of others, a much younger Bob Brown in Vietnam, where he had completed two tours.

Other walls in the building were lined with pictures of him with any number of army units, on assignment in Afghanistan sitting behind a captured anti-tank missile or back from a hunt in the Zambezi Valley complete with rifle and trophy, in this case, a splendid sable.

Wherever you looked in the offices you found hardware. These included carbines with stacks of 30-round magazines, hunting rifles, .45 ACP pistols (usually complete with loaded clips) and even more revolvers. In between lay a variety of all-purpose Special Forces blades including WWII K-Bars and a host of survival knives. The entire arsenal was thrown about in disarray, usually on the floor or leaning against cupboards, behind doors and even in an alcove under one of the stairs.

The lasting impression was that Lieutenant Colonel Robert K. Brown really did cater for the professional adventurer. His rigmarole was gung-ho and very much in keeping with Brown's macho image. Unfortunately, these Rambo-type sentiments also resulted in several spin-offs, not all of them welcome, especially where there were people murdered as a result of 'do anything for money, legal or otherwise' advertisements that were carried by the magazine in the early days.

Bob Brown soon put a stop to them, but the consequences were severe and ultimately cost both him and his company millions. A couple of legal cases included actions brought by families because a husband or a mistress had been shot by someone who had placed an advertisement in the magazine. One of these was headed 'Guns for Hire'.

It was obvious that Bob Brown attracted his share of crazies, especially since *Soldier of Fortune* made an issue of extolling the virtues of Vietnam vets. Consequently, there was invariably an aspiring wannabee knocking at the door at 7535 Arapahoe Avenue just about every day.

For the trip to El Salvador we went to Brown's house in Boulder in November 1985. There we were joined by Bob MacKenzie and John Donovan, a powerful, bald-headed chap with a neck like a professional wrestler, a sport which, I gathered afterwards, he'd also tried. Donovan's forté in those days was trying to punch holes into concrete walls with his bare fists. Interestingly, 'Big' John was a major in the United States Army Reserves.

Bob Brown, our host and Paul Foley, who had spent 12 years in the

French Foreign Legion, headed the team: 'My A-Team', Bob explained with a wicked smile.

Foley, in his fifties, was a tall, sinewy man who thought nothing of a 30-mile hike through the mountains as a preparation for a Saturday night thrash. Most of the time he was quiet and reserved, but that could change when he'd been at the bar a while. Then he could spring into action in a moment, whether eating dinner with us or in one of the bawdy bordellos that the men liked to frequent in the seedier parts of San Salvador.

I'd followed Foley's progress over the years and frankly, I doubt whether the man would ever have been comfortable in anything but a military uniform. He was decorated for bravery when he jumped with the Legion into Kolwezi in Zaire at the time of the Katangese invasion. As he tells it, it was an attack by rebels that left scores of Belgians, including many women and children, dead. *Les Paras* whipped them in 48 hours. Those few rebels still alive, fled back to Angola and as is the custom in these African uprisings, very few prisoners survived the night.

We flew in a group, eight or nine of us heading first to Houston, where we'd been booked on an airline that I had never heard of before: TACA. To me, that wasn't reassuring, considering that we would be arriving at El Salvador in the dark and I'd been told by one of the men that there had been several foul-ups involving commercial airlines in the mountains that surround the country's main international airport in recent years, especially during bad weather. It was raining when we left Texas . . .

Our route included a stop in Belize, a former British colony that was regularly used for tropical warfare exercises by elite British units such as the SAS and the SBS. In those days, Belize was constantly under threat of attack from Guatemala, its bigger and more belligerent neighbour, which regarded the little stretch of mangrove swamp and jungle fringing the Gulf of Mexico as its own.

Arriving after dark in any country where there is a war usually presents a unique set of conditions that you're usually warned about beforehand.

For one, you don't wear camouflage when you travel. Second, you never travel with an empty pistol holster on your belt. Some of our group had both, even though we were being met by American military aid personnel who were already working there, including Harry Claflin who was in-country, having volunteered for an assignment with the El

Salvador Airborne Battalion, Reconnaissance Platoon. Among his other duties was involvement with the so-called 'PRAL', a clandestine infiltration group funded by the CIA and based at Ilopango, the country's largest military air base.

'Great group of young kids', said Harry when we asked him about his job, 'But they've had no training in Recon'.

We'd barely entered the airport concourse before it became clear that we were scheduled for a grilling by the authorities. A bunch of officials viewed us warily, with good reason, I suppose. We certainly weren't your usual run-of-the-mill tourists, even if there were any coming to El Salvador in wartime.

'These boots, of yours', said an official dressed in a khaki uniform, also with a holster on his belt but with the appropriate hardware, 'are they for climbing *montañas?*'

'Yes' I said.

'Which *montañas?*'

Of course I couldn't tell him because I didn't know. I wasn't even certain that El Salvador had any accessible mountains, and in any event, this was no holiday jaunt.

'We're here to see action against the Gs', interjected Brown in Spanish. He'd fought for a while with Castro in the Sierra Maestra, but that was before the Cuban leader had begun to refer to his intimates as *camaradas.*

It was to be expected that the airport functionary would view this very vocal, crapulous bunch of Gringos with suspicion, especially since Donovan had warned us earlier not to take anything for granted. He made the point – valid as it turned out – that while America supplied El Salvador with all manner of assets, the severest critics of El Salvador's civil war also had American passports.

Another customs man found a pair of Vietnam combat boots in Foley's baggage. This caused the arrival of a new lot of officials. Brown then identified himself and produced a letter from the El Salvadorian Minister of Defence, at which point all the officials went into a huddle. Calls were made to their superiors and in an hour, we'd become heroes. That done, and after more beers, we set out in a decrepit old bus along a deserted road: we were heading out on the first stage of our journey to the city of San Salvador.

One of the reasons for all this kerfuffle, apparently, was the discovery some time before of combat gear in the luggage of a

Scandinavian mercenary on his way to join the FMLN guerrillas in Nicaragua. His travel agent had unwisely booked him through El Salvador. Instead, he should have gone to Managua. We never did discover his fate.

San Salvador, the capital, lies about 35 miles from the airport. There were several army roadblocks and, not all that surprising, precious few streetlights along the way. Guerrilla ambushes, we'd been warned, had been frequent. Not long before we got there, three American nuns and a lay worker had been killed on that very same route by a rebel group. It was an accident; the FMLN told a newspaperman in Managua afterwards, they'd believed they were army.

Anyway, somebody else declared, they shouldn't have been travelling that road at night.

Harry Claflin eventually saved the day. He'd brought along to the airport half a dozen M16s and enough ammunition to start a war. With these passed around, the men settled themselves comfortably in the bus at seats alongside open windows, each one of them hoping desperately for an ambush which never came.

Brown's crowd were an odd bunch, not all of them likeable. It was their whim to look for trouble wherever it might be encountered and they did so in South and Central America, Asia, the Middle East, parts of Europe during the Balkan troubles and, of course, Africa. Their yarns over the years were the stuff of schoolboy fiction, but let it be known that Brown also made a good living from this kind of vicariously tipped armchair adventure.

In the 40 years of the existence of the magazine, quite a few people associated with *Soldier of Fortune*

Harry Claflin, former American Special Forces operative-turned El Salvadorian-mercenary, made most things happen for us while we remained in country. He was attached to US Military Group, El Salvador while in country, or USMILGP-EL. (Author's collection) had been killed, not all of them in action. Bob MacKenzie was one. Another was Craig Nunn, a former Special Forces sergeant and a street-fighter in Chicago. While he was with the magazine, Craig was its art director and would listen to Bach and Bartok at full volume in his studio with a pair of earphones over his head. Craig was killed in a motor-cycle crash in the Rockies.

Some years before, *Soldier of Fortune* martial arts editor, Mike Echanis – while chief military advisor to Nicaraguan President Samoza – was killed when the Aero Commander in which he was travelling was sabotaged in mid-flight shortly after take-off from Managua.

Another freelancer, Lance Motley, was working on a story for the magazine when a Burmese mortar exploded close to where he was standing: he was covering the extended campaign being fought by a group of Karen rebels operating out of Cambodia. The poster in Bob's office back in Boulder encapsulated it for that particular bunch: *'Happiness is a Confirmed Kill'*.

Also in the group was 'Sweet Michael', the only psychopath with whom I've knowingly travelled to a combat zone. A particularly menacing individual, we soon discovered, that he liked to present a world of silent intimidation that was always tinged with violence. 'Sweet Michael' didn't fly into El Salvador with us, because he'd been 'doing a job' and considered it more opportune to take the roundabout route. However, he was waiting for us at our hotel.

A burly, surly, pale creature whose eyes you avoided because he was usually playing with an open, double-edged blade that every now and again he'd throw across the room, 'Sweet Michael' was the ultimate real-life bad 'un. He narrowly missed me with the knife twice and I didn't like it. It was evident from the first moment that the guy was in trouble with the law and, after a few days in El Salvador, we were to discover that he'd made a living of sorts doing 'jobs', some of them for the Mafia. True or false, we were hardly likely to ask him directly, especially when he was drunk, which was most of the time.

'Sweet Michael' liked to flash a big roll of hundred-dollar bills in his pocket anytime there was somebody around. Bob indicated that he'd recently done some 'wet work' that had left a widow and two kids behind and for which he'd been paid $10,000. Like other jobs handled by this misfit, payment came in cash.

He would frequently hint at something devious that he had just 'accomplished'. Then he'd take out his roll and utter something like 'where the hell d'ya think I got this load'. He was a loathsome man, and Alwyn and I always avoided him if he was around. Brown would comment when the psycho started to get to you, that he was 'one of the boys', which was why he'd invited him along.

While 'Sweet Michael' might have been just the man to ice people back home in New Jersey or Georgia, he never went out in the bush in El Salvador. Frankly, he didn't seem to have the balls for it, said one of the others. I agreed. As they say, he might have been interesting specimen, but his presence tended to be fortified by a generous slug of booze. Always a difficult bastard, last heard, he was doing time for a Federal offence. They never apparently got him on any of the murder raps.

Not yet, anyway . . .

The city of San Salvador in those days was not a grand place in the tradition of Rio or Havana. Nor is it today.

It snuggles untidily between two rows of hills in the Valle de las Hamacas – the Valley of the Hammocks – and while there, it seemed to be the only city in Latin America with no colonial buildings left intact.

Once it had been the capital of the United Provinces of Central America. Then there had been plenty of fine old buildings erected by the successors to the Conquistadores, but all were destroyed by a succession of earthquakes and floods which had levelled the region several times during the past few centuries.

I'd expected to find a modern, progressive kind of place. I was disappointed, as were others who also hadn't been there before. Of course there were plenty of tall buildings, as there are everywhere in the New World. However, San Salvador was no Manhattan. Most of these stunted, unattractive glass and concrete blocks looked like they'd been plopped down at random in the expectation of another catastrophe.

Driving into town from the Sheraton was like going back to earlier decades, because there was pollution everywhere. Also, the streets were full of splintered packing cases (all new cases were used to build shacks in the *barrios*) together with more garbage that one would have thought possible. Street urchins – dirty, unkempt and clearly homeless – came running whenever we stopped.

The traffic, sometimes on the wrong side of the road, was a perpetual problem. There was no visible control like we know it in Europe or America. Cars were speeding, dodging, cutting in front of others, often through dangerous intersections or lines of traffic or alternatively, like teenagers at a rave, intent on playing chicken or dodgems. I'd seen something similar in Beirut when that city was at war with itself and somebody commented that it was a symptom of a war psychosis. Trouble was, it only got worse as hostilities progressed.

On the whole then, San Salvador was not the most attractive place in which to find yourself for an extended stay, though Harry Claflin told me afterwards that having spent nine years there, the place had kind of grown on him.

Our hotel, the Sheraton, was situated in one of the better hillside neighbourhoods and from our rooms we could observe the whole untidy sprawl. Thankfully, while we could see it, we couldn't smell the stench or hear the noise. Yet, the hotel was an interesting experience in itself and it's surprising that none of the visiting correspondents devoted a line or two to it in the *New Yorker* or *Rolling Stone*, since almost everybody who reported on the war found themselves there, if only to use the bar.

San Salvador's Sheraton had a rough resemblance to the Commodore Hotel in Beirut, or Meikles in Salisbury. After the Presidential Palace it was the most heavily guarded structure in the country.

On arrival we were carefully frisked by security guards. There was no problem with the weapons we were carrying, they told us, but we ought to be discreet. If anybody was to be shot, it should be left to them to do the shooting, was the gist of it. Also, we were warned, no strangers were allowed into the hotel compound unless they had good cause to be there. Rebel bands, they told us, had put a price on the heads of certain Americans and four US Marines had been killed with grenades in a bar not far from where we were sleeping each night. That had happened only a few months before.

The extensive security pleased us, though nobody enjoyed being frisked. But then I didn't relish the prospect of getting killed or crippled either, and certainly not in a conflict that meant very little to me. After all, I'm supposed to be British.

All this rigmarole comprised the *visible* layer of security at the Sheraton. There was a less obtrusive, 'covert' layer underneath and that, I discovered by accident.

One evening I needed to get some film out of the cool room next to the kitchens for the next day's shoot. I barged through a door into a corridor that led off the main lounge, straight into the muzzle of a sub-machine-gun. I backed off quietly, trying to explain my presence in

English to somebody who spoke only Spanish. The wielder of the gun said nothing, but he wasn't happy. Once somebody had explained to him why I was there, he ordered me with a nod of his head to get on with it. Gringos were to be forgiven such gaffes. Thereafter, I took a good look before entering any other area of the hotel and I'd usually first inform the front desk of my intentions.

Later I was to find out that there were half a dozen of these G-men on duty around the clock. They were apparently all members of the country's *Equipo de Reacción Especial*, or ERE, which might have been roughly equivalent to America's Secret Service, though obviously, far more active militarily as befitted their security role. But for them, I'm certain, there would have been many more murders in San Salvador's hotels.

Security in the city must have been horrendous for those in charge. Every senior government official, every military officer above the rank of major, every minister and his staff had his or her personal bodyguard. Even short journeys between the suburbs sometimes required two or three vehicles, most of the time travelling in convoy. The guards were usually dressed in mufti, which was deceptive, and still didn't detract from the fact that San Salvador was an armed camp. There were even soldiers patrolling the botanical gardens.

The houses or apartments of all these functionaries were guarded around the clock. There must have been thousands of men so employed. Kabul at its worst never deployed that kind of manpower in protection roles.

Even so, there were still attacks taking place, if not all the time, then regularly enough to cause unease. On the second night of our stay, the rebels hit a house a few blocks from the hotel. We could hear the firing and the battle went on for some minutes. A few of Brown's entourage emerged from their rooms, one of them with an M16 in one hand and spare clips in the other. They were all keen to join in but the hotel guards had other ideas.

When cameraman Alwyn Kumst asked about it next morning at Army Headquarters, he was told that one of the guards had had a malfunction with his automatic weapon. It was an unlikely story and symptomatic of the kind of obfuscation that passed for propaganda. The El Salvadorians eventually became masters at disinformation, and little of what they offered was even vaguely plausible.

The government of El Salvador incensed many correspondents both with their lies and a level of censorship that was intrusive. Quite a few of my colleagues were journalists with years of experience of other wars. Some, like Holger Jensen of AP and later *Newsweek,* had been wounded several times. We all knew the rules, and in general we worked by them. But it didn't help that there wasn't a single member of the media who wasn't initially treated like a juvenile.

When we responded accordingly, there was fury on both sides, though eventually things did ease up.

Covering the war in El Salvador was different from working in most other Third World 'brush fire' conflicts. For one, because there was always something happening, it was never boring.

When we were in the interior we went on operations in the mountains and the valleys of the east, flew over the jungle on air strikes or went on naval patrols in the Gulf of Fonseca, all well within sight of the Nicaraguan coast and some of the biggest maritime defences in the region. In those brief weeks we were sniped at, managed to avoid the odd landmine, and 'survived' at least one ambush (which distressed some of our budding heroes).

The best part of it was sleeping under the stars, usually within the constraints of some really rough conditions in isolated villages in the foothills. As the sun set, we ate beans and chillies, shared a few beers

While on patrol in the interior, life went on for the locals, much as it always had done. Our patrol was sniped at several times and after dark, out in the open, the threat of a concerted attack by the guerrillas was real enough for the troops to take guard duty seriously. (Author's collection)

with the *campesinos* as they stood guard at the edge of their settlements and, now and again, listened as attacks or ambushes were taking place in the distance. There were people dying out there, we knew.

We never felt personally endangered, whether at base or on patrol, but the fact is that this was one guerrilla war in which the rebels remained undefeated on the battlefield until the Americans stepped in with their MilGroup aid programme. This clandestine operational group involving Special Forces became Washington's uncompromising Central American Cold War initiative and finally turned this war around.

Whatever the ultimate consequences, it would have been a great thing for the FMLN insurgents to have been able to kill or wound one of us *extranjeros*; a propaganda victory that could have been significant, especially if the link to *Soldier of Fortune* were to be exposed. The 'mercenary' syndrome was never distant in minds of any of us, since Bob Brown was financing some of his own people to train irregular units in other wars. The government in San Salvador was aware of this and as a result the army and the air force took good care of us.

We were all 'carrying' and none of us took chances. The majority in our ranks had the advantage of having had good combat experience.

The daily events of conflict in El Salvador were close enough for us to be acutely aware of them.

Once, while being ferried in a Huey towards a hillside village to the west of the Volcan de Conchagua, we were fired at from the ground, but the pilot couldn't see where it was coming from. On a second pass, tracers could be spotted rising from a thick clump of tall trees.

Later that day, *Fuerza Aérea* – the El Salvador Air Force – tried a ploy of their own. They sent in as a decoy one of their little two-seater Bell scout choppers, with the intention of drawing fire and then have their Huey 'Mikes' (circling nearby) rake the area with their Gatlings. A few thousand rounds in five- or eight-second bursts would do the necessary, was the way an American air force officer attached to a local squadron briefed us. While it sounded simple enough, it wasn't. Such attacks were precision-guided and needed luck. Several times one of the Bell pilots offered me his observer seat but I declined with thanks, though Alwyn was happy enough to go up with him once and was half-deaf from blast for days afterwards. He declined the offer of a subsequent flight with a smile.

At other times, it seemed that the guerrillas were conspiring against us personally. Perhaps they were. They would wait until after we'd left an area before hitting a target. They certainly knew we were around because some of their leaflets specifically mentioned us.

It wasn't direct contact with the enemy that Alwyn and I feared. Indeed, we would have welcomed a bit of action, especially when others were doing the fighting and we had to keep our heads down. What worried us the most was that we might be mistaken for Americans, with a good chance of a bomb being lobbed through the window of a bar or restaurant where we might have been eating.

There was also the prospect of taking a hit while eating lunch with Colonel José Rodriques of the Arce Immediate Reaction Battalion in a little bistro along one of San Miguel's backstreets. Five or six soldiers always took up defensive positions with automatic weapons at the windows and doors of any bar he frequented. Still, the rebels would try. Drive-by shootings seemed to have had their origins in this war. The ploy was probably devised by the Sandanistas and later exported to the streets of Los Angeles and Washington DC.

I didn't appreciate how dangerous San Miguel was until I began to take photos in the centre of the town on the morning of my third day there. I'd gone out alone and wandered down some side streets looking for options. What did surprise me was that there were almost no soldiers around. Within minutes, while focusing on the twin steeples of the cathedral, two Jeeps screeched to a halt alongside where I was standing. Out tumbled a squad of soldiers who fanned out round the courtyard. The officer in charge ran towards me.

'You come!' he demanded, seizing me by the arm. He was wearing one of the El Salvador Army battlejackets.

'Give me a couple of minutes', I begged. 'I'm nearly finished.'

'No, come now! This place is very dangerous . . . there are *campesinos* everywhere . . . some have been turned . . .'

Although he was barely 20, his face was surmounted by a pair of bushy eyebrows that gave him the severe expression of somebody much older. I complied.

Back at base, the camp commandant had apparently received a call from one of his informers in town that I was wandering about on a private jaunt. I'd been through San Miguel often enough by then for just about everybody in this frontline town to know that I was working from the Arce Battalion base with the rest of Bob's troupe.

Obviously annoyed, the commander told me that the rebels had shot

The main entrance to the Arce Battalion barracks in San Miguel. I was struck by the number of young men who were semi-permanently housed there who had lost feet or sometimes their legs to landmines. (Author's collection)

at (and missed) an English couple working as missionaries in one of the government schools a few weeks before. It was obviously a case of mistaken identity, for the rebels rarely intentionally killed those 'helping the cause'.

But then, he added, 'It's the mistakes we worry about.'

Battalion headquarters at San Miguel, our base (or more commonly, the *cuartel*), was a fort in the old tradition that might well have featured in one of those movies originally made about Mexico's Pancho Villa.

The walls, 15 feet high, were painted in a gaudy combination of brown, green and yellow dazzle. The corners rose into French Foreign Legion machicolations and this Disneyland effect could not have been intentional since it had been built more than a century ago to defend the eastern part of the country when insurrection was endemic.

Over the main gate was a sign: yellow letters on black:

BATALLON DE INFANTERIA DE REACCIÒN IMMEDIATA.

166

The name Arce (pronounced Arcey) commemorated one of the fathers of the nation, General Manuel José Arce. It was a tough, efficient special unit that had seen its share of action in the war and, until then, hadn't disgraced itself.

Security here too was tight. A strongly held sandbagged guard post about 50 yards from the main entrance commanded access to two roads leading directly to the fort. Almost always, the guards looked as if they expected trouble. It was an exposed position and they were occasionally sniped at, although that didn't stop mothers and sisters from hanging about outside while waiting for a chance to visit their menfolk.

Once inside the great doors, things were more relaxed. Soldiers not on duty lounged about in T-shirts and shorts playing board games or *futbol* on the soccer field out back. Much of the rest of the area was dominated by cavernous warehouses which also served as barracks. Officers were billeted more comfortably near the battalion HQ, set somewhat apart. All windows in the outer walls were covered with wire mesh for protection, though occasionally someone would manage to throw a grenade over the walls.

I was surprised how crude the barracks were, terribly overcrowded and none too clean. The men slept in long rows of stacked iron beds; three, four, even five levels high. There was almost no space for stowing uniforms or equipment and the troops made little heaps of their belongings along the walls. Anything of value was carried in pouches on their belts.

We ate with the troops and the food was execrable. Even in the officers' mess the cuisine was deadly dull; again mostly beans. The colonel, as we'd been made aware before we arrived, preferred to eat out.

It was at the Arce Battalion headquarters that I first saw large numbers of men who had become landmine casualties.

'Why don't you send the crippled ones home? They're no longer of any use to you in this war,' somebody asked our escort, a major.

He answered without hesitation:

The first and most important reason why they are still here is that they are mostly peasant boys from this area. If we sent them back to their villages in the mountains, they'd be fingered as having fought against the guerrillas . . . obviously they would be killed.

More important, this base – this camp – was their home before it all happened. If they want to go, of course they can. At any time. Meanwhile, they stay here. We're happy to have them.

In any event, he added, they were family, and the unit took some pride in looking after them. 'Maybe some time there will be money and we can get some equipment to help them.'

The battalion had a proud combat record. Situated as it was in one of the most contested zones of the war – with Nicaragua just across the bay – there was a lively esprit de corps. Every evening at stand-to the men would sing the regimental chorus, lustily and with good effect. It was stirring stuff and could be heard by everybody in town.

Every one of these younger *compañeros* (few of whom had reached their majority age) willingly went about his duties. That could not always be said for some of the other units we visited. If one were to judge by the number of Arce crests about (a yellow dagger on green surrounded by red) each one of them understood exactly where his loyalties lay.

El Ejercito Vivira. Mientras Viva La Republica was the battle cry. It, too, was blazoned in bold yellow letters above the main gate.

CHAPTER EIGHT

Patrol in No Man's Land

John Hoagland on the war in El Salvador: 'I don't believe in objectivity. Everyone has a point of view. But I won't be a propagandist for anyone. If you do something right, I'm going to take your picture. If you do something wrong, I'm going to take your picture also.'

During the Vietnam War, John Hoagland filed for and received conscientious objector status. Paradoxically, nine years after that war's end, he was killed in El Salvador by a bullet from an American M60 machine-gun.

ABOUT A WEEK AFTER ARRIVING in El Salvador, several of us were taken by a Huey 'Mike' helicopter to one of the small settlements in the north of Morozan Province, where we were to join a company of soldiers of the Arce Battalion. Our squad included Bob MacKenzie, cameraman Kumst, Paul Foley, and a handful of others, but not 'Sweet Michael'.

The 20-minute hop above 3,000 feet was instructive; we flew just high enough to avoid small-arms fire, though that placed us within what Harry Claflin casually called the SAM-7 envelope. Envelope or not, it was the first time we'd been able to examine clearly the terrain we were working in, for it had been overcast before.

The mountains near San Miguel were almost all volcanic, though most were extinct. Others emitted intermittent puffs of smoke and apparently some had recently erupted. Every day slight tremors could be felt. The biggest volcano of them all, Cacaguatique, sat dormant but ominously brooding near the coast, its peak perpetually in cloud or surrounded by sulphur fumes. Recent lava emissions were visible on its flanks though nobody would hazard a guess as to when the somnolent beast would go active again.

Before we left, we'd been told to prepare for a long haul. We'd walk in column from dawn to dusk for three or four days, said MacKenzie

San Miguel, as with quite a few other towns in the interior of El Salvador, was dominated by a volcano; none were dormant and many tended to constantly emit fumes. (Author's collection)

and our route would lead us into the same mountains we were now traversing by chopper. The idea was to take only bare essentials, together with as much water as we could manage, as weight was a factor. The army would supply the rest, Bob disclosed, though he warned that it would be tough. 'Take your malaria tablets', he added. 'If you don't, the mosquitoes will devour you, it's that bad!' That said, we didn't have a mosquito net between us.

The Huey dropped us in a clearing in the forest that seemed to stretch all the way to the foothills. It was an unusual feature in a country where so much of the terrain seemed densely overgrown. Once it had been a dairy farm, but the cattle were gone, all eaten, either by the troops or the insurgents.

The pilot chose his LZ carefully, principally because one of the army units on the ground would provide us with cover. As in Vietnam, choppers in this war were most vulnerable when in the flare or lifting off. Once down, the pilot kept his machine on the ground only long enough for passengers to disembark, perhaps load a casualty or two and then take-off again. Throughout, the door-gunners ranged their twin-

170

barrelled 7.62s across the surrounding countryside.

First Lieutenant Carlos Alfredo Soto came forward to greet us, his light-brown face smudged with sweaty lines of camouflage paint. An M16 was cradled in one arm, the other held the straps of a brown canvas map case.

'You are very welcome', he said as he shook hands with each of us in turn. Youthful, energetic and obviously on top of what was happening around him just then, he seemed genuinely pleased to have us with him. His English was the best we'd heard yet.

'Come this way' he called. 'We've got coffee.' Lieutenant Soto led the way to a small temporary base that had been set up in a clearing next to some old buildings. Most were covered in graffiti. One of the signs read: *Soldato no Defendas Altos Ricos*. Another was a commemoration: *Viva El 55 Aniversario de PCS*: the 55th anniversary of the Communist Party of El Salvador.

Half a dozen soldiers got up off their haunches to extend a welcome. All were dressed in the same wavy green and brown camouflage uniforms and carried American automatic weapons. Their webbing was similar to that used by the Yanks in Vietnam and well suited to the tropics. An 81mm mortar tube was propped up against a tree trunk, but the bombs had been discretely stowed a short distance away. Another officer was talking loudly into a field radio with a map spread out on the dirt between his legs.

The coffee was a cinch, prepared in an old aluminum kettle balanced precariously over a small fire. ('Not too much smoke', suggested the lieutenant.) Tin mugs, freshly scrubbed, suddenly appeared – we were apparently the second or third lot to use them – and Paul pulled a packet of biscuits from his kit. This was a good start.

The column we'd joined was larger than usual for this kind of high-country patrol: about 100 men all told. They were in constant touch with base and they could have a 'Mike' over us in 30 minutes.

Soto reckoned that he would welcome some contact, but he had to be wary of overextending his lines. The rebels sometimes liked to attack in great charges of 300 or 400 at a time, occasionally more. Although a government patrol in the interior had never been overrun – in contrast to some towns – there were times when it had been close. Whenever there were attacks, he assured us, there had been casualties.

FMLN guerrillas had overwhelmed some army and naval bases in that fashion, attacking in depth, and always at night, he explained. The

La Unión naval base, not far from where we'd been put down, was mentioned. 'So I never allow the men to extend beyond 400 yards. Then we can consolidate quickly if we have to. And of course I can call in air cover.'

Standard patrol routines in El Salvador's so-called 'Red Areas' were rigorously applied. The men were taught never to bunch up or stand about in groups. There might be snipers in the area and they could be very accurate, he assured us. Any river or valley crossing was well reconnoitred beforehand. That usually involved a small scout group that would make a bridgehead before the main body arrived.

'Still, we have to be cautious . . . there is always a danger of ambush . . . it's necessary for the patrol to work to an efficient routine', were Soto's words.

The American influence was definitely there, MacKenzie noted. Many of the procedures perfected in Vietnam were now being applied to this Central American conflict.

'And the guerrillas?'

It was a serious business, Lieutenant Soto replied. He didn't need to elaborate.

Before we'd left the barracks at San Miguel, a medical helicopter had brought in a soldier with a gaping wound in his thigh. The femur had been shattered and the right side of his body was riddled with splinters. He'd already lost a lot of blood and the man was in great pain despite a morphine double-dose. Any more and it could have affected his heart.

They laid him on the stone floor of the medical room and it wasn't long before he was lying in a pool of his own blood. To our untrained eyes, it seemed that he would die. He'd taken the full force of a POM-Z grenade that had been primed as a booby-trap inside the

Government troops were generally willing, loyal to their commanders and efficient. Were that not the case, the rebels would have overrun the country soon enough. It never happened. (Author's collection)

door of a building. That was within a mile or so of where we then were.

'His own stupidity!' said the officer, obviously annoyed at the loss of one of his men which he regarded as unnecessary. 'He should have looked! Each one of them has been trained for that kind of thing.'

Lieutenant Soto's men were a mixed bunch. Some carried 3½-inch bazookas, the same M20 'Super Bazooka' that *Jane's Infantry Weapons* describes as being of 'elderly design'. Nevertheless, they were useful weapons in this kind of primitive country and if not always adequate for retaliation, useful in a tight spot.

While the rebels had the more versatile RPG-7, the men with the M20s were pleased with what they'd been issued, especially since the weapons were made of aluminium and relatively light. Also, they could be dismantled when not in use. According to the instruction manual, the maximum practical range was a bit more than 1,100 yards, though I've yet to see it hit anything at that distance.

There were also a number of M60 general-purpose machine-guns spread along the length of the column. Those hauling them would spread-eagle their 7.62mm ammunition belts across their chests and over their shoulders. To the casual observer, it looked glamorous, but was it practical? Probably not, but as in most Third World conflicts, the image was appropriately macho and the men had faith in their Gringo weapons, though with all that ammunition, these were inordinately heavy loads to lug across mountains.

When questioned about an enemy presence, the lieutenant was candid. There was no doubt there were guerrillas around, 'but you won't spot them easily', said Soto. He swung an arm expansively about the countryside. 'There!' he pointed across a rare stretch of open ground at a tree-line some distance away. 'And there', indicating a valley at the edge of our vision, 'and there', at the mountains nearest us. 'Everywhere!' he added with emphasis and we had to smile because the way he talked, we were surrounded . . .

'You saw what took place this morning?' he asked. We nodded. 'Well it can happen again. It will, if not today, then tomorrow. Or the day after . . . that's the way this war goes', he declared.

Lieutenant Soto was not the typical Central American conscript officer. Well-educated and reflecting some of the attributes of the class into which he'd been born, he intended to become an architect when the war was over. 'Much to rebuild!' he said.

His was a rich family, with land in the west. He'd been to a private school in Mexico City where English was compulsory. After having been commissioned in the army he'd done a few months at an American military school on the East Coast, but wouldn't say where. It wasn't the sort of thing he'd have liked the rebels to get to know about, as if they didn't already.

'What's the strength of the rebel force here?' somebody asked. Soto was vague: a hundred, maybe 200. He had his ideas, but there was nothing specific.

The FMLN was obviously in the region in some strength, for when we passed through a little village in the afternoon and his men asked the usual questions, the *campesinos* were uncooperative. Some were aggressive, every face a portrait of grief. They told us only enough to get us on our way again.

'You see for yourself what they think of us', he said after we'd taken off again. 'They are frightened . . . the guerrillas are nearby.'

I was glad to be out of there.

Once we'd begun walking, it became a hard slog. I'd taken the trouble to get myself into shape, but already I felt done-in and it was only midday. I had to compete with men half my age who'd been nurtured from childhood in these mountains: most were local boys.

We followed no determined route. Soto indicated to the north-east on his map and the man at point went off in that general direction. He wanted to reach a particular village before nightfall: Carlos something-or-other. He knew the people there and said it was safe, or reasonably so.

Nothing in the war, he stressed several times then and later, was really secure. It was all a question of degree, he suggested. And preparedness. He'd been instructed by the colonel back in San Miguel to see us through it all safely and he was taking no chances.

So we walked. Within three hours I had my first cramp. I sat down for a little while and said nothing because you don't want to let the side down. The undulating hills were the worst. We often had to climb out of gulleys and ravines using our hands. There was also the heat, a hot-house clammy humidity that made my clothes stick to my body, as if I had been doused by a bucket of warm water.

There came a moment when I sought the first bit of shade ahead and lingered. Then one of the soldiers nudged me on. There was always a note of urgency in their voices.

The column marched at good speed considering that it was supposed to be a 'casual' four-day patrol. Once they were on their way, the men stretched the pace. Taking pictures became difficult. I was beginning to lag and it worried me. That's when Paul came to my rescue and took my pack, the one that MacKenzie had offered to carry earlier. I declined the offer the first time but I didn't hesitate when he suggested it again.

Every hour or so, the column halted. Then some of the men would light up a cigarette or throw themselves to the ground for a ten-minute break while others spread about on the perimeter. We all sought shade and even in those few minutes some of the troops would fall asleep: these youngsters had adapted well to a rigorous routine and they made good use of sparse opportunities.

When we reached the intended village late that afternoon, I was exhausted. In about 90 minutes it would be dark. Lieutenant Soto dispersed his men carefully and indicated strongpoints and who would be responsible for what. Wrist watches had been allotted to section leaders before the squad left San Miguel (very few El Salvadorian soldiers could afford such accoutrements, even if they were essential) and the men knew their duties. But first, he sent out several patrols to look for evidence of an enemy presence: fresh tracks or food wrappers would be enough, Soto reckoned.

We 'slept' – for want of a better word – that night in a tiny hamlet of about 20 adobe and leaf-roofed buildings clustered round a small square. The village, one of the older settlements, lay on a gentle slope in the foothills surrounded by some big trees that ran in a ragged line along what would have been the main drag. Some of these were traditional forest giants, gnarled and scarred. Others had been stunted by wire, or had spikes driven in to hold a cable or to support a wall. Bunches of onions hung between the leaves of those closest to 'town'.

Pigs were everywhere. Since the rebels like to help themselves when they passed through, I was surprised that there were still so many around. Once there had been cattle, herds of them everywhere, but now there were few left, which was a pity because, as in Africa, livestock in Central America is a moveable asset.

As it got dark, a marvellous aroma enveloped us all: wood smoke mixed with the scent of frangipani and bougainvillaea. The air was suddenly fresh and cool. Elsewhere, someone was frying eggs. The village was poor and not at all clean; but I felt, as I sat in the gathering dusk, that it would have been a great place to rest for a few days. Not just yet, though.

There weren't more than 60 people in the place, all of Indian or mixed stock, which wasn't that unusual in a country where more than 90 per cent of the population was officially listed as *mestizo*. Before the war, in UN demographical studies, only one in a hundred El Salvadorians had the dubious distinction of being classified 'white'. Until then, I'd thought that only Israel and South Africa still categorized race.

My first impression of these people was that while many looked frail and emaciated, they'd done very well for themselves for many centuries without outside help. It was the white man who had brought his usual afflictions, including smallpox and STDs as well as his guns and rum. Like those across the water to the north, these natives too had suffered.

Nevertheless, as rustic as they may have looked to us interlopers, they seemed a good deal happier than their compadres in the cities. They were a lot more content and possibly more sedate, and that in spite of the troubles. They smiled when we arrived and were still at it when we left early the next morning.

As promised, the army fed us – beans. There was pork-and-beans, tomato-and-beans, greens-and-beans, beans-and-beans! In fact, we were treated to beans for breakfast, lunch and supper. After four days of it I was beginning to get a little tired of the menu. However, I still like beans, especially with plenty of chilli. Besides, now and again, there was a bottle of warm beer that one of our team had stowed in his bags, to wash it all down.

How did these people manage? I asked Soto. They were friendly to the army, yet this was bandit country.

'This is a protected village. They defend themselves. They ask us for weapons and we give them to them.' At first the rebels had tried to force their own stamp of authority on them and other communities and there were many fierce exchanges. Afterwards, when it seemed pointless to lose people for a cause that would be settled anyway after the glorious victory, the FMLN tended to avoid the place. However, any *campesino* caught in the open or unarmed was killed, always, as was explicitly stated, as an example to others.

'It's a price they pay', he said. The villagers were most vulnerable when they went into town, as they sometimes needed to do for medical, family or other reasons. 'Then the rebels set up road blocks . . . they murder anybody they suspect of having dealt with our people . . . quite brutal', said the lieutenant, and added:

It's merciless. It can also be impersonal and cold blooded, which is what has really caused so many of these peasants to revolt. Talk to them yourself . . . you'll quickly see that it's the system that the guerrillas are trying to impose that they despise. One and all. That and the fact that they're all Christians . . .

The Church in El Salvador, we'd learnt even before we arrived, was opposed to most things linked to government, often diametrically, so. It blamed the politicians for the war and in a sense, the priests were right because it was greed that lay at its roots. That said, there is hardly a country in the Western Hemisphere that is not battling corruption in all its forms, though everybody was aware that El Salvador was probably a lot more crooked before hostilities started. For this and other reasons, the Church – or the Liberation Gospel as it came to be called – seemed to have a ready ear both for the revolution and the rebels, especially in some of the rural areas.

The argument propounded went along the lines that the FMLN offered a better prospect for change. But nobody could reconcile the peasants' fundamental belief that Marxism was anti-Christian; not even the Holy Fathers. Some of the more passionate ideologists, the so-called 'worker priests', tried, but they never really succeeded. To these simple people, a communist was an atheist. End of story.

One got the impression after a few weeks in the country that it would take a lot more than a guerrilla war to change many of these deeply entrenched beliefs, which went back centuries.

It all came out while we sat talking about the war after dark. Often we were joined by some of the NCOs and one or two officers, none of whom could speak much English, so Soto would translate. There were probably guerrilla groups doing much the same thing in the mountains within sight of us that beautiful moonlit night. The people with us in the village were as curious about us as we were about them.

As an aside, many of these simple folk, some of whom might see a single movie a year – and then on an open screen in the countryside with a small generator providing power – were admirers of the American movie hero and cult-figure Rambo. Even among the peasants of remotest South and Central America, this kind of ubiquitous and inescapable junk-culture prevailed.

Next day we reached Santa Cruz, one of the three or four towns by that name in the region, which was all very confusing to us strangers.

The going had been hard on us all from early in the day, first marching in a thick clinging mist that obscured everything and later, in rain and mud. It was miserable. I badly needed a shower and I also seemed to have been the only one to have been the focus of mosquitoes, almost the entire night.

After a brief stop for something to eat (beans again) we climbed slowly up a long path leading into another series of foothills. Twice, single shots rang out. The soldiers would hurry forward in the direction of the sound, but they wouldn't see anything. The bush was too thick and any kind of response was out of the question, reckoned Lieutenant Soto. At times, he said, if he had an idea of where the firing was coming from, he'd lob a few mortar bombs. But not this time . . .

Ghosts walked by night in Santa Cruz, the troops said. It had been abandoned for a year by the time we got there. There had once been a new administrative block and what appeared to be a fine, two-level school, complete with playing fields and a boarding establishment for children who would arrive from outlying districts. The buildings echoed voices eerily and one of the walls in front had a huge hole in it. It was creepy.

Santa Cruz had been heavily damaged by both sides as hostilities progressed. There was as much graffiti on the walls as shell-pocks. Artillery must have been used at some time or another, or was it rocket fire from the 'Mikes'?

A rebel had written in red paint across one of the open spaces of the main building the words, a foot high: *Joven Ingresa a la Escuela Militar del FMLN*. They'd apparently used it as a training base and there were ammunition cases and cartridge shells everywhere. A Cuban party had even lodged there, another of the officers said.

'Why did you let them keep the town for so long?' I asked Soto. 'Once you knew they had it, why didn't you take it again? Or at least try to do so?'

'Ah', he said smiling, his usually infectiously convivial self. 'Thereby hangs a tale.' Using his bush hat with a red band around it to shade his face against the sun, he pointed down the valley from which we'd just emerged. 'You see where we came through . . . it's all tough country like that around here. The approaches too . . . very difficult . . . lots of jungle . . . and the mountains behind us. Look!' A large range of hills did indeed undulate from one horizon to the other and there was only one road leading up from the floor of the valley and that was a good 20 clicks away. It wasn't metalled either, which suggested mines.

The guerrillas have all the cover that they need. Working as they constantly do from improvised positions, they have the initiative, here, at least. Anyway, when we arrived they just withdrew: tactical retreat . . . good communist procedure. They'd wait until we'd left, then they'd come back. Once we depart tomorrow, they'll be here by mid-morning again.

'So why didn't you stay here; in force? Occupy the place? Permanently.' He replied:

Because then they would fight like hell to drive us out. They did it two, three times. It became a point of honour. They shot down one of our helicopters and killed the three men in it. Although the crew survived the initial impact, they were executed on the spot. They displayed their bodies in a public place . . . wouldn't let anybody bury them.

It was a bad mistake, he said, because such barbarism didn't go down with these simple village people, who know instinctively what is right and wrong.

That was when the military commanders in San Salvador decided: 'Enough! If we cannot keep a permanent force occupying Santa Cruz, then the guerrillas won't use it either.' Soto had warned earlier that none of us should wander about unaccompanied and it wasn't the enemy he was concerned about just then: *his* mines were laid about in the dirt outside, he intimated.

It was a pattern that had become all too common throughout the country where regions or large towns were being contested. Santa Cruz, close to the Honduran border (which remained a conduit for men and arms as long as the war went on), retained a high priority for both sides.

Steve Salisbury, an American journalist friend who covered the war in those parts for several years – and was still around when I last heard – told me of another village that was destroyed by the rebels. The town was Cinquera, which lay about 50 miles north of San Salvador and, at the time, was being defended by a squad of soldiers. All the men and boys who could carry a rifle had been formed into a makeshift self-defence unit, but they had received little or no military training. Like much else in this war, it was all half-cocked, he reckoned.

While there, he'd met Maria Lydia Solis, a widow who had gone to fetch money and who had not only lived through it all but had survived.

The battle kicked off at sunset and went on all night, with the rebels entering the town in the morning. Although there had already been many casualties – including a dozen women and children – the rebels lined up the survivors and killed them all. Only a handful of women and children were spared and Maria Solis was one of them.

'We begged the soldiers not to kill us all but they said we must pay.' They took everything of value.'

FMLN cadres stayed four days and then left and there were any number of horror stories afterwards. Since Cinquera was only an hour's drive from San Salvador, that sort of thing inevitably lead to questions being asked by the populace: what was the army doing all this time?

'The worst were the wounded that they executed', reckoned Salisbury. 'The mayor and his secretary [who was Mrs Solis' husband] were both badly hurt. Señor Solis had stepped on a mine some weeks before so he was already in a bad way, but no matter, they dragged him outside and shot him in the head.'

The survivors abandoned Cinquera for good as soon as government forces eventually arrived and the place remained deserted until the end of the war. Few who knew it before were eager to return.

We didn't stay long in Santa Cruz either. For one, Soto wasn't happy. Also, he was worried about us. Radio intercepts had disclosed that the FMLN knew that a bunch of Gringos, some with cameras, were with the column. Once before he'd been mortared while passing through: his platoon had lost a couple of men. He didn't want that to happen again.

So we picked up our things and went off again, if only to keep out of trouble.

In the old days coffee had been a source of wealth to the people who worked these uplands. There was much evidence of the old plantations, although most of the smaller bushes had long ago gone to seed.

The graceful haciendas that hugged hillsides and offered magnificent views over the surrounding countryside were still intact, although their owners had fled. None of the old homes we passed were occupied, and from what was lying about, it was evident that guerrillas had been there too.

'Be careful where you walk', Soto said earnestly whenever we came to an area that had formerly been inhabited. 'They see us coming from a long way off . . . then they lay their mines and set booby traps . . . just like in Vietnam.' Worse, he maintained, the guerrillas had plenty of time to do it.

'So, let my men search the place before you start filming or taking pictures because we don't need to be calling in a chopper to haul your body out of here . . .'

While MacKenzie and Foley were nonchalant, we civvies tried to follow instructions. We'd follow the soldiers and, where possible, try to step in their footprints, but it wasn't easy.

We could see from the trappings that life in the old days must have been good. It had probably been a tasteful combination of opulence and a feudal tradition that went back centuries. Naturally, there had been servants galore; their quarters invariably clustered tidily behind the main residence.

I asked Soto what would happen after the war. Would he and the other landowners go back to the old ways? He evaded the question; it was clearly embarrassing. But then he himself had been a member of the privileged class so it was understandable.

Of course, the plebeian soldiers who served under him knew it, but in some countries other than communist ones, officers still command more respect if they are gentlemen. Even the Russians, having destroyed the old upper class, found it necessary to invent a new one.

Some of the farmhouses, though ransacked, were remarkably well preserved. One, on a hill-top that commanded views all the way across to the distant mountains, lay only a short hop by helicopter from San Miguel and looked as if it had been abandoned only recently. In fact, it had been standing empty for years. We weren't allowed in there because of booby traps, and didn't complain.

I heard afterwards that some government troops on another farm, not too far down the road, had been badly burnt by a phosphorus grenade set above a bathroom door. It was triggered by the light switch, even though there hadn't been any electricity there for years. Old habits die hard, it seems.

When the time came, getting us out of what had once been a minor paradise wwas a risky exercise. Again, it would be by helicopter, the colonel in San Miguel had decided.

On the morning of the fourth day, we'd been warned that a chopper

An array of different types of aircraft was used against the FMLN guerrillas. Even former civilian planes like this one had rockets fitted to their hard points. This photograph was taken at Ilopango Airport, outside the capital. (Author's collection)

would arrive at a particular time and we were to wait at one of the concrete slabs where the coffee was once laid out to dry in the sun. But as always, Alwyn was still filming and he needed more time. He took a while to make his way down to the improvised LZ and I could see that Soto was annoyed.

The Huey, meanwhile, kept circling. The crew were in radio contact with the ground, very much in a hurry to get the job done. They felt exposed in those mountains because others doing the same thing in the past had become targets. Also, we knew, there had been a chopper or two shot down.

The Huey refused to land until we were all bunched together. Then it was a quick touchdown followed by an immediate lift-off. We were exposed for only a few crucial moments and, as the gods willed, nothing happened. Not that day, anyway.

I never did find out what happened to Lieutenant Soto after the war, though a scandal soon enveloped San Miguel's commanding colonel and he was relieved of his command. It had nothing to do with military matters, some said, and they cited corruption.

Which is the way things sometimes go in wartime . . .

CHAPTER NINE

A Central American Conflagration

'The civil war raged on in El Salvador, fuelled by US aid to the
Salvadoran military. The government harshly repressed dissent,
and at least 70,000 people lost their lives in killings and
bombing raids waged against civilians throughout the
countryside. The country's infrastructure had crumbled and the
nation appeared to be no closer to its goals of peace, prosperity
and social justice than when the process began. Then in 1989,
the murder of six Jesuit priests, their housekeeper and her
daughter at the University of Central America shocked the
international community into action.'

Enemies of War, PBS, Washington DC, 2006

THE GUERRILLAS HIT THE NAVAL base at La Unión on the Gulf of
Fonseca along El Salvador's Pacific coast some months before we
got there. They killed dozens of young conscripts for the loss of a
handful of their own.

It was a remarkable victory for the rebels. Their fighters entered the
base some time after midnight and they'd evidently reconnoitred it very
carefully over a long period and knew exactly what obstacles had to be
overcome. First they cut the throats of the guards. Without firing a shot,
they moved quickly among the barracks buildings and hurled grenades
into open windows before anyone could even begin to assess the threat,
or how to counter it. The raid made a great stir throughout the country.

A year later, in March 1987, a similar raid was carried out on the
headquarters of the 4th Brigade at El Paraiso. Altogether 20 soldiers
were officially said to have been killed, though the actual figure was
something more like 70.

An American instructor, Sergeant First Class Greg Fronius, died while
trying to rally a defence after their El Salvadorian officers had abandoned
their charges. Guerrillas attempted to overrun the camp and kill everyone
there, but they weren't as successful as they might have been.

Once it was over, enemy losses, said Harry Claflin, were estimated to be close to 100, though the actual number remains in dispute because in keeping with revolutionary ideology, the guerrillas would always try to take their casualties with them. The reason for doing so was to avoid giving their adversaries any kind of moral or propaganda advantage.

While these attacks happen every now and again, the consequences were seldom as critical as at La Unión. Some people believed the attack on the naval base might have been the turning point of the war. There were those who claimed that the FMLN had gained an almost irreversible advantage.

The reality was that the attack was admirably coordinated. Even with more moderate losses, it would have been the kind of operation that any guerrilla commander would have been proud of. For the Salvadorian *Estado Mayor* (General Staff), it exposed a critical lack of order and discipline that was demoralizing and one of the reasons why the base at San Miguel was on such a high alert while we were around.

Following those developments, one of the American military observers suggested that the attacks made clear that government forces were getting very little real-time intelligence. He made the point in a report that was widely circulated that nobody in the country knew what was going to happen next. The comment, objective and clearly well-intentioned, resulted in his being labelled a guerrilla 'fellow traveller' and his reports were subsequently viewed with scepticism. But of course, he was perfectly correct.

The fact was that the FMLN had executed the La Unión raid with great precision, preceded by months of excellent planning. They had come undetected across the broad waterway between the two countries after dark in several small boats, which meant that their radar images must have been minimal and were probably not picked up by shore monitoring stations. And even if they were, the operators did not report in. Also, their weapons were waiting for them in safe houses on shore. There was nothing tell-tale that might have alerted anybody on watch at the time.

One of the immediate consequences of the La Unión debacle was that it sharpened American resolve to take a more active part in the war. There were gaps in the defences of El Salvador that Washington proposed to plug. Ultimately, it did.

Many of the men with solid experience of other wars in South-East Asia, whom I encountered in remote places, were sent to Central

America on training missions. If they got into a few scrapes in the course of their duties, or accounted for a few gooks along the way, ran the argument in certain Washington circles, then so much the better. Each time it happened, the authorities tended to look away. There were no Gringos involved in this Central American war . . .

The media was another story. American journalists made a thing of 'aid' people with weapons in their baggage arriving in El Salvador, much as they might have done with us had there been somebody from the *New York Times* or one of the other major American dailies when we touched down. It would probably have been front page news in both Washington and New York the next day, especially if it were also shown that one of our members was a member of that ultra-exclusive little band of warriors known as USMILGP-EL, or in the lingo, US Military Group, El Salvador.

In our circles, we would use the phrase Mil Group – or MilGroup – among whom Harry Claflin was one of its more successful members. In the end, American veterans attached to units of the El Salvadorian Army under MilGroup's auspices did outstanding work. Effectively, they had a hand in turning the war around.

Harry Claflin had done solid time in South-East Asia, which included two tours with US Marine Reconnaissance in I Corps, where he ran recce patrols along the Cambodian and Laotian borders. Certainly, he had his own views on what was going on just then in Central America. I shared a room with him at Ilopango Airport during some of our forays and was aware that he'd been badly shot up during one of his 'Nam tours of duty in 1966. You couldn't miss it when he got dressed.

Harry's 'home from home' at Ilopango was pretty simple as digs go, but it was secure. Though on a military air base, we were unlikely to take 'incoming' so close to the capital. More importantly, it cost us nothing. When we didn't go out, we pulled out a few boxes of Meals, Ready-to-Eat (MREs) – ubiquitous, any-army meals that are ready for immediate consumption. All I had to do each morning was roll up my sleeping bag.

Harry – with loads of combat experience – and never one for chit-chat, was as terse about his personal background as he was about what was going on around him. 'Sometimes you win and there are times when you lose', were his words. But in El Salvador just then, he suggested, 'the insurgents are starting to get hurt'.

Years later he and I shared a few retrospective notes and his revelations are interesting.

Claflin stated:

I worked with these local troops about a year and though it took a while, I gradually brought them up to speed. The stuff that I'd originally done with Recon Platoon came to the attention of quite a few people. In fact, the MilGroup people took a lot of interest. So did the El Salvador Chief of Staff, which was probably why I was asked to put together a programme to train a reconnaissance type element for the El Salvador Army's 4th Brigade.

The idea was to prepare the guys for special missions and they gave me a free hand. I suggested that I prepare the men by combining two programmes that the Marine Corps had run in Vietnam: the Stingray Project and the Small Unit Action Forces Program. Stingray was run by Force Recon, and in its day was pretty damn successful.

It was on this basis that I finally helped to create GOE, or *Goupos de Operaciones Especiales*. By the time we were done, we'd trained them from their bootstraps to their eyeballs. I can tell you now, they were sharp!

Other, similar GOE units followed and no doubt these initiatives helped shorten the war. Claflin also commented:

You must remember that by 1983 – when Washington first sent military advisers to help the El Salvador Military – the country, like all Central American states at this time, was simply not prepared for war. Two years later, because of US assistance, the El Salvador Military was up to the task of kicking the shit out of the gooks.

What our 55 American advisers did, was to take a Third World army and remould it into a modern combat force. The success of the military with which we were involved at a very basic level (and here we're talking about 1989) – led to what the media termed the Final Offensive. By then many FMLN cadres were getting desperate.

Their leaders, sitting comfortably way back behind the lines

– most of them in Sandinista country anyway – wouldn't believe any of it. They couldn't accept that a tiny nation like El Salvador was fielding seasoned troops and getting results. This was a real blunder on the part of the enemy, because they'd started to believe their own bullshit.

They actually still held out the ideal of the people rising up in unison with them and overthrowing the government . . . didn't happen . . . couldn't happen. Those same people on whom the guerrillas were counting had had more than a gutful of the FMLN.

We ended up destroying the FMLN Military Wing. It was never again to become as active as it had been in the past.

As to the Political Wing, the first Presidential elections in which the FMLN was able to participate, the results said it all. Because of the peace accords, they carried only one percent of the vote . . . a single percentage point! So much for the glorious fucking revolution . . .

And today, into the New Millennium, many years after the fighting has stopped, El Salvador is by far the most modern of the Central American countries and certainly the biggest friend we have in the entire region.

Our Huey pilot approached La Unión with circumspection at dawn a few days after we'd been lifted out of a position in the hills north of San Miguel. He circled twice before landing and looked carefully in all directions as he did so. It wasn't that he was nervous, he said: in fact, he would have welcomed the chance to give his gunners something to shoot at.

Only afterwards did he confide that one small guerrilla unit – an elite bunch of fighters – had taken to firing at Air Force helicopters from the foothills each time they flew over. Nobody could get a fix on their position in order to retaliate. Even worse, he suggested, the FMLN had got their hands on some SAM-7s. It was not impossible that this same bunch of operatives had them too.

That, in itself, was a good deal less disconcerting than it might have been 12 months earlier, because South Africa had become a clandestine partner in the war. There was already some cooperation between Pretoria and Military Headquarters in San Salvador and some of the lessons learnt fighting Russian-backed insurgents in Angola had been passed on. One of these was that if a pilot saw a SAM-7 coming, he had perhaps a second or two to take evasive action. It had been proven often enough that it was easier for a chopper to get out of the way of a ground-to-air missile than a fixed-wing aircraft. Another pointer was that if there was a real, or suspected, anti-aircraft threat, tree-top level flying was the preferable option. It is extremely difficult to get a bead on an aircraft if you only have it in view for seconds, never mind still knock it out of the sky, the South Africans explained.

From the ground, as we drove through the town on the way to the naval base, we found that La Unión was very different from how it appeared from the air. It should have been a big place, with coffee factories and warehouses on the outskirts. The suburbs were modern, extensive and well laid out, though quite a few had been abandoned because of the war.

With its distinctive red tiled roofs, friezes and Spanish architecture, La Unión before the war had been allowed space to grow. There was none of the congestion of San Miguel or some of the other conurbations in the region.

On closer inspection, it was smaller than we'd expected. Also, it was run-down. The harbour, by contrast, was relatively new; because of the war it had been renovated and extended. Nicaragua lay across the bay and the port clearly had a certain strategic value. One also got the impression that La Union must have been an active commercial harbour before hostilities. On our visit there were only fishing boats and half-a-dozen naval craft tied up alongside. No small cargo boats or oil tankers, like we saw at La Libertas farther to the west.

Some of the smaller fighting boats were US Navy Island Class patrol craft; high-speed aluminium boats with crews of 14. They'd all been delivered to El Salvador after the attack on La Unión, which underscores the assertion about war changing the nature of conflict in a particular sphere, sometimes irrevocably.

Apart from soldiers on patrol, La Union was hardly a town at the business end of an increasingly acrimonious civil conflict. All the buildings in the central business district, many with plate-glass windows, were still intact. Also, we found that early in the day, life seemed slower than elsewhere in the country, though things were happening: shops and cafes were opening, a postman started his rounds and a group of kindergarten children were being taken to school. To many of its residents, if there was any fighting, it might have been taking place on another continent.

Naval patrols became a vital adjunct to the war effort in El Salvador as they combated the smuggling of personnel and war materials to the guerrillas from Nicaragua. There were few questions asked: if an unknown vessel was suspicious or acting strangely, it was sunk. This policy eventually caused huge logistics problems for the FMLN. (Author's collection)

There were no formalities when we reached a gunboat attached to one of the El Salvadorian Navy 'Reaction Force' flotillas. The blue and white flag on the mast bore the words *Dios, Union y Libertad* across its broad, white horizontal stripe.

Within minutes we were heading out towards the far side of the gulf. The shores facing us, said the youthful captain, Byron Roberto-Rivas Alfonso Pinto, were Nicaraguan. Having passed round his card, as protocol demanded, he suggested that we call him Captain Bob. With Brown and MacKenzie, we now had three Bobs onboard.

The 110ft naval patrol boat was immaculate. The crew probably knew we were coming and had prepared accordingly. There were two .50-cal Browning machine-guns, mounted fore and aft, and the weapons were well greased. There were more automatic weapons mounted alongside the bridge. Aft, strapped down, was a 14ft Zodiac. It performed a double function: as a lifeboat and for use in shallow inshore patrols among the mangroves. The crew was dressed in camouflage, with nothing to distinguish sailors from soldiers; no formal whites anywhere. Best of all, the heads down below had been scrubbed.

Life on board consisted almost solely of patrolling a fixed area out to sea. They would intercept and stop small boats and fishing smacks that crossed the bay, which, at its widest was about 30 miles across. These craft were sometimes searched for weapons and illegal entrants and if the crew had a bit of luck, the captain told us, they got themselves an insurgent or three.

'We can't search every boat or arrest every suspect. But we know that the other side are using these waters to bring across their people and their weapons. It's a very active area', he told us through an interpreter.

'Sometimes, when we're sure, we let one or two of the suspects pass to see where they lead us. But that's a big operation and it can get complicated . . . it needs lots of men on the ground to follow through. And the enemy is not stupid.'

We were offered breakfast, American style, with bacon and eggs and a gritty grey bean paste instead of hash browns. The coffee was percolated, local and good.

Captain Bob told us of something that had taken place a month before. He'd stopped the same shallow-draught boat for the third time in about as many weeks. It was always in the same area, usually towards sunset. 'We were even on nodding terms with the crew of two,' he declared.

This time she had her lines out and somehow, I sensed something wrong. There was nothing I could put my finger on, but I felt it . . . in my bones . . . these hombres were up to something. But they were too clever for me. I knew it . . .

So, the third time I came on them, I did something I hadn't done before. We had some soft drinks and I offered them some. So they came on board. We talked a little: about the weather, the fishing, the war, even about Nicaragua. And since it was getting late, the taller of the two men, a young fellow with sharp eyes and not much to say, offered me his hand. He had to go, he told me.

They shook hands and the pair turned to go. Then Captain Bob realized that the hand he had grasped was not the callused paw of a fisherman. The palms were soft, the grip flabby. This was no tarry sailor. 'I had him, I knew. But we had to be careful.' We steamed on, but not too far away. Meanwhile we inspected several other boats, keeping our suspect in sight. I radioed to headquarters and asked for a helicopter and a couple of marine commandos with diving gear.' An hour later most of the support team was ready and waiting at La Unión, but the helicopter had to come from San Miguel and that took a little longer.

The fishing-boat didn't move, but light was now fading and the commander feared that they would lose them since it gets dark quickly in the tropics.

'The one advantage that we had was that the sea was calm and there was no wind.' Not long afterwards the familiar roar of the Huey could be heard. It approached from the shore, directly towards them. 'We told it to lower a winch, and in two minutes I was in the air. Meanwhile the officer of the watch kept the boat in his sights. We made straight for it.'

Still in touch with the naval craft, a lookout said that the two men were hauling in their lines. In another minute they would have made off.

'We had only seconds to drop a marker. My vessel was following as fast as her 26 knots allowed.'

What happened next is in the record books in San Salvador. The helicopter dropped its marker alongside the boat and the two men, now covered by a twin-barrelled 7.62mm machine-gun, were ordered through a loudhailer to sit tight and await the navy while two frogmen went into the drink.

They found a weapons cache wrapped in double plastic bags that had been attached to the fishing-boat. The two on board had slipped the cable the moment they spotted the inbound chopper. Too late: they hadn't counted on navy divers. The sea was barely 15 feet deep.

This particular pair had been smuggling weapons into El Salvador from Nicaragua for months. On a previous occasion, when things looked like going off kilter, they'd simply jettisoned their cargo and it sank to the bottom without trace. Never mind: they would go back to Nicaragua and get more. At that time the Sandinistas were getting all the weapons they needed from Cuba.

The manner in which the hardware was being shipped is interesting. Attached to the harness that held the loads, there were two small flotation bags that supported them just below the surface. In a cumbersome manner the 'fishermen' were able to tow their loads ashore. If challenged, it was easy to turn over a bag and lose it.

In those calm waters they had enough warning. Visibility was invariably excellent and when your engines weren't running, you could

Every boat working the area between El Salvador and Nicaragua had to be checked. It was a bit like the situation in the Eastern Mediterranean with the Israeli Navy. (Author's collection)

hear a man talking a mile away.

We were never told what happened to those caught trying to infiltrate the country from Nicaragua, either as smugglers or combatants. Harry Claflin let slip at some stage while I was staying with him at the Ilopango air base that it was unlikely that they would have survived.

'They make them talk', he told me one evening, 'and then they disappear . . . just like that . . .' he declared

Towards the end of the decade, the Americans became much more involved in interception work along the coast, especially off La Unión. US Marines were brought in to man island-based electronic observation sites in the Gulf of Fonseca.

SEAL teams were also drafted. These crack navy specialists, the equivalent of Britain's SBS, would probe Nicaraguan defences, which, at the time contravened both American and international law. The United

States was not at war with that country and in any event, the US Constitution didn't allow for such things. However, that didn't seem to bother President Reagan. In those days the American defense establishment could do such things and get away with it. Most times, anyway . . .

At one stage, Washington even sanctioned the mining of the Nicaraguan port of Corinto, which had become a major FMLN staging post for the struggle in the neighbouring country. The US Navy LST *Sphinx* was detached for this purpose and there was much damage caused.

All these forces coordinated their activities under the auspices of Harry Claflin's MilGroup, run from a discreet San Salvador headquarters by one of those shadowy figures of the Cold War who, years later, is still regarded with respect and fondness by those who worked with him. John Waghelstein, a Jewish boy from Brooklyn, even got on well with us scribes.

'Teflon Warrior', American author Jim Morris called him. One of his attributes was that he liked to speak like a real person and not in the anodyne sound bites of the staff college. Last heard, Waghelstein – or 'Waggie' as his friends and colleagues called him - was lecturing at the Naval War College at Newport, Virginia.

By the time we arrived in El Salvador, in the mid 1980s, the country was in a state of upheaval. It was going through a period of transition from possibly the worst army in Latin America to one of the best. Jim Morris' old pal Waghelstein was to play a pivotal role in behind-the-scenes command and control.

Other Americans who saw service there remember the epoch as a period of confusion. Still more regarded the dedication of some Americans involved as foolhardy. There were crazy missions into rebel territory that shouldn't have worked but did. Had they been launched anywhere else in the world, they might have been regarded as suicidal. Some of these operations were well behind enemy lines, usually linked to possibly killing one of the combat commanders or perhaps destroying war materials recently arrived from either Cuba or the Soviet Union.

Even the medals these brave young men were awarded were the peacetime equivalents of the Bronze Star or the Meritorious Service Medal. It was an insult. Every one of these individuals was a dedicated volunteer to a cause.

Conditions weren't helped by the fact that it was all surreptitious. If any of these irregulars were taken captive by the enemy, they were peremptorily warned, neither the Pentagon nor US government would know anything about them, never mind their clandestine roles. As it was, operations in most Third World countries in which American nationals were involved or possibly implicated were disavowed by Washington. There was simply no other way with a Congress that was hostile to any form of American military involvement abroad.

Certainly, it was a peculiar era. Colonel Oliver North had direct access to the Oval Office and, looking back, it couldn't last. Nor could Ollie.

In Central America, Ilopango Air Force Base on the outskirts of San Salvador enjoyed the kind of mystique that had previously enveloped Da Nang and, possibly, Ondangua in Namibia's northernmost region of Ovamboland, adjacent to Angola. All had been operational air force bases and, in their day, had enjoyed a certain notoriety, in part because nobody knew for sure what aircraft or other assets such as advanced munitions were at hand.

The same was true of Ilopango, where some strange events took place: midnight flights, squadrons of gunships lifting off or landing around the clock, helicopter airlifts involving large numbers of troops – who could usually be clearly seen sitting at the open doors of Huey 'Mikes' – together with an occasional ambulance, sirens wailing, that would mysteriously arrive and depart. We knew that attack C-130 gunships with Gatlings and heavy guns provided ground forces with powerful top cover after dark, but these aircraft were very rarely spotted on the ground in El Salvador.

Under normal wartime conditions, we shouldn't have been allowed near the place. However, our party was 'protected'. Our patron was Señor Bob Brown and he could go anywhere! So, in effect, could we.

Other Americans also frequented the place; grey, nameless entities with grey nondescript faces, who did not communicate with anybody.

Part of the problem in El Salvador as hostilities dragged on, was that both sides became steadily more desperate to make some kind of mark. At the same time, Washington was openly reviled by the rebels. Any Americans in El Salvador at the time – whatever their politics – were linked to the ruling junta, which wasn't difficult to comprehend since there were so many Gringos in the towns and bases of the interior and, most of all, in the capital itself.

Few were tourists or journalists. A number were closely shorn members of the Outer-Beltway Establishment. The majority were attached to military missions or acted as diplomatic 'observers' and almost all enjoyed dubious cover. Here and there were the usual pairs of CIA 'twins'.

I am not sure whether it was the official policy at Langley or not, but each time I ran into CIA staffers in remote places like the Congo-Brazzaville, Tanzania, Islamabad or the Namibian border with Angola, they always seemed to wander about in pairs, in itself a giveaway. The same was true when I handled a contract for Langley in Afghanistan in 1985: I never ever met either of my handlers singly while the job was in progress.

The reality about the tendency of duplication is that while a couple of interlopers might find each other's company comforting in a hostile area, it also presents the enemy with a double target.

We had a remarkably free rein at the Ilopango Air Force Base considering that it was the nerve centre of the war. Decisions were made by the Chiefs of Staff at military headquarters in San Salvador, the country's capital, but it was at Ilopango that these orders were put into effect. Nothing happened without close air support, which included TacAir squadrons of A-37 Dragonflys.

It was strange indeed that Alwyn Kumst and I were allowed to wander about the base with our cameras and take whatever footage we pleased, which would be difficult in any other conflict these days. Even in Somalia during that early 1990s 'rescue mission', I was stopped from taking photos by an Italian Air Force unit at Mogadishu Airport and, later, by some Turkish soldiers on board armoured personnel carriers.

In El Salvador, by contrast, the authorities didn't even ask to see what Alwyn had shot. Since they had only Brown's word for it, everything we filmed could just as easily have been handed over to the guerrillas and nobody would have been any the wiser. However, Bob had known me for a long time.

To one side of Ilopango there were several helicopter squadrons, mostly Huey 'Mike' assault choppers, several armed with 7.62mm twin-barrelled guns: the *Escuadrón de Helicopteros*. In our time they flew raw; no Kevlar floor matting to protect their crews or anything vital round the engines or hydraulics. Later, specially designed and mounted engine armour was added; also AN/ALQ 144 infra-red jammers to deflect SAM missiles.

We'd head out in single-aircraft sorties, which didn't excite me. In the Angolan War all sorties into the distant beyond were handled by two-ship operations, sometimes more. My first question was who would get us out if we went down? The second was, if we went out on our own, without backup, who would know *where* we'd gone down . . .

When the El Salvadorian Air Force began to lose more of its machines to ground fire, they adopted the two-ship practice as well, in part, because as the South Africans had explained, it was the more secure option.

As in other wars in less-developed countries, it was air power that finally tilted the balance towards the government, for no other reason than that the FMLN had nothing to counter it. As we were all aware, no guerrilla force can indefinitely withstand continual pounding by combat helicopters or even what was thrown at them from fast-aging AC-47s with their clusters of heavy weapons, usually AN-M3 .50-cal Browning machine-guns mounted adjacent to the cargo door.

These antiquated 'Puff the Magic Dragons' would arrive within the hour if a unit in the interior considered itself under threat, although they usually worked at night, circling in 'pylon turns' from above 10,000 feet, or just beyond SAM-7 range. They would sometimes be supplemented by C-130s, flown in from what we suspected were other locations in the region, usually Honduras.

Any Vietnam vet who has spent time at the Sharp End will tell you that the average C-130 could put down enough saturation fire to wipe out half a battalion at a time.

It took a while, but we eventually familiarized ourselves with the various systems, like the pattern of fire laid down by a DC-3 being evenly spaced with one bullet or flechette every eight inches or so. If the guerrilla leaders weren't unnerved, their men in the field must have been. Those in charge in San Salvador told us so, and ultimately they were proved right.

Also based at Ilopango were a couple of squadrons of A-37 light-support jet fighters. Designed as trainers, they provided solid ground support, often swooping in low and dropping ordnance where needed. I was made aware that they used napalm, but the authorities denied it; it was uncivilized, they suggested. The insurgents in the mountains who were at the receiving end would have agreed.

Moving about with the 'Mikes' had its moments, especially in the eastern mountains. There was one particularly well-defended hilltop

Gunner on board one of the El Salvadorian helicopter squadron's Hueys searched for targets of opportunity while we were heading towards the east of the country. (Author's collection)

position near the Honduran frontier that the government liked to attack. However, the rebels were well entrenched. It must have taken a lot of effort but they'd built a defensive system that included caves and trenches and were able to beat off several onslaughts.

After a Huey had been lost to ground fire there, some of Brown's troupe suggested that we go out on one of the operations then being planned. It would be an in-depth strike to unseat the enemy. 'Get some kills too', reckoned one of his number.

Brown would have none of it. 'We're not here to try to get ourselves killed', he said when the issue was raised for the third time. An old soldier – Bob Brown was a reserve half-colonel by the time he retired – he could pull the guys up sharp when he needed to do so.

For me, flying in helicopters in El Salvador was always interesting. I'd done it over much of Africa and written a book on the subject, *The Chopper Boys*. At one stage I had thousands of helio combat shots on file.[1]

In El Salvador, I was soon to discover, helicopter warfare was quite different from elsewhere. The same machines were employed but the terrain was dissimilar: much of it was intermittently jungle-covered mountain. Also, we were up against a more resilient adversary.

In the earlier period, the Hueys would fly at an altitude that the Americans liked to call 'avoidance radius'; a planning figure used to determine the distance that an aircraft should keep from a particular air defence weapon or system to avoid effective fire. It sounded complicated. Yet, looking back, it seemed that we must have presented fairly easy targets. At 4,000 feet, we were certainly well within range of any of the SAM-7s that we knew the other side had acquired from Moscow.

We were also well within range of any heavy enemy machine-guns, such as the 12.7mm DShKA or the 14.5mm KPV, both of which the FMLN had in abundance. While the equipment was hauled in on foot, invariably on the backs of men and occasionally mules, the rebels never appeared to be short of ammunition. They even brought in some multi-barrelled ZSUs of the kind that had awed me in Beirut and elsewhere in the Middle East often enough in the past.

Still, while the guerrilla gunners didn't appear to be all that well trained, they chipped away steadily at the resources of the *Fuerza Aérea*. The losses were never made public and one only heard about particular incidents on the grapevine, usually after a Huey or some other helicopter had been lost. Waghelstein's MilGroup knew exactly what had gone out. They also kept tabs on what came back to base, but they weren't telling us scribes.

One of the advantages of being airlifted in these choppers with their side-doors open was that, because of the noise, we never really knew if we'd become a target. We only really became aware that something was happening when tracers were spotted, quite often heading in our direction. One of the pilots once said that if they really counted the number of times they'd been fired at from the ground, the majority of air crews would probably have looked elsewhere for work. Another commented that it was all part of the fun. He actually meant it, because he and some of his buddies had come to relish the tension that had become part of the everyday drill.

None of it was easy, though. By the time we'd arrived in 1986, it was clear that most El Salvadorian air crews were under strain. That was when Washington stepped in and brought in the 'Pigs': American air-crews working in rotation from Honduras in 45-day tours of duty. The name came from their referring to themselves as 'Danger Pigs'. They called the Hueys 'Pigs' too, because by then those choppers were out of date. Obviously, they would have preferred a few of the same Blackhawks that their colleagues sported in Honduras, where a less-intensive guerrilla war was underway.

The Americans came into El Salvador as B Company, 4th Battalion, 228th Aviation Regiment in July 1987, but their home base, for the duration, was Soto Cano Air Base in Honduras. It was a clever piece of diplomatic sleight of hand to keep the US Congress off their back, even though officially these people didn't fly combat missions. As Harry Claflin reckoned, their main role was to ferry about MilGroup personnel.

Door gunners were drawn from the 193rd Infantry Brigade and they did tours of six months. While in San Salvador, this very committed group of individuals lived in a 'safe house' which, some say, was the third best-defended structure in the capital. The crew were discreetly taken to work at Ilopango and back home again in a van with heavily armour-plated tinted windows.

All these Americans followed complicated procedures that soon became part of the daily routine. Targets were jointly assessed by MilGroup and the Chiefs of Staff. The crew would then assemble on the night before an assignment to discuss routes, intelligence reports and other relevant information. Each team used a complex assessment matrix to project the level of danger likely to be experienced, whatever that might be.

It was superior military training, organized and implemented by American advisors, that swung the war in favour of the government in the end. It took a few years, but El Salvador eventually emerged with one of the best military establishments in the region. Here, a patrol moves warily through one of the towns in the eastern part of the country. (Author's collection)

Some South African pilots who had been at Ilopango said it was like having a photograph of somebody's lungs who had died of cancer in front of you while you were enjoying a cigarette. 'You knew there was danger; there was always danger', he told me, 'but you learnt to live with it', he added nonchalantly.

A number of aircraft were shot down over enemy lines in this war; both helicopters and fixed-winged machines. If a crew survived the crash, they were not treated kindly. In one attack, long after we'd departed, ground fire brought down a Huey 'Mike' outside the village of La Estancia about 12 miles north of San Miguel, the same area where we visited derelict coffee plantations while on a ground patrol. The enemy did to the air crews what government troops did to the guerrillas: they were almost always executed after having been made to talk.

The senior pilot, Chief Warrant Officer Dan Scott, was taking Lieutenant Colonel David Pickett, Officer Commanding (OC) of the 4th Battalion, 228th Aviation Regiment back to his headquarters in Honduras. He'd been on a staff visit to El Salvador and, as a shortcut, had flown from San Miguel towards San Francisco Gotera, and then tacked towards the north-east.

That way, he had reckoned, they'd reduce flying time and slip inside the established 'Green Three' route into Honduras that led directly to Soto Cano.

The twin M60s with which the Hueys were customarily armed, were strapped to the floor of the machine because officially, American air crews could not fly with guns mounted. Thus, for the duration of that trip they were inoperable. Again, it seems, the Yanks were the only guys in the street playing by the rules. The fact that the helicopter traversed a hotly contested region of conflict didn't appear to matter and, in any event, nobody told the guerrillas that the helicopter wasn't armed. They shot it down anyway.

As the war dragged on, the FMLN endured some formidable casualties. In the first six months of 1985, the El Salvadorian Armed Forces were responsible for about 3,200 insurgent losses (out of about eight or nine thousand). That included more than 1,500 of the enemy who'd surrendered. In the same time period, government forces lost 810 men killed, wounded or missing.

When the war began the El Salvadorian Air Force barely existed, even on paper. By 1983 it had 20 operational helicopters; less than two years later there were 60. Obviously, with that kind of potential, pilots had to come from elsewhere, which was when quite a few foreign aviators entered the picture, including a number from South Africa, all of them true-blue mercenaries.

This kind of escalation must have put enormous pressure on the guerrilla command. The attrition rate to their forces was clearly unacceptable. Like it or not, there came a time when the FMLN had to answer to the families of the dead. This was a people's war.

It was consequently no surprise that Nidia Diaz, a seasoned guerrilla commander with years in the field who was captured by an Air Force helicopter hunter squadron (it combined air operations with special ground forces missions), was found with a document showing that the rebel command had already abandoned all hope of an outright military victory. The gist of it was that a negotiated peace was the only way and some cadres were already beginning to say so publicly. Still, it took almost seven more years of fighting before that happened . . .

The 'Permanent Offensive' by the government compelled the rebels to reduce their forces from battalion-sized units to sections of anything from five to perhaps a dozen men. This transition became more marked when their objectives started to become more economic than military. What followed was an intense round of sabotage: bridges and power lines were knocked down; assassinations increased; there were ambushes in the field and agitation among students and labour movements.

As we flew between Ilopango and San Salvador we could observe some of the consequences. In one area, close to the capital, there were long lines of power pylons, each knocked over by an explosive charge laid at each concrete base. Also, we flew over numerous bridges that had been blown up. At one stage we were able to land where a huge structure straddling the Trans American Highway had been destroyed. It had once been a bridge, but it had been so badly blasted that little of its original form remained intact. Because of mines, we weren't allowed to move about.

By then about a third of the population was unemployed and in spite of governement military successes, conditions had deteriorated economically. That happens when so much of the army is tied up in guarding static assets, like bridges, electric plants, dams and so on. Consequently, more ordinary people were voting with their feet and taking their money with them. Things couldn't continue like that much longer.

The rebels, despite heavy losses, remained active till the end. Throughout, they showed remarkable versatility, coupled, in true Castro fashion – the Cuban leader was one of the architects of what was called the 'People's Struggle' – with an utter ruthlessness of purpose.

There are those counter-insurgency pundits who consider the FMLN, in its day, as one of the best unconventional armies of the time. They reckon, even now – and despite having lost the war – that when the guerrillas fought, there were no restrictions. They waged their war in the age-old traditional manner of using every means at their disposal to harm the enemy. There was never a question of its having one arm tied behind its back, and the fact that the international press gave them tacit support counted for an awful lot.

CHAPTER TEN

Somalia: Wars of No Consequence

'As a trouble spot, Somalia is a familiar name to many people in America. Yet even before the Mogadishu warlord, self-appointed 'General' Farrah Aideed had become a real issue, a drama of horrific proportions was in the process of unravelling in this troubled corner of East Africa. It's a place where violence always appears to have been the norm.'

Al J. Venter, *The Chopper Boys*[1]

E VEN BY POST-IMPERIAL STANDARDS in Africa, Somalia is in an awful mess. That's nothing new because the Horn of Africa has been a battleground for as long as it has been inhabited by man. Judging by what's going on there now, it remains ungovernable. As we go to press, there are more abductions there than ever before, more assassinations than ever make the news, an intrusive al-Qaeda presence and, more recently, an ever-growing list of ships taken by pirates operating almost with impunity from bases on the Somali mainland.

I'd been visiting the place off-and-on from the late 1960s. The first time I landed at Mogadishu was the morning after American astronaut Neal Armstrong took his momentous 'giant step for mankind'. I returned with my wife Madelon in the mid 1970s. She found it a fascinating, if disturbing, backwater that reflected ominous undertones for the future. She was actually glad to return to Nairobi after a week because the writing was already on the wall that the place meant trouble.

In those days, the few journalists who made the effort to get to Mogadishu from Addis Ababa (usually on their own initiative, having managed to persuade their editors that the country was newsworthy) found themselves in an altogether different environment from that to which they'd been accustomed elsewhere in Africa. Even then, Mogadishu – a city that had once been a quiet little Italian colonial outpost – was extraordinarily remote.

Little had happened in Somalia since the British and the South

Africans drove Mussolini's fascists out in 1941. The people then were just as surly and unkempt as they are today (which might be expected when there is no work), the cars on the road are decrepit – often with 12-year-olds at the wheel – the electricity supply is erratic, plumbing in hotels (if you could find one worthy of the name) is capricious and more often than not, their loos don't flush.

As the late Lord Bill Deedes once said about the place, it 'was an uncovenanted mercy'. It is much worse today . . .

The main post office, when we got there in the 1980s, had a single bulb in its cavernous roof with no doors or windows. It was closed for the day when the official felt like it, or when the regular shipment of *Qat* arrived by air from the Ethiopian highlands – an unsurprising event since much of the nation is addicted. It had a single public telephone for all communications with the world outside, cemented to a concrete pillar in the middle of the hall. Since satellite phones were still in a

Aerial view of Mogadishu taken from the sea. The city was formerly a peaceful colonial haven, a first for the Italians (prior to World War II) and then for the British. However, in the 1970s a series of army mutinies intervened: these were coupled to fierce exchanges between rival groups of Islamic militants which eventually crippled the country and left it without an effective government for decades. (Author's collection)

development phase, it meant that if my wife wanted to talk to our children, she had to wait in a long line, often well into the night.

Mogadishu, built solidly on a range of white sandstone cliffs that stretch back into the desert behind, was different in other respects. About a quarter of the size of Nairobi, it was remarkably expansive and faced onto a broad lagoon bounded by a reef about half-a-mile out. The place was like one of those tiny colonial blips on the map that we read about at school when Conrad was prescribed. However, it was safe, and it stayed that way, at least until the Jihadis arrived.

In those distant days, as my wife and I discovered, we could sleep securely. Nobody stole anything from our hotel room, such as it was. Twice my wife had to walk some distance to the post office and back after dark to call home. She was never molested or insulted in those mysterious, malodorous streets that reeked of a combination of urine and cardamom.

Before the war levelled the town, the Italian imprint was ubiquitous. There were raffia-clad bottles of Chianti on every dinner table, the chemist's shop bore the legend *Farmacia* and was manned by knowledgeable expatriates who had been born in Bari or Palermo and the police wore the same peaked caps issued under the rule of *Il Duce*.

In the 1960s and until fairly recently, Mogadishu reflected a dilapidated sun-bleached mixture of European, African and Muslim buildings, some with high walls and steel gates that enclosed delightful tropical gardens. It was a bit like parts of the Coté d'Azur, only all the faces were dark and the inhabitants wore the kind of garb that Somalis like – long, easy-flowing robes from which the East African *kikoi* was adapted long ago.

At the heart of the city stood a magnificent Roman Catholic cathedral, the biggest, it was said, south of the Mediterranean. Like much else in Mogadishu, it was gutted during the civil war. There was also a fine old Imperial Arch in the Italian tradition, complete with marble columns and enriched with bas-reliefs. It was modelled after the fashion of such things since Caesar's Rome and ensuing pseudo-Romes.

Il Villaggio Anzilotti was the suburb that boasted the best brothels and lay west of the old harbour that Gaius Plinius Secundus – otherwise known as Pliny the Elder – mentioned in his writings almost 2,000 years ago. The streets were all *Via*; Via Damasco, Via Roma, Via Congo and so on. It was an ancient place, perhaps the oldest settlement on the east coast of Africa south of the Sudan and was said to have had a Chinese quarter a thousand years ago.

Towards dusk we foreign waifs would drift along 'sunset strip' towards a succession of diplomatic beach clubs that stood in dozens of neat rows, each commanding its own few square yards of yellow sand fronting onto the lagoon. The British encampment was next to the Russians, or was it the Poles? Alongside that stood a kind of American 'home-from-home', the only place in that staunchly Muslim land where you could get hash browns with your eggs on Sunday morning and female staff could still wear bikinis without having stones thrown at them.

Nearly every night was party night. With the Cold War in full swing (Somalia having thrown out the Russians and embraced the Americans, and let it not be said only for material reasons), we tended to favour Western establishments, while those of the Eastern Bloc remained stiffly aloof from the sometimes raucous goings on a few feet away. We'd wave amicably at each other if we caught an eye.

I made the Italian Club my base: a flimsy shack with a grass and corrugated iron roof and electric fans big enough to make life bearable. There was obviously no air-conditioning since all the doors and windows stood permanently open. Whatever breeze there was, arrived from the sea, usually towards evening, though it could be stifling in the dry season, which was for eight months of the year.

The real thrash would begin a little before midnight, when first Franco and later Gino – both local boys of Italian parents whose families had settled in Somalia between the wars – looked for volunteers for the regular cheetah shoot. I called it a cheetah slaughter and they didn't like it. It was of such frequency while I was there that I and my American friends were surprised that there were any of these big cats left along this desolate stretch of the coast.

I'd enjoyed good hunting in Africa in my day, and I might have been tempted; but they were using floodlights and running these beautiful animals down in four-wheel-drive vehicles, like an Australian kangaroo romp.

Towards midnight Somali ladies would appear out of the dark, almost every one of them tall, graceful, stunningly alluring and actually quite modest. Most reflected an air of diffidence, almost as if the world belonged to them, which, I suppose it did. They were strikingly beautiful. They were also incredibly slender in their *kikoi* skirts, usually with nothing on underneath. Some had the grace of a desert gazelle.

Somali women generally are blessed with high cheek-bones and beautiful soft eyes; any one of those that we encountered along the beachfront on the outskirts of Mogadishu could easily have stepped out of a Pirelli calendar.

Many of the journalistic tribe found them irresistible. Cheap, too; for those inclined it was two dollars for a 'quickie', or knee tremblers, we called them. The alternative was ten dollars for a night in a hotel, but then you had to fork out for breakfast as well. Two breakfasts on an expense sheet submitted to your editor invariably raised questions, so it was generally a no-no.

Since all these women were Muslim, they wouldn't drink in public, which was another attraction, for whisky in Mogadishu was expensive, usually three or four times what it cost in Nairobi. Still, everybody had a party and some scribes with more money than sense would take along two of these ladies at a time. Not surprisingly, they got the clap or worse. Such afflictions could be cured with antibiotics, but that was before AIDS rampaged across the African continent. It was only a matter of time . . .

Internecine strife put a stop to all the fun. The generals who took over Somalia after they murdered President Abd-ir-Rashid Ali Shermarke in the 1970s were soon squabbling among themselves. Then the killings started and it became almost obsessively brutal. An obscure new kind of artificial 'nationalism' was invented – as well as a written language, which looked like something out of *Star Wars* – and those who ensconced themselves in Mogadishu's long-defunct parliament laid claim to a lot of territory that belonged to their increasingly unfriendly neighbours.

In particular, they eyed Djibouti, which had been a French colony as part of what they liked to call 'Greater Somalia'. Then they demanded the 'return' of fairly large chunks of land that had been ruled almost forever by a no-nonsense and exceedingly belligerent government in Addis Ababa. They blundered badly when the Somali ruffians who ran the show sent their army into the Ogaden in Ethiopia, and it was Soviet hardware and training that drove them out of that useless strip of desert where nobody lived anyway.

That was the start of it. Subterfuge, insurrections, intrigue by the bucketful and army mutinies have continued ever since. More recently, al-Qaeda got into the act and Mark Bowden gave us a pretty good insight into that mayhem in his classic *Black Hawk Down*. The book is as accurate a depiction of any I've seen of Somalia before or after the

American attempt to try to inculcate a bit of sense into a nation that will probably never understand the word. Not in my lifetime, in any event.

There were other, less dramatic aberrations, but the final crunch for the people of Mogadishu came when some idiot allowed a local businessman to build a slaughterhouse just outside the town and dump several tons of camel guts into the lagoon every day. Soon every other shark in the Indian Ocean seemed to have assembled off the Somali coast and attacks on humans became so frequent that foreign embassies forbade their staff and their nationals to swim in the sea.

Horror stories followed. Boats coming through the cut in the reef would overturn if the weather suddenly turned nasty and everyone on board would be taken by the sharks, sometimes within minutes. Children sitting on boats with their feet in the water sometimes lost them. On 'sunset strip' the rule was that kids on the beach were not even to wet their toes. The Italians paid two million dollars for steel shark nets, but by the time the politicians had siphoned off their percentages, there was hardly enough left for a tennis court.

I went back to Somalia early in 1993, not long after the first American soldiers landed on Mogadishu beach in a spectacular show of force:

By the time the Americans arrived in Somalia at the start of Operation Restore Hope, there wasn't a window pane intact in Mogadishu's International Airport. Not much worked either, though the US Army presence was manifest. (Author's collection)

their faces blackened, flak-jackets in place and M16s at high port. They were astonished to be greeted by dozens of television crews who had been watching this pantomime from the shore. Among those awaiting them was my old pal Mohammed Amin.

It was planned as an amphibious invasion and though it was exactly that, the whole caboodle ended in farce. While some officers were expecting trouble, there was none. It stayed passive until a group of GIs started banging Somali heads together as they fanned out across the airport. The trouble was, the Somalis they encountered happened to be legitimate: almost all of those already at the airport were in the employ of the United Nations units in the country. Some sharp words were exchanged between the UN commander and the American officer in charge before these Rambo wannabees were curtailed.

American participation in Somalia, Operation Restore Hope, could hardly be rated as a war, at least not until events got out of hand and several US helicopters were brought down by dissidents in the main part of Mogadishu. There were 22 nations directly involved, many of them Western – including France and Italy – as well as quite a few others such as Turkey, Egypt, Oman, Saudi Arabia, Zimbabwe, Pakistan and Botswana. The trouble was, very few of these soldiers had ever heard a shot fired in anger, much less fought in a war.

Altogether 30,000 strong, they faced a mixed bag of Somali warlords who were always at each others' throats, including a crafty rogue and former US Marine by the name of Mohammed Farah Aideed, who, with his equally duplicitous father, had done much to cripple the country. For years this totally unscrupulous executioner had been stealing food intended to feed Somalia's starving millions. At one stage he was even exporting it to neighbouring states for profit.

Meanwhile, all these tribal *padroni* had acquired a formidable arsenal of modern weapons from many different countries. They included British and Russian mines (the former from World War II, mostly taken out of the Libyan desert); Russian small arms and rocket-propelled grenades; Italian, Spanish, Brazilian, Chinese, Portuguese and American rifles and a miscellany of heavier weapons from South Africa, Germany, Iran, Syria, North Korea, France and elsewhere. If it could kill or cripple, the ferocious rabble in the streets of Mogadishu wanted more of it.

The foreign troops in Somalia were more of a rescue mission than a fighting force. However, it didn't take them long to forget that it was the

The aircraft 'graveyard' at Mogadishu Airport included scores of more recent Soviet fighter aircraft as well as several British Canberra bombers and bits and pieces from several transport aircraft. In Somalia's dry climate, the place holds a trove of perfectly useable spare parts which ongoing hostilities have prevented anybody from exploiting. (Author's collection)

plight of a million or so starving children that had brought them there in the first place. As soon as things turned nasty, most of those countries couldn't wait to get their soldiers out of there. They argued that since the killings had become rampant, the Somalis could settle their own differences as they pleased. It was their pigeon anyway, and I suppose, they were right.

As it happened, the Americans led the retreat. In spite of the loss of life that Mark Bowden wrote about, it was quite a commendable effort, even if it cost more lives than it should have. Washington's role amounted to a brief footnote in contemporary African history.

Remarkably, my own visit at that time was not prompted by any wish to experience another war, or to join hordes of journalists already packed into the few hotels that were still open for business. I had nearly finished my latest book, *The Chopper Boys*, which deals with helicopter warfare in Africa and I wanted something unusual to take it right into the 1990s. What better place than a troubled corner of Africa where Washington had deployed 100 modern and well-equipped American helicopters. The choppers were responsible for most of the communications, supplies and air combat roles in which the UN had become engaged.

My first impressions after landing at Mogadishu Airport were instructive. I hadn't expected to find dozens of wrecked aircraft lining the runway. There were Chinese and Russian MiGs, Sukhois, British-built Canberra bombers and what was left of American C-47s lying at the far end of the runway. The place was an aircraft junkyard and curiously, most of it was salvageable, even if the Somalis didn't yet know it.

The airport looked as if it had been repeatedly bombed and nobody had bothered to repair it. In fact, each time anybody tried to fix something, more mortars or RPG-7 rockets would come shuddering in.

I recall that the words 'Welcome to Mogadishu Airport' were still legible, with a few of the letters missing on the terminal building. I also remember writing that not a single pane of glass was intact.

When we got out of the USAF Hercules that had brought us from Mombasa, we were met by an Arab soldier who didn't bother even to check our papers before herding us into a rattletrap bus that had once belonged to the Mogadishu Municipality. He deposited us at what was left of the old terminal building.

It took me hours to cadge a lift to the United Nations Operation in Somalia (UNOSOM) headquarters north-east of the airport. There, I reckoned, I'd be able to put phase two of my plan into effect.

211

The force guarding the airport was about to be relieved, I was told. I could go into the city and from there to the UN compound. 'But first, you must sign this indemnity, if you please', an Egyptian officer ordered: If you get killed or wounded, there can be no claim on the United Nations.'

I signed: what else could I do?

Since we'd all be travelling through hostile territory on the back of a truck, the pre-convoy briefing was specific: 'Keep to the middle of the vehicle. Stay well down. Don't expose yourself. They snipe at us from time to time . . . if we stop and they climb on board, hold onto your bags, your wallet and your spectacles. If you don't, they'll steal everything that isn't bolted down.' The order came from a cynical Canadian NCO who had clearly been through the mill.

With that we were off into Mogadishu proper, or what American grunts liked to refer to as 'The Dish'. The column of five UN vehicles was escorted fore and aft by French armoured personnel carriers with their hatches shut. I sat behind a group of Gulf soldiers manning a .50 Browning and the rest of the troops had their weapons cocked, facing outwards.

We drove past the old Russian compound, and then turned left before we reached the *Villaggio Quattro Chilometri*.

Suddenly I was in a world a lot more outlandish than anything I'd known before, even second-hand. Nor was it for lack of experience. I had been in Beirut when the Israelis invaded Lebanon in 1982 and though war raged, the city and the people who lived there had some sort of shape to their lives. It was dangerous, sure, but the chaos, as one wag wrote, was ordered. Mogadishu, in contrast, was utter pandemonium.

The city sprawls. Approach it from the sea during the monsoon and it is an awesome mish-mash of muddy pools, piles of garbage, open sewers coupled to the turmoil of hoards of the kind of pullulating crowds that only Africa can sometimes produce. The conglomeration stretched as far as you could see and it really did intimidate.

Just about every building that we passed had been blasted. The road was lined with the wrecks of cars and trucks blown apart in who-knows-how-many battles for control. A burnt-out Humvee, already speckled with rust, spoke of the events of months before. There was a time when any American military vehicle was fair game for Aideed's rag-tag horde.

As I – and the rest of the world – was only to discover afterwards, there was no clear line of demarcation between the various factions. In

American troops – in this case female soldiers – loading ammunition at one of the
military bases in the interior. (Author's collection)

a sense, it was Beirut incarnate, only worse . . .

Every man carried a weapon, and that often included youngsters not yet ten years old. Women, children, the old, crippled and the maimed milled about on and off the road and in and out of narrow alleys. There were hundreds of paths and improvised weapon-pits between the few structures that remained intact. The road itself was impassable in parts because jagged blocks of concrete, oil drums and wrecked cars had been hauled across the pot-holed tarmac to slow movement. Pools of filthy green water remained from the monsoons and children played in the muck.

When we reached the marketplace after what was listed on the charts as 27th October Square, the throng overflowed onto the road and the convoy was forced to slow. There were times when we were limited to a crawl. One felt terribly vulnerable in that mishmash of humanity where just about every other male was armed, if only with a pistol secreted in the belt or a switch-blade in the pocket. The fact that the entire route had suddenly become a kind of Middle Eastern *souk* was worrying.

Arms flailing, the people alongside were in our faces, shouting, gesticulating at us, at each other. Their expressions were contorted, their eyes glazed or bloodshot, the effects of *Qat*, no doubt.

One of the soldiers on board told me that near this same market, American Blackhawks had been hit by RPGs, twice in past weeks. One of the aviators had been killed and those who'd survived were savagely mauled.

He pointed to a mass of twisted metal. 'That was once a helicopter, a Blackhawk', he intimated. It was almost unrecognizable. It took a little longer before we eventually pulled into the American diplomatic compound with its heavy weapons bunkers bristling with firepower.

'We go here', said the soldier. 'You go now', he pointed his carbine towards some buildings and smiled when I thanked him in Arabic: *Shukran.*

The big UN flag on its pole on the roof of the tallest building hardly stirred, but it did tell me that I'd reached the headquarters of the American commander of UNOSOM.

I didn't stay long in Mogadishu. Following an identity check, I was sent to the office of Lieutenant Colonel Fred Peck, a Marine officer who dealt with the foreign correspondent community in what had already become a dubious enterprise for the Americans. Congress was baying for 'our boys' to get the hell out of that African shit-hole. Placating journalists every day, Colonel Peck couldn't afford to put a foot wrong.

A charming, forthright veteran of several American military ventures of his own, including Vietnam, this professional soldier handled this delicate assignment with aplomb. What he didn't do was stand on ceremony.

He looked me up and down for a few seconds when I told him that I wasn't too much interested in East Africa's starving millions, a comment that raised a few eyebrows among those nearest me. Instead, I explained what I wanted and showed him a dummy copy of *The Chopper Boys* that I'd prepared for the Frankfurt Book Fair.

'Yep,' said Peck: 'Reckon you do have different needs.' He addressed one of his officers nearby.

'Take Mr Venter here to Marty [Major Martin Culp II] and let's see whether we can get him up to Baledogle. They can fly him out on one of the Hawks', he ordered.

Baledogle, as I was to learn, was the main American helicopter base, about 150 clicks north of Mogadishu and situated alongside a remote

US Marine helicopters formed about half the complement of roughly 100 choppers that operated out of Baledogle. Many were CH-53s, which played a valuable transport role during the war. (Author's Collection)

village in the interior. It had formerly been used as a staging base by the Soviets before Somalia switched sides halfway through the Cold War.

'Everything that happens with choppers you'll find there', a female major told me. The Army flew mainly UH-60 Blackhawks and the Marines CH-53 Sea Stallions as well as Super Cobra AH-IW gunships. Baledogle had originally been chosen by the Russians as a strategic air base because of its isolation.

It took a couple of days before I was flown north and I entered a part of Africa that had never been kind to man. In fact, it reminded me most of the Sahel: almost all of it desert with sparse grass cover, but more than enough stunted thorn bushes. Here and there an ill-nourished acacia poked through, the only foliage not ravaged by goats. This was a hard place in which to survive, one of the most inhospitable I've encountered on any continent.

The town by the base – more of an assemblage of low buildings that appeared to be held together by bits of twine, plastic bags, animal skins and wire – was typically Somali hardscrabble. Its signature, like most settlements in the Somali interior, was rotting heaps of garbage that surrounded it. There had once been a clinic, distinguished by its whitewashed walls, but the doctor had long since gone. A clutch of vultures perched on its roof.

From the air, the base looked impressive, but this was misleading. There were a few barn-like concrete buildings that had been built by the Soviets, but that was long ago. Some looked like barracks, others had clearly been headquarters of one form or another. The control tower was skeletal, its roof held up by a dozen steel struts. Above flew two flags, that of the United States and that of the UN.

As with Mogadishu Airport, almost every fitting had been ripped out of the walls. It had clearly been years since the windows had last seen glass and the doors had been smashed for firewood long ago.

Once the Americans arrived, they erected several huge tent-like sheds along the perimeter; in fact, these were the first structures we spotted as we approached by chopper from the south. Always assiduous on foreign soil, it hadn't taken the Yanks long to set up their own hangars and workshops, each of them portable and flown in from America. Alongside were hundreds of cargo stacks, some two or three storeys high: enough stores, containers, vehicles, aircraft and spare parts to keep the war going for a year. In between stood the tents for the men and women who worked there.

Rows of what were once to have been engines for a Soviet aircraft factory to be built in Somalia lie scattered in the bush at Baledogle, about 100 miles north of the capital. (Author's collection)

As we circled, the pilot pointed at dozens of circular metal objects below: jet engines, dozens of them, neatly laid out in the bush and some half-buried in sand.

'Russian . . . MiG-21 engines', he shouted into the mike. He explained afterwards that Baledogle was to have become an assembly point for MiG-21 fighters, the first of its kind in Black Africa. This gear originally included thousands of cases of machinery, spares and other equipment that had been hauled up to Baledogle in a succession of truck convoys, the entire operation taking a year.

'We were ecstatic', said the Somali interpreter. 'We were to have our own factories for those planes. Somalia was to be a leader in Africa. We thought at the time that there would be work for everybody. Somalia would become a power. The Russians told us so. Like fools, we believed them.' His eyes blazed. Then, he added, some bureaucrat killed the project. He didn't get the bribe he'd been offered, or perhaps it ended up in somebody else's bank account. 'The project was stillborn even as we were digging the foundations.'

Nobody in Mogadishu knows the whole story. Most of those

217

involved were dead anyway. From what I could make out, cover-ups in Mogadishu and the universal corruption of Africa smothered the project before it got properly under way. Yet, my informant ventured, millions had been spent in getting as far as they did, to which all this abandoned hardware testified.

'All wasted. Think of the hospitals we could have built . . . schools.'

None of us had even heard of Baledogle until Operation Restore Hope. It was the best-kept Russian secret in Africa and I could see why.

The Blackhawk had been late in getting to Mogadishu Airport to pick me up. I had to be taken there in a Humvee, one of a new generation of American military vehicles that became familiar during Operation Desert Storm and afterwards, throughout Iraq and Afghanistan.

From Colonel Peck's UNOSOM headquarters, we retraced our previous route back to the airport. This time there was a Marine sergeant standing in a 'well' at the back of the infantry carrier with an extremely useful wooden staff that he used to dissuade hopeful Somalis from clambering on board. Even so, one made a dive for my Nikon. We struggled for possession until a smart blow knocked the thief sideways and he fell almost under our wheels.

If the Humvee had been moving at speed, we'd have driven over him in the middle of the main market, among thousands of people. Certainly, the mob would have turned on us in a flash. The troops on board carried live ammunition for just such an event, and they would have used it had they needed to. Their instructions were clear: don't hesitate to use your weapons if your lives are threatened.

It's worth mentioning that all the journalists in Mogadishu knew about rough measures handed out by the troops, especially to robbers and thieves who wouldn't think twice about sticking a knife to your throat if they thought they could get away with it. Consequently, because these scribes were at the receiving end, and being continually threatened, few ever mentioned anything about this kind of retaliation in their reports.

We all knew that we needed these soldiers for our own security, especially those of us who couldn't afford personal bodyguards. If it involved a few cracked skulls to keep the rabble at bay, then so be it.

CHAPTER ELEVEN

Air Operations in the Horn of Africa

'It seemed like another 10th Aviation Brigade field exercise as a
3-17 Cavalry Scout weapons team lifted into the blue African
sky. Crew Chiefs of the 3-25 Assault Helicopter Battalion
serviced their UH-60 Skyhawks, staff planning continued
without a break in the tactical operations center, mechanics and
cooks carried out their tasks . . .'

Captain Tom McCann reports from
Baledogle, Somalia, early 1993

BECAUSE WE ARRIVED LATE AT Baledogle, at one stage the largest
operational American air base on the continent of Africa, we missed
dinner. Somebody organized some fruit, a can of sardines and bottled
water and we were grateful, for there are few favours meted out in most
military establishments I've visited.

I shared a tent with the padre and his first words to me in the fading
light were: 'Watch out for scorpions in your boots in the morning. And
snakes in the dark, when you take a leak.'

Baledogle, I quickly learnt, was serpent country. Quite a few of the
troops had been bitten and a handful had to be flown to the military
hospital in Mogadishu. None had died from a bite, though, so it could
have been worse. According to the padre, they killed snakes every day,
cobras of ten feet or more and sometimes a viper. There were enough of
the venomous variety around to start a herpetarium. The men towed a
dead cobra at the end of a length of nylon gut through the women's
showers one evening with the satisfying result of several naked ladies
bolting into the night.

One of my first impressions of the base was that there were a lot of
women at Baledogle, including senior officers. Major Pauline Knapp
commanded the 159th Medical Company. Her husband, also in the
army, had stayed behind at the base in Germany, 'to play golf' she joked.
Hers was the wing responsible for most medical evacuations in Somalia.

The unit's motto, she pointed out, was appropriate: *Anywhere, Any Place, Anytime – You Call, We Haul.*

Pauline Knapp was a firm, sassy and very professional lady who boasted that she hailed 'from the wrong side of the Hudson in New Jersey'. A graduate of Rutgers, much of her time off duty was spent preparing for her Masters.

That said, she had her time cut out for her. With her crews, the helicopter unit covered almost the entire country (except the north-east, where the French operated their Super Pumas). Her medical company, she reckoned, was there to bring back casualties – as well as the dead – to field hospitals 'as quickly and as humanely as possible'.

The work kept her busy. If she and her husband could manage a weekend a month together, they were lucky. 'But when we do, it's quality time', she joked with a delightful smile that said it all.

'I run a lot . . . keeps me sane', she added quickly.

At Baledogle I also met Captain Yvette Kelly and her husband Colonel James Kelly, Executive Officer at the base. They'd met some years before at a military base in California and served together through Operation Just Cause in Panama, where Yvette flew combat helicopters.

Each week the couple shared two important events: a film, and thereafter, 'big eats', which comprised some cans of food from home that might even include a good-quality imported *pâté de foie gras*, all nicely laid out on a table – covered by a spotless white tablecloth – and decorated with a few bottles of Evian water between them. It usually happened in the mess where there was much coming and going, but these two lovers – a couple of ordinary Joes anywhere else in the world – were oblivious to anything else.

I was soon to discover that routines at Baledogle rarely varied. The first call came shortly after five in the morning and entailed an five- or eight-kilometre run depending on the mood of the duty officer. Nobody was excluded, unless with good reason. It wouldn't go on your record if you didn't make it, but the omission would be noted. Likewise with the last run of the day towards evening, not compulsory but conscientiously observed.

There were two meals: a regular brunch and a dinner, both adequate, but hardly memorable. The cooks had a job to do and they weren't looking for stars, though I never heard anybody complain.

In Mogadishu and Baledogle officers and men alike ate together. In Mogadishu the mess hall was vast and pre-fabricated, fitted with only two doors, one for entry and another for those on their way out. In Baledogle, by contrast, everything took place outside, under whatever shade could be found.

We ate standing up to make room for those who came later and there was no loitering. As with everything else, you did what you had to and got on with your duties.

If you didn't like the menu, there were always MREs which provided variety and you could eat them, hot or cold, anywhere you liked. 'Dishes' – such as they were – were all freeze dried and included meatballs and spaghetti, sirloin and mushrooms, a variety of chicken prepared every which way and neatly presented in little vacuum sachets that could be heated on a solid fuel cooker. It was the same sort of thing that American astronauts and their Russian counterparts ate when they were aloft.

Apart from the need to exercise, life at the air base was about as laid back as it might be with a unit serving under difficult conditions. All ranks used the same showers and toilets, although there were particular times reserved for the women to wash. Since water was controlled it was only available for an hour a day.

The latrines at Baledogle, plastic 'porta-potty' boxes, faced each other with a modest hessian screen separating the sexes. It was the job of one of the female soldiers each morning to empty night soil into a great pit on the edge of the camp, douse it with kerosene and put a match to it; an unenviable task in that heat, but somebody had to do it.

There was one difference in rank. At Baledogle the warrant officers – almost all of them chopper pilots – managed to set up a rudimentary open-air mess for themselves a short distance from the rest. In that remote wilderness it was an extravagance to which only a select few were invited. Since I was the first journalist to stay over in the camp, I was inducted by a ritual that also included something a little more potent with our coffee afterwards.

The outdoor senior NCO mess – it was actually more like a mobile canteen – was operated by CW4 Dave Coates, an old Vietnam hand who, in Somalia, flew AH-1 Cobra helicopters. He was a veteran soldier typical of any army and junior officers tended to steer clear of him because he wasn't afraid to say what was in his head. As head honcho, Dave dominated his little coterie with scant regard for rank. As he blandly stated while pouring us another 'wee dram' long after the others had got their heads down, he was due for his ticket anyway.

The senior NCO mess had the only working fridge outside the sick bay and it was kept locked. That might be why there were always beer cans in the unit's garbage bags each morning.

Alcohol was forbidden among American forces while serving in Somalia, ostensibly because it was a Muslim country. That was nonsense of course, since the French, Australians and Italians all got a drinks issue. No Mediterranean native would start a meal without his half-litre of red, but for the Americans, one couldn't help but get the impression that booze seemed to be a taboo left over from prohibition.

It was the same with tobacco. The no-smoking rule at Baledogle, while not promulgated, was effectively enforced among these adult men and women serving their country thousands of miles from home. No drink, no smokes, and (for most) no sex. Small wonder then that some of the troops needed counselling halfway through their deployment.

Naturally there were those who smoked. There were even cigarettes and Skoal chewing tobacco for sale at the base PX, but it was clear that those who partook were 'observed' by those who didn't. Like outcast lepers, they'd wander about the camp looking furtively over their shoulders whenever they pulled out a pack. Since I smoked occasionally, I joined them, if only to offer moral support.

For all that, just about everyone at Baledogle – and Mogadishu – was on first-name terms, officers included. A walk through the operations centre, where I spent quite a few days while still at headquarters, was as casual as a country club in Miami.

Martin Culp II, Captain, United States Army, was Marty to everybody. Yet he was a senior air force officer with a good deal of responsibility for what was going on in the country at the time. A helicopter pilot himself, his job at HQ was to lead a group of officers who planned daily strikes against hostile groups in the interior. It entailed flying armed helicopters against both Aideed's men and those Somalis who opposed him, like the Qat-chewing Colonel Morgan and the irascible Ali Mahdi Mohammed.

If there was a line of demarcation between officers and the men and women under their command, I didn't detect it, except routine salutes when moving about base. Culp would ask, rather than command, somebody to do something. More accustomed to British military tradition, the level of familiarity astonished me.

There was a limit, however, and to a large extent it applied to the sexes. Any officer who used rank to entice a female soldier into his bunk did so at risk. 'Career terminators' was the phrase most often used, but judging by the number of women soldiers who were sent home pregnant, discipline couldn't have been that well enforced. As they say, love laughs at locksmiths and military regulations.

Part of the problem lay in the isolation of the base. It was a rough and tumble reality that Somalia must have been one of the few countries in which UN forces were never able to have 'R & R' within its borders. Even in Angola, had these soldiers been serving there, they would have been able to get away to some of the most beautiful beaches in Africa, all within a day's drive south of Luanda.

In Somalia, most of those who wished to escape the strain of living

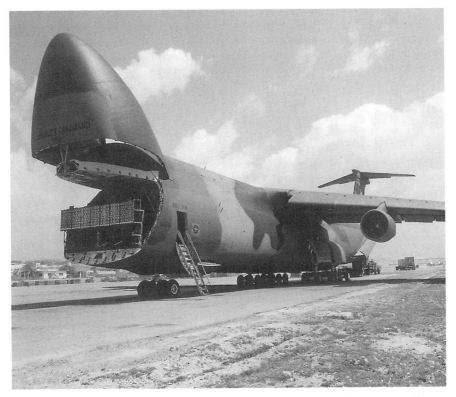

One of the giant USAF transports bringing in supplies to Mogadishu Airport. These aircraft didn't linger: they came in, unloaded, took on passengers and the wounded and took off again. Turnabout would be measured in minutes rather than in hours. It was the same later in Iraq and Afghanistan. (Author's collection)

within an arm's reach of some of the worst violence anywhere, had only one option and that was Kenya. Troops could sometimes get onto one of the C-130 transports that ferried supplies between Mogadishu and Mombasa. There were also flights to Nairobi.

I met Colonel Mike Dallas, commanding officer of the 2nd Brigade HQS of the 10th Mountain Division on my first morning at the base. Small, wiry and fit, he had a pair of eyes that missed nothing. 'Intimidating' was how Dave Coates described him.

Mike Dallas was the ultimate soldiers' soldier and it showed. He tolerated no laxity, not when you're that far from home. If an officer couldn't do what was expected of him, he was out on the next flight.

Colonel Dallas was one of the first of the American field commanders to arrive in Somalia and had been instrumental in putting together this expeditionary force while the unit was still at Fort Drum, home base in upstate New York. After I left, he returned to the Horn for a second tour, and again, was one of the last to leave.

We exchanged letters afterwards, when he'd been transferred to the Pentagon. A few years later I spotted him in a CNN newscast leading a unit on its way to Haiti. His eagle will have been replaced by a star by now, or who knows, perhaps even two. A healthy cut above the average senior military officer that we writers are likely to meet in present-day US military postings, Mike Dallas perfectly fits the stereotype of an American commander in foreign parts.

It was interesting that journalists who covered the Gulf War were expecting cigar-waving, loud-mouthed, leather jacketed smart-asses in uniform when they first set foot in that military theatre, especially among aviators. Then, when there was a lull in the fighting, the generals decided that it might possibly be in everybody's interest to introduce some of the young combatants to the scribblers. Most journalists who had never had any kind of contact with military people before – except in the movies – were astonished.

Instead of a bunch of gung-ho war heroes, they discovered a body of quiet, efficient and, more often than not, self-effacing airmen. The majority had just returned from sorties over Iraq and had seen a lot of action. Quite a few had been seriously shot at, yet there were very few in their ranks who took themselves too seriously. Rather, most declared, it was a job that needed to be done. More to the point, commented several, what was happening just then in Iraq was the culmination of all their training and frankly, they enjoyed doing it. Not a word was said about the extraordinary measure of dedication that made the whole thing work.

They still chewed their gum, liked root beer with a float, enjoyed Sunday football, spoke to their families back home almost every day and some would even admit to being extremely nervous whenever the situation over the battlefield became awkward. When asked about this operation or that, or what they thought might have transpired behind enemy lines, there emerged a very balanced and well-educated crowd of young men and women who were not only professional in their approach to what they did, but actually enjoyed the challenge.

Moreover, there wasn't one among them who did not have a thorough grasp of the situation, not only on the battlefield, but also in the world around them.

What also came to light was that the majority were university graduates, quite often a good deal better educated (and better-informed) than the journos who were throwing cynical questions about. Some of the hacks in our pack were so churlish that it made some of the older professionals cringe.

There were several developments that surprised us all while working with American forces in Somalia. One was the decision by the US Congress to pull out most of their troops halfway through the campaign.

From an initial deployment of 28,000 soldiers in the Horn of Africa, the American in-country command was finally left with just 6,000, a large proportion of whom were not combatants. Also, they were very much on their own because, with some notable exceptions, the support they got from the majority of UN contingents was lukewarm. One observer called it a strategic *coitus interruptus*.

Perhaps it was inevitable that Somalia should revert to anarchy even before the last American chopper had pulled out.

What is not generally accepted about the American effort in Somalia is that while Washington had men on the ground in this vast north-east African state, it was they and not the rest of the multinational force who ran the show. The Americans took a while to get their act together, but after that everything became proactive. For a start, US forces played a vital role in separating the factions and if any of the warlords stepped out of line, he took a beating.

UH-60 Blackhawk assault helicopters regularly hit rebel positions in

Afghoi, Jilib, Belet Uen and Marka. The recalcitrants were dealing with hard men armed with some serious weapons. History, one of the unit commanders told me, had long since proved that the only response to such people was strong and sustained action.

The bloody battle that eventually ended Washington's role at the vanguard in Somalia was the 'Black Hawk Down' incident that resulted in the loss of 18 American soldiers – several of them Special Forces as well as some air crew – all of whom were involved in trying to capture one of Somalia's most notorious warlords.

By some accounts, the Americans were lured into an ambush that appears to have been planned a long while ahead, which also gives the lie to reports that Somali rebel leaders were incapable of planning. Suddenly, from nowhere, up popped hundreds of Soviet-supplied RPG-7s. While they weren't used to best effect, it was numbers that counted in the end: thousands of irregular Somali fighters ranged in full tilt against a squad of young Americans who did what was necessary when the chips were down.

The weapons used by the Somalis against the American troops – in particular, the RPG-7s – had been smuggled into Somalia by forces hostile to the United States in the months prior to that fateful day. We have to accept that it required considerable effort because much of this activity took place under the noses of the occupying force.

Within days of that event – which involved some American soldiers being dragged naked through the streets of Mogadishu – the Pentagon had made its decision: it was time for the troops to come home. Once the American force had been reduced, there was no possibility that the UN could control developments as effectively as before. As a consequence, the international community was faced with another UN fiasco.

For those of us involved on the periphery of conflict in Somalia, and who experienced combat in other parts, regarded the country as arguably more dangerous than the majority of the minor wars of the 1990s. The uncompromising and brutal nature of the Somali way of life ensured as much.

At a conservative count, conflict within this East African society has so far cost about half a million lives. There are some aid organizations who maintain that you could probably double that tally. In truth, nobody can be certain of the real figure because there wasn't anybody

Even along the beaches to the north of Mogadishu there were the remains of crashed aircraft that had been forced down. Some of these planes had been on the daily Qat run. (Author's collection)

keeping tabs.

The bottom line has always been the excesses of people like Aideed. Kill or be killed were the watchwords of these factional heads that neither recognized nor were circumscribed by any convention. Geneva might have been on another planet.

In a peculiar way, the Somalis seem always to have been adept in dispensing violence. Since the end of World War II, they have fought with each one of their neighbors. Indeed, they continue to do so and have since expanded their revolutionary interests abroad. It tells you a lot that several Somali nationals – all of them Muslim fundamentalists – were arrested in Europe following acts of terror. One Somali youth was taken into custody in 2007 under British anti-terrorism laws after police found in his apartment containers of a chemical used in the July 2005 London bus and Underground blasts that left scores dead.

In Somalia itself, there was never a 'front line'. Most of the time, battles just 'happened', sometimes at a cross-road, or because of a woman or perhaps a dispute over *Qat*. But for the presence of a UN force during the initial stages, losses would have been far greater, though as soon as the last of the Blue Helmets had departed, the bloodletting escalated once more.

If the drama that we encountered was sobering, the succession of conflicts that followed the departure of the Americans and their Allies defied description. No fewer Somalis died with their throats cut while they slept or were stabbed in the back in the marketplace than in outright battles, which often took place outside a village, in any one of the dozens of towns, or on the roads linking them.

Others were killed, sometimes in their hundreds, in a single fire-fight on the imaginary 'Green Line' that ran through Mogadishu and which was originally supposed to separate the combatants. With time, the war seemed to borrow some of its jargon from the Beirut of the 1980s.

Earlier, while the warlords maintained a strangle-hold on food dis-tribution centres – as well as access to foreign aid compounds – they milked the situation until it haemorrhaged. Not that it mattered much in the end because the monster that was created by all these shenanigans ended up feasting on itself.

Within a short time after the Americans left to fight in Iraq, there was still more violence and more bloodletting. In fact, in the past decade and a half, it has got much worse...

CHAPTER TWELVE

Somali Aftermath

The Battle of Mogadishu (also known as the 'Battle of the
Black Sea') or, for the Somali people, *Ma-alinti Rangers* ('The
Day of the Rangers') was a clash that was part of Operation
Gothic Serpent. It was fought early in October 1993, in
Mogadishu. Involved were forces of the United States
supported by UNOSOM II against Somali militia fighters loyal
to the warlord Mohammed Farrah Aideed.

FOR ALL THAT WAS HAPPENING just then in Mogadishu, as Third World,
or more pertinently, African conflicts go, there were a number of
significant firsts for this so-called Somali peacekeeping force. In fact,
apart from the Americans and, to a lesser extent, some of the European
countries, it was a presence-under-duress, much like Darfur and the
Congo today for those involved in still more horrific debacles.

Women played a significant role throughout the Somali campaign.
Often under threat in an Islamic community that sometimes regards
females as inferior chattels, they served in many capacities. They did
duty as helicopter pilots – both in gunships as well as at the controls of
medevac aircraft – and as members of British air and ground crews,
Australian military police and convoy escorts.

Additionally, there were female Scandinavian and Canadian flight
engineers, medical personnel, health specialists, drivers, general duty
soldiers, guards, and the rest, and all these women played sterling roles
in keeping the wheels of a fairly extended military operation oiled. In
American military uniforms still more women performed all these duties
and more. In fact, while there were quite a few sceptics to start with,
even among some of the developed countries, the women soon proved
to be every bit as competent as the men with whom they were deployed.

Somalia was also the first conflict in which both aid personnel and
the media took the first tentative steps either to arm themselves demon-
strably or, at very least in order to stay alive, acquire weapons for guards
who were hired for their protection. While there were critics who were

By the time Operation Restore Hope was in full swing, there were hundreds of helicopters operational in Somalia, the majority American. Most were stationed at the main US Army base at Baledogle, about 100 miles north of Mogadishu: the facility also included a large US Marine chopper contingent. (Author's collection)

opposed to these actions and very vocally condemned them, they simply weren't where it was all happening. For a start, from their comfortable offices in Europe, North America and elsewhere, they couldn't even begin to appreciate the serious threats that some of these people faced.

My old friend and colleague Mohammed Amin managed the Reuters Television and News Service in Somalia from Nairobi and was candid enough to admit that he had done the unthinkable and acquired four AK-47s at $100 each for the protection of his crews. His journalists weren't armed, he told me, only their guards. Not that these weapons didn't prevent three members of a Visnews team, including Dan Eldon, from being hacked to death by Somali militiamen in mid 1993. Three months later, five CNN drivers were slaughtered in broad daylight by a militia band; they had been armed.

Other journalists, though reluctant to be drawn on the matter, were known to have been carrying weapons, but they would skirt the issue when questioned. Not to carry a weapon for self-defence in the streets of Mogadishu, or Kismaiyu in the early days of the UN presence, could lead to serious consequences, such as getting yourself murdered, one of them explained.

While I was in Mogadishu, a French journalist who approached the US Military Headquarters compound next to the American Embassy was accosted by a Somali with a pistol. Without warning, the gunman shot the Frenchman in the arm, an event that took place within sight and sound of a US Marine guard post.

The journalist fell to the ground and seconds later the Marine on duty killed the Somali with a burst of automatic fire.

In this regard, Somalia was hardly unique. Journalists in Vietnam, Rhodesia, Lebanon and elsewhere would occasionally arm themselves, but that was a matter of choice. It was certainly not commonplace and inevitably involved a measure of opprobrium from fellow scribes.

I carried a .45 ACP in the Rhodesian War and thought nothing of it. In some of the attacks against insurgent or government positions in Angola, I was armed, as I was when I went into combat with some of the mercenary groups that I accompanied over the years, particularly in Sierra Leone, where there was a hefty bounty on the heads of any white man involved with the mercenary force.

Chopper gunship pilot Neall Ellis had evidence that the Revolutionary United Front (RUF) rebels had issued a $5 million reward for either killing him or shooting down his Mi-24. Since I was doing duty and flying with him, I would have been naive to believe the rebels would have treated me any differently from Neall, or other members of his crew, had they forced us down. I'd always argue that you didn't wave your press card over your head when you had a hyped-up gook coming at you with an AK-47.

Somalia was a good deal worse. The country had regressed to an obscure medieval fiefdom where only might was right. It was the single example that underscored the age-old premise that even the worst kind of government is better than no government at all. Frankly that's exactly the way it was: there was no control, no order, no government and no law enforcement.

Ostensibly the United Nations presence that arrived in Somalia in the early 1990s was there specifically to do something about the situation. On a strictly humanitarian level, it had devolved into one of the biggest human disasters since the end of World War II. It didn't help to argue that the country appeared to thrive on chaos. Even Cambodia's Pol Pot regime, inhuman as it was, had a few fundamental systems of control in place. So too, to a lesser extent, had the Congo almost a generation earlier. The Somali people, by contrast, existed in a self-made limbo that might easily have been equated to a vacuum.

One of the first operations launched in Somalia was a bid to clear weapons off the streets. In principle the idea was commendable, but whoever conceived it from the comfort of his or her desk somewhere in the civilized world had no idea that while it sounded fine, it almost was like asking the average Somali to stop breathing. Nobody told the original planners that in Mogadishu, a man without his AK-47 was not a man. Take his gun away and it is almost as if he's been emasculated. In hindsight, there was a lot else they weren't informed of either.

While some firearms were recovered, usually by coercion, the Somalis seemed to have an endless supply of them, including some of the larger hardware like 12.7mm or 14.5mm heavy machine-guns, which they mounted on the backs of pick-ups and appropriately dubbed 'technicals'. By early 1994 it had become obvious to just about everybody in the region that in spite of efforts to counter the trend, more arms shipments were reaching the warlords each month than ever before.

Like today, a good deal of these shipments came from the Yemen, ferried across the Red Sea by small, high-powered boats, the same type of 'Go-Fors' used by drug smugglers in the Caribbean. Which begged the question: who was paying for all this largesse which didn't come cheap? Most of it, we discovered afterwards, came from Iran.

As a relief operation, the Somali campaign was, as one wag phrased it, 'an unmitigated calamity'.

By May 1993, when the main body of the American force had left, conditions deteriorated even further. But then, with all effective control over the aid process having been terminated – the main initial objective was to get food to people who needed it – the country again reverted to anarchy. It wasn't long before there were more people starving in the interior than there had been before UN soldiers arrived and there was nothing anybody could, or would, do about it.

Observers who are familiar with the country pointed to several problems which were never properly resolved. The first and most significant was the inability of the UN (or anyone else) to limit the power of Somali faction leaders, One foreign correspondent who was in-country while I was there, said that the only way to bring peace to Somalia was to put all the warlords against a wall and shoot them. Either that, he suggested, or pull the UN out and let them continue fighting among themselves, which happened shortly afterwards anyway.

American troops wait on the airport apron at a military base in the interior to be airlifted north by chopper. (Author's collection)

Sadly, little has changed in the almost two-decade interim and the consequences continue to be horrific, especially among those least able to fend for themselves.

Most civilian and military personnel in Mogadishu with whom I spoke knew exactly what was going on in the country. They told their bosses in Europe and America that these tribal leaders were both primitive and excessively brutal, that they'd taken countless lives and so on, but nobody believed them. They do now, but I'm pretty sure there won't be another Somali rescue mission any time soon.

A look at the track records of some of these belligerents is instructive. The most obstreperous of the bunch was Mohammed Farrah Aideed who, before he died in a firefight in Mogadishu in mid 1996, was a relatively well-seasoned military tactician. He'd survived scores of firefights where others hadn't. At the same time, as the UN quickly discovered, he was a seasoned psychopath who was extremely cunning, totally unreliable and not averse to confrontation when the mood took him. Aideed's father drove the former dictator Siad Barre out of Somalia and 'ruled' over parts of Southern Somalia as well as the southern half of Mogadishu for many years before the UN arrived.

The northern sector of Mogadishu was in the hands of Ali Mahdi Mohammed, a former hotelier who, like Aideed, was also addicted to Qat. That wasn't unusual; almost every adult Somali chews the leaf, categorized as a drug by UN agencies.

Colonel Mohammed Said Hersi Morgan – he called himself General Morgan – had been closely linked to the former President Barre (Morgan was his son-in-law) and controlled Bardera and parts of the region round the port of Kismaiyu, some hundreds of miles south of Mogadishu.

Morgan's principal adversary, for a while, was Colonel Omar Jess, the man who dominated most of Kismaiyu. Jess, another militant lunatic, waged war against every one of the 14 warlords at some stage or another, but just then he was allied to General Aideed; at least until he was murdered and replaced by another tyrant. Washington was aware at the time that Aideed and Jess proposed to split the country between them: Aideed would take the north, and Jess the south.

The list goes on. Few of these self-appointed leaders, megalomaniacs one and all, had any kind of military experience, nor was there anybody in their ranks who might even vaguely have resembled a politician. But, as we now know, they had the hardware and they were ruthless.

Until the Americans and some of the other coalition forces began to use force to separate the hordes (or at least to deprive them of their arsenals) they tended to regard all foreigners with contempt. Also, they displayed this animosity with great enthusiasm. If they believed they could get away with it, they would fire at every UN patrol that came within range, often using women and children as shields. When the UN retaliated, they would shout foul. However, Somalia has never had a monopoly in this kind of duplicity, since there are other nations to the immediate east of Somalia that have also shown themselves adept at using the ploy.

The arrival of the American force initially caused a number of changes, many of them for the better. Within the first two months, there were more than a dozen air and ground attacks, mostly lead by US, Belgian and French forces, on known warlord strongpoints all over the country. Quite a few were successful and huge quantities of weapons were seized.

Elsewhere they failed dismally, mainly because the Americans had a self-defeating habit of dropping leaflets on the towns they intended to attack in an attempt to warn innocent people to keep clear. That, of course, was like telling a criminal that the cops are on the way. The warnings gave clan leaders the time and opportunity to stow their goods.

The French, with generations of experience in African conflicts, weren't prone to such senseless protocol and always went in without prior warning. If there were civilians in the way it was simply bad luck. It's hugely instructive that of all the forces deployed in Somalia during this critical period, Paris took among the lowest number of casualties. The warlords knew better than to goad the Elyseés Palace into action.

While the stoning of Coalition Forces and an occasional sniping attack continued unabated in some parts (mostly where the US forces were active, because initially they were not allowed to use live ammunition to retaliate), they rarely happened wherever there were French (and French Foreign Legion) troops on the ground.

The same, coincidentally, held true for the Turks and the Australians; neither took crap from anybody.

Looking back on the tragedy that Somalia became – and still is – it was clear from the start that the Americans and the United Nations entered a country that was possibly beyond saving. There was no drinkable water until it was produced by the Coalition. Nor was there any electricity to speak of. The roads throughout the entire country hadn't been maintained since the early 1970s. Mogadishu, the capital – and other towns along the coast and in the interior – displayed on their walls the consequences of years of barbarous fighting.

Because the removal of the dead was way down the list of priorities of any of the warring leaders, the danger of epidemics was real enough for Washington to take some extraordinary precautions. That included vaccinations for all personnel on a scale that had never been implemented before, as well as draconian health measures, largely because in some areas where bodies had been buried, the cadavers were barely covered. It wasn't unusual to find skeletal hands and feet sometimes protruding from the country's soft, shifting sands after a strong wind.

Although there were no dogs in Mogadishu (they had all been eaten), jackals, vultures and hyenas dug up many corpses. It would never occur to the average Somali to do something about it, like reburying the dead. That would have meant work . . .

P.J. O'Rourke had his own take on these things after a visit to Mogadishu, at about the same time I was there. He said something along the lines of people not dying like flies in Somalia because with all those bodies around, the flies were extremely well fed . . .

On a more serious note, there were reports of cholera and other

Mogadishu, and its environs, was almost totally destroyed by ongoing hostilities. There were broken and abandoned aircraft and garbage that hadn't been collected for years. Travelling anywhere without a substantial armed escort could be risky. (Author's collection)

infectious diseases from every aid centre that fielded a presence. There were also huge increases in the incidence of tuberculosis, measles and meningitis in the population, especially among starving children and adults. This was a country that had already been battling to cope with kwashiorkor and rickets for decades.

Malaria had been endemic in Africa since the beginning of time and in Somalia it had become a serious issue by the time the Americans arrived. In the first months there were many reports of the disease among Allied servicemen, some of them critical enough to be relocated to hospitals in Europe. The fact was that almost all anopheline malarial strains along the Indian Ocean coast showed strong resistance to available anti-malarial drugs.

As a prophylactic, the medical officer at Baledogle gave me antibiotic doxycycline hyclate tablets, which is more generally used to cure light venereal and amoebic infections.

The result of all this dislocation was that both American and the rest of the UNOSOM command was obliged to take in every single item that they might need for their deployment. That included food, equipment, fuel, power, spares, machinery and all the water necessary for the maintenance of tens of thousands of men and women.

Drinking water became an immediate factor after the landing and it needed urgent attention. Most of it, in plastic bottles, was shipped or, initially, flown in from the Gulf or from Kenya, and sometimes from Europe.

From the start most European contingents supplied their personnel with bottles of water from home. The Italians and the French were immovable; they would drink nothing else and ultimately they were proved right.

Bottled water that arrived from Saudi Arabia was found by chemists attached to US forces to be contaminated by faecal matter. Mountains of water pallets, some 50 feet high and stacked near Mogadishu Airport, were destroyed. That operation ended costing the US taxpayer millions of dollars because so much of it had been airlifted.

That was when Americans took a few alternative steps. Accompanying their force was a ship specially built for desalinating seawater. It took a little while, but the engineers onboard eventually made a connection to a shore station with a flexible hose. Within a month they had established two more desalination plants on shore, each capable of producing almost a quarter of a million gallons of fresh drinking water a day. Even so, it was rationed.

Up-country, in places like Baledogle, Bardera or Kismaiyu on the coast to the south, the solution was not quite so simple. Some local water sources were purified for washing and bathing. All potable water, almost for the duration, was still ferried in by road or air.

During my time at Baledogle in the interior I counted several C-130s landing or taking off each day, many of them hauling loads of drinking water packed on pallets.

Postscript

At the time that the United Nations withdrew its forces from Somalia in the early 1990s, there was hardly anybody who believed that this chronically afflicted, dyspeptic nation – then said to be in the final throes of a self-induced death rattle – could ever be a threat to anyone. They were wrong. After the Americans moved on, Osama bin Laden's al-Qaeda cohorts discreetly moved in. Their cadres set about establishing a series of powerful Jihadi cells in Mogadishu.

In some respects, conditions in this vast country then began to resemble what had been taking place in Afghanistan prior to 2003. Once American and European intelligence agencies started to focus on the

The Russians had originally built a sophisticated air base at Baledogle, intended to play a strategic role in the Indian Ocean and adjoining Red Sea areas as the Cold War progressed. However, when they abruptly departed in the 1980s, the locals moved in and stripped the place of everything except the bricks and mortar. (Author's collection)

Horn of Africa, it was discovered that Somalia's revolution, like a miasmic virus, had infected an entire region, all the way down the Indian Ocean coastline of Africa.

As we've already seen, the destruction of two American embassies in Nairobi and Dar es Salaam in 1998 with hundreds of fatalities was an almost immediate consequence. That was followed in November 2002 by another group of Islamists who tried to destroy an Israeli-owned Boeing 757 passenger jet with 261 passengers and ten crew on board at Mombasa, one of the largest harbours in East Africa. Incompetence coupled to bad judgement caused both rockets to go wide, but a suicide bomber did ram a truck loaded with explosives into one of that city's Israeli-owned seaside complexes later that morning. A dozen tourists and staff were killed.

Gradually, there were issues linked to Somalia that began to unravel. For instance, US Embassy officials in Nairobi were able to demonstrate that al-Qaeda had been moving into other East African countries in the region and used mainly Saudi money to buy the allegiance of poor

Muslims. More of bin Laden's operatives passed themselves off as simple men looking for a quiet place to lead a devout life. They continue to do so because the East African coastline is historically Islamic, preponderantly so, in fact.

'These people put large amounts of money on the table, and sometimes marry local girls with the idea of establishing a bloodline. In this way they forge a formidable network throughout East Africa', I was told.

What also emerged were the identities of the people who were involved in some of the East African attacks, the majority with Somali connections. For years, Fazul Abdullah Mohammed, mastermind of two Kenyan bombings, together with his co-conspirator Saleh Ali Saleh Nabhan, sought out like-minded compatriots in the thousand or so mosques that dot this remote coastline. Fazul, a national of the Comores Archipelago, even financed a soccer team in the Kenyan coastal village of his choice and, in a brash moment, called it the al-Qaeda team.

By all accounts, says a UN report published by *All Africa Global Media*, Fazul remains in hiding in the Somali capital, though he slipped back into Mombasa for a short while, prompting terror alerts from Britain and the US. Like some of his co-conspirators, Fazul survives on cash allowances provided by an al-Qaeda financial controller living in Sudan.

Following the uncovering of caches of al-Qaeda documents in Afghanistan, several Somali sites – including bases at Las Anod in the north and El Wak near the Kenyan and Ethiopian frontiers – have been pinpointed as two of the most important al-Qaeda training bases in Africa. It has been common knowledge in Nairobi for some time now that another al-Qaeda staging post was south of the port of Kismaiyu, not far from the Kenyan border. Explosives used in the American Embassy attacks came from there before being sent by road to Kenya and Tanzania. Each time, according to US diplomatic sources, there were Somali couriers in charge.

The suicide bomb attack on the USS *Cole* in Aden harbour on 12 October 2000, had Mogadishu connections. A Somali woman was identified as the paymaster; she acquired all the vehicles needed for the operation.

An important consequence of these developments is that American defence planners have established several sites in the Horn of Africa for expanding a military presence in the region, including one or two on Somali soil. Though Washington is not saying exactly where they are,

Somalia has regressed to become the most backward and least-developed country in the world. It has huge potential, but these days its only wealth lies in herds of camels that are found wandering about everywhere. (Author's collection)

they are close enough for some of the warlords in Mogadishu to move their place of residence on a regular basis.

The most important of these military establishments is the Combined Joint Task Force – Horn of Africa (CJTF-HOA) headquartered in Camp Lemonier, formerly the French Foreign Legion operational headquarters in Djibouti. Effectively, this modest harbour, linked by rail with Addis Ababa, serves as the focal point for DoD anti-al-Qaeda efforts in the zone, while CJTF falls under the jurisdiction of the United States Central Command (USCENTCOM).

On average, its HQ staff at the Red Sea base totals about 250, while the number of assigned troops, though classified, vary between one and two thousand. Additionally, the US Navy – in conjunction with various countries including many from NATO as well as China – conducts surveillance patrols and missions in the Red Sea.

Thus, on an altogether different level, this war goes on . . .

CHAPTER THIRTEEN

Search and Destroy in the Eastern Mediterranean

The Israeli Navy today reported seizing a cargo boat with 50
Palestinians described as guerrillas trying to sail to Lebanon.
The boat, intercepted outside the Lebanese port of Khalde, was
taken into custody with its passengers and crew. Military
authorities said the ship flew a Honduran flag, had an Egyptian
crew onboard and Lebanese owners. An Israeli Navy patrol
became suspicious of the merchant ship after she sailed from
Cyprus. Those arrested [were described] as members of Al
Fatah, Yasir Arafat's guerrilla organization.

New York Times, 8 February, 1987

THERE WAS A TIME, NOT that long ago, when we journalists on
assignment in the Middle East would complain that Israel must be
the last Western nation to insist that foreign correspondents submit their
copy for censorship.

Iraq and Afghanistan changed all that, to the extent that Israeli
strictures today are mild compared to what some countries countering
insurgency are likely to demand. More often than not, even getting to
report on military issues in parts of Asia and Africa is impossible
without a letter of authority from somebody at the top.

Journalists who arrived in Israel were required sign an undertaking
that included a proviso that any copy intended for publication was
vetted by a government official. Quite simply, it was a matter of no
signature, no press card. There were no exceptions, which is why we all
signed at some stage or another. We, like the Israeli officials with whom
we dealt, knew that signing your rights away as an independent observer
was tantamount to censorship, though in reality controls were pretty
limited. Also, the strictures were almost impossible to enforce.

As a visiting 'fireman' I never complained. I would do my story, take
my pictures, get back on the plane and go home. Nobody at Ben Gurion

241

Airport would ask about the notes in my briefcase or what I'd filed while on Israeli soil, or possibly whether the films in my hold-all had anything that might compromise the security of the nation.

However, don't be fooled that you can enter the country incognito, do your job and leave again unnoticed. Everything in Israel is 'noticed'. It is also recorded. You'll get past immigration, but you only need to file once to have someone knocking at your door, and not necessarily in the early hours of the morning.

Military reporting in Israel has always been a fairly low-key affair, with accreditation handled by the appropriate authority at the Government Press Centre at Beit Agron in downtown Jerusalem. If your intention is to report on security matters, you'd deal with the office of the Israel Defense Forces (IDF), or, as it is called, the Spokesman. For foreign correspondents permanently based in Jerusalem in the first decade of the New Millennium, the situation is no different: the government has a grip on them, intangible perhaps, but perceptible.

'Recalcitrant' news providers are pigeonholed in a category of their own, especially when those who might be giving too much prominence to 'the other side', i.e. the Palestinians.

That situation might involve some kind of leverage, like unobtrusively restricting access to IDF units, or not being provided with information that might be passed on to other hacks as a matter of course. It doesn't take long for the message to get across and if that is not working, then a quiet word with the newspaper or network's senior management or owners, most of whom are Jewish anyway, will do the trick. Or the unhappy soul is sent packing, possibly on assignment elsewhere in the world.

For decades *Ha'aretz*, a left-wing daily, has routinely highlighted what it terms 'the Palestinian plight' and because it has a strong following, they get away with it in the face of public opinion, which was why I rate the newspaper among the best in the Middle East.

As a consequence of these tactics, my colleagues tend to tread warily. If they meander too far off course in what they submit to their editors in London, Washington, Helsinki or Tokyo, they're aware that while they won't be deported, they might have a tough time renewing their residence permits next time round. That's fine in the normal course of events, but it might be intimidating if you emerge with a scoop that might have a bearing on national security. Generally, this is not likely to happen, but conceivably it might, especially in this epoch of instant international communications and the Web.

Consequently, the last time I visited Israel I had my picture taken, completed the requisite forms and went along to Beit Agron to fetch my government press card. The questions asked were perfunctory. Apart from how long I intended to stay, I was required to detail which areas I intended to visit. Did I know any Palestinians or did I intend to contact members of the community? These were some of the questions asked by a female sergeant. She remembered me from my last visit and that I had a British passport. I'd been there several times already for Britain's *International Defence Review*, part of the Jane's Information Group stable.

My track record was in the computer, but she was required to ask anyway. At the same time, you couldn't avoid getting the impression that under the brittle crust of this female soldier's friendliness lay a magma of paranoia, especially when dealing with foreigners.

The object of my assignment then was to spend a week on board one of the smaller Israeli Navy patrol boats searching for insurgents along the

Spending time with the Israeli Navy in the Eastern Mediterranean was one of the highlights of many visits to this corner of the Middle East. We went on a week-long patrol with a Dabur gunboat: the word means 'hornet' in Hebrew and suggests a powerful sting in its tail. (Author's collection)

Lebanese coast and it had all been arranged months beforehand. Named Daburs, the Hebraic for hornet, these were fast, functional and though only lightly armed, adequate for their envisaged security role.

It was the mid 1980s and there were about a dozen of these small gunboats which could easily maintain 30-knots for extended periods while out on patrol. Searches would sometimes take them hundreds of miles from home, but that involved planning and back-up and only happened when intelligence indicated that something was happening in distant waters. Some operated out of the naval base at Haifa, a moderate-sized, well-fortified complex north of the main harbour. As with all Israeli military establishments, security was stringent and uncompromising. You didn't go near that section of the harbour unless you had very good reason to do so.

Since the 1980s, naval gunships doing that work have been replaced by larger, faster, better-armed and equipped warships. They're described in *Jane's Fighting Ships* as light missile cruisers, which confirms that the level of security throughout the Eastern Mediterranean has escalated.

The threat of infiltration by armed enemy agents is constant and usually involves a few zealots at a time who try to infiltrate the country. These efforts, too, have become more sophisticated. The Israelis have widened their searches to look for one-man submarines as well as some fancy propulsion devices that might propel a scuba diver for miles, perhaps 30 or 50 feet under the surface of the sea.

At one of the border camps I visited near Metullah in the far north, there was a poster on the wall of the radio room, which detailed some of the gadgets. Hizbollah, it seemed, had acquired a dozen mini-subs. The one displayed was made of stainless steel.

At that time, I was also able to run through some of the scuba equipment acquired by Israel's foes and, being a diver, I found pretty advanced equipment. There was some of German manufacture, mainly from Draeger, together with American stuff, the kind you can rent at any dive club.

Said, my military escort, whom I'd picked up earlier at my hotel in Tel Aviv, said: 'They've used some of it to get through, but for every action they take, we've had to devise a reaction.' I was aware that a year before, some aspirant infiltrators had used jet-skis in a bid to run the blockade from Tyre. They were blown out of the water and nobody survived.

Jet-skis, miniature one-man submarines, microlights, light aircraft and 'Go-For' speedboats have all been brought into action by Hizbollah in their efforts to penetrate Israeli defences. Most of the time the assignments were suicide jobs. Like many such operations, Israeli shore radar installations tended to pick up insurgent groups within minutes of their leaving Tyre, or whatever other Lebanese port the insurgents used. That set the chase in motion. However, with time, even this routine has evolved into something more complex.

For some years the IDF had a sensitive radar station at Al-Bayyadah in Lebanon, some miles north of Naqoura, the main UN base in the Mediterranean. Those who took the coast road built by Alexander the Great 2,000 years ago from the border to Tyre, couldn't miss this sophisticated electronics facility with its tall masts and multiple antennae on high ground on the mainland side of the road. It was illegal under international law, since the facility was not on Israeli soil, but the IDF was the most powerful presence in the region and nobody could do anything about it.

That was the way it stayed until Hizbollah exerted pressure and took enough young Israeli lives to force the IDF back across its own lines.

Our skipper, Lieutenant 'Motti', was an Israeli Navy regular, barely into his twenties. He took us into Sidon harbour several times and that only stopped after we'd come under sniper fire a few times: fortunately the shooters were bad shots. (Author's collection)

I spent a good deal of time with the IDF, both in Israel and with specific units in Lebanon during and after the 1982 invasion that took the Israel Army all the way to Beirut. I visited the country dozens of times and rarely left without something solid on which to report.

The most interesting, and probably the most exciting, jaunt was the week I spent on board the Dabur which was assigned to patrol offshore Lebanon.

I was introduced to the commander of the Dabur that was to take us out, a mature 22-year-old regular who liked to use only his first name in our presence: 'Motti', or more formally, Lieutenant Motti. I was with him for a week, yet I never did discover his family name.

Motti was on his last tour as a ship's captain. Thereafter, he told us, he was destined to take command of a flotilla of six Daburs: not bad for a youngster who had finished school four years before. But then, as he said, so much in Israel is different. Having taken us onboard at the Haifa base, he called a shore station on the radio. It was all staccato and in Hebrew. Then he turned to the two of us, smiled and said: 'We're ready to go to Lebanon.' Before we left the quay he addressed us. 'I've got just a few orders for you', he said:

> When we put to sea, we start our patrol where the harbour wall ends. Also, we're at sea for the duration even though we might go into one of the Lebanese ports, either Sidon, south of Beirut, or Tyre. If that happens, we'll stay at anchor but only during daylight hours and you will remain on board and not go ashore. At sunset we head out again and get back here in five, maybe six days. We'll see . . .

I learned later that this was a standard routine, and it took place after the invasion of Lebanon. The entire coastline, all the way up to Beirut was under Israeli control, including the two ports that included the harbour further south, which the Arabs like to call Sur. To us, it was Tyre.

'Questions?' It was the typical Sabra approach, blunt and unequivocal. Lieutenant Motti was not particularly strong on protocol and while his English was only functional, he did pretty well, often using his hands to make a point.

The next issue involved communications. Did we speak any Hebrew? We shook our heads.

'OK. No problem. Your flak jackets are there', he said, pointing towards a cluster of olive-green battle jackets and army helmets that lay towards the stern.

If we go into port or the crew is called to action stations, you wear them . . . they are necessary . . . no exceptions. No action is likely, but we take no chances. In port – either in Tyre or in Sidon – they sometime shoot at us. It is the same when we approach anything at sea, even fishing boats . . . they are the worst . . . sometimes loaded with explosives.

When George later complained about the weight of his jacket while filming, Motti retorted sharply: 'You are on board with me. You are my responsibility. You take off your shirts, your pants, if you like. No women on board. But your protection you will wear it when I order you to do so!'

The radio rattled and Motti called out a string of orders. Within minutes we were heading out of the naval base at half-speed. Perhaps half-an-hour afterwards – with Haifa still very much in sight – all the

Every boat within our operating range in the Eastern Mediterranean had to be searched for weapons. It was a slow, sometimes dangerous business because some of the insurgents were willing to give up their own lives to cause damage to their sworn enemy. (Author's collection)

Dabur's guns were cleared and prepared for firing. It was a routine procedure on leaving harbour. Then, when we reached a reasonable distance offshore, the crew manned the boat's two 20mm cannon – one aft, another forward – and fired bursts. They also tested the Dabur's two .50 Brownings on either side of the bridge, after which they were dismantled and taken below. These larger calibres were only hauled topside during interceptions, or while in a Lebanese port.

Lieutenant Motti and his crew worked in conjunction with a host of other Israeli gunboats and patrolled a large area which, according to demand, might extend all the way to the coast of Cyprus or beyond. Once a blip appeared on the radar, it would be rated on a scale of one to ten, according to the nature of the target and its threat potential. Israeli Navy intelligence and surveillance systems – then and now – are integrated with an even more complex network ashore and as with everything else, covered much of the Middle East.

Each target picked up by shore radar was classified for possible response and perhaps one in a thousand might be hostile. Nonetheless, all were studied and aerial or satellite photos called for if necessary.

Foreign craft that had not been security-classified were rated no lower than five and it stayed that way until some kind of contact or observation had been made. Until then, the men on the Daburs regarded every contact as a potential threat, especially at night when attempts at infiltration were most common.

On detecting a blip, the Dabur would warn one of the shore stations of its intention to intercept, but by then the order would probably already have been given. If the unknown factor was possibly an enemy presence, another gunboat – or perhaps three or four, again depending on threat level – might be diverted to provide backup. Meanwhile the radios would buzz . . .

The work done by these vessels was likened to that of an air force patrol, flying in ever-diminishing circles over a vast expanse of sea. It was no less time-consuming and, to most of the sailors, just as boring. But this was work that had to be done. These days, the craft are bigger and much of the work is electronic and space-age configured.

During a subsequent visit in August 1996, it quickly became clear that while there appeared to be very little visible insurgent activity, there was actually a good deal going on. Not a week went by – sometimes not a day – without Israeli intelligence picking up reports of projected

Action stations on board a Dabur as we approached an unidentified fishing craft. Because of suicide attacks, the Israeli Navy took no chances. (Author's collection)

Hizbollah raids. As one Israeli intelligence officer explained during a briefing in Jerusalem, Hizbollah – Hassan Nasrallah's much-vaunted Party of God – had very effectively replaced both Amal and Palestinian attacking forces, though both organizations still launched occasional raids, if only to keep their men in a state of readiness for what they liked to refer to as 'The Big Push'.

Over the years, there have been numerous attempts to breach the Israeli maritime cordon, part of which can be clearly seen from the beach at Nahariya or from the observation point on higher ground at Rosh Haniqra.

During one of my stays in Naqoura, I was awakened one morning by several lengthy bursts of machine-gun fire. Later, I learnt that an Israeli gunboat had warned off a bunch of Lebanese sponge-fishing boats that were drifting too close to the Israeli coastline. The firing went on for minutes.

While almost none of the attempts by fundamentalist forces have succeeded, the game goes on. In the past, when a hostile group did manage to penetrate – whether by land or sea, and occasionally by air, perhaps using balloons or microlights – these efforts got the full media treatment. One such was the attack on 11 March 1978, by a small group of Palestinian zealots who came ashore from a small boat near the kibbutz Maagan Michael.

After killing an American girl, Gale Robbin – she had chanced upon them on a deserted stretch of beach – they set off along the main coastal highway and fired on a bus headed for Haifa. It stopped and the terrorists boarded, shooting three civilians in the process and wounding eight others. A fierce gun battle followed when the hijacked bus was later halted at an Israeli roadblock. A marble monument alongside the road where the incident took place stands there today and I see it each time I travel the road.

By the time the drama was over, there were 34 Israelis dead and 72 wounded. Two of the Palestinian attackers survived. Their task, as fighting members of al-Fatah, their interrogators were later told, was to penetrate Israeli defences, take civilian hostages and attempt to free Palestinian terrorists in Israeli prisons.

An even more bizarre incident took place six months later, when the Israeli Navy managed to stymie a massacre that the terrorists had hoped

Motor vessel *Ginan*, one of several acquired by the PLO on the European market. They would use them to try to smuggle weapons into Gaza and, in several notable instances, attempt to detonate them at the approaches to an Israeli harbour while primed with tons of explosives. (Official IDF Photo)

would make international news. A squad of seven Arabs manned the *Agios Dimitrios*, a modest-sized Greek coaster, which had several tons of high-explosives stacked on deck. It was intended that the charge be detonated in the Sinai port of Eilat.

The insurgents hoped initially to hit the harbour with 122mm rockets and then ram the ship into the quay before setting off the main charge. It was discovered afterwards that there was enough TNT to destroy much of the city and clearly, had they been successful, the loss of life would have been enormous.

About the same time the Israeli Navy captured another cargo ship, the *Ginan*, a Palestinian-owned mother ship from which al-Fatah intended to launch amphibious raids along the Israeli coast. A relatively small craft, she'd set out on her mission from the Lebanese port of Tripoli, north of Beirut.

A month later the *Stephanie* arrived off the Israeli coast. It too was intercepted by a Dabur and another attack was averted. This time an al-Fatah team admitted having been sent by Abu Jihad, head of the military wing of al-Fatah, then opposed to the relatively 'moderate' Yasser Arafat. In this strike, a quartet of enemy combatants did get through. They entered Israeli waters in a rubber dinghy and disembarked at Nahariya on 22 April 1979, where they killed a father and his daughter as well as an Israeli policeman.

The significant message that emerged from these attacks was that drastic situations involving security demanded drastic action, even if it meant cutting off the maritime approaches to Lebanon. Israel has been doing that for decades. Usually, a period of intense naval activity follows an attack, warnings are issued that the situation will be repeated if there is no let up and eventually, the Israelis withdraw. Until next time.

As fundamentally unstable as the Eastern Mediterranean may sometimes be, the IDF has achieved a fair degree of control over the region, though as we all know, there is little in modern warfare that is iron clad. During the summer invasion of 2006, Hizbollah combatants targeted an Israeli warship that had crept too close to the shore and was bombarding Hizbollah shore positions. The ship was hit by a missile that set it on fire and almost sank it.

With a variety of assets that include patrol planes, drones, satellite tracking as well as above-and-below water monitoring, Jerusalem has been able to maintain a reasonably effective security presence. For all that, the occasional attacker or group of them still manages to get through . . .

Leaving Sidon harbour behind us at sunset, our Dabur gunboat continued on its patrol. A few miles out, the crew test-fired all weapons onboard. (Author's collection)

During Israel's infamous Operation Grapes of Wrath, which sent the IDF into Southern Lebanon with a powerful series of armoured columns, the Israeli Navy blockaded all Lebanese ports. That measure had a direct bearing on subsequent discussions which, while not leading to anything substantive, did result in curtailment measures being implemented by the Beirut government.

Security measures were not easy to maintain then, nor are they now, especially since there is regular sea traffic between Israel, Turkey, Cyprus, Syria, Greece, Egypt and all points in-between. Less than half-an-hour's flight out of Ben Gurion Airport lies the Suez Canal, one of the busiest waterways on the globe. Minor ancillary matters also warrant consideration; Israel has undertaken not to interfere with the livelihood of hundreds of Lebanese who work legally off the coast, fishing, trading or sponge-diving.

With the Suez Canal, the Israeli intelligence machine needs to cope with thousands of ships, large and small, that pass through the strategic channel each year. In the case of the *Agios Dimitrios*, there was good evidence that Israeli agents had been watching the ship long before she sailed from Syria. She'd called at several Mediterranean ports, including one in Greece, before she made her way south through the canal and into the Gulf of Eilat.

The *Agios Dimitrios* was destroyed by long-range naval gunfire halfway up the narrow waterway and everyone on board was killed.

The first interception by our Dabur took place not long after dark that first night at sea. Roughly five or eight clicks off the Lebanese coast, the men were called to action stations.

By the time George and I had hauled ourselves on deck, the covers of the 20mm cannon had been removed, the Brownings shuffled up from below and all were manned. The rest of the crew took up positions along the gunwales armed with Galils, the standard IDF infantry weapon.

A flare pistol and a bunch of grenades were placed within easy reach of Lieutenant Motti on the bridge. 'I've used them before', he disclosed. His mind was clearly elsewhere so we didn't press for details.

About a cable-length from a small, unlit boat, a searchlight on board the gunboat was switched on. We recognized the distinctive lines of one of the many fishing smacks that regularly line the sea wall at Tyre. The lieutenant ordered that the Dabur's engines be stopped, removed a loud-hailer from a position alongside where he stood and, in fluent Arabic, addressed the crew of the boat, by now only a short distance away.

Nowadays, Israeli ships don't come under fire as often as they did in the past. Naval gunboats are bigger and better equipped for trouble. In 1985 the Daburs were fired on several times a year, sometimes by offshore batteries manned either by Druze or Amal forces. One of these modest-sized patrol boats was hit by RPG-7 fire, which meant that it was less than 1,000 yards from the shore because the rocket self-destructs at that range. A few years later, a Dabur came under accurate shore-based artillery fire and took heavy casualties. The shelling stopped when the batteries were rocketed by Israeli Air Force jets.

The boat we'd stopped that night was clean. The men answered the usual questions and lifted their nets from the water for inspection and were allowed to continue. More interceptions were made before midnight.

Motti's orders in the event of hostile action were clear. He had the authority to return fire. If taking incoming, there was no need to request permission to retaliate. Air support was a constant on all operations and available night or day. In that heady period, with the IDF dominant in these waters, it very rarely came to that.

The crew on board the boat with us were a mixed bunch, and the skipper was the only regular. The rest were doing their compulsory 30-days a year and were from diverse backgrounds.

The engineer, for instance, was a plumber. The first officer (the equivalent of a petty officer in British or American navies) was an architect. The rest included a cab-driver, two medical orderlies, a store assistant, a graduate student and one crew member without regular work. Their commander was the youngest of the lot, but they listened and trusted him and there was never a quibble when orders were issued.

'If somebody fires at us from a small boat and there are women and children on board, do you shoot back?' my cameraman asked. De'ath was known for his outspoken 'liberal' leanings, which had several times got him into trouble in his native South Africa. 'I won't answer that', Motti said. 'You ask the others what they would do.'

He had evidently been primed for that question by the Spokesman's Office. Later, speaking to the crew, we were left in no doubt how they would react. Most had lost kin in one or other of the wars in the Middle East and they wouldn't hesitate to blow up a boatload of guerrillas who sheltered behind hostages; kids or no kids.

'Even if it meant killing everybody on the boat?' was George's retort.

'It would be better than the suicide bombing of our own people if we didn't stop these animals here, at sea, where they can do no harm except to us. That's why we're here.' This came from the plumber, as forthright with his own questions to us as his answers. He seemed to be enjoying his month away from home and his family of five.

What was interesting about the Dabur crew was that every man onboard had been cross-trained. Lieutenant Motti commented: 'We haven't got space for specialists, so each member who serves on a Dabur must be able to do the work of at least four should any of the others be wounded.' The same applied to him, he disclosed. If he were incapacitated, there was always somebody who could take his place. Training in the Israeli Navy, as we were to see, made for efficient crews. Additionally, they could use each others' weapons and, if needed, run the ship for long enough to get replacements. Anyway, he explained, the gunboats rarely ventured far from home and it was not often that they worked alone.

Motti reckoned he could probably have another gunboat come to his aid in less than hour. 'They're out there', he disclosed, 'just beyond the horizon.'

Everybody on board had also been comprehensively trained in signals procedures. His men could identify the ships of all navies together with their respective aircraft, whether operational in the Mediterranean or not. They could distinguish between an October-class patrol-boat of the Egyptian Navy and similar vessels in French or Syrian naval service, some of which had earlier been reported active off Tripoli, to the north of Beirut.

Early on the morning of the third day at sea we headed into Sidon harbour for a break that would last until nightfall. We might have gone in again, but the patrol boat was sniped at while leaving port.

Although there were IDF forces in the city at the time, the Israelis enjoyed only a tenuous hold on the town. Also, there had been several suicide bomb attacks and quite a few Israelis had been killed.

I'd actually passed through Sidon not long before a car bomb had demolished the regional Israeli headquarters building there and scores of people had been killed. A massive cache of explosives had been secreted in the ground floor of a building and cleverly cemented over before the first Israeli units arrived on their way north towards Beirut. The explosives were command-detonated some days after a headquarters detachment had moved in.

In Tyre things weren't nearly as bad. Though there was somebody targeting the gunboat from one of the pock-marked buildings near the mosque, his aim was poor. On that July early evening, we were the only boat setting out to sea and probably presented an easy target; there were two shots which broke the silence just before the muezzin called the faithful to prayer. One ricocheted off the bows, the other missed us altogether.

There was another rifle shot soon afterwards, but by then we were a third of a mile or so out to sea. Meanwhile, some Israeli troops on shore had retaliated and we continued into the setting sun.

Motti quipped: 'We get sniped. Often. There's not much we can do. They fire their guns, then they disappear into the old town . . . they're not very good as marksmen go . . . or possibly they're markswomen.'

Meanwhile, in Lebanese waters, we enjoyed a relatively tranquil patrol. In Sidon, Motti even put out his rubber duck inflatable boat and we circled the harbour several times, more in search of good fishing than much else. We were below decks again before noon to avoid the heat.

From the boat, we could see that the town had taken a hammering, almost all of it during the invasion. Several ships had been sunk in the harbour by Israeli jets; their masts protruding untidily above the surface. Lieutenant Motti used them as markers, as did some of the troops ashore. Not all of these wrecks had been removed by the time I returned in 1996.

'Could we go ashore?' George De'Ath asked.

'Not a good idea', said the captain. 'You'd need an escort. I have no men to spare.' We left it at that.

From where we were moored we could see something of the security problems that Sidon presented. When the Israelis finally decided to pull out of Lebanon, the soldiers based in all three Lebanese ports were glad to be out of there.

Sidon, in particular – which dates from Phoenician times – was a warren of narrow alleys, bunker tunnels and strongpoints. Every vantage point was dominated by half a dozen hills that overlooked that venerable old settlement that today plays host to one of the largest Palestinian refugee camps along the Mediterranean. Those who had targeted us were probably among thousands who were waiting for just such an opportunity.

They were to get a lot of practice by the time the Israeli government pulled its forces back in the mid-1980s. And still more when Jerusalem decided to go in after Hizbollah guerrillas in the summer of 2006.

CHAPTER FOURTEEN

Israel's Border Wars

'If as a result of the war in Lebanon, we replace [Palestinian] terrorism in Southern Lebanon with Shi'ite terrorism, we have done the worst [thing] in our struggle against terrorism. In 20 years of PLO [activity] no one PLO terrorist ever made himself into a live bomb.'

President Yitzak Rabin while still Israel's Defence Minister in 1985

AFTER THE ISRAELI INVASION OF Lebanon in 1982, I'd go to Beirut three or four times a year. I'd head there too when I'd been working in the south of that trammelled land, usually when I had reports to get out. Or it might have been the wish to quaff a few beers with friends like Claude, Fadi, Rocky and the rest.

For peace of mind, I'd try to link up with an IDF convoy going in that direction, since these were times when Islamic Jihad movements were abducting Westerners. Their numbers included British journalist John McCarthy and Terry Waite, the peripatetic envoy of the Archbishop of Canterbury. Moving about with the IDF was the sensible thing to do.

Coming in from Israel, I'd usually pass through the Rosh Haniqra border post and follow the coastal road north to Tyre. From there it was a short hop to Sidon and then along the highway to the outskirts of Beirut. Occasionally, the Israeli Navy would open up on cars travelling that way, so it could be hairy and there were lots of road accidents. We'd joke that if the snipers didn't get us, then some lunatic behind a wheel would.

In Sidon we'd seek out our contacts and ask to be shown the latest bit of Fatah or fundamentalist mischief; perhaps where a roadside bomb had been laid and detonated from a nearby orchard (as so often happened); or where a mine had been planted, though that was usually done on gravel roads; or maybe somebody had thrown a grenade at a patrol from a high point overlooking the route.

There would be much commotion about follow-ups or possibly a roadblock afterwards, but few of the perpetrators were caught. They'd be gone in a moment after doing their thing though, even then, ambushes would sometimes be laid by some of the bolder Jihadis.

It was interesting to see how the Israelis coped. By then the war had swung full circle, from hands-on electronic warfare to weapons-in-your-hands. Although there were always casualties, the majority were Arabs. Many more Lebanese were killed by Israeli Air Force bombs or rockets – or by Israeli snipers – than members of the IDF.

Even so, the number of young Israeli men who died in that war mounted steadily. Then, one day, the Knesset decided to withdraw them all. However, not before about 800 or so IDF soldiers had been killed and something like five times that number were wounded, of whom another 500 – as this kind of statistic goes in modern war – would be permanently maimed.

Meanwhile, there were many incidents that accentuated the trauma of what was taking place just beyond the frontier line in the north, quite a few involving dissenters. Hersh Goodman, defence correspondent of the *Jerusalem Post* at the time, suggested that among the biggest doubters were brigadier generals who refused to serve in Lebanon, as well as pilots who returned to base with their bomb loads undropped.

Even more revealing, a nation is in serious trouble when, no matter what else was going on in Israel or the rest of the world at the time, all nightly broadcasts began with the funeral services of the latest combat deaths in Lebanon.

It was strictly a personal choice, but for me the most interesting route to Beirut was not the direct road north, but by way of the fundamentalist stronghold of Nabatiya. I'd usually get there through the foothills that separate the coast from the interior after entering Lebanon at Metullah.

To most journalists, Nabatiya was bad news. It wasn't a big town, perhaps a little larger than Marj'Ayoun, the Christian stronghold in South Lebanon, and a lot more compact. Like Maarakeh, another strategic Shi'ite centre – which, like others, had its own command centre or *Husseiniyeh* – it was certainly big enough to keep the IDF from 'sanitizing' it militarily. They could always surround these settlements easily enough, systematically go through the various compounds and houses and arrest all the men and boys, but the leaders will always have planned a way out, sometimes using tunnels that led into the hills.

Israel's frontiers are the most thoroughly patrolled in the world. There are a dozen or more security measures including: landmines; electronic monitoring and listening devices; three, sometimes six, sets of fences; and the always-present human element. Twice each day, the entire border region is scoured by men and women searching for evidence of infiltration. This was a scene along the Lebanese border, where there is also a likelihood of being sniped at by Hizbollah militants. (Author's collection)

Tactically, the Israelis told us, the town was impossible to secure properly even though there were regular attacks on their people emanating from the place. Consequently, Nabatiya acquired a sinister reputation. Had the same thing happened to the Germans, they would have dragged ten men out and shot them for each one of their own casualties, but such things had become passé after 1945. They still are, though I believe it will happen again when things deteriorate still further – if not in the Middle East or Central Asia, then in some other trouble spot. History has a curious way of repeating itself.

We would drive along the narrow main road through Nabatiya, always in daylight. The eyes that met ours were Shi'ite, surly, aggressive and clearly incensed. Many of these people had lost kinsmen in the war and there was no mistaking their sentiments: they despised us Western types who, uninvited, had come scratching about on their turf. To be sure, there would be a good sprinkling of Hizbollah among their ranks, many trained combatants who were biding their time for the opportunity to show their mettle.

Men and women would stand firm on the side of the road, arms folded, heads held high and give us the evil eye. I saw that look often enough in South Africa in the apartheid era when riot police went into the townships. As they say, creed really does sometimes spawn as many bigots as race.

The people of Nabatiya and its surrounds believed that there was a special place in Hell for what they termed these 'Jewish intruders' in their American trucks with their American .50 Brownings and American M40 106mm recoilless rifles mounted on American Jeeps or APCs. There was an even deeper loathing – be that possible – for IDF troop-carriers and, as might have been expected as the war progressed, it was those vehicles that became 'preferred' targets, as they still are when Jerusalem takes the war to the enemy.

It's worth mentioning that some of the very first of the improvised explosive devices of the modern period (IEDs as we know them today) were planted in these same foothills, usually laid along the same southern Lebanese byways that we travelled. The IDF called them side bombs, which was appropriate because they were always laid at the side of the road, usually with wires attached.

Nabatiya was then – and still is – a city very different from all others in Lebanon. In a sense it might be compared to the holy city of Qom in Iran, apart from when the Shi'ite populace would celebrate Ashura, which marked the martyrdom of the grandson of the Prophet Mohammed. Then great swathes of the faithful would draw blood as they flagellated themselves across the chest and back with chains and pieces of broken wire, after which the town would sometimes be ominously quiet.

It was not at all like the rest of Lebanon and though we didn't know it at the time, much of what we observed underscored the fanatically religious commitment that Hizbollah – also largely Shi'ite – exploited so efficiently in later years.

It was also at Nabatiya that the IDF, purposefully or otherwise, on 16 October 1983 committed what must arguably be the worst single tactical blunder of three decades of conflict in the Middle East. In military terms, in the minds of Israeli field commanders and their seniors, it was an almost insignificant event; a simple faux pas that happens in wartime. To Shi'ites, worldwide, the offence was the most damning assault on Shi'ite Islam.

On that bright October day, an IDF military column arrived in
Nabatiya, where some 50,000 to 60,000 Shi'ites from all over the region
had worked themselves into a frenzy of chanting, wailing and bloody
self-mutilation. There was no possibility of even trying to reason with
such a mob; they were in the throes of what some have termed 'the great
cleansing process' and the crowd was mindful only of their total
religious commitment.

Impatient at not being able to pass, the Israeli convoy commander
decided to force a passage through the crowd anyway and he ordered
the column forward. That was when the mob turned on them.

In seconds there were tens of thousands of people screaming
obscenities, throwing stones and then setting tyres alight in a bid to prevent
the column from passing. Once an IDF troop carrier had been set alight,
the shooting started and left two dead with more than a dozen wounded.

That the officers responsible were subsequently disciplined was of no
consequence. A terrible religious atrocity had been committed, declared

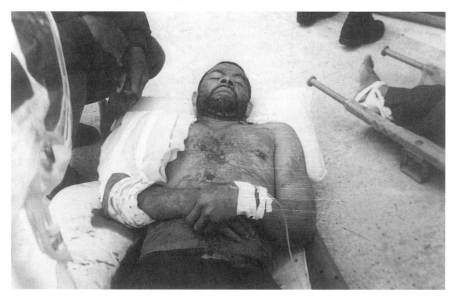

The Israelis have been known to be indiscriminate in their use of artillery. More than
100 people – almost all of them civilians including large numbers of women and
children – were killed when a cluster of IDF shells hit the Shi'ite town of Qana in
South Lebanon. There were no apologies and the investigation that Jerusalem said
took place afterwards yielded little. Among the seriously wounded were several
members of the UN Fijian Battalion. (Author's collection)

the head of Lebanon's Higher Shi'ite Council from Beirut. He also issued a *fatwa*, a religious edict that made it illegal for any Shi'ite, anywhere, to cooperate with Israeli troops. Effectively it was a declaration of war.

Almost three weeks later at the IDF headquarters at Tyre, a place I would visit often on my way in or out of the country, the Shi'ites took their revenge by detonating a truck loaded with explosives at the front entrance of the two-storey building. Altogether 61 people were killed by the blast, roughly equal numbers of Israelis and Arab political prisoners.

In her book, *Sacred Rage*, my former colleague Robin Wright tells us that it was the largest single toll Israel had incurred since the invasion: 'A lone Shi'ite suicide bomber had killed more in one day that the PLO had claimed in the five years leading up to the invasion.'[1]

She goes on: 'As one of the most hard-line Shia mullahs explained, "Israel could have won the southerners' hearts and minds, but instead, its warlike style has turned people against it".'

Looking back, one was always left with the impression that Nabatiya was a most unusual place. Other Lebanese towns – then and now – are noisy and rambunctious with everyday activity. There were always people fixing things, women calling, children shrieking and, if you listened carefully towards late afternoon, Arab flutes, which, to our Western ears might have sounded a little discordant. It was the kind of music you needed to get used to, as, with time, I did. To me these were reassuring echoes, some still resonating long after we'd left a settlement.

In Nabatiya, by contrast, you could almost feel tingles of hatred on the back of your neck. While going through the place, nobody spoke as we passed, there was no music, no kids playing in the street and you just knew that there was trouble waiting to happen. Most often, we couldn't wait to get out of there, yet time after time we'd go back, almost as if we were tempting the gods.

The IDF soldiers who travelled with us felt much the same. When they returned to Israel from Beirut, they'd groan when they were told that their route would take them through Nabatiya. Unpleasant things happened there, they would comment among themselves and, as we approached, they'd be that much more vigilant.

When I visited the town a decade later, very little had changed. Nabatiya had become a regional headquarters for Hizbollah and, according to Jerusalem, almost all attacks launched into Upper Galilee were planned from there; which is why the town is still blasted so often by the Israeli Air Force today.

To me, Sidon wasn't much better. I once spent two days there, ostensibly to visit some of the Palestinian camps south of the town. What an experience that was.

The camps – which were like concentration camps without towers and manned by troops with machine-guns – were appalling. They were cesspits of misery, as I wrote in one of my reports. The children looked as though they were starving, the majority clad in rags and playing in some of the slimy pools that formed during winter months. Most families were housed in little more than shacks that gave almost no shelter from the cold and the wet. Even so, in this inner circle of purgatory, the occasional incongruity of a youngster bubbling with enthusiasm couldn't be missed.

It was during one of my earlier visits that I joined an Israeli patrol checking vehicles and civilians in the centre of Sidon, which was not unlike some Israeli towns in the north, perhaps 40 years before. A section of eight paratroopers was doing a fairly good job of a distasteful task and hating it. It was as much an insult to unit elán as to the civilians who were subjected to their pawings.

De'Ath and I went about with them, filming or taking stills, and we soon saw that the people viewed us just as they did the soldiers who were making their lives a misery. We were regarded as the enemy, because we'd arrived with this hated 'Zionist Scum' as Lebanese propaganda leaflets called the Israeli Army. We were in the process of recording on film their activities as they stopped traffic, searched vehicles and persons, checked IDs and asked impertinent questions. It mattered little that we were foreign journalists with foreign passports. The local Arabs even had a name for us: *jundi*, which in their dialect meant hated foreigners. That we were hobnobbing with the aggressor spoke for itself; by our very actions we were darkening shadows within shadows.

What the Israeli troops in an occupied area were doing to the locals was harassment, pure and simple, and things sometimes turned violent. When George and I spoke about it afterwards, we agreed to give the opportunity a miss should it be offered again. Journalists in other parts of the world have had similar experiences and generally, you cannot avoid seeing it, because it is part of the job.

During the course of many years of visiting the region, much had taken place, especially after I returned to the Israeli border in 1996. I met some members of an IDF unit that had had a few uncomfortable moments with a landmine. Earlier, one of the soldiers had found some wires alongside the road, which was something nobody ignored. Each potential bomb had to be investigated and it was invariably a

A UN soldier at Naqoura in South Lebanon displays one of the IEDs that had been placed alongside a road used by Israel forces. It was almost indistinguishable from the rocks among which it had been laid. (Author's collection)

risky process. Experience had taught that anything involving batteries or wires could be attached to command-detonated bombs. It was also apparent that those opposed to these occupiers, quickly learnt to excel in the unconventional, as they do today in Iraq and Afghanistan.

I arrived shortly after the foot patrol had gone some distance into Lebanon, well beyond the 'Good Fence'. It was the same tedious routine, the men keeping good distance, one group watching the left and the other the right. They were all within hearing distance; no need for the radio, though it was there.

The sergeant had noticed something in his path, nothing in particular that he could remember afterwards, but something different. He'd been doing the job long enough for it to become almost second nature.

'You get the feel of it after a time . . . you sort of just know', he told me in good English. On that occasion he didn't know why he'd stopped where he did. Then he spotted the wire at his feet. 'It's instinctive', he reckoned.

His name was Avi, a cockney from Limehouse, London, he'd tell us with a chuckle. He and his family had done their *Aliya* when he was eight and, as is customary, he'd been called up for his regulation 36 months of military service after leaving school.

Whenever he saw that the ground in an area where he was working had been turned or freshly dumped, he would raise his hand and tell the others to get back. 'Far back!' he'd shout. He did so this time too. Five or six others in the patrol positioned themselves in two shallow dips in the road after making sure that they too hadn't been booby-trapped. Hizbollah sometimes purposely leave visible signs in one place, which, when disturbed, blow up in another nearby location – perhaps a ditch, or alongside some rocks that offer potential cover. Often enough it might be where the rest of the patrol had taken shelter. It's a smart trick in this filthy game.

The sapper sergeant spoke into his lapel to the command post. He had a problem, he told them, his Hebrew as fluent as any of his Sabra mates.

As he had done possibly a score of times in the past, Sergeant Avi Issel moved slowly forward and studied the untidy little mound of soil that had caught his eye. He moved a tuft of grass and with a small metal probe, poked about until he clinked against another metal object, and that little gesture triggered the biggest alarm in the region in a month.

It took the Israeli engineers who stepped into the breech a short while later about 30 minutes to expose the device, but by then, more troops had begun scouring the surrounding hills. They found nothing.

Later, I was able to establish that a Hizbollah strike unit had been around, probably attached to the Islamic resistance that was operating out of the Beka'a Valley. By the time we arrived, they'd all melted into the hills.

Just as well. The TM-57 landmine of Soviet origin that was eventually uncovered was linked by wires to still more explosive devices. There were mines and artillery shells dispersed along the length of the road over a distance of about 200 feet. Had the sergeant not found that bomb, the next IDF convoy that used the road might have been targeted and there would almost certainly have been casualties.

My old friend Uri Dan, an Israeli political and military commentator whom I interviewed for one of my television documentaries, told me a few years before that South Lebanon was the fulcrum upon which the future of all Israeli relations with the rest of the Arab world would ultimately hinge. I've quoted him on the subject often enough, and with good cause; Uri believed that any arrangement without watertight guarantees for the security of Northern Israel would be suicide as long as Syria was fomenting war against his people. It was difficult to argue against such logic.

Israeli forces along the border with South Lebanon. Specially converted road moving equipment was sometimes used to check for mines and IEDs. (Author's collection)

His conviction was branded short-sighted by some and it may well have been. Only time will tell whether the Israelis did the right thing by pulling back behind their own frontiers a decade ago because while they were there, South Lebanon offered the IDF an outstanding – if brutal – training ground. There was round-the-clock experience of the real thing, at a price, of course.

It was not to be. Those 70 square Levantine miles next to the Israeli border where the IDF occupied what it referred to as its Exclusion Zone (or as some liked to say, its Zone of Influence) were a welcome if uncomfortable buffer. Eventually, Hizbollah cadres became so active in South Lebanon that the pundits in Jerusalem thought they'd cut their casualties and pull out. They dismantled their radio and radar masts, as well as the early-warning radar station near Naqoura, blew up their bunkers and living quarters, set booby traps and left.

Nobody had counted on the IDF going into South Lebanon in force again in the summer of 2006, with disastrous consequences. Casualties that resulted from that experience – altogether 3,000 troops were deployed – were horrendous. It lasted a bit more than a month and was Israel's first real military defeat in a ground campaign of that duration.

While legends of the Six Day and Yom Kippur wars remain potent in the minds of Jewish people everywhere, the Arabs learnt from the 2006 misadventure that Israel really was not the indomitable megapower that Western media so often liked to portray in the past. Instead, the country was shown to be vulnerable and the fact that there had been one terrible IDF tactical or command blunder piled atop another while the shooting lasted, compounded issues.

Suddenly, it was demonstrated to Arabs everywhere that the hated enemy was not invincible. That alone gave Hizbollah an impetus like no other event had done in decades.

It has also made things difficult for those who report on such things. Although the shooting war was halted soon enough, the entire region south of Beirut suddenly became much more of a restricted area. It had always been a tough region to visit, but since the summer of 2006, those with dubious agendas were regarded with greatest circumspection. Simply going by the experiences of some of my colleagues, it would appear that nothing is likely to change very soon.

South Lebanon, impasse or not, is not only a dangerous place for strangers, it is also difficult to get to. You can try to get in overland from Beirut, or possibly across the Shouff from Damascus. Either way you will end up on the coast road, which will take you through Sidon and Tyre. Apart from the roadblocks, of which there are scores, chances are your embassy will be making enquiries about you after a week or two, especially if there is no good reason for being there in the first place.

Some lucky people, with the right clearance, might be able to pass through Israeli lines at Rosh Haniqra, north of the town of Natanya, like we did, many times. But then again, you have to be doing something that passes Israeli scrutiny. There are many documents to be completed and the number of questions asked by the IDF can be stupefying. The chance of getting that kind of clearance today is almost zero. I tried again through the Israeli Embassy in Washington in 1999 and was denied.

Then again, it's like that almost everywhere you go in the Middle East these days. Try moving about in Egyptian or Syrian sensitive areas and it can be a good deal more frustrating.

In March 1996, and once more that August, I crossed into Lebanon at Rosh Haniqra and it wasn't much fun.

Both young men and women do compulsory military service in the IDF. The girls play a vital role in communications, logistics, support and in certain medical spheres. This young lady sits in the radio room of an Israeli Army unit on the border with Lebanon, to the immediate west of Metulla. (Author's collection)

Four suicide bomb attacks had just taken place in Jerusalem and Tel Aviv and there had been attempts by Hizbollah to enter Israeli territory by such ingenious means as small hang-gliders and jet-skis. Everybody was nervous. I wasn't shot at, but others were. So, as it was throughout Lebanon before the shelling, everybody was on edge. Something was brewing but nobody could be specific.

There was good reason for all this concern. Just before I arrived a young Lebanese Hizbollah zealot with the name of Ali Amsher who hailed from the village of Addayseh, had strapped a case of explosives garnished with ball-bearings to his body. He waited for the first IDF patrol to arrive.

When the column stopped at the crossroads where he had taken up a position, he walked forward towards an Israeli patrol, saluted once and blew himself up. He took a Druze captain of the IDF with him and wounded several others. In its broadcasts from Beirut, a Hizbollah spokesman claimed a remarkable victory. Ali Amsher, his report stated, was in Paradise with his just rewards.

This was also a time when I covered much of South Lebanon by car, usually in the company of a UN official. Many of the places we visited were those mentioned by T.E. Lawrence in *The Seven Pillars of Wisdom*. I read it again recently and was surprised at its lucidity, even though that work will soon be a century old. Lawrence admirably captures the mindset of many of those who were involved in his war and, had he been alive today, *El Aurens* would probably have said something about very little having changed where it concerned the people.

Lawrence too, went to Damascus through Tyre, Al-Hanni Cheba'a, Marj'Ayoun, Rshaf and Dyar Ntar, all towns that subsequently found themselves in the sharply disputed IDF Zone of Influence, where Arab and Jew exchanged fire almost every day. In the weeks that I was there, I saw the Israelis regularly use artillery against suspected rebel positions in the Norwegian area. That was not long before Operation Grapes of Wrath.

While visiting South Lebanon, I've always made a point of trying to attach myself to one of the UN battalions. Even then, we were hassled by Hizbollah.

One of my hosts while Operation Grapes of Wrath went on was a young Swedish dynamo called Mike Lindvall, a civilian who worked for the United Nations and went on to Afghanistan when it was still under the Taliban. Judging by the speed at which he got us through a dozen roadblocks, including those manned by the Syrian Army, South Lebanese Army and what was then an extremely inept Lebanese Army, Mike knew everybody, both within the UN command, as well as those irregular Muslim units with whom he had to contend. Hizbollah was familiar to him too.

As we approached Tyre, he asked me whether I'd removed all evidence that I had come through Israeli lines. I hadn't. My hip pocket contained a wad of Israeli shekels and my passport had been stamped at Ben Gurion. He wasn't pleased. I'd better 'watch it' if we were searched, he said. As it happened, we weren't.

I was to go back there some years later under the auspices of General Emile Lahoud with Hassan, a young Shi'ite captain in the Lebanese Army, and conditions were much changed. There was still an overbearing suspicion towards all strangers entering the area, but there had been progress. But for the war, modern Tyre might have been one of those lugubrious semi-tropical vacation spots that you see advertised in the Sunday papers, though the tall buildings were still pock-marked from the scores of battles over decades.

Along the port city's Corniche, a real attempt had been made to clean up. Several banks had opened their shutters and there was a handful of new restaurants. Prices were high and in US dollars. There was even a routine Sunday afternoon market in almost-new European cars, mostly BMWs and Mercedes. All had been stolen and shipped to the Eastern Mediterranean from the Adriatic.

In fact, had I wished to do so, I could have bought a seven-series BMW not yet a year old for $12,000, but only if I didn't ask questions. The only problem was what I would do with it once my assignment was over.

I certainly couldn't drive it across the border to Tel Aviv . . .

Hizbollah has been running Tyre ever since it became an effective force in the region and, fundamentalist or not, they have done a good job of it. They had also imposed their own form of government based on Sharia Law; alcohol was already forbidden to all by the time I last called, even to the handful of Christians who'd stayed behind.

With the end of the civil war and the integration of the Lebanese Army, Christians had begun to return and there had even been a few wine shops that opened, which is not unusual for a country that produces its own vintages. There was little that the Mullahs could do about it at first. However, gradually the word got about: if those selling alcohol didn't conform, things would happen. A few bikinis were even seen along local beaches, usually attached to female UN staff – but they too have since been declared *verboten*.

Being a scribbler, all my actions in the area were coordinated through Timur Goksell, spokesman for the UN in Lebanon, a tough-talking, three-packs-of-Lexington-a-day Turk. By then he'd been responsible for liaison with the press at Naqoura for more than a decade. Though since retired, the UN consults him when there is need, as they did during the 2006 invasion.

It was Timur who first put me in the picture about Hizbollah. Ever since *Sayyed* (kin to Mohammed the Prophet) Abbas Moussawi, the original leader of Hizbollah, and his family were rocketed in a sneak attack by an Israeli helicopter while travelling from the town of Jabship in 1992, the fundamentalists have become paranoid about the movements of strangers entering the area. Somebody had shopped Moussawi and they had no intention of it happening again, which was why the movement has always suggested what they like to refer to as the 'real agenda' behind some of the work done by Western journalists especially.

I was in Naqoura when the UN media chief in the Middle East made contact with the man who replaced the late Shi'ite cleric-turned fighter. For that historic Hizbollah meeting, Goksell and Lindvall drove from Naqoura to Tyre, but first they had to make contact with a Hizbollah militant at a neutral address in the port city and transfer to an unmarked car. For 40 minutes they were moved around in circles, calling first at one house and then another. At last they were led down a back street to one of the half-dozen safe houses in the town to meet *Sayyed* Hassan Nasrallah, Secretary General of the Party of God.

Afterwards, neither of the two UN officials were prepared to comment about the discussions, but I did gather that the Hizbollah 'Supremo' told them that Southern Lebanon was about to enter a new and dramatic phase.

So, too, it did, with the guerrillas having subsequently emerged as an incredibly focused, semi-conventional military force. The guerrillas had somehow inculcated the kind of iron discipline and determination which, in years past, was as much a part of IDF élan as the history of the Jewish state.

What has also since become apparent is that the Israeli ground

On the slopes of Mount Hebron, on the border between Syria and Lebanon, stands this sign, used for target practice by soldiers from a dozen nations in the past. (Author's collection)

fighting machine is a shadow of what it used to be. It is manned by young men who, unlike previous generations, are more accustomed to the good life. They take their cell phones into battle with them – as they did in 2006 – and end up compromising the security of the unit because Hizbollah listens while they talk to their mother or their girlfriend. They don't begin to compare to the resolute IDF fighters who took and held Beirut in the early 1980s.

More importantly, a new kind of enemy has emerged; one who is prepared to sacrifice one life – or many lives – if real loss to their enemies is achieved.

It was during that visit that I left with Lindvall for the mountains of the east where the borders of Israel, Syria and Lebanon converge near the modest little village of Cheba'a. The journey took us from Tyre through an area supposed to be controlled by Ghanaian UN forces and on to the Finnish HQ near Srifa. From there it was east again to the Israeli border post at Metullah and north-east to Marj'Ayoun and the South Lebanese Army.

At times, the road would meander almost to within spitting distance of the vast array of security measures that the Israelis had installed. Every 300 feet or so there'd be yellow and red warnings in Hebrew: mines. There were several rows of electric fences and razor-wire, ground sensors, video cameras, early-warning detection devices and, of course, still more mines. All were intended for men with guns and explosives who tried to cross.

Of course, Hizbollah knew we were there. We would come to one of the small towns along the way, Dayr Qanu an Nahr, or Ett Taibe further towards the east, and Lindvall would gesture towards someone sitting by the roadside.

'Hizbollah', he'd say, with a nod of the head.

'How do you know?'

'He's always there. You won't see his radio, but as soon as we've passed he'll warn the people ahead that we're on our way.' Mobile phones were the medium.

It was much the same at towns then not under the 'control' of the Israelis. Earlier, Lindvall told me about an American student who'd hitch-hiked through South Lebanon with the stars and stripes conspicuously displayed on his back-pack. He got through Hizbollah country without mishap; but as soon as he reached SLA territory they seized him and handed him over to the Israelis, for his own safety, they told him. That youngster was fortunate because other Westerners had disappeared in the region, some permanently.

Hizbollah intelligence, I discovered soon enough, was efficient. All movement, all travellers, were noted, me included. Earlier, when some of their security agents swooped on hundreds of suspected Israeli informers, they knew their movements to the last foot over the previous two or three years. Many agents were caught and executed.

Yet it wasn't quite that simple, Mike added. Many innocents died too, which was one of the reasons why relations between the Party of God and the Lebanese government remained fractious. The authorities would prefer Hizbollah to leave police work to those in charge of such matters, but Nasrallah has always had his own views, which underscores the notion among non-believers in Beirut that the pervading Hizbollah presence is both revolutionary and autocratic.

On the ground, during my last independent visit out of Naqoura (as opposed to my 'official' trip with the Lebanese Army later), hostilities in South Lebanon had not been going well for Israel. I'd been there when the relief of about 20 soldiers from a camp in an area north-east of Bint

Jubayl – a big Muslim town in the western sector and well known for its commitment to the fundamentalist cause – was taking place.

The Israeli fortification on high ground overlooking a large wadi had been attacked several times in the past year and those soldiers who were being sent home were replaced by 20 others who would come in by road. The work they did was not hard or overly dangerous, but at the end of a three-week tour of duty, they'd had enough.

The changeover began at dawn with the first South Lebanese Army ground patrol, backed by two APCs, moving over a specific route. They inspected the road, its adjoining gullies, overhangs and bridges. This patrol was followed by a squad of Israeli sappers who repeated the process. More soldiers fanned out in the surrounding hills and took up positions held overnight as observation posts by both the Israelis and the SLA. These were preliminary security assessments it was explained, with more to come.

Only about midday did the IDF road column reach the 'Permanent Violation' (as Israeli military strongpoints in South Lebanon are designated on the UN map). One group of Israeli youngsters would

Youthful Israeli troops, doing their requisite period of military service after leaving school, form the backbone of Jerusalem's national defence initiative. Here they are seen on patrol along the South Lebanese frontier. (Author's collection)

disembark and another would board the troop-carrier. There were few formalities and the mood was subdued. By some accounts I've since read, it could be a disconcerting experience.

After exploding mines and roadside bombs had become almost routine, IDF commanders liked to vary their procedures. I never saw it happen, but I was aware that the route was often changed at the last moment, whether swept or not, and then only to confuse the enemy. Or the men would be taken out by helicopter, which they preferred anyway. IDF columns that entered South Lebanon in the 2006 invasion simply repeated the old process, but this time they were dealing with an adversary who'd had the time and patience to call the shots. Unlike the Israeli newcomers, Hizbollah cadres were waiting when the strike eventually took place.

As before, roads to and from camps, many of them unsurfaced in the final leg, which made them ideal for land mines, still had to be traversed to bring in supplies. Most of what IDF units needed to fight had to be hauled in by truck, with the usual support and escort: fuel, ammunition, razor wire, weapons and food; even water, because local supplies might have been poisoned.

With long experience in such matters, IDF officers learnt to adopt measures to limit the movement of guerrilla fighters. The first was the use of armour on all high points overlooking the routes used by convoys. Tanks were deployed, fitted with special equipment such as radar, infra-red sensors and a variety of detection devices. In addition, convoys would be accompanied by vehicles with jamming systems that prevented the detonation of bombs by specific radio frequencies. At that stage, Hizbollah had cottoned on to using simple walkie-talkies for the purpose, many traded or stolen from UN troops who were supposed to be there to stop such things happening.

Over decades, vehicles were constantly modified to cope with the changing nature of conflict. By 2006, IDF troop-carriers weren't much like those they had used even a decade before. Protected by steel panels round the cabs, drivers were now encased in capsules said to be able to absorb the full blast of a roadside bomb. They were mine-proof as well. Trouble is, almost nothing is impervious to the high-explosive, anti-tank (HEAT) rounds much favoured among some insurgent groups.

In earlier days, I remember an Israeli trooper telling me that an approaching Sagger missile (a Soviet weapon which is obsolescent today) 'is a huge ball of fire coming at great speed. You can't miss it! But if you see it coming, there's just time to take cover'. It was frightening and it made a tremendous blast, he conceded. 'But when anybody sees one, the cry goes out and we all get down.' The man had been at the business end of a Sagger twice before, but like the Katyusha – a larger, unguided rocket with a longer range but also with a powerful blast – 'there's often more noise than effect'.

Israeli officers to whom I spoke after the 2006 invasion confirmed that as in Afghanistan, it was sophisticated command-detonated bombs that were most feared. In the old days many of these bombs, which could hold 20 kilos of high-explosive, looked like chunks of rock. Those that I photographed were barely distinguishable from the sandstone boulders among which they were laid. They were cunningly camouflaged, the majority filled with quarter-inch or half-inch ball bearings that could pierce sheet steel.

Cuttings or overhangs near the road were much-favoured as they are ideal for ambush in primitive surroundings since they tend to funnel the approach of the enemy, making them vulnerable to attack. Before they pulled out of South Lebanon the previous decade, Israeli specialists had partly solved the problem by shifting embankments and cuttings back 50 or 60 feet. The cost of such earthworks, which, in turn, had to be protected, was tough on Israeli taxpayers.

Meanwhile, Hizbollah devised other strategies. Instead of using some of the more complicated (and expensive) weapons available on the market, they sometimes laid 100 kilos of plastic explosive as a single bomb, buried in the middle of the road to cripple the vulnerable under-bellies of Israeli amour. A little before my tour of the region in 1996, nine Israeli conscripts were killed by a single explosion that lifted a modified counter-mine M60 tank 20 feet into the air. Other favoured targets for such bombs were APCs and fuel bowsers.

Problems faced by IDF elements in those days would be similar today. For instance, large clumps of high-explosive are difficult to detect by conventional means because there is almost no metal. Detonation is either by pressure from above – a kilo or two will do it – or possibly by wire from a remote position overlooking the target. Radio frequencies are still used, but the Israelis are masters of electronic disruption. Occasionally, Hizbollah will employ a small metal contact detonator, again connected by wire but buried in the road ten or 15 feet ahead of the charge.

Israeli Army M60 tanks modified for mine-clearing were brought in for the job some years ago with turrets and main armaments removed and their flanks strengthened with steel and ceramic panels to withstand RPG-7s or wire-guided missiles. Additionally, upper hatches were toughened with steel plates to withstand air bursts and mortar bombs.

Many such adaptations were put into effect after Israeli intelligence found that Hizbollah had acquired Yugoslav TMPR6 penetration mines, supplied by Iran.

Towards the end of the 1990s, I visited a forward Israeli post on the security fence. It was the last year that the IDF sent their conscripts into South Lebanese postings and the experience was notable because such things are likely to happen again.

All terrain immediately beyond the unit's defences was regarded as hostile. While snipers weren't yet a significant problem, it was not impossible to get hit by a marksmen possibly sitting on high ground half a mile away. In wartime, such issues are of concern, a youthful lieutenant told me.

The camp in which I found myself was responsible for observing and stopping Hizbollah attempts to cross into Israel by air. They had

Armoured troop carrier used by the United Nations on the slopes of Mount Hebron during winter. The temperature can fall to 20 below when the weather gets really bad. (Author's collection)

knocked a microlight out of the air earlier in the year: it had taken off from the village of Bani Hayan, and exploded soon after lifting off.

'We know exactly when they launch. They aren't in the air a minute before we hit them. *Poof!*' the Israeli sergeant gunner in our group explained.

Israel has other not-so-secret weapons in its armoury: 'spies in the sky' that can read the brand name on a packet of cigarettes from three miles up. These remotely piloted vehicles, or RPVs, can stay aloft for up to nine hours and transmit information to banks of monitors on the ground. Some are now being used by Western governments to follow the movements of terrorists elsewhere, or to keeps tabs on items that float and that might be considered 'dubious' in European waters.

Should members of the unit cross into South Lebanon, they would have with them infra-red sensors that would be able to indicate whether there was somebody hiding camouflaged in a wadi, or what equipment was being unloaded from the trunk of a car many miles away. All transmissions are in code, which the Syrians have been trying to jam for years.

This air force station in the hills east of Ayta Ash Sha'b was not named. It was called the 'Volcano Contingent' and appropriately so. The principal weapon, mounted on APCs, was the American six-barrelled 20mm 'Vulcan' Gatling and there were two of them.

The camp, right up against the Lebanese fence, was reached by a narrow road, again lined on both sides with signs that warned about mines. The entire perimeter, about a third of a mile long, consisted of bulldozed earth ramparts. In the distance there were several towns, all Muslim, their minarets reflecting the sun in the early morning light. The only human movement was that of locals weeding the tobacco crop in adjacent fields.

Like most other Israeli camps in the region, there were 35 soldiers at the post; five were women who were responsible for communications and intelligence. Also of note was the fact that almost none of them were over the age of 21. The commander and my host was a 21-year-old electronics expert with the rank of a lieutenant; his second-in-command was about a year older and also male.

Breakfast was being served when we arrived, good old-fashioned yoghurt, herrings, pita and green salad with cucumber predominating. There was coffee, lots of it, black and strong. I could just as easily have been back at the King David in Jerusalem. Meanwhile, in the arrivals area outside, more vehicles had just come in: a new contingent had taken over from the night shift.

Things started with a brief overview. The men spent a maximum of three weeks at the camp, after which they went home on leave, which was compulsory and couldn't be accumulated. The only exemptions from call-up were on medical or religious grounds; almost 20 per cent of the population was so exempted, I learnt afterwards from an article in the *Jerusalem Post*.

'We work to fixed routines', said the commander (who asked whether I spoke any Spanish). He was from Argentina and though he said his English was 'not too good', it was fine.

'At first light we all stand-to. In the past, if it happened at all, the terrorists would attack at dawn or at sunset. Then everyone must be ready . . . no other way.'

'Have you ever been attacked?' I asked. I didn't expect an answer but he gave me one anyway.

'Not directly; but we have been mortared. And in April there were many Katyushas', he told me

'On the camp?'

'One or two, but we were in the bunkers. Most of them hit outside.' He pointed to a nearby kibbutz.

'Not on the people. In the fields. But near.'

'And mines?'

'Over there, plenty.' He pointed north. 'None in Israel.'

The work was not boring, he suggested. At first he had some difficulty with the diverse group of people under his command. There were Falasha Ethiopians, Jews from India and Canada, some British and quite a few from Arab states such as Morocco, the Yemen and Iraq. Some were Sabras, second-, third- and fourth-generation Israelis. The lieutenant's family had originally come from Rosario.

Also at the camp were handfuls of Americans and Russians and occasionally there were problems. 'Nothing serious: but you know how us young people are.' He was enjoying the session, in part because I was genuinely interested. Most journalists, he'd found, went to the operational area for the ride and the pictures.

An interesting aspect dealt with men or women who'd simply had enough of the routine and who wanted to go home. As I was to discover, the IDF had its own way of dealing with such people.

'I had one of these people two weeks ago, young guy, about 19 or 20 and he said he was going crazy. He had to go home.'

Those dissatisfied with life in the army are never prevented from leaving, he disclosed. 'They're taken before the camp commander and warned that when they came back, whether it is after a week or a month, they'd be charged and jailed . . . all done under military law and two weeks in detention usually follows.' The time of absence and in detention is added to the period of compulsory military service and it had to be served, one of the officers explained.

'When he gets back to his unit afterwards, life goes on as usual, both for him and for us. No hard feelings. We all just get on with our jobs.' he said.

The obvious role of the camp was to pinpoint enemy fire. For that it was equipped with an American 'guidance' system called 'Unit 37' the operators of which had been trained in the United States. The majority of specialists served three months at a stretch Stateside. It has since been superseded by other weapons systems.

While details were classified, I was told that Unit 37 used a method of 'saturating forward areas with radio frequencies and analyzing their

In winter it gets bitterly cold in parts of Lebanon, particularly along the ice-clad slopes of Mount Hermon, where I spent a week with DanBatt, the Danish UN detachment. (Author's collection)

disruption by an explosion'.

The response was automatic, effectively within three minutes. This was one of the reasons why Hizbollah units bombarding Israel like to disappear as soon as they've launched their rockets, missiles or mortar bombs. A conspicuous feature of the camp was the stacks of liquid nitrogen tanks placed around the periphery at irregular intervals. They were used for cooling infra-red instruments, essential in the heat.

Life at all Israeli military establishments along the Lebanese border, of necessity, is focused on the eight or ten mmiles of security fence, with each camp responsible for its own stretch. Some of the control panels in the operations rooms were electronically linked to the fence and were geared to give warning of a breakthrough. There were also regular patrols along a well-maintained security road; two vehicles in the day and three at night, when the patrol is customarily led by an officer.

Targets are all graded according to threat level. Some warnings are electronic; a pressure on the wire of about 10 kilos, for instance, will set off one signal; anything over 30 kilos triggers something else. There are sensitive sensors for ground movement as well as infra-red, radio and TV monitors and quite a few that the IDF does not talk about. At any point along the border there are at least a dozen different impediments.

Apparently, it was easier for Hizbollah to cross farther towards the east, because the terrain was less uniform and more difficult to guard because of high points, valleys and steep gradients. In this area, a machine sprayed fine dust adjacent to the fence so that patrols could spot any kind of disturbance. All was constantly checked.

A chart on the wall of the camp operations centre categorized some of the tactics that Hizbollah had used to cross the frontier into Israel. Besides the usual array of small boats that included high-speed racing craft, there were several acoustic and contact mines depicted (all Israeli patrol boats now carry depth charges) and among about 30 others, photos of the pair of sleek, powerful jet-skis, used by the insurgents who had tried to run the naval blockade from Tyre the previous year but were killed by gunfire from a patrol boat; their craft was found to be packed with explosives. IDF intelligence sources later reported that the objective had been to ram a pleasure craft off Haifa; another suicide operation.

Various types of scuba equipment were also on view, including some well-known brands made in America. One was a Farallon diver propulsion vehicle, state-of-the-art for this kind of unconventional warfare which, said the lieutenant, was what this affair was all about.

I was made aware of the sinking of a small submarine in Israeli waters in the late 1970s by depth charges, even though Jerusalem never released details. It took place in deeper water off Tel Aviv, all of which adds a new dimension to this ongoing low-key conflict.

However, anti-submarine tracking systems have improved a hundredfold-fold since I spent my three years in the navy. Even Hizbollah would be aware that if America has the most advanced undersea tracking systems, then in all probability so has Israel. And while using suicide bombers is encouraged by Party of God commanders if tangible benefits are derived from actions, sending people to almost certain death in risky, unproved maritime exploits is another matter.

This could be one of the reasons why so little use has been made of the dozen underwater craft it is known to possess. But then again, since Iran is involved in all of this, who knows what long-term plans are afoot for their deployment.

CHAPTER FIFTEEN

Marj'Ayoun and the South Lebanese Army

'At Israeli behest, the South Lebanese Army was set up as a
Christian militia under the command of Major Sa'ad Haddad
in 1978, its prime role being to assist the Jewish State counter
Palestinian terror. After the Lebanese War, and once Jerusalem
had established its so-called security or "exclusion" zone, it was
the job of the Israeli Army to help the SLA maintain its
dominant position in the region.'

Globalsecurity.org

HE WAS A BOY, NOT more than 18 years old, and he kept firing at the
UN position until his magazine was empty. Nobody shot back from
any of the strongpoints that surrounded the base.

One moment the youngster was walking down the road towards
Ebel es Saqi, the next he'd levelled his M16 and was firing on full auto.
He obviously wasn't Hizbollah because they've always preferred the
AK-47 to anything Western.

At the time I'd been in one of the battalion halls, a few hundred feet
from where all this was taking place, with my UN escort, Captain
Fredrik Amland, Norwegian Battalion (Norbatt) in South Lebanon. The
also youthful Amland was one of about 1,000 Scandinavian soldiers
deployed in South Lebanon with the United Nations Interim Force in
Lebanon (UNIFIL). Half were Norwegian, the rest from Finland.

The firing surprised us all. Though we didn't take cover, the fusillade
halted everything in the mess where we were eating at the time,
automatic fire in the Levant tending to have that effect. Some of the
soldiers stopped what they were doing, which was when the captain
went out to check.

'It's one of those fuckers, shooting at us', Amland reported when
he'd returned to his meal. He spoke in an accent that reflected time spent
in Newcastle in England and, clearly, wasn't much bothered.

'Who's shooting?' I asked. He didn't answer immediately. When I asked again he said brusquely: 'fucking DFF. Just walked up to one of our OPs [observation posts] and started shooting . . . no reason at all . . .'

DFF or De Facto Forces was argot for the South Lebanese Army, which their Israeli patrons referred to as the SLA. In fact the abbreviation signified a good deal more: DFF meant anyone 'on the other side' with weapons.

'Someone hurt?' Another officer queried

'Nobody. Not even a scratch.'

Didn't his people return fire? No retaliation at all? I asked.

He hesitated a moment, clearly annoyed at the inference and then replied in the negative.

'So what's the upshot? What you going to do about it?'

Silence. Now it was the captain's reticence that had become bothersome.

'Nothing. Absolutely nothing', he finally declared. He then added, almost as an afterthought, that since the shooter was DFF, there was nothing to be done. Were they to take any kind of action against the man such as arrest him or keep him in a cell a day or a week, the local community would be in an uproar. The UN might be accused of siding with the 'hated fucking Jews across the border', my escort suggested and he was quite serious.

'What about next time? It might be you or me that's in his sights?' I declared warily. It could easily happen and he knew that. In fact, it already had, just weeks before. Then a sniper – not a very good one, mark you – had targeted several UN soldiers and wounded one of them. The man only stopped taking pot shots when the UN commander demanded a meeting with the elders of the man's village and from what I gathered afterwards, the man shared the views of the majority of South Lebanon's Christian population at the time: UN troops were regarded as interlopers and were not properly doing their job.

Still, it wasn't my problem and Lebanon, we were all aware, could be a dangerous place. Each of us had accepted that much within hours of getting there. Look askance at somebody on the open road and he might draw a gun, was the usual bar-room comment. At a hint of a pretext he'd probably kill you, happily, and then go home to his wife and kids and possibly first stop off at his mosque along the way.

I'd seen something similar take place once to a car ahead of me while driving through the Shouff during a visit to Druze positions a few years before. A car had pulled abreast of another and the two drivers were having a chat, oblivious of passing traffic trying to get through. Eventually another driver got out of his car, pulled a pistol from his belt, put it against the head of one of the culprits, a juvenile, barely old enough to qualify for a licence.

All I got was the gist of what was perhaps a 20-second discussion: if the youngster didn't move, he'd blow him away. Moments later, in a screech of burning rubber, the car pulled away.

'Where's the guy now?' I asked Amland.

'His own people have taken him away.' It was an absurd situation, like the war in the adjoining countryside.

Later the captain said something about it being typical of these irregular hostilities. He confided that he'd rather the whole fucking Lebanese business had never happened. As it was, he was embarrassed at having to talk about something that officially didn't happen, probably wasn't even entered into the log, and with an almost total stranger to boot.

Later, the captain admitted that there would be no official protest.

For decades Marj'Ayoun was at the heart of the Christian Lebanese struggle in South Lebanon. A short distance from Metulla in Northern Israel, it was the headquarters of the South Lebanese Army. Then, without warning early in the New Millennium, the Israeli Army pulled its forces back behind its own borders, leaving this community to be dealt with as Hizbollah saw fit. It was a bitter betrayal. (Author's collection)

No questions had been asked, nor would any be. Nor were any apologies asked for or given, because at that stage the 3,000 members of the SLA were held in contempt by the UN, even though they constituted half the military forces in this low-key guerrilla insurgency in an area a good deal smaller than Greater London. The other half was Hizbollah.

I wasn't the only one who thought that the situation was bizarre. To disregard the presence of an Israeli-supported military unit, much as the UN was trying to do, was almost like the British government ignoring every Roman Catholic in Northern Ireland during the Troubles.

That was Lebanon then. It is also Lebanon today, where anything but the most serious kind of bloodletting rarely gets the attention it might deserve.

I discovered afterwards that the man who'd let fly at the guard post came from Marj'Ayoun, a stark hilltop town of cinder blocks and rutted streets. This was the most Christian village in the eastern part of the security zone. It was also Israel's forward command and control centre in the region and the headquarters of the SLA while that element was still active.

Modest, even by Arab standards, Marj'Ayoun was a rather nondescript Middle Eastern village which boasted barely 12,000 inhabitants. With Hizbollah today dominating the entire region, only a fraction of the original Christian families remain. The majority have suffered the same fate as other Christian communities in the Arab West Bank further to the south, like Nazareth, Taibe, Ramallah and Beit Jala.

Marj'Ayoun was an important focus to many Lebanese Christians then, just as staunchly Shi'ite Nabatiya is to Hizbollah today. Before Israel pulled its troops out of South Lebanon, Marj'Ayoun was the nerve centre of all SLA operations in the region. Most of the senior officers of this Christian militia lived there. Almost all its houses were gathered in untidy clusters round several large hills, some half-finished, others two or three storeys high and still unfinished, in large measure because of ongoing hostilities. Marj'Ayoun saw a lot of action in its day and many of the men with whom I came into contact, a few of whom became friends, ended up dead because of it.

The main road wound through the town. Near the centre, even today, it is sometimes only wide enough for a single vehicle as it twists and turns on its north–south axis. In the old days, roads branching out from Marj'Ayoun would shoot off in all directions and stop where the minefields began.

There were scores of shops on either side of the main road, but not as we know them in the West. These are adjuncts to the family dwelling, so there were always old people and children about, the latter playing almost under the wheels of passing cars. Elsewhere, there were cluttered little workshops, usually with two or three men sitting out in front drinking coffee or pulling from a hookah.

The smell of cooking was everywhere; falafel, or mutton ribs or a shank over an open fire by the roadside, much of it dominated by the powerful scent of cardamom.

In those days, if you sat on the flat roof of one of the houses near where Samy Talj ran his little garage, you could see much of the surrounding countryside, usually with a couple of GPMGs covering local ground from behind clusters of sandbags. Anybody who has used a 'Gimpey' in combat knows what a comfort these guns are in a scrap.

These were Western weapons though, and the SLA used captured Soviet stuff. I concluded from the deafening silence from my escort on this subject that they'd probably been filched from one of the UN squads.

Unlike Beirut, where everything leads up to the mountains, the country around Marj'Ayoun is largely rock-strewn. Many of the high points were defended, though you saw little of those fortifications from the town. In the valleys and wadis between them, there had been some hard fighting.

To the south, on the road to Metullah and what was known for many years as the Israeli 'Good Fence' border crossing, you could just make out El Qlaiaa, another Christian town. The place became unsafe after Ahmed al-Hallaq, the SLA security chief, was abducted by some of his own men who had been got at by the Hizbollah command. They were paid good money to hand him over to the Party of God. In Israel such an act would be roughly analogous to Hamas partisans kidnapping the head of Shin Bet, torturing him and then putting him to death.

That is what Hizbollah did, I was told often enough. They forced al-Hallaq to reveal the names of many of his agents, who were then rounded up or killed. He couldn't resist their entreaties, they said afterwards, because they had their own ways of making him talk and the human body can only take so much . . .

From the same roof you could also see some of the buildings on the outskirts of El Khiam, with its notorious prison that during the Israeli period of occupation drew a lot of attention, especially from human rights groups. There was plenty happening at Khiam when I was around – a bit like Guantanamo today – but it wasn't the sort of place that visiting journalists made too much of.

Both the Israelis and the SLA always maintained that the prison inmates were criminals who had committed what were euphemistically referred to as 'military crimes'. There were no details given, even if you asked, except that if Khiam did not exist, 'then the war would go badly for everyone', an Israel colonel told me. Then Hizbollah might be within small-arms range of Israeli settlements, he warned. He was probably right because now that the IDF has finally pulled back, many Jewish settlements, moshavs and kibbutzims are being fired at from across the fence.

What was disconcerting was when some people in a couple of villages adjacent to Khiam told me that they could sometimes hear prisoners screaming at night. Who knows what went on behind that structure's 13-foot walls topped with razor wire?

All this was happening in an area roughly 30 miles from east to west and about 8 miles deep and officially under UN control. Those Europeans operating in South Lebanon at the time knew very well about what was going on at El Khiam when the Israelis were still in South Lebanon, but they tended to look the other way whenever this reality faced them. In this peculiar never-never-land, most UN contingents pretended that the place simply didn't exist.

The man who created the SLA south of Beirut was an Israeli officer, Colonel Yoram Hamizrachi, who was originally a journalist, a very good one, we were told. For the purpose, he was given the rank of lieutenant colonel and told to get on with it. Initially the new unit was called the Christian forces, and only later the South Lebanese Army.

Hamizrachi, whose idea it was in the first place, was an impressive fellow and I got to know him well over the years. After his tour of duty with the IDF, he stayed with me for a while in South Africa and then went on to live in Canada.

Some journalists who arrived at Metullah – where Beata, his German-born wife, and he operated out of – suggested that Hamizrachi's job with the SLA had all the makings of something quite glamorous and derring-do. It was anything but.

The man was tall and, frankly, far too heavy for the popular notion of an Israeli Army officer. He usually wore a billowing kaftan at home,

A journalist and a lieutenant colonel in the IDF Reserve, barrel-chested Yoram Hamizrachi almost single-handedly created Sa'ad Haddad's South Lebanese Army. Several times my wife and I visited him at his home in Metulla, Israel's northernmost town. On one occasion, he took us across the border into South Lebanon. (Beata Hamizrachi)

where he received most of his callers – Jewish or Arab – and that would sometimes give him an almost brooding, Buddha-like image. He was also impressively well-read and as fluent in Arabic as if he'd been born to the culture.

His mien was disarmingly frank, which would sometimes belie more immediate concerns. His house, he used to say, was on the very last spit of land that nudged Israel's northernmost security fence. 'The most northern house in the State of Israel', he would joke and then offer us a drink.

When Fatah and, later, Amal and the others began lob Katyushas across the fence, the Hamizrachi family would take shelter in one of the back rooms. The idea was to always have at least two walls between them and anything heading their way.

'We don't worry about it too much', Beata would say. 'They are not very accurate and we always have time to move when the first one whistles through.'

Hamizrachi could also be unconventional, especially in his handling of 'predators', as he liked to refer to members of the Fourth Estate. In the late 1970s, no serving Israeli officer would take a journalist (certainly none with foreign passports) across the border into Lebanon. We were considered to be imperfect correspondents by the authorities in the Middle East and were treated accordingly. Yet he led me across the border on my second morning in Metullah.

'I want you to meet somebody', he said in his booming baritone that always set the scene, if not for a confrontation, then for something about to happen. I was to meet the leader of the SLA, he told me. So it was that I was, for the first time, ushered into the presence of Major Sa'ad Haddad, a self-effacing Lebanese regular officer who had given up a promising career in the army to throw in his lot with the Israelis.

This Arab officer was the antithesis of Hamizrachi and a very different kind of individual. He spoke imperfect English and almost needed to be nursed through an interview, suggesting little and volunteering almost nothing except platitudes. He'd use phrases like 'my boys are brave' and 'the cause is just'. His Israeli 'controller' meanwhile, trod his own narrow path in Arabic when dealing with the man.

Haddad must have been good at what he did, for the SLA – which initially emerged as an ineffectual mob of ill-assorted strays with guns – was ultimately to become a reasonably efficient counter-insurgency unit. The force would go on to develop a measure of clout that could match anything the Palestinians or Amal threw at them, if only because the SLA operated in the backyard of many of the men in its ranks. Most had grown up in South Lebanon.

In the early days, after the SLA had been constituted as a fully fledged fighting force by the IDF and given much Soviet hardware captured from the Egyptians and Syrians, serious difficulties emerged, some of them bad enough for Jerusalem to consider abandoning the project.

There was initially little order or discipline among the first recruits mustered at Marj'Ayoun. Factional differences gave rise to friction: one group supporting the *Ketaib*, powerful Christian Phalangists who dominated the Lebanese Force Command, while another Christian grouping fancied those who not only opposed them, but also supported the dissident Franjieh hierarchy of the north. This group was later exposed to Syrian infiltration.

In those days both groups were generally regarded as thugs. Ruffians I'd heard them called, who would murder for a nickel. I found them pretty good fighters the first time I went out on ops with one of their patrols.

Taken into the hills flanking the old Crusader castle Fort Beaufort, the patrol became disconcerting when the soldiers started taunting Palestinian units on the ridges above. It was a bold but asinine show of strength. What worried me was that that all we had between us and 'them' was a thin-skinned M113 APC which trundled along lines that were hardly demarcated. The APC would certainly have been no match for any of the 23mm heavy guns that Fatah was able to deploy.

Although the Palestinians shot at us from time to time, there was never any kind of concerted attack. Both sides knew that the Israeli Air Force needed little provocation to respond. Nights were different and were when most Hizbollah, Palestinian Fatah or Amal elements would emerge.

Over the years many questions were asked about why the SLA was actually created in the first place. It seemed a paradox: Jews employing Arabs to protect their northern flank. 'Simple', said Hamizrachi after I'd returned to the Israeli side of the fence. 'It's there to protect the southern Lebanese from Beirut and the north. Since there are thousands of people dying each month, it makes good sense to recruit these people.'

As Hamizrachi explained, the SLA was conceived to prevent hostile penetration of Israel from Lebanon. At that time, in the late 1970s, Israeli farms and settlements came under frequent attack from across the border. Moreover, the frontier was porous; Fatah could sometimes ambush

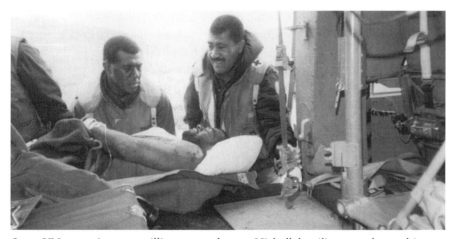

Some UN countries were willing to stand up to Hizbollah militants and casualties mounted steadily. The Fijians, in particular lost quite a few lives because they stood fast in the face of Arab intimidation; here a Fijian soldier is airlifted out of the operational area. (Author's collection)

vehicles on Israeli roads. When they did, casualties could be serious and often were. A Fatah guerrilla group once attacked a bus full of Israeli children and took hostages. Many young innocents died that day.

'We could put an end to all that *schlimazel* by creating a secure border zone', were his words. 'And what better way to do that than by using the people living on the other side?'

It was decided by Jerusalem that since the area round the Litani River, the largest water course in Southern Lebanon (though barely a trickle in summer), was inhabited mostly by Christians, they could be mustered, also for their own protection. They would be brought together as a group, trained and armed and used to deal with the kind of terror then creeping south. In fact, it made good sense. As Hamizrachi said: 'Lebanon was on the rubbish tip of history, anyway.'

So it was that the Christians in the south began looking after their own interests and, indirectly, those of Israel. Since the Muslims living in the region were aghast at what was happening elsewhere in the country, they did not oppose this new development. In fact, so many of them supported it in the early stages that the SLA opened its ranks to members of the local Shi'ite community. Hindsight demonstrated afterwards that this was a bad mistake.

Part of the problem inherited by Hamizrachi was that despite the fighting, many Lebanese government institutions were still in place, if only nominally. There was still a Lebanese Army as well as a police force, although by now, both had been marginalized by civil insurrection. For many, to join the newly established SLA would have meant abandoning their careers. Some long-serving officers were worried about what association with the SLA might do to their prospects of promotion, never mind their pensions. Crumbling security and the collapse of the Lebanese economy finally decided it for them.

Slowly the SLA matured, but it was a demanding process. For a while American, German and French mercenaries were allowed to join (conditions were hard and the pay derisory; about $100 a month with no perks), but few stayed long. One was Dave McGrady, an American who had fought in Rhodesia and with whom I went on a bounty hunt in Ian Smith's rebel territory (as described in Chapter 19). He came to hate Lebanon.

Some of these 'volunteers' were infiltrated into the SLA by radical groups then active in Europe and the Middle East. Those whose cover was blown were quickly liquidated. Others just disappeared.

Many South Lebanese Army strongpoints were fortified by the Israelis, who passed on captured Soviet armour, taken from the Egyptians or the Syrians, to help fortify these positions. (Author's collection)

On a broader canvas, there is little doubt that the Muslim people of southern Lebanon have always been an entity unto themselves. Proud of their southern origins, they can almost be compared to southern Italians who regard their northern cousins with disdain.

Though Shi'ite, these people are known as *Metawillah* and have been referred to as dissenting followers of Islam. Past travellers have noted their toughness and treachery, due to the number of times their culture has been uprooted by invading armies, from the early Egyptians on. In the few dealings I had with these people, I found them forthright. If not overly friendly they were always correct in their dealings. By contrast, there was no curbing the vicious hostility projected my way by their children, particularly after Israeli artillery had been active and casualties resulted.

Colin Thubron deals with the region and its inhabitants in sumptuous detail in his book *The Hills of Adonis*. Though published almost half a century ago, it was clear even then that turmoil was imminent.

Yet, as the SLA gathered strength, still more Shi'ites were recruited. Like Christians serving in the SLA, they were allowed to send their families across the Good Fence into Israel to work. Initially, as I was to see, things worked well. Because of the war there were times when their wage packets provided the only economic support.

By the mid 1980s the SLA had evolved into a cocky and well-knit little army. By now the IDF had strengthened its defences by providing its surrogates with captured Russian tanks, scores of American M113s and a variety of tracked and half-tracked vehicles. Many SLA officers were sent to Israeli military training depots. It was not long before SLA cadres were almost indistinguishable from the Jews, except for language. Their uniforms and small arms were the same and to cap it, every IDF soldier working with the SLA was fluent in Arabic, since most of these troops were of Sephardic origin.

Meanwhile, the Israelis had built a string of secure fortifications that stretched from the mountains along the Syrian border to the coast north of Naqoura. In UN jargon, these were the installations that were referred to as PVs: 'Permanent Violations'.

Most lay on high ground and dominated a likely infiltration route. In keeping with Israeli strategy, all approaches were mined. The same was true of IDF strongpoints on the Golan, one or two of which were able to hold out until relieved during the Yom Kippur War, even when completely surrounded by the Syrian Army.

Though the Israelis are now back in Israel, the minefields they left behind still present problems and will continue to do so for a while, especially as not all are mapped.

At one stage an international mine-clearing group headed by Lionel Dyck, a former Rhodesian Army officer, was contracted to deal with some of them. His brief included some Hizbollah-controlled areas in the Beka'a Valley. By all accounts, it will still take many years to finish the job properly.

Meanwhile, the casualties still occasionally roll in, the majority of them civilians.

The 1990s initiated a different set of problems that also obfuscated the intentions of those with fingers in the proverbial South Lebanese pie. Yoram Hamizrachi was long gone and while the SLA continued to remain a factor for a while, it was less so than before. Again its future was scrutinized, and for several reasons.

'It's essentially a problem of security', said Joseph P., regarding me carefully with his single eye: he'd lost the other in a firefight with a bunch of Palestinians who'd ambushed his patrol. He was an old friend from the period when Samir Geagea had been head of the Lebanese Forces, now also dissolved, and had been a key man in his hierarchy. He'd actually been my contact when I first entered Lebanon during the civil war period. Because he was from the Christian south and still had many members of his family there, this former demolitions expert took a great interest in that region. At the same time he didn't want to be named, which was absurd since everybody knew who he was and the role that he played in this internecine conflict. Still, he was deadly serious when he turned towards me shortly after we first met and warned: 'You identify me in print and I'll have your balls, even if I have to send someone to cut them out!'

Lebanon was still at war when we met in Baabda, a suburb of Beirut, in a little coffee shop. I'd called Rocky, the officer in charge when Christian was killed. He had told me where to find Joseph P.

'The problem is that the SLA is no longer secure. Before it was a Christian force; about 90 per cent. Now it's mostly Shi'ite. Some members have been subverted.' He looked surreptitiously about him as he spoke, a characteristic trait, always suspicious, always checking. By his own admission, it had probably kept him alive over the years.

'Some Christian villages have even tried to reach an accommodation with Hizbollah's Nasrallah. It's all a question of survival . . . staying on top.' It was the customary conspiratorial touch, typical of Joseph P.

'If the Israelis pull out, then what? There will be a massacre . . . a serious killing. Thousands! All the old scores will be settled.' The scar high on his left cheek where he had been hit by shrapnel stood out in sharp profile as he spoke. Then he added: 'Discipline has become slack. It's not like the old days when we were doing a competent job'.

Joseph P. defined the scope of the Israelis in South Lebanon. Because the SLA was no longer working properly, increasing numbers of security roles fell within the ambit of the IDF. That meant more patrols, more searches for mines and more booby traps. The result, he declared, was still more tension and an increasing number of Israeli casualties.

'My friend', he added, 'it is no longer a secret that more SLA and Israelis are being killed there than Hizbollah. You can read it for yourself in the *Jerusalem Post*'.

Joseph P. was correct. Simply speaking, the Jewish State was losing too many of its young soldiers in what was clearly an army of

Israeli patrols throughout South Lebanon were constant until roadside bombs – or in more modern parlance IEDs – started taking lives. The IEDs currently being used against Coalition Forces in Afghanistan were originally blooded by Hizbollah in this area adjacent to the Israeli frontier. (Author's collection)

occupation in South Lebanon. Though the IDF was on the ground in hostile territory, its presence under almost constant fire was achieving very little. Not long afterwards it didn't surprise us that the Israeli Army pulled back and security in the entire South Lebanon region fell under the control of Hizbollah. Because cross-border hostilities then began to escalate markedly, the IDF launched its disastrous invasion in the summer of 2006.

I have since heard that in the aftermath of that debacle, Joseph P. was assassinated outside his Beirut home.

It should be noted that when the IDF suddenly withdrew, the SLA was disbanded. Worse, it was an unconscionable last-minute decision that left the entire force both vulnerable and exposed. Without the protection of their sponsors, there were an awful lot of SLA cadres killed, quite often together with their entire families.

Several things impeded the 'Peace Process' in the Levant in the late 1990s. The most notable was inextricably linked to the Golan Heights, which – historically and politically – belongs to Syria. It always has. The right of conquest, even the Israelis admit these days, cannot prevail for all time.

I'd visited the Golan at the time when I had first met Hamizrachi. After many requests, the Israelis took me into one of their strongpoints on the cusp of the escarpment that overlooks a distant desert of grey stone on which Damascus was originally built. I stood outside, on the edge of a great minefield surrounded by razor wire, cold and silent. It was a grim winter and Damascus was a hazy cluster of buildings in the distance.

The inside of the fort – for that is what it was – was damp and gloomy, a warren of defensive tunnels built to keep an invading army at bay, as it did in 1973. It was manned mostly by older men who were required to give so much time each year to the defence of the nation.

When the visit was over, I wasn't allowed to linger. As it was, everything they wished to keep hidden from my prying journo eyes was covered in canvas. They fed me a bowl of hummus and tahini with pitta, which was when my escort, an army officer from Natanya, suggested that we move on.

President Bashar Assad has said many times that there can never be peace in the region until the Syrian flag again flies over the high ground that we know today as Golan. He has repeatedly argued that Sinai, captured in the selfsame Yom Kippur War, was returned to Egypt years ago. Obviously a different case, the two issues are linked, yet who can argue so long after the Camp David Accords?

Stresses Assad: Golan should likewise have been vacated by Israeli settlers. While there is little regard to history in his thesis, to the average young Arab intellectual – be it in Damascus, Cairo, Amman or Riyadh – it makes very good sense.

For their part, the Israelis reckon that they are not the ones who are intransigent, but rather, it is President Assad who impedes the implementation of a long-term peace settlement. On the one hand, he makes conciliatory noises. Simultaneously, he arms Hizbollah with rockets to strike at Israeli towns across the border and assassinate Lebanese political leaders. If the Syrian leader chose to do so – even Assad's enemies acknowledge – he could put a stop to it all with a single wave of his hand.

There is another, less widely known aspect to this imbroglio which, for a while, was linked to both the SLA and the future of Northern Israel: this one involves water, arguably the single most valuable asset throughout the entire Middle East. In one of his last public speeches before he was assassinated, the late President Yitzhak Rabin declared that the uninterrupted supply of water in Israel was 'even more important than peace'. Without it, he declared, 'the nation cannot and will not survive'.

Rabin was always of the view that since the Golan Heights supplied a large proportion of water to Israel, Syrian demands for the return of the Heights, as a quid pro quo for peace along the northern Galilean frontier with Lebanon, was incompatible with the reality of the situation. He also declared that while President Assad was of the opinion that the position of the Golan Heights was not negotiable, things were not quite so simple.

Assad only needed to look at a map to understand the ramifications surrounding this process. It goes something like this: The high ground to the east of Galilee is directly coupled to the defence of the source of water. Again, there are two factors to be considered: the first is Lake Kinneret (Lake Galilee) which is entirely in Israeli sovereign territory but is dominated by the Golan Heights above. Second, there is the flow of the Jordan River, whose headwaters and tributaries lie in the Golan and adjacent parts.

An article in the Israeli newspaper *Ha'aretz* (21 January 1996) spelt it out:

The matter of Lake Kinneret is vital since it is the largest (and only) water reservoir in the state of Israel. Israel can in no way agree to the Syrians' returning again to the shores of Lake Kinneret.

It may be recalled that up to the Six Day War, the international border passed about ten meters from the north-east part of the lake. In fact, the Syrians took over the narrow strip and saw themselves as partners in the lake. They interfered with fishing activities and harmed [and killed] both civilians and security personnel. They even threatened to contaminate the water if Israel attempted to pump water from the lake without their agreement.

These two paragraphs lie at the core of the problem of the entire northern region of Israel. It also highlights ancillary security issues that relate to the country's social, political and economic infrastructure.

Nearly all of the Golan lies within the Galilee Basin. The lake supplies roughly a third of the water that Israel needs. Two of the three main sources of the Jordan River, the Dan and the Hatzbani rivers, rise on the slopes of Mount Hebron, nearby. The mountain and the Heights are inseparably linked and they are all integral to the package claimed by President Assad.

As the Syrian leader says, there can never be peace in South Lebanon until they are all returned to Syria. A third river, the Banias, another tributary to the Jordan, also rises in the Golan Heights.

All these factors together, Jerusalem concedes, have little to do with Syrian tanks or soldiers. Here, it insists, it is necessary to look at the historical record. *Ha'aretz* again:

Syria talks about international law, but it already knows from its ongoing dispute with Turkey on the joint use of river water [along their boundaries] that this law is not clear. Also, if Syria were to try to divert the course of any waters emanating from territory under its control, another war will be inevitable. It has happened before. It will do so again.

For these reasons, a senior official from the Israeli Foreign Ministry told me, nobody is prepared to rush into any long-term settlement with Syria without having looked very carefully at all possible permutations. 'Israel is not averse, at some point, to perhaps exchanging the Golan

Mainly Christian South Lebanese soldiers gave as good as they got from Islamic radicals who were gradually replaced by Iranian-backed Pasdaran revolutionaries, who would soon call themselves Hizbollah. (Author's collection)

Heights for a secure South Lebanon. But in order to achieve that, he said, we must have the right guarantees.'

The man who can provide those assurances sits in Damascus.

CHAPTER SIXTEEN

Uganda: Africa's Killing Fields

In the past half century, the continent of Africa has spawned
political tyrants like some modern societies produce visionaries.
As we go to press, President Omar Hassan al-Bashir has been
indicted by just about every international body of consequence.
The man is a brutal oppressor. He has caused the deaths of
possibly half-a-million people in Sudan, the majority in Darfur.
Before him, there was Idi Amin Dada of Uganda.

NOR SHOULD WE FORGET PRESIDENT Robert Mugabe of Zimbabwe.
While his tally of killings are nowhere near those of el-Bashir – who
has all-but obliterated an entire people – Mugabe has managed to lay
waste to a country on an almost apocalyptic scale.

Sadly, much of what has taken place at the hands of these African
vulgarians was – and still is – racially motivated. In the Sudan, for a long
time, it was black people who were being massacred, by a staunchly fundamentalist Islamic government. Mugabe's campaign, by contrast, was
initially aimed at getting rid of white people living in Zimbabwe, though
in the process he ended up persecuting millions of his own black
subjects, many of whom fled.

The pivot of Amin's initial fervour centred on his bid to expel
Uganda's Asian community, the majority of whom, in a gesture of
British magnanimity, moved to the United Kingdom. Brutal dictator that
he was, he then turned on his own black people.

When this oppressor eventually died in Saudi Arabia, African
journalist Makau Mutua went on record as stating that Idi Amin had
ravaged Uganda as thoroughly as any leader in modern history has
ravaged any country and that he almost single-handedly turned a
nation's prosperity into economic ruin plunging a peaceful society into a
nightmare of chaos and terror. Mutua goes on to tell us that while ruling
by decree, Amin was one of the first post-colonial dictators in Africa to
unleash mass killings as a response to internal opposition and that
during his eight years as president, beginning in 1971, his government

was responsible for the deaths of as many as half-a-million of his countrymen. Another 100,000 fled into exile while thousands languished in prisons and underground torture chambers. Before Amin, Mutua tells us, Uganda's economy was regarded as one of the healthiest in East Africa. Like Zimbabwe today, it was soon in utter ruin.

There is no question that Amin, who in 1951 won the Ugandan heavyweight boxing championship while serving as an NCO in the then still British-dominated East African Army, was certifiably mad. It was also one of the reasons why those of us who reported from Uganda at the time believed he was suffering from an advanced form of syphilis. What made his rise to the top that much more astonishing was that he would never have achieved power had his British mentors, of all people, not encouraged him to oust his equally demented predecessor, Milton Obote.

That equally contemptible ogre, it should be noted, ended his years in exile in Zimbabwe and enjoyed both the protection and the patronage of his host, Robert Mugabe. It says much that Westminster was also responsible for bringing Robert Mugabe to power.

Of all Africa's dictators, Idi Amin was arguably the most unhinged. While in power, he awarded himself the Victoria Cross and announced that he was adding to his list of titles – which included 'Lord of All the Beasts of the Earth and Fishes of the Sea' – that of 'Conqueror of the British Empire'.

Perhaps then, and not altogether surprisingly, it was Amin the buffoon, not Amin the butcher, who first caught the world's attention. He raced around Kampala in a red sports car, watched Tom and Jerry cartoons, plunged into swimming pools in full military uniform during diplomatic functions and boasted that he had fathered 35 children.

A cruel, ruthless man, Amin presented himself to the world as a ridiculously absurd figure. He volunteered himself as King of Scotland, so that the Scots, as he liked to say, 'could be free of British rule' – a theme which resulted in a brilliant film that went on to win an Oscar. Then he would send telegrams to the Queen of England, insulting and taunting her and he once challenged the President of Tanzania to a boxing match.

When the capital, Kampala, fell on 10 April 1979, Amin, along with his wives, mistresses and a very substantial quota of children, had already boarded a plane for Libya. From there the entourage was quickly dispatched to Saudi Arabia. Muammar Gadaffi, another African

Some of the soldiers in the army of future Ugandan President Yoweri Museveni, when he ousted Idi Amin, were barely into their teens. These were the forerunners of the 'child soldiers' we were to see much of in later years in Sierra Leone, Liberia and the Ivory Coast. (Author's collection)

delinquent very much in the spotlight, really did not need Amin's presence to tarnish further his dubious reputation.

Uganda was an interesting place to visit in the old days and as others discovered, it could also be perilous.

My old *rafiki* Mohammed Amin, Idi's namesake but certainly no relative, ran his illustrious news agency, which he called CameraPix, out of Nairobi. He would regularly tell me that his latest source of news or photos in Kampala had 'copped it'. There were six or eight of these stringers murdered by the general's goons. A couple disappeared without trace.

As a journalist, Uganda was part of my unofficial news-gathering brief, which suited me because you never came away from Kampala without something to write about. I went there with my wife once and the pair of us were probably among about only a score of tourists to have booked a visit to the Murchison National Park that year. Despite the risks, it was a memorable trip, with boating on the Upper Nile and taking pictures of crocodiles. Amin, we were to learn later, fed many of his victims to these beasts.

What disturbed me most about this visit was that we were under surveillance by the Ugandan secret police from the moment we stepped off the plane at Entebbe. Even at Murchison, where we slept in a tented camp – there were obviously no doors to lock – I was aware that Amin's men were on the periphery. My wife was the proverbial innocent in paradise, so I said nothing, though I got very little sleep.

Using Nairobi as a base, I went back to Uganda repeatedly over the years, both before and after Amin's rule. Sometimes we media types would score pay dirt, perhaps by being invited to State House, where we were expected to grovel before this uncouth idiot. Most of the European scribes would cower and smile, usually sublimating their fears in booze, of which there was always plenty. I never did, which might have been why Amin remained reasonably civil towards me during the few times we did make contact, one such time being at his home on Nakasero Hill which overlooks some of the better parts of Kampala, including the diplomatic quarter. Towards the end, he even sent me the Muslim equivalent of a Christmas card during Eid, which I still have.

Getting into Uganda during Amin's rule was, at best, problematic. Everybody who arrived from abroad – and even from Nairobi – was watched. This meant that I preferred using alternative routes, such as overland through Rwanda and several times by ferry across Lake Victoria.

Going in by lake steamer was always a delightful voyage, but only if you travelled first class. I'd customarily board at Kisumu in Kenya – usually at the end of Kendu Road, in a harbour affectionately named Port Florence in the colonial epoch. There were stops a-plenty en route, some in Tanzania further south. Throughout, we'd keep a sharp eye out for lake flies, which could descend on the ship in dark, noxious clouds, often a third of a mile wide. People have been suffocated by these dense, slow-moving swarms.

Once berthed at Entebbe, I'd join the rabble and try to get through customs and immigration without fuss. Usually, I'd latch on to some backpackers, who were always around, and most times I'd succeed. Then I'd take what might have passed for a cab along one of the most dangerous roads on the continent of Africa, to Kampala, though that would usually begin with a ten-minute haggle over fares.

Whenever I used local transport in East Africa, there was always a strict routine that needed to be observed, like holding on to my baggage and first checking both tyres and brakes. Quite often the intended car would be faulted on both counts: the treads on an astonishing number of vehicles on Uganda's roads were down to their canvas underlays and blow-outs were as commonplace as fuel stops.

During the dozens of times that I made this hazardous journey, there were often accidents along the way. The bodies of victims would be carefully laid out on the verge for the families to collect and if there was no family, or the word hadn't yet got out, the cadavers would be buried somewhere nearby a day or so later. Because putrefaction sets in within hours in that heat, it was the sensible thing to do, not that anybody concerned themselves unduly with graveyards . . .

Then followed the invasion of Uganda by the Tanzanian Army in 1978, which led to an abrupt change of government.

There were several events that led up to that debacle and while it went on to be labelled a 'glorious military victory' by Dar es Salaam, it was a disaster for the entire region. It bankrupted Tanzania, then being ruled by President Nyerere and, ultimately, the war led to his unpopularity as a leader, even though the Tanzanian Army methodically stripped Uganda of just about every piece of machinery, equipment and furniture that hadn't been bolted down.

If it could be pillaged it was. The booty was then hauled back to Tanzania, as it was euphemistically phrased in local papers, 'to help pay for the war'. Only massive efforts on the part of the West got the economy on its feet again, this time with a new man at the helm, former guerrilla leader, Yoweri Museveni.

What eventually caused Idi Amin's downfall was the murder, at his command, in February 1977 of Uganda's Anglican Archbishop Janani Luwum, together with two senior cabinet ministers. They all died in what was described as a car accident, but there was evidence that the Archbishop was clinically butchered. In fact, I was told by several former members of Amin's cabinet that parts of this eminent ecclesiastic were later fed to guests at a banquet held for members of the diplomatic corps in Kampala.

By then, world opinion had turned against Amin and for the first time, several African nations broke their silence about the excesses of a fellow African leader. In fact, they were far more outspoken about Idi Amin then than they've subsequently been about Zimbabwe's Mugabe.

Also, matters weren't helped the previous year when Israel launched a spectacular operation at Uganda's Entebbe International Airport to rescue passengers of an Air France jet that had been hijacked by pro-Palestinian guerrillas. Amin, and the rest of Africa, was deeply embarrassed at this so-called foreign intrusion onto 'sacred' African soil.

Finally, in October 1978, this bumptious executioner, who was inordinately cunning, capricious and also a consummate liar, made his biggest blunder. He invited almost 3,000 Libyan troops to Uganda to enlarge his army and facilitate a national switch towards Islam. At the same time, he dispatched his rag-tag army into Tanzania. By all accounts, Idi Amin hoped that a regional war would divert the attention of the international community from a succession of domestic problems, but then Tanzanian President Julius Nyerere did the unthinkable. He retaliated by ordering his own so-called People's Militia into action. Within months it was all over and Idi Amin was accorded refugee status in Saudi Arabia.

During the Uganda/Tanzanian war, I arrived in Kampala at roughly the same time as the invading forces and found myself a room in what had originally been the Kampala Intercontinental Hotel. While it was also eventually stripped by the Tanzanians – of everything from electric light switches to toilets and washbasins – it was still better than average as far as some African hotels went. We also had to watch for missiles each time we returned to the hotel, especially at night.

As part of his war effort in support of Uganda, the Libyan leader had donated tens of thousands of Holy Korans to the people of this Central African state. All were beautifully case-bound volumes in Arabic, complete with English translations on opposite pages. I still have one in my library, duly stamped on the title page with the imprint: Socialist People's Libyan Arab Great Jamahiriya. Things were fine for a few days, at least until members of the Tanzanian Army took rooms in the hotel. Being mostly Christian, they'd make short shrift of these tomes by hurling them over the balcony without checking if there was anybody below. At more than a thousand pages each, they were pretty bulky items; taking a hit from one of them would almost certainly have floored the recipient.

As for the rest, it was a typical African conflict, with us hotel residents sitting on our balconies after dark, gin and tonic in one hand, binoculars in the other, watching the 'fireworks'. Almost every night there were tracer patterns that arched into the sky.

Once hostilities had moved on towards the east and the north, few of these volleys were fired in anger. More likely, there would be a group of soldiers on a bender. They'd fire for effect in the air each time somebody got clever or perhaps needed another round of drinks. However, we'd quickly duck inside if the hot stuff headed our way, but in the end, our hotel was spared much of it.

For its part, the Tanzanian Army worked to a series of set plans which, we soon concluded, must have involved an awesome amount of ammunition.

Led by several hardscrabble armoured units – whose equipment included T-55 tanks, a few T-34s, Soviet half-tracks, and 122mm 'Stalin Organ' rocket batteries – the Tanzanian invaders would trundle into position every morning, pulverize a real or suspected concentration of Ugandan troops for an hour or two, and then spend the rest of the day consolidating new positions 10 or 20 miles up the road. The procedure would then be repeated the following day, and so it went until the Ugandans were finally routed.

In the middle of all this mayhem were the few thousand Libyan troops who, though still in Uganda, never played any real part in the war. In fact, for much of the time, armed to the teeth as they were, they were little more than bystanders.

Their leadership was equally inept because we could all see fairly early on the direction this war was heading. Instead of getting on the first planes out, the Libyans hung around until the end. When they finally did make their move, it was too late.

They headed down that same Kampala–Entebbe road to the airport that I'd used earlier and ran straight into the Tanzanian Army units that were waiting for them. Ambushes would be set at several likely spots, and once in the killing zone, the APCs the Arabs used would be the first to be destroyed. Those Libyans who managed to survive these initial onslaughts would rush into the jungle.

At that point, local people – civilians, one and all – would go into action. With their long machetes, they'd slaughter any Libyan they found hiding in the banana plantations or the long grass. Each time somebody reported an Arab presence, the old, the young, male and female would pile into Land Rovers, buses, trucks or even tractors and hunt them down. It says much that not a single Libyan prisoner was taken.

I watched one such hunt from a taxi on the main road to Entebbe out of Kampala. Word had it that there were a bunch of Libyans holed up in a building just off the main road.

Eventually, a group of local 'head-hunters' arrived, eager for battle. They all had long knives and were shouting, whistling and chortling, with some of the women around the periphery ululating as if there was no tomorrow. It was scary, even though I wasn't the subject of their ire.

Gradually, the crowd got bigger and whoever was cornered in the building did the obvious and stuck a white cloth attached to the end of a stick out of a window. With that, the crowd went berserk and surged forward. There was no stopping them and while some of the youngsters tried to break through a window, the group out front managed to batter down the door.

Moments later, three or four camouflage-clad figures were hauled out to whoops of joy from the crowd. Everybody who could do so laid into them with their blades; the unfortunate Libyans were dead in minutes.

For these soldiers, a large part of the problem was that while Libya was an African nation, its troops weren't black. Nor could many of them speak English. This meant that even though some of these poor souls tried to worm their way into the woodwork, so to speak, they were very easily spotted, especially in the kind of under-populated bush country that makes up so much of Uganda's interior.

Consequently, their fate was sealed and almost the entire force ended up dead. The few who did get away managed to board the last flights back to Libya early on. A few of the more imaginative fugitives managed to steal a boat and slip across Lake Victoria to Kenya.

Moving around Kampala during that uncertain time of transition had its moments. There was nothing to stop us going into what was then still innocuously referred to as the Ugandan State Research Centre, the ultimate misnomer.

In reality, this relatively modern cluster of buildings, which had several deep dungeons and was surrounded by a tall concrete and razor-wire fence, was equated by many Ugandans to Moscow's old Lubiyanka

Prison. It was a grim, austere sort of place; anybody taken through those iron gates on Nakasero Hill while the tyrant ruled, very rarely emerged alive.

With Idi Amin out of the way, the security system so assiduously cultivated over the years simply fell apart. Those who had previously been in charge became the hunted and families settled old scores with a vengeance that almost equalled some of the earlier violence.

An immediate consequence was that there was nobody around either willing or able to shred many of the documents that implicated thousands. There were piles of files and papers lying scattered about on the floor of every room in the State Research Centre, some two feet deep. Many were marked 'Top Secret' and I grabbed some that looked interesting because they dealt with serious cross-border security issues with the Sudan and other neighboring states.

Early on, I was also able to make my way through several dark corridors to the dungeons in the basement. It was an appalling experience. They were still removing the dead from below during my first visit and the stench was awful. It took me a little while to do the rounds

Entrance to Uganda's notorious State Research Centre, the innocuously named head-quarters of both Idi Amin's and Milton Obote's secret police which contained torture chambers. We were to witness some horrible realities once we got into the building. (Author's collection)

and it was obvious that there wasn't a cell where there hadn't been inmates shackled to the walls, many naked, each one of them emaciated. While males predominated, there were women inmates as well. Who will ever know to what abuses those poor creatures were subjected; the walls of all the chambers were caked in dried blood. We didn't need to be told what it was. A water main had broken somewhere in the building and the lower floors were lightly flooded. Where the water reached up onto the walls, the black mucous that was scattered in irregular patches everywhere reverted to its original crimson.

What came next surprised even a few of the hardened correspondents who had observed human rights abuses in other parts of the world. There was a large room at the end of the deepest tunnel that had obviously been used for torture. What appeared to be a home-made wooden chair stood in one corner, complete with canvas buckles on the arm rests and still more to clamp the feet of the victim. All around were wires that protruded both from the walls and from a device that looked like a small generator.

We were already aware that Amin liked to be present when some of his victims had electrodes clamped onto their heads, ears, nose and testicles. Whether they talked or not was irrelevant, all were dead within days.

Long before he had been deposed by the Tanzanians, we were aware that Idi Amin had taken over the day-to-day procedures involved with running his government, much like Zimbabwe's Robert Mugabe in more recent times. This monster consolidated his power under three security groups: the military police, his so-called Public Safety Unit, as well as the dreaded State Research Centre. All enforced his decisions with the kind of terror that had Amin still been alive, would have probably led to his standing trial at the International Court of Justice at The Hague. Indeed, the State Research Centre conducted some of its 'public executions' at its headquarters, in the heart of the capital.

The diplomatic corps in Kampala was, without doubt, aware of what was going on. Nakasero Hill was the suburb of choice of many diplomats, as well as some of the well-heeled businessmen who had decided to stay. In fact, the residence of the French Ambassador was only across the way and the screams of prisoners were so bad that his wife had to be flown out for treatment at a clinic in France.

But this, it was argued at the time, was Africa. The country was newly independent and in the main Europe and America, much to their discredit, tended to turn a blind eye to such horrors. While South Africa was being castigated about its apartheid policies, hardly a word about Uganda was whispered in the corridors of power at UN Headquarters in New York.

Black people, the apologists would say, didn't do such things. In fact, they were only emulating some of the excesses that Europe had experienced in its recent past at the hands of Hitler. History went on to repeat itself in the Congo, then in Liberia and, finally, in Zimbabwe.

In Uganda, meanwhile, Idi Amin's systematic intimidation of his people continued and he ended up murdering many Ugandans. Quite a few foreigners were also killed, including a couple of Scandinavian journalists who tried to enter the country illegally, by boat from Kenya. They were arrested, tortured, put up against a wall and shot.

Then his 'killer squads' murdered two Americans, Nicholas Stroh, a journalist and heir to the Stroh Brewery in Detroit, and Robert Siedle, a sociologist who had been studying the care of the elderly in Africa while teaching at Makerere University in Kampala. Years later, Siedle's son – who was 16 when Amin came to power – reported that he had been living with his father in Uganda at the time. He also disclosed that his dad had come to know Amin before the general took total control of the country and was initially impressed with him.

Everything that happened to young Siedle appears in his book, *A Tree Has Fallen In Africa*. As Siedle tells it, rumours of unspeakable cruelty such as murder, torture and rape, committed by Amin and his poorly disciplined army, began to circulate in the months that followed Idi Amin's putsch. About then his father and Stroh became suspicious of the thunderingly gregarious general:

> When rumors that hundreds of soldiers at the army's Mbarara Barracks, some 250 kilometers outside of Kampala, had been slaughtered on June 22, 1971, filtered through to Kampala . . . [they] set out into the African bush to seek confirmation of the atrocity.
>
> So on July 7, 1971, the two men cranked up a battered pale-blue Volkswagen station wagon with a hand-written 'Press' sign attached to the windshield and drove off into the tangled heartland of Uganda, never to be seen again.
>
> Their disappearance alerted the world for the first time of the policy of mass murder of the Amin government that came to be referred to by the International Commission of Jurists as Amin's 'reign of terror'.

WARNING!

LETTER AND PARCEL BOMB RECOGNITION POINTS

■ Foreign Mail, Air Mail and Special Delivery
■ Restrictive Markings such as Confidential, Personal, etc.
■ Excessive Postage
■ Hand Written or Poorly Typed Addresses
■ Incorrect Titles
■ Titles but No Names
■ Misspellings of Common Words
■ Oily Stains or Discolorations
■ No Return Address
■ Excessive Weight
■ Rigid Envelope
■ Lopsided or Uneven Envelope
■ Protruding Wires or Tinfoil
■ Excessive Securing Material such as Masking Tape, String, etc.
■ Visual Distractions

In a house adjacent to that of President Idi Amin on Nakasero Hill, we were to find the local headquarters of the PLO. There we discovered drums of explosives in the basement that caused powerful fumes to permeate the entire house. In another part of the building, I found a number of timing clocks intended for use in pipe bombs, one of which had already destroyed the plane of Kenyan Minister Bruce Mackenzie in mid-air after he had displeased President Amin. Elsewhere on the premises were details, clearly from a Western source, that indicated what to look for when there was a threat of letter bombs: these explosive devices were also being 'manufactured' at the PLO house. (Author's collection)

On June 22, 1971, I had celebrated my 17th birthday in Africa without my father. A few days later, I returned to the United States alone. Neither my father's body nor Stroh's was ever found. Pleas by the US State Department to the Ugandan Government to have my father declared dead so his estate could be settled and life insurance benefits paid were met with denials by Idi Amin that my father was dead.

My father and Stroh, the hefty general said, had simply left the country, gone on holiday.

Twenty-six years later, in May, 1997, I returned to Uganda as a guest of General Muntu, commanding officer of the Ugandan People's Armed Forces, to interview the soldiers who murdered my father and dig for my father's body . . .

I went often into Uganda's interior, both before and after the Idi Amin epoch. It was usually a dangerous exercise, all the more so because the roads were always treacherous. Of the three drivers that I regularly used off and on with my hire cars over a three-year period, two were killed in road accidents.

This was also a time when AIDS first became an issue and we could see that there were people dying in numbers throughout the country. All of East Africa was being increasingly affected by the disease, but for some reason, Uganda suffered the worst, in part, it was said in Nairobi, because it actually originated somewhere along the border with the Congo.

True or not, I ended up making a television documentary called *Aids: The African Connection* and spent months in and out of Uganda doing research and filming, the first time with Dr Jack van Niftrik who ended up writing a book on the subject. My film eventually ended on the documentary award shortlist at the Shanghai Film Festival. I didn't make it to the awards table, but the film was seen throughout China for a month.

For the week while working on that film, I ate breakfast every morning at the Hellenic, the same little hotel on the outskirts of Kampala that had ABC's 'World News' anchor Diane Sawyer seated at the table next to mine. Though she had not yet risen to her subsequent giddy heights in the hierarchy, she was working on a network production on the virus at the time and barely spared us a glance.

In 1994, I went in again. I declared afterwards that I didn't think I'd be going back any time soon and I was right. There were two reasons. The first was the Ugandan Army. the second was a rebel group that called itself the Lord's Resistance Army (LRA). At the time it was run by a lunatic called Kony and, after Amin, one couldn't help thinking that Uganda certainly spawned these types. This ogre's specialism was abducting children from local schools. Some, not yet into their teens, were 'moulded' into what he termed his 'Volunteer Army'. Almost all ended up sporting automatic weapons and murdering innocents.

Kony has obviously been successful in his efforts to dispense mayhem because the LRA is just as active throughout Central Africa now as it was then. Not only does this revolutionary movement wish to unseat the existing government, but it would like to take over power throughout a region that includes parts of Uganda, Northern Kenya, the Congo, Southern Sudan and the Central African Republic.

We would often be shown mass graves, left behind by Ugandan President Idi Amin's goons. These skeletons were in an abandoned house and many were children. (Author's collection)

The rebel movement had an attention-grabbing background. Kony took over the LRA from where his equally demented aunt and mentor Alice Lakwena left off. Her specialism was dousing her soldiers with 'holy water', which she claimed would make the opposition's bullets bounce off their chests. The fact that they didn't was of no consequence; enough of her soldiers survived the occasional battle because of bad marksmanship on the part of the other side to credit her with some remarkable successes.

Prior to Khartoum's assistance, Kony was operating from a head-quarters deep in Uganda's Kidepo Valley National Park. This he shared with Karamoja cattle rustlers who regularly exchanged fire with the Ugandan military and the occasional Kenyan Army patrol that came across the border to retrieve stolen livestock.

Not everything went his way. At one stage Kony's force was down to about 500, including child warriors. Then he, too, started 'anointing' his troops with various concoctions to make them 'invisible'.

The effect was that it made Kony's warriors fearless; to frightened and inexperienced government soldiers, the enemy's crazy disregard for death sometimes caused them to break ranks and run. A Ugandan editor, Charles Obbo, described the LRA as 'a few hundred rebels [who] are giving a division of 10,000 Ugandan soldiers a right run around.'

It got worse – thanks to Khartoum. Having slipped into the Sudan and befriended the Khartoum government – who saw the rebel as a useful pawn in their fight with Kampala – Kony returned to Uganda with what Western intelligence agencies at the time estimated were 6,000 guerrillas. In their first encounter with the Uganda People's Defence Force (UPDF) in the north of the country, the LRA killed between 250 and 500 UPDF soldiers. That was a year or two before I got there.

In addition to carrying modern Kalashnikov assault rifles, LRA guerrillas were also planting mines along roads and paths used by UPDF forces (with Sudan supplying the wherewithal). Kony's fighters would haul light artillery pieces and RPG-7s into some of the better-coordinated attacks.

Overnight, Kampala was faced with a new and revitalized enemy who was not only well-disciplined, but used the same kind of weapons that they had issued their soldiers with. Also, LRA guerrillas had been taught how to ambush and they used these tactics to good effect along many of the major roads of the north, as far west as Pakwach and east to Lira.

Kony's guerrilla force bore some distinctive hallmarks. The LRA then, as now, was divided into brigades. These, in turn, were split into smaller groups of 15 to 50 men at a time, depending on the nature and size of the task ahead. Each unit had its own political 'commissar' and the men in this formerly staunchly Christian force were now allowed to adopt the faith of Islam; more of Khartoum's meddling.

In other respects, not much else has changed over the years. Children in the ranks of the LRA – kids of 10 or 12 years of age – are known to be responsible for some of the worst atrocities, often laying waste to entire villages. The stacking of human skulls alongside roads was always a hallmark of the LRA, largely to intimidate those who tried to bring them to book.

As in other parts of Africa, the LRA revolt has some ugly tribal undertones. Kony, an Acholi from Northern Uganda, believed in the resurgence of the warlike Acholi nation as a dominant force throughout the country. This, in turn, resulted in the slaughter of other tribal groups, though that seems always to have been a problem in Central Africa. Anyone within the ranks of the LRA who was even vaguely suspected of disloyalty was murdered.

For many years, conditions were so bad that no Western correspondent dared accompany the LRA on its forays and for once, I wasn't going to push that envelope, not this time anyway . . .

My connection to both the rebels and the Ugandan Army took place in the small town of Gulu south of the Sudanese border, a tough five- or six-hour drive north of Kampala.

At that time Gulu was at the frontline of Uganda's war against the LRA, who would sneak over the border from the Sudan to stage attacks. The main crossing point between the two nations, then and now, was Nimule, about 150 clicks north of Gulu, a route that has been closed to ordinary travellers for years.

Gulu had once been one of my favorite stops. Before 1986, when I made a television documentary on the region and the town represented a tiny oasis of sanity in the crazy turmoil that had overtaken Uganda, I'd go there from time to time.

The main watering hole for us hacks – and a very good one at that – was the Acholi Inn; it offered reasonable food and ice-cold Tusker beers. There was even a hospital worthy of the name, complete with permanent staff, many of them expatriate. Moreover, Gulu's children were all at school thanks to the local Roman Catholic Mission, some of whose Holy Fathers were later murdered by Kony's people.

Other attributes included a foreign-aid contingent drilling for water in some of the surrounding villages and, most spectacular for those of us who travelled up by road, a requisite stopover at the Murchison National Park, in its day one of Africa's finest. All that ended when the first cadres of the LRA arrived on the outskirts of Gulu.

A few years passed before I returned to the town, this time with a French film crew from Antenna 2. By now, unfortunately, Gulu existed in name only. Curiously, not all was bleak. As it lies on one of the major routes linking other parts of Africa, some transients had returned. Also, there were aid specialists trying to make a go of it, but all felt the effects of the war. The Acholi Inn still stood and offered me a bed without a mattress for $25 a night. The food was inedible and the alcohol was suspect.

Because of the nearby LRA presence, the Ugandan Army was in control and foreigners and locals alike ignored military orders at their peril. On arriving in Gulu, we all reported to the local field commander and he gave us the usual claptrap. The war against the LRA was in its final stages – or so we were told. Also, the last dissidents had been driven into Southern Sudan. What we were seeing, said the colonel, was a 'mopping-up' operation. Then he got unpleasant.

'No pictures', he warned pointing a finger at each one of us in turn. 'Not even one!' If we were caught filming, the man continued, we would be arrested and charged with 'sedition' (a favourite word in some of Britain's former colonies in Africa).

We were told to wait at the Acholi Inn. Meanwhile, a couple of surveillance men kept tabs on our movements. By the third day, we decided that we had to do something. Each night there was firing about town and on the outskirts, but we were not even allowed to ask questions, let alone investigate.

Our French producer, an equally devious schemer as the dreaded colonel, had a plan. We invited our two 'minders' for a beer shortly after breakfast and we could all see immediately that they enjoyed the break. Then a bottle of whisky appeared. An hour later they were drunk and we were off to town.

By noon, we had filmed the centre of Gulu, snatched a sequence of the military camp while driving past and ended up in the railroad yards where half-a-dozen trains stood abandoned. The LRA had sabotaged the line some miles distance of town, which meant that the region no longer had a rail link with the south.

It was there that a Ugandan Army officer caught up with us and demanded we accompany him back to the army camp, a very bad place for a uncooperative foreigner to find himself, he assured us.

When we refused, he went off for reinforcements. We hot-footed it out of town in the direction of Kampala, several hundred miles to the south, our two cars keeping pace with each other.

It was a calculated risk, abetted by the fact that while the Ugandan Army at Gulu had radio contact with military headquarters in the capital, they were having trouble transmitting. This much we were told by a British expatriate whom we met at the hotel and who had come to Gulu to service the equipment.

However, we all knew there was also the LRA. At that stage, we'd been assured by the British expatriate that Gulu was completely surrounded. Cars moving through the region were being shot up, though most ambushes took place in the late afternoon. It was still lunchtime and we were prepared to chance it. All these factors had been carefully discussed the night before.

The author with the French television crew on the road to Gulu and the war with the Lord's Resistance Army in Northern Uganda. This crew helped me with filming when my own team refused to budge from Kampala because of 'danger'. (Author's collection)

Barely ten minutes out of Gulu – with the two vehicles moving one behind the other, about 300 feet apart – we suddenly became targets. Automatic fire sprayed both sides of the road. Neither car was hit in that first salvo, but it was close enough to see that the LRA were using green tracers. A short distance on there was more firing.

By now I was lying flat on the floor of the car directly behind the driver and being the hero I am, I urged him to put his foot down even harder.

We covered the 12 miles to the next town in about eight minutes: the longest journey of my life. All of the villagers, almost as a kind of welcoming group, were gathered on the edge of town to greet us. They could follow our progress along the undulating low hills through which the road twisted, and there was no missing the shots. A great roar went up once we reached the outskirts and for the moment we were safe.

Once we had reached Kampala we split up. I wasted no time and went overland by bus and taxi directly to the Kenyan border and crossed at Malaba early the next day, on foot.

The French crew managed to persuade a charter pilot to take them to the Kenyan capital the same evening. At least we got our film out . . .

CHAPTER SEVENTEEN

Bounty Hunt in Rhodesia

One of my crazier ventures was to accompany Dave McGrady,
an American mercenary from Michigan, on what he would
have liked to think was a 'bounty hunt' in the wilds of
Rhodesia while that bush war raged. In theory, he would have
been paid good money for every 'terrorist' scalp. In reality, the
adventure almost got us all killed.

MCGRADY WOKE ME AFTER MIDNIGHT. The American grunted softly
and nodded in the direction of the river. 'Gunter and the Greek are
asleep', he said quietly.
'So much for those fuckers guarding our butts . . .'
From my sleeping bag tucked next to a couple of large boulders, the
night seemed less oppressive after the rains. From dawn onwards, it had
been a tough slog. Much of the hike had taken us across difficult thorn
and mopani country speckled by giant outcrops of granite, some as high
as multi-storeyed buildings. *Gomos*, they called them up Mount Darwin
way and probably still do: it's a Shona word.
There'd been a few stops, usually to brush tsetse flies from our backs
and catch a breath, but nothing long enough even for a brew: always tea,
because you can smell coffee for miles in the African bush. When we
found a temporary camp site we opened a few canteens and drank some
of the water we'd taken earlier from one of the few streams we'd
crossed. One of the guys tried to filter some of it through his bush hat
and while it tasted muddy, the filtering got rid of some of the grit.
Too risky to start a fire, McGrady ventured. I agreed, in part because
of the goats we'd heard a few miles back. In that kind of backwater, a
single goat equates to human presence. Also, we weren't quite sure how
these people would view a quartet of strange whites spending time on
their turf; we were all in camouflage and shouldered an assortment of
weapons. News of strangers in remote areas travels fast, especially in the
African bush, so we kept out of sight and never crossed open ground if
we could help it.

Domestic animals might also signify a gook camp. McGrady had mentioned as much earlier out of earshot of the other two, because they were already on tenterhooks. We two should take extra care, he suggested. I couldn't argue, especially since these were unknown factors in a land that was being disputed both by the guerrillas and the government.

Now that we'd moved in, McGrady was hoping for a kill or two of his own . . . if they didn't get us first . . .

The insurgents in that area, north-west of Wankie, were a tough, seasoned bunch of fighters, or so we'd heard back at the Quill Club in Salisbury – Harare today. This was the land of the Matabele, distant cousins of their belligerent Zulu forebears; the majority of rebels operational in that region were loyal to the portly Joshua Nkomo. Many, we knew, had been trained abroad, some in Iron Curtain countries. Also, we took it for granted that they'd have been issued with some heavy-duty hardware.

While the four of us were adequately armed for any normal kind of contact – between us we had two FN-FAL rifles, McGrady's converted AR-15 and my own Mini-Ruger (the last two in .223 calibre) – we really weren't properly equipped as a hunting party in a war zone. Even with our clutch or two of grenades, we'd never have matched anything sophisticated like the guerrillas used. McGrady had read some of the intelligence reports that passed through his hands from time to time: all emphasized the sophistication of the weapons being lugged by this guerrilla force. Among hardware regularly brought back from bush forays were a profusion of AK-47s, as well as RPDs, RPG-7s and POM-Zs, never mind the usual batch of anti-personnel and TM-46 anti-tank mines. McGrady had been warned by some of the Rhodesian regulars that the guerrillas knew how to lay them too.

The mines were always a consideration, which was why we moved as cautiously as we did. We slept uneasily as well, because in doing his customary hourly rounds, McGrady discovered the Greek slumped fast asleep over his rifle on his two-hour watch on the first night out.

With McGrady creating a dark shadow at my side – he lay on his sleeping bag rather than in it – I peered into the darkness in an effort to see what it was that had caused him to rouse me. It couldn't have been all that serious because my slumber had been pretty intermittent anyway.

I leaned over towards him: 'You hear anything?'

'Negative', he whispered.

'Had a bunch of something come through . . . must have been wildebeest . . . moved on towards where *they* are', he said, pointing at a position perhaps 500 feet away '. . . probably spooked when they smelt the Greek's aftershave . . . galloped off quickly. That's what got me on my elbows', he added.

McGrady wasn't enamoured of the Greek. Within a day or so the sentiment was reciprocated and from then on the two hardly exchanged a word. The European didn't like being told what to do, which was one of the reasons why the American felt he could have managed better without him.

Just then some heavy cloud moved in and covered what little moon was left over this stretch of Matabeleland. It would rain again, probably soon, he'd told me earlier. If it did, the people we were looking for wouldn't find yesterday's spoor. Trouble was, if they'd left tracks in the direction we were headed, we wouldn't spot theirs either.

David G. McGrady, a private American citizen with no military background, had originally arrived in Africa by way of *Soldier of Fortune*, that Colorado-based magazine that catered to what it liked to term 'Modern-Day Adventurers'. These were mostly former military veterans, most of them gung-ho and who had done a tour or three in Vietnam. Almost to man they sought action, legal or otherwise, preferably under a foreign flag.

By McGrady's time, the magazine had published several features on the ground war in Rhodesia and McGrady, always the iconoclast, got hold of a copy of one of my early books on guerrilla warfare in Africa, titled *The Zambezi Salient*.[1] A bit of a pace-setter for its time – it highlighted several wars then creeping inexorably southwards – the book covered some of the hostilities in Rhodesia as well as Portugal's military campaigns then ongoing.

McGrady obviously liked what he read, and through my publishers he was given my address and dropped me a line. His first question was: are there any military opportunities in which I can get involved in Southern Africa?

I replied that there were plenty, but that he'd not only have to get himself across the Atlantic, but he'd also have to consider carefully whether this was something he'd really like to do, especially since he had no military background. I suggested that he arrive reasonably well

American mercenary Dave McGrady on the improvised raft that took us across the river into Injun Country, as he put it, 'to hunt gooks'. They almost got to hunting us . . . (Author's collection)

equipped: 'you're going to need your own kit and the kind of heavy stuff that might be useful for fighting in the bush', was my suggestion.

Perhaps two months later, a youthful Dave McGrady arrived in Johannesburg, where he met three other American adventurers, all with solid military experience under their belts: Drenkowski, Cunningham and Bolen. All three ended up doing freelance military work in Rhodesia.

Dana Drenkowski was a USAF pilot who'd flown more than 200 combat missions over South-East Asia in Phantom F-4s and B-52 bombers and had then gone on to work briefly as a hired gun for Libya's Colonel Muammar Gadaffi.[2] Tom Cunningham and Jim Bolen, by contrast, were both former members of US Army Special Forces units. Jim was a member of a CIA/ Studies and Observation Group (SOG) Team in Vietnam and Tom had left one of his legs behind in South-East Asia following a rather serious contact with the Viet Cong.

With this group on my doorstep, I had to do something to assist them in their quest for a bit of action. Since I was working for a local magazine at the time and spotted the opportunity of something possibly happening with these guys in Rhodesia, I suggested to my editor, Jack Shepherd-Smith, that we perhaps had the makings of a story here. That was when I was given one of the company cars and McGrady and I set out for Salisbury. The others had already gone ahead.

Once in Salisbury, McGrady tried to join the army. He'd hoped to get himself posted to the Rhodesian Light Infantry (RLI) but was dissuaded from doing so by the recruiting officer who suggested, in part, that because the American was a married man with children, and had neither combat skills nor a military background, he might possibly be better suited to some kind of rural protection work instead. This was when he was pointed in the direction of the Rhodesian Department of Health.

There he was given the job of riding shotgun with his 30-round AR-15 carbine and a Colt Commander .45 ACP in a shoulder holster. In typical Yankee fashion, he'd sport a Gerber Mark 2 survival knife, usually suspended from his webbing. Later, he acquired a clutch of grenades, which he liked to keep strung within easy reach on his Vietnam-era nylon webbing.

'Reckon I'll save one of them for the terr who rolls me over to see if I'm dead or not.' An unlikely situation, because McGrady always carried magazines loaded with nearly 900 rounds, enough to keep a minor gook army at bay, he reckoned.

While working for the Deaprtment of Health, it was his job to offer protection to some of the department's units required to enter Tribal Trust Lands in specific areas. It was the only way they could work, which was essential if tabs were to be kept on immunizations, outbreaks of cholera and even an anthrax epidemic in cattle at one stage, which also ended up affecting some humans.

'It was actually pretty interesting stuff', was one of his asides. 'But we didn't see much action. The gooks were there all right. I expected them to react, but there wasn't a helluva lot of risk.' At that stage, he explained, the insurgents preferred soft targets; they were probably intimidated by his arsenal, he would joke.

It wasn't long, therefore, before McGrady, by now a blooded American mercenary and bounty hunter, became typical of some of the freelances we might encounter in Rhodesia's bush war during the 1980s. Though never attached to any regular 'Rhodie' force, he saw enough action in the former rebel state to qualify eventually for a job with Sa'ad Haddad's South Lebanese Army.

Once in the wilderness, Dave McGrady missed little of what went on while he was in the bush. He was prone to quoting what one of his Selous Scout buddies once told him: 'Develop a knack for looking beyond the obvious . . . try to spot anything thing out of place . . . look for the unusual . . .'

Also, in this kind of work, he knew that if you were slack, didn't pay attention to the small things that mattered and do the necessary when required, you ended up dead. It was as simple as that, he'd say, because this kind of conflict conflict was unforgiving.

By his own admission, much of what he had learned in the African bush came from the process of trial and error. He admitted to some serious blunders which, under different circumstances, might have cost him his life.

'But I learnt and had to do a lot of it on my own because there's usually only a modicum of input from others, mostly from some of the guys who have been doing similar kind of work.' Most sobering, he acknowledged, was the fact that he was strictly a bounty hunter and could count on no military support from the Rhodesian authorities.

That means, whatever happens, I'm on my own. I can't call in for any support. No air strikes if I run into the enemy . . . no RLI, no Fire Force . . . even if I'm completely surrounded. Nothing! Obviously once I've made contact and I'm able to put the word out, they'll come running. But how do you do that without radio comms?

And considering all that, I don't exactly think I've fallen down on the job. Some of the folks out here believe that I've been into this business a lot longer then I have and, judging by results, I reckon I've been pretty damn successful.

On that point McGrady refused to elaborate, except to say that in previous months he'd been active in several areas in Matabeleland that had been declared 'hot' by defence planners back in Salisbury.

In a sense, this American had become a thoroughly competent military man. He was a perfectionist who relied solely on both instinct and his natural skills to stay alive. Had he remained on in the United States and perhaps turned his talents to crime – something he admits crossed his mind on occasion – he would almost certainly have given local law enforcement agencies grief. McGrady was also determined not to add his name to the long list of mercenaries and other adventurers who had perished in Rhodesia.

His one lasting regret was that he'd never fought in Vietnam. He knew it would have provided training and experience to make things easier in Africa. 'It'd have to be one of those Special Forces units', he said. 'I'm too much of a loner to put up with this grunt-bonding crap. Give me the essentials and leave me to my own devices.'

It was his eyes, he explained. Bad eyesight had prevented him from being drafted to South-East Asia. Meanwhile, the war in Vietnam was winding down, 'so the draft board was rejecting guys like me . . . but it hasn't held me back from doing my thing here in Rhodesia'.

Rhodesia's war, which had sporadic beginnings in the late 1960s, finally developed into a full-blown guerrilla struggle in December 1972 when insurgents attached to the Mozambique-based Zimbabwe African National Liberation Army (ZANLA) attacked Altona Farm in the Centenary area north of Salisbury. The conflict that followed lasted seven years. Soon the entire north-east of the country was grappling with an escalating insurgency that resulted in the country being mobilized for war.

Militarily, the conflict in this Montana-sized African state spread from the north-east and then towards the south of the country. Finally, with Zimbabwe People's Republican Army (ZIPRA) guerrillas coming in from the west, a new front was to open that used Zambia as a staging post.

However, for all the numbers of trained insurgents, financial and material aid from China and the Soviet Bloc, together with vaunted claims that were sometimes reminiscent of Lord Haw Haw's broadcasts to Britain in World War II, the terrorists were never able to capture or even properly infiltrate a single Rhodesian town.

Essentially, the war was largely contained by the country's miniscule armed forces, but after years of fighting and huge demands made materially and time-wise upon the tiny white community, many of these people ended up voting with their feet. That was followed by the insurgents managing to gain footholds in some of the Tribal Trust Lands, which became no-go areas for the security forces. As a consequence, some bitter battles ensued.

In the overall combat situation, the insurgents were rarely a match for the professionals. In the final phase of the war (sandwiched between the election of the Muzorewa government in April 1979 until the ceasefire arranged by Britain in December that year), the few hundred men in the Rhodesian Light Infantry's four commando units killed almost 1,700 enemy troops. Then it became what some observers liked to call a 'numbers game': there were just too many of the enemy.

In one of my last discussions with former Rhodesian Prime Minister Ian Smith at his home in Harare – prior to his move to Cape Town where, in 2007, this former Battle of Britain pilot died – he said it was the flow of whites leaving Rhodesia that got to him in the end.

'Once I found I was losing the equivalent of a company of fighting men a month, I knew that I wouldn't be able to sustain the war indefinitely. I had to settle it, and that had to be done by talking with these people, something that London eventually facilitated.'

What motivated that development was the harsh reality that by 1979, the last year of real hostilities, there were about 2,000 whites leaving Rhodesia each month. With almost nobody moving the other way, the country had become seriously stretched with the inexorable loss of skilled and trained manpower. At the same time, Smith admitted, it was a pretty close-run thing.

The guerrillas took heavy losses in the final stages of the war. They had thousands of their comrades killed in combined-operations, cross-border strikes into Mozambique. The first cross-border raid in August 1976, for example, was headed by the Selous Scouts at Nyadzonia, a ZANLA camp, and ended up with 1,200 enemy killed. At the same time, enemy morale plummeted. Their leaders had told this very substantial insurgent army that Salisbury would soon capitulate, but it wasn't happening.

Also, the surrounding states, at first eager to help in what was first termed in Dar es Salaam 'The Liberation Struggle' (which had already seen off Lisbon's rag-tag armies in Angola, Portuguese Guinea and

Mozambique), were becoming increasingly nervous of being dragged into an all-out war with the 'White South'.

Zambia was already playing host to something like 25,000 fighters. Apart from Joshua Nkomo's ZIPRA troops, these included forces from South Africa's ANC as well Namibia's SWAPO, and like those fighting in Rhodesia, they got their succour from Moscow and Beijing. What made President Kaunda touchy was that these foreign combatants actually outnumbered the Zambian Army by a ratio of something like three-to-one.

One of the sentiments that emerged in Lusaka only afterwards was that if things didn't go the way it was expected with the war then being waged in Rhodesia, the presence of these insurgents could ultimately threaten the political stability of Zambia. It was an issue, we now know, that was even discussed with guerrillas leaders at a fairly high level by Moscow.

Dave McGrady had no illusions about the kind of work in which he'd be involved in Africa. Or that his limited experience of a sophisticated

Three members of our four-man 'stick' that went into an area adjacent to one of the Tribal Trust Lands in Rhodesia's north-west. After being dropped by Land Rover, we crossed the river and from there on, we marched through a huge, sparsely populated region looking for insurgents. (Author's collection)

guerrilla struggle might impede this mission. In the brief time he'd spent in this guerrilla struggle, he'd developed an appreciation for the wilderness that a year before might have been as alien to him as the jungles of Brazil and which sometimes takes others decades to assimilate.

At first glance, the youthful American, then in his late twenties, appeared to slot perfectly into his new-found job. He had brought his own stock of firearms and boxed ammunition to Africa, and having done his homework – he was an avid reader – he'd arrived reasonably well prepared. The work was tough, but he was in superb physical shape. That, a solid sense of bush craft, and a level of stamina rarely found outside the ranks of the Green Berets made for an enviable package. Certainly, his physical ability and fairly recently acquired bush craft put the rest of us to shame.

From the start, we were aware that McGrady was certainly not prone to that common failing to which most Americans are susceptible: underestimating the enemy:

I know what I'm up against. I also know what they can do as well as what they've done. So, before I get involved in a scrap, I scratch everywhere for background research on the particular brand of gook active in the area in which I'm going to operate. And in the broader picture, I like to make sure I'm supporting the right cause . . . can't do something you don't believe in.

Then I get to try to understand their culture, which is essential if you're going to avoid misunderstandings which are most-times unnecessary. And when I'm on ops in the bush, I kind of go into what I like to call my sixth, ultra-alert sense . . . keep's me alive and well.

He had his own personal philosophy about motivation: why he was there. It went something like this:

Both the ZANLA and ZIPRA terrorist groups are pretty brutal when it comes to killing anybody who might be opposed to what they stand for. Here I emphasize the 'might' part of the equation because you can die very easily for what they *think* you might be thinking, not what you really are. It's the same kind of totalitarianism that we've seen in Cambodia and parts of Lebanon: the

'all or nothing syndrome'.
    If you're not for them, it is assumed you must be against them
. . . it's all black and white and not a single grey . . .

He'd long ago learnt that the insurgents, on average, killed a dozen or more blacks to every white. He was opposed to that kind of anarchy. He went on:

I'm not in Rhodesia to keep the power in the hands of the white minority. I just didn't want a despot taking over and making life miserable for everyone.
    Those bastards will take a village chief from his hut, cut off his ears, his lips and sometimes other parts and force his wife and other family members to eat those body parts. Then they'll murder him and often deal with the rest of the family in the same way, simply because they're family.
    We've had some of the white people captured who have been similarly brutalized; women were raped, babies hung from trees and bayoneted. Not the kind of people that I'd ultimately like to see running any country . . .

The first few days out in the wilds had been difficult. The immediate difference between the American and us was that McGrady had his bush legs and it was all us city folk could do was to keep pace. But then he'd been doing this kind of thing for a while. He'd been trying for months to get himself a kill, or as he phrased it, 'a terr, two preferably, both dead.'[3]
    That kind of jargon was pretty specific to the bars around Salisbury. A dead gook could bring in $1,500 in Rhodesian dollars from the authorities, or at least that's what the posters promulgated, only in less abrasive lingo. Moreover, this American wanted a piece of the action.
    McGrady acknowledged that while it all sounded fine, it was a two-way street. 'They' might get him first, he conceded, which was why he'd invited us along for the ride. And then, when things started going sour with the other two, he thought the better of it.
    'Bad mistake,' he would comment, usually late in the day. 'Could have done better on my own . . .'
    He was annoyed that the Greek didn't know how to move silently through the bush. Worse, he couldn't keep his trap shut, especially

towards sunset when the bush went quiet. Or that Gunter – whom he called the German – demanded to fill his water bottles each time we crossed a stream.

Gunter wasn't actually a German as his name suggested. He'd been born in South Africa and for a fitness freak who was supposed to have spent time with the Recces, he didn't strike us as being among the sharpest of Special Forces honchos. On the second night out, about half way through his watch, McGrady spotted him standing tall in the moonlight doing windmill stretching exercises to limber up. Eyes rolling, the American wondered out loud if the man had ever been anywhere near one of South Africa's crack reconnaissance regiments . . .

Also, his constant need for water worried us. The man perspired like a hog. We'd walk a mile and his entire uniform would be soaked: clearly, that wasn't normal. Whereas the rest of us could manage on between three and five water bottles a day, he needed 20. Only later did we hear that it was a medical problem that had precluded him from long-range ops with the army. A couple of years after our little jaunt in the bush, we heard that Gunter had died of a heart attack, which was unusual because he was otherwise fit and strong.

Those first few days were tough. Though it took time, we adapted quickly and were able to keep pace with McGrady from the second day. Like the American, we soon became accustomed to this strange and sometimes curiously muted world, where conflict had intruded like no other modern-day influence. To those involved, McGrady included, it was almost a game: men on the hunt, intent on destroying each other. In another sense, the chequerboard had enveloped us all: an uncompromising game, as someone called it, 'Them or Us'.

Some, like McGrady, did it for a cause. Others were into it for the money. These new-style Africa-bound bounty hunters could make a good deal of cash. Moreover, it was all tax-free.

Our first-night ambush position near the Gwaai River wasn't ideal. Rushing water from the adjacent stream tended to conceal any noise we made, but then, as McGrady pointed out, it would do so for the enemy as well if they crept up on us.

While the position alongside the river wasn't too exposed, there were fresh tracks in the vicinity and they worried him. Earlier, we'd crossed an even bigger waterway, the Shangani River, swollen now by six weeks of heavy rain to a torrent that defied crossing in anything but the improvised pontoon we'd used to get to the other side. It was a bulky and unwieldy device made of 55-gallon drums which barely floated properly and which we had to propel across with a long pole.

A local Rhodesian rancher took us across the river and his four African employees had to push hard against the current.

'When you get back, fire three evenly spaced shots and we'll come and fetch you', the rancher told us. 'It'll take me about 45 minutes to round up the crew so don't be in too much of hurry', were his parting words to us.

The rancher said nothing about what we should do if we were on the run, possibly with a squad of rebels at our heels. Because of crocs, swimming wasn't an option, or shouldn't have been, although I hadn't yet totally rejected the idea. No question they were around, because the rancher had almost lost one of his dogs a few days before we got there when it jumped into the water and swam across to be with its master.

In the days that followed, we saw a lot of tracks. Some reflected the linear chevron design that distinguished ZIPRA from their Mozambique-orientated ZANLA counterparts who owed their allegiance to Robert Mugabe.

Occasionally, McGrady would lay his assault rifle on the ground as an improvised measuring stick to pick up the spoor after it had trailed off into different directions. It was another aspect of the game: nobody walked in a straight line any longer than they had to in this kind of counter-insurgency warfare.

We also noticed a few figure-of-eights left in the deep mud by recent visitors wearing Czech boots. They worried McGrady because the Czech-trained insurgents had already garnered a reputation for stealth and ruthlessness. The American estimated that because of the rains, none of the tracks were more than a day old. Our black tracker, who boasted the illustrious name of Montgomery, concurred.

Obviously, while we saw nobody in that vast Rhodesian bush, we weren't alone. On the face of it, the entire region looked abandoned, or possibly just sparsely inhabited because of the war. However, there were people about and, as McGrady suggested when the Greek thought otherwise, that had to be expected on the fringe of Rhodesia's Lupani Tribal Trust Land. Whoever and wherever they were, he quietly declared, he hoped we'd find them before they spotted us. I liked that about the man: few things fazed him, and in the bush he took nothing for granted.

As the American ruminated after our little jaunt was over, just about wherever you go on the continent of Africa, 'there'll always be a face somewhere, peeping out of the bush at you . . .'

The second night out, we'd taken up a position further towards the north. The sun had barely set before the drums started. Obviously emanating from one of the villages we'd circumvented, they were closer than we'd initially suspected. That accentuated our problem.

Gunter wanted to know if this was a warning to other villages that we were in the area. 'We'll know the answer to that one if they attack', McGrady retorted.

Which meant that none of us slept easily that night.

There was another issue. We were all aware that the war had entered a new and more aggressive phase than before. Even cursory evidence of an army presence in an area might have set the infiltrators on the run in the past. As hostilities progressed, things changed. By the time we arrived in this remote region north of the main highway between Bulawayo and the Zambian border post at Victoria Falls, those doing the hunting, we'd heard, were increasingly becoming the hunted.

Barely a week earlier, McGrady had lost one of his Rhodesian buddies in just such a counter-attack. It had come as a surprise, if only because nobody believed that such a small guerrilla unit could be quite so assertive: there were only about six or eight of them. The man's unit had been following tracks, but the enemy they were after doubled back. They attacked at sunset just as the four-man 'stick' settled down for a night ambush.

The event was instructive and McGrady made the rest of us take note: we were no longer dealing with a bunch of amateurs, he averred.

'They're good, these guys . . . bush savvy . . . this is their land and they're familiar with just about all of it. They get the locals to be their eyes and ears, even if it needs a little coercion from the business end of a barrel. If that happens, we're going to have no option but to reckon with them.' For once there were no questions from either Gunter or the Greek.

With these thoughts in mind, an hour or two in the rain-sodden bush, perched as we were alongside a fast-flowing river, sometimes seemed to last half the night. There were two watch spells for each of the two groups: McGrady and I covered the first three hours of darkness, followed by the other two and then us again. The routine would be repeated until dawn and the process would be reversed the following night. After we'd discovered that the Greek had dozed off over his rifle, none of us got any real rest.

I asked the American what we needed to do to remedy a situation that could become critical. His reply was unequivocal: 'shoot the bastard the next time it happens', which was what he'd already told the man the first time he'd kicked him awake while he was supposed to be on watch.

The presence of goats didn't help either as they added to our edginess. In the dark it was easy to mistake their deep, throaty grunts with a human cough, or possibly somebody clearing his throat. When that happens, you sit up, move your finger across the slide towards the trigger and try to peer through the fog of night to see what's going on.

Also disconcerting were the screams of a baboon troop in the bush after dark. Were they fighting or was it a leopard on the hunt? With so many of these big cats about, one would have thought the primates would have preferred not to broadcast their presence . . .

It seemed like an eternity before they would move on.

There was also a mysterious wild creature that would wake us with a start every hour or so when it would jump into the water within yards of where we were stretched out, usually accompanied by a loud splash. It was probably a water monitor and the noise would startle those who weren't already lying there with their eyes open. It would take a minute or two for the muscles to slacken again. Meanwhile, the mind would remain taut.

'As tight as a guitar string', was how McGrady succinctly phrased it.

By first light, we were up. By then, Gunter had usually already crammed his soggy sleeping bag into his pack and shouldered it. He'd hang about

Cursory patrolling of an intended bounty-hunting area was usually done from the back of a Land Rover, a system that had built-in disadvantages. The vehicle could be, and was, ambushed by the guerrillas. (Author's collection)

and wait for us to get ready. Almost every morning we were out, he'd complain that the weight of his pack had doubled, which was when one of us would remind him about the rain. McGrady would shrug and mutter something about us putting our lives at risk with this man . . .

Minutes later, on that third morning, we were on our way towards the improvised bridge we'd crossed the night before, a narrow tree trunk that hovered precariously above the current. One by one, with the others covering, we worked our way across. On the other side, McGrady took point with the tracker following. I followed up in the rear because I needed photographs.

Once on the far bank, the American pointed to a fresh set of boot prints in the dirt, hours old. Montgomery slowly lifted his head and, with the kind of gesture that comes with experience, sniffed the wind. 'Nothing', he said quietly. Then he turned to the Greek and quipped in his quaint, fractured English: 'Dey long time gone . . .'

Since there wasn't a whiff of those who'd come in the night, we had something more with which to occupy our thoughts as we trudged through a succession of broken forest country that stretched back all the way to the Zambezi. For some reason – clearly inexplicable but of immense consequence to us – our unknown 'visitors' had wavered in taking those final few steps across the water. Probably a gook reconnaissance team, McGrady ventured.

What had stopped them? We pondered the matter when we halted briefly for a break. There were no conclusions, though the incident sharpened everybody's senses. By now we were moving even more cautiously than before, each one of us intent on putting more distance between them and us in the tall elephant grass that dominated large open areas adjacent to some of the clearings. We didn't exactly expect to be ambushed – that was to have been our job – but there wasn't a man among us whose safety hadn't been flicked off in anticipation of what we believed to be inevitable.

After being on the road a few hours, the rest of the trail seemed clear. Several times it meandered towards clusters of tall rocks that you could see at a distance above the flat terrain. Even to this unseasoned eye, these landmarks were distinctive.

About noon that day, McGrady pointed towards a rocky outcrop ahead, much bigger than the rest. It was used as a collection point by groups of insurgents who entered from Zambia, he'd been told. He underscored its position on the map that he'd kept in a waterproof holder tucked into his webbing.

For the rest of that day's patrol we kept well within the tree line. If there was any spotting to be done, we'd do it from the kind of cover that our Rhodesian Army friends embraced. Then, to be doubly sure, McGrady decided that we should occasionally double back on our tracks. We did that several times, but found nothing.

About an hour before sunset on that third day, we halted briefly for the customary snack. The march had been difficult and the heat had slowed our pace, but there was no stopping, not this deep into a totally unfamiliar terrain.

Dinner was simple: tea and kudu biltong,[4] bought before we left civilization from the small fresh-produce store behind one of the big hotels in Bulawayo. It was enough to sustain a man for a ten-hour march.

'It's the only food I carry, light and full of protein and best of all, it never spoils in the sun', said McGrady.

South Africa, and home, I felt, were suddenly rather distant, even

McGrady with one of his earlier bounty-hunting 'successes'. He always liked to work with one of his trusted African assistants. (Author's collection)

though it had taken us only nine hours by road to reach the place which was to be our stomping ground for the next eight or ten days.

Almost nothing goes to plan in wartime and the Rhodesian War was no different. It was the same with our patrol. By that third day, the hunt had lost its allure. In the words of the Greek, 'it has become a totally fucking bore . . . I came here to kill and all we do is walk through this shitty bush country. We find nothing and then we walk some more.'

The rain poured down intermittently, often in buckets, and that didn't help either. In fact, there were times when it never seemed to stop. We'd trudge a while, always moving silently along the bush trail, stopping occasionally to rest, and McGrady would compare compass bearings with the map. Then we'd take off again and a few hours later, the routine would be repeated. It was tedious, but that's how these things happen in this kind of irregular conflict.

Several times we crossed human tracks that might be fresh if the rain stopped long enough, but of their owners, we saw nothing!

We'd brought enough food to keep us happy for about a week. Gunter had suggested prior to setting out that we might possibly shoot something for the pot, but the American vetoed him. 'Fire off a shot in this bush and they'll pick it up five miles away . . . maybe more . . . then they'll end up tracking us' was his comment. When the mood took him, McGrady could be acerbic and pretty much to the point. To which he added: 'I'd imagine that by now, they already know we're in the area. Perhaps not our exact location, so let's just keep it that way.' He didn't hang around to debate the issue.

Our single biggest problem from the first day out was keeping Gunter and the Greek from continually chatting while on the march. McGrady's demands were basic and the need for silence in that remote bush country, where sound can travel for miles, was number one. It would be that way throughout the march – no talking – especially towards nightfall when nobody was certain who or what was out there. He wasn't asking much, but those two had great difficulty in complying: they'd always be nattering among themselves and it was usually a gripe.

On the third day, when the Greek decided at sundown to cut down some branches to make a fire, which was not only absurd, but under the circumstances risky, his clumsy efforts caused the American to lose his cool. It was the only time I was to see him angry. Grabbing the cocky little Greek by the throat, he told him that if he continued with this kind of bullshit, he'd cut him loose and leave him to the deal with the enemy on his own. There was no argument and, to be fair, things did quiet down a lot afterwards.

From then on, McGrady, Montgomery our guide and I slept a good few hundred yards downwind from the other two. We'd prepare our own meals and stand our own watches. If there were going to be problems because those two couldn't keep their mouths shut, said the American, they could handle it for themselves. He phrased it in typical McGrady fashion: 'Then we slip away and pretend they never existed. I don't think they'd be missed . . .'

By the fifth or sixth day we knew it was over. We were getting nowhere. Nor was there any prospect of a decent ambush, not once the locals had become aware that we were around. That and the fact that we'd spotted gook tracks in our area . . . there was no doubt that by then they'd seen ours.

The fact that Gunter and the Greek couldn't bring themselves to slot into a fairly tough regimen, finally put an end to it. That, together with Gunter's constant demands that he fill his water bottles while rain pounded down around us, was the final straw. We'd head for the pontoon and the farmhouse the next morning, McGrady told the other two before dark. He came back to our position with the news that they seemed quite happy with the change of plan and it pleased him.

Before noon the following day, within sight of the old farmhouse across the river, we fired off three shots. Little more than an hour later I was under the shower and the old man's cook was preparing lunch. Gunter and the Greek were nursing their blisters and wondering aloud what was on the menu.

It was a year later that I would get the full story of our little escapade. Apparently we were lucky to have 'got out of there without having been attacked', as one Rhodesian officer phrased it when he collared me afterwards in Johannesburg. In his view, we'd been on a military operation that was not only stupid but was hare-brained. He believed we were saved only by the fact that the insurgent group in the area was equally dumbstruck, the gook commander simply didn't know what to do about us.

The Rhodesian who passed on this news had spent some time at Wankie with the man who temporarily commanded the regional Joint Operations Centre, more commonly known as the JOC. He'd admitted that the army was aware of what we'd been trying to do: they'd actually intercepted a message from the insurgent leader to one of his squads that was active in the Tribal Trust Land after we'd gone in.

In brief, they mentioned to their superiors in Zambia the presence of 'four members of the security forces, two of them bearded, together with a black scout'.

The gist of that radio report was that the guerrilla group initially thought we'd been sent in by the Rhodesian Army to lure them into an ambush. They believed that there were possibly other Rhodesian Security Forces in the area waiting to strike; feints and counter-feints that took place often enough in this conflict, for such is the essence of this kind of counter-insurgency in Africa. They were right about the ambush, which had been our original intention. Fortunately for us, they were wrong about everything else.

As I was told during that chance meeting a year later, on the sixth morning of our patrol – the same day that we decided to call it quits – the ZANLA squad that had sent the original message received an order from Lusaka to take us out. In fact, said the officer who confided these details, they were perhaps a half-a-mile behind us by the time we boarded the pontoon. They were on their way to get us, a squad of about 20, every one of them well-trained and armed with more weapons than we would have been able to shake a stick at.

That wasn't the end of the story. The head of Rhodesian forces in that specific area – headquartered in Victoria Falls, not being aware that we'd crossed the river and were comparatively safe – went on to send a platoon of troops, all members of the Rhodesian African Rifles (RAR), into the Lupani Tribal Trust area in a bid to search for us. There was also talk of using spotter planes to make contact, though I'm not sure how successful that might have been in the thick bush country of the north-west.

The RAR troops arrived in the area in two trucks, which were promptly ambushed on the way in. Twice! Only after an RLI Fire Force call-out was pressure finally lifted, but by then there had been casualties on both sides.

It was as a result of that little escapade that I was banned from entering Rhodesia ever again, though I was to get over that little hurdle a year later.

As Dave McGrady will tell you today, more than a quarter century after leaving Southern Africa, things were reasonably relaxed in Rhodesia in the early days of the war. For much of the duration of hostilities, nobody gave the guerrillas a cat's chance of winning anything, never mind taking over the country.

Also, he was glad that he hadn't joined the Rhodesian Army. Towards the end of the war, the desertion rate among Americans who had joined up was something like 50 per cent. One of his comments about the period was:

> Initially, I knew that I could get a job guarding someone's ranch or farm from attack. I did a few jobs, but nothing much, probably because most farmers were just not prepared to pay a few hundred bucks a month even though I was quite happy to split whatever bounty I made with them. Most were broke themselves . . . the war.
>
> All I really wanted was an opportunity to help fight terrorism. I knew, once I'd made contact, possibly registered a few kills and so on, that the word would get out that farms in that area were no longer easy targets. I believed it might deter future attacks.

It was a naïve approach, but that's been the way that McGrady has always rationalized. In any event, nobody took him up on his offer, which was why he drifted into the Department of Health.

The last quarter of 1977 saw McGrady volunteering to look after the vast open land of several ranchers nearer Bulawayo, a region that had seen a considerable escalation in terrorist activity. Some of these ranches had been abandoned, others temporarily vacated and quite few stayed unoccupied for many years after the war ended. For long stretches McGrady was the only white – with several hundred African labourers – in an area of roughly 200,000 acres.

A letter he wrote at that stage read:

> For the past month I've been doing farm security work on a ranch 60 clicks north of B [Bulawayo]. Plenty of terrs. Same 'ole problem though; no can find, and believe me, I've been out looking. Been laying night ambushes on known terr paths leading from the TTL [Tribal Trust Land] and also doing bush patrols during the day. So far no luck . . .

Insurgents there certainly were, only McGrady never found any – not then, anyway – probably because he'd been working on his own.

When he set up his one-man night ambushes, he had no one to help him share the load.

Another letter followed:

A few days ago our neighbour's African boss boy's pick-up truck was ambushed by three terrs. Armed with AKs, they fired on the truck, stopping it. They then dragged the black guy out, before setting it on fire to spite the rancher. The fuckers made off into the bush, though the good news is that they didn't kill the driver. The night before they burned down this same guy's hut and rifle-butted his brothers to put the fear of God into them . . . he told me that as many as 30 terrs will be crossing the Shangani River soon to attack the ranches. So I'm expecting them at any time.

While McGrady went about his business on the ranches, the drama of war continued to unfold on an almost daily basis, some of it in the vicinity of the ranch. A subsequent letter reported:

Last week a ranch and an Internal Affairs 'Keep'[5] were attacked on separate nights. Also had another ambush in the Wankie Game Park on a South African family's car. You probably read about that one in the papers.

Then two nights ago I heard a heavy explosion while sitting in the house . . . next day found out it was an Army vehicle that'd hit a TM-46 landmine; one soldier killed, two wounded pretty badly . . . these attacks took place just a short distance from where I'm based at present.

It was that incident that prompted McGrady to provide protection for the ranchers in Matabeleland. It was soon afterwards, that I wrote to him and enquired whether Gunter, the Greek and I could join in on one of his patrols. The rancher with whom he'd been staying had been ambushed in a dry river bed not far from the house. There were eight or nine guerrillas who fired on the farmer and his son while they'd been driving in their Land Rover.

The old man was shot in the arm and back. His son was hit in the head, but luckily it was only a scalp wound. He ended up concussed. The attackers also fired an RPG but it missed.

While the Land Rover was still rolling forward the old man fell out. As he was lying in the sand a terrorist came up to within three or four yards of him and started firing away with his AK . . . full auto. Shows how well these fuckers shoot . . . the terr missed the old guy every time. Instead, he was splattered with sand thrown up by bullets landing all around him.

At that moment, according to McGrady, the farmer managed to unholster his .22 calibre pistol and shot his attacker in the stomach. 'The gook buckled over and then took off with the rest of his gang . . .' The next day, the rancher and his son returned with a British South Africa Police (BSAP) stick, followed a blood trail and found the terr. He was dead, having been finished off by his comrades. The rancher proudly showed McGrady the terr's cap insignia that he'd claimed as a souvenir.

To McGrady, that incident was part of a war that was becoming increasingly brutal. It was his contention that hostilities had devolved into a no-holds-barred affair and that too much of it, as far as the Rhodesian Security Forces are concerned, was being fought 'by the book'.

'But not the enemy', he wrote in one of his letters. 'They were pretty damn ruthless . . . stopped at nothing to achieve their aims . . . savage brutality is only a small part of it.' And that, he added, was probably why he was still in Rhodesia, still looking for what he liked to call gooks.

Nobody was under any illusions of what was expected of Dave McGrady while he remained in Rhodesia.

Danger apart, the average bounty hunter needed to be as good as, or superior to, those he was after, while also having a healthy dollop of guile and luck. It was obvious that he needed to be superbly fit. In the bush, it was his legs that would do most of the work and, when the time came, they would also get him out of trouble. At his peak, Dave McGrady was one of the few infantrymen that I knew of who could stay on a track in the bush for four or five hours at a steady jog.

As he commented, it could be an extremely tough regimen because everybody was aware that the average insurgent was also in superb physical shape. Also, he could survive on very little while out in the bush, sleep rough for months at a time, survive on his own in this primitive land and call on the locals when there was need to. When targeted, he would often enough survive wounds that would kill the average white man.

One member of Colonel Ron Reid-Daly's Selous Scouts who was

doing a little freelance bounty hunting was caught on his own in a forward position by a squad of about a dozen insurgents. In the end, he had to spend more than a day dodging them. It was only because he was in such fine physical shape himself that he was eventually able to elude them and get away.

The Scouts, apparently, got paid extra for this kind of effort, which usually took place while they were on leave. It annoyed some of the other units who weren't offered the option. Brian Robinson, the penultimate commanding colonel of the Rhodesian SAS, got himself kicked out of the office of General Peter Walls when he protested. It was none of his business what the Scouts did when they were back home – or where they did it – he was peremptorily told by the irate Supremo, Brian told me many years later.

While McGrady enjoyed no tactical support from the authorities, he did enjoy a small measure of input from local security forces. As he explained, if he were to enter an area that had been 'frozen' without disclosing his intentions to the right people, he could be targeted by both sides. Also, apart from possibly of being killed by the Rhodesian Security Forces, he could just as easily end up getting Rhodesian soldiers in his sights.

Which begs the question: how did the Rhodesians regard the majority of bounty hunters? To most, McGrady concedes, 'we were superfluous. We might have been necessary under some circumstances, but generally, we were regarded as more of a hindrance than a help. Too many of them regarded us as a bunch of misfits, and obviously they were partly right . . . there were some mercs that were so way out that they simply didn't fit the bill.'

From my own observations, there were also precious few McGradys, because only a tiny handful matched up to the kind of demands that Dave took in his stride.

The American had the last word. 'Let's not underestimate what this job entailed. It was hard. Also, it could be totally unforgiving. One mistake and you were a dead man.' Which was probably why the average American who arrived in Rhodesia intent on making his fortune lasted only three months, he added. Some held on a bit longer, but then disillusion would set in and they'd go on home.

Later, following his stint with the South Lebanese Army in the Levant, McGrady spent a while in Nicaragua.

CHAPTER EIGHTEEN

On the Ground in Rhodesia's Bush War

'It's easy to fight when everything's right It's a different song
when everything's wrong . . .'

Comment in an e-mail from Colonel Lionel Dyck discussing the
Rhodesian war

BOB BROWN WAS TWO HOURS into his flight back to New York from
Southern Africa in the summer of 1985 when he was given a message
from the cockpit by one of the flight attendants. I'd persuaded an official
at South African Airways to pass on by radio the news that Arthur
Cumming, a Rhodesian with whom we'd been hunting a few days
before, had been murdered.

Dapper, brave and a veteran of this bush war, Arthur had been
dubbed 'Gentleman Jim' by some of the members of his unit, the
Rhodesian Light Infantry or, as we knew it, the RLI. Whether in civvies
or in the distinctive mottled green cammo gear worn by Prime Minister
Ian Smith's 'rebel' army, he was always impeccably turned out.

First details of his murder, which took place at the Cumming hunting
concession not far from Wankie in Rhodesia's north-west region, were
sketchy. However, since we'd got to know the Cumming family quite
well – we'd been hosted by Arthur and his wife, Sandy, in their home in
a region that had had its share of hostilities in the ongoing guerrilla
struggle – we were able to relate to what little we'd been told. With
another American adventurer of repute, Big John Donovan, as part of
our group, Bob had even managed to bag a decent sized kudu bull and,
to the chagrin of us all, a sable antelope.

The routine at the old Cumming ranch – it had been in the family for
a couple of generations – was the same for each of the five or six
mornings that we had hunted. We'd go out in Arthur's Land Rover before
dawn each day. While we'd have to travel across dirt roads to get to our
destination, which was troubling, we weren't deterred: Arthur had been
using those roads just about forever and he was fine, so far anyway.

It was worrying that there had been landmines laid in many of the surrounding hunting areas during the previous couple of years, but so far none on the Cumming's concession. In several cases nearby, insurgent mines had been triggered by vehicles and some of the occupants, children included, had been killed. We were also aware that a few weeks before we'd arrived, insurgents active in the region had used a couple of TM-46s to boost an explosive charge that they'd use to drop a bridge across the nearby Matetsi River.

Our tracker on this leg of our Rhodesian adventure was Tickey, a senior member of the Matabele tribe who'd been with the Cumming family for more than 30 years. Small and wiry, with a pinched face, Tickey could read the bush like you or I might scan a newspaper. He'd follow a trail through thorn and scrub brush and tell you how many animals had used it, exactly what they were, how they were moving, in haste or passively, and when last they'd passed that way.

Tickey could spot a lioness in the long grass even before she knew he was there. As Arthur said, he was the best in his league and the man was justifiably proud of his ability. He was very much 'part of the family' he told us.

When asked about his loyalties, considering that so many of the other African folk in that area had been subverted by insurgents, Arthur was unequivocal: 'I've grown up among his people. So did my dad and his dad. I speak his language like his own children. Consequently *his* people are *my* people.'

He went on to say something about a bond of understanding between the folk on his ranch that he'd seen demonstrated over and over again. In fact, the family was on such good terms with its 'native' staff that Arthur actually declined a government offer to erect a security fence around the homestead.

So who were we to argue when Tickey rode shotgun on board the four-by-four while we hunted the big stuff?

What we didn't know – and which was only to emerge afterwards – was that Tickey was already a fully paid-up member of the guerrilla force active in the region. Had he been a bit smarter, he could probably have led us into an ambush. That would have been a jackpot all-round: a handful of Americans and a journalist to boot.

He could certainly have done so had he wished: subsequent reports spoke of a squad of ZIPRA guerrillas some 30 or 40 strong that had entered the region from Zambia a short while before we'd arrived.

Furthermore, they were armed with some of the best squad weapons in the Soviet armoury, including RPG-7s.

In the end, Tickey waited until we'd left the farm to head home before he led his group of terrorists into the Cumming home. That happened shortly after Arthur's brother Lawrence had gone off to Bulawayo earlier in the day.

At about nine that evening, according to Sandra Cumming, Arthur got up to lock the outside doors, much as he always did about that time of night. Moments later, she recalled, three black men wearing the uniforms of the Rhodesian Army – complete with camouflage cloth caps – entered the room. They'd come in from the kitchen, which meant that somebody had opened the outside door for them.

Sandy's first words to her husband were 'Arthur, what's the army doing in the house?' All that Arthur could do was shout: 'Run Sandy! Run for your life!' Then all three intruders opened up on him with their AKs and this Rhodesian farmer crumpled in a heap on the cement floor.

Sandy, almost nine months pregnant, had meanwhile slipped out of the house through one of the side doors. Roughly 30 seconds later she heard more shots, some of them ricocheting off the concrete. The terrorists had delivered the *coup de grace* and she knew that her Arthur was dead.

By slipping into a low clump of foliage at the bottom of her garden, Sandy Cumming managed to survive the onslaught, even though her husband's killers spent a good while searching for her. Finally, even though the insurgents were still in the house, all of them gathered together in the sitting room and plundering the booze cabinet, she was able to sneak back into the house and activate the recently installed Agriculture-Alert system – we used the term Agric-Alert.

While Sandra Cumming played hide-and-seek with her husband's murderers, a nearby army patrol rushed to her rescue. But even that took time.

The favourite insurgent ploy in that war, immediately prior to an attack on a farmhouse – as with Malaya while its guerrilla emergency lasted – was to lay a pattern of mines, usually an anti-tank mine surrounded by a cluster of anti-personnel mines (APs) in the approach road to the farm. If nobody had been able to check beforehand, one or more of these bombs might be detonated by the vehicles heading in.

Arthur Cumming, though critically wounded, didn't die immediately. And because the entire farming community of the north-west – for a radius of more than 100 miles – was connected to the same radio-based security system, they could follow the drama in real time. They'd all heard Sandy's first call for help once she'd emerged from hiding, the killers having returned to the house after their fruitless search outside. Finally, after the attackers left, she came onto the link again: 'Arthur's dead' were her words.

Bob Brown was to learn all of this after he returned to the United States. He communicated with both Lawrence as well as Sandy Cumming. Not long afterwards, he was to get news about her newborn.

Reports that subsequently filtered through from Rhodesia indicated that Tickey, who had often hauled young Arthur about on his back while still a child, had been arrested. He was tried in court and executed by the authorities a short while later.

I covered the Rhodesian war almost from the start of hostilities. I was to go north of the border from South Africa – based as I was in Johannesburg at the time – scores of times in a dozen years. Sometimes I'd fly or sometimes I'd go by road, which I did often enough, occasionally with my wife. We'd travel the lonely road between Bulawayo and

The Rhodesian Light Infantry's Fire Force was brought in by Alouette helicopter gunships to try to follow up on the Cumming murder, but the attackers had already fled back to Zambia. (Author's collection)

Beit Bridge, just praying that we didn't run into the guerrillas. Along the way there would be ready evidence of the low-key insurrection that then gripped the country, including burnt-out vehicles abandoned in the bush and others that had obviously been raked by gunfire. Occasionally, we'd spot a car or a truck that had tripped a landmine, some of them blasted by mines that had been laid on tarred roads. The guerrillas would drill out a small section of tar, lay their mine and then with great care, make it look like a pothole that had been filled with gravel.

On one occasion, Madelon and I travelled about 100 miles across a dirt road to Gulu to visit a friend; her husband was then serving in the army and he was based there. It was mid-afternoon when we set out from Fort Victoria and halfway there, I realized that what we were doing was possibly a mistake. We could be ambushed at any time, never mind the mines. The road was in bad shape and huge swathes of bush partly covered it in places. All we had for protection was her little .38-Special snubbie and my Colt .45 ACP: no match for even a single AK-47.

However, we got through, spent a few days in the officers' quarters, and then headed back on the Sunday morning, this time with an escort for part of the distance. We did that kind of thing in Southern Africa in those days because we were young and in love and fate took good care of us.

It was on the trip back to civilization that we had a serious run-in with a bunch of insurgents on the main road between Francistown and Ramatlabama. They were all ZIPRA guerrillas and they used their weapons to stop us along a lonely stretch of road. All they wanted from us – about six or eight of them – was a lift to the next town. I said we'd take two.

No they countermanded – we were to take them all. It was clearly an impossible situation, which was when I told their leader to get fucked and drove off. I was pretty sure they wouldn't gun us down in a country that was already playing the role of an uneasy host to their forces. Fortunately, I was proved right.

Asked to do that sort of thing today, I'd probably offer to take the lot and buy them their meals and beers as well.

War or no war, the 1970s were magic times in Africa. I was working for Republican Press, the largest magazine group in Africa that published magazines like *Scope* and *Farmers Weekly*, both of which had substantial circulations in Rhodesia and it helped a lot that the company had had almost all its foreign assets frozen in Rhodesia. Republican

Press couldn't take its money out of the embattled country at war, but that didn't prevent me spending bundles of it each time I was assigned to go north. Following a phone call to the local representative of Republican Press, we'd make contact each time on my first morning in Salisbury and she'd hand me rolls of Rhodesian dollar bills, usually thousands of dollars at a time. I would always make very good use of it.

Location expenses it was called, but the trouble was, I couldn't take any of it out of the country, which suited me fine. For the best part of a decade, I was able to cover Rhodesia's war almost continuously and in the process gained an astonishing amount of experience in military matters. I was also able to feed a host of publications abroad and earn the kind of extra money that eventually allowed me to build a rather beautiful home in Noordhoek, one of Cape Town's better suburbs.

Using company money with no restrictions whatsoever, I'd hire cars, stay in the five-star Monomatapa Hotel (which the army had dubbed 'The Claymore' because it had the curiously rounded shape of one), eat like an epicure at Meikles and move about the country as and when I pleased. If Bob Brown didn't arrive to do the same thing himself, he was constantly sending over Americans to experience Rhodesia's war and I played host to many of them, courtesy of Republican Press.

'Brown's Reprobates' – as local and foreign media dubbed our exclusive little entourage – ended up a familiar sight in town. Each one of these Americans toted at least one large-calibre 'piece' and most eventually became members of the only recognized media centre in the country. The Quill Club was as much a hangout for local and foreign journalists and spooks as the inevitable 'Guns for Hire'.

By then there were already quite a few Americans in the Rhodesian Army. Among the best known was Bob MacKenzie, who served with distinction in the Rhodesian SAS. Once that was over, Bob went on to become second-in-charge to former Selous Scouts founder-commander Colonel Ron Reid-Daly in the Transkei Army.

There was also Major L.H. 'Mike' Williams. Following some unconventional stints in Asia, Mike served as the tactical commander of the Grey Scouts, the country's famed mounted infantry. Others included Chris Johnson from Houston, Texas, who'd originally served two tours with a Marine Recon Battalion, as well as Airborne/Ranger qualified Bob Nicholson from Fortune, California, both of whom eventually found a home in the RLI.

The 1st Battalion, The Rhodesian Light Infantry (nicknamed 'The

Saints' or 'Incredibles') was a regular airborne commando regiment in the Rhodesian Army that became a parachute battalion in 1977. Regarded in its day as one of the world's foremost proponents of counter-insurgency warfare, its regular duties included both internal operations and external pre-emptive strikes against guerrillas based in the neighbouring territories of Mozambique and Zambia.

Organized into four company-sized sub-units called commandos, with an average fighting strength of about 70 men, their characteristic deployment was the Fire Force, a reaction operation called out by radio whenever enemy units were spotted, usually in remote locations in the bush.

RLI 'troopies' soon became the country's most effective rapid-deployment helicopter shock force. Small combat elements would consist of four-man 'sticks', each consisting of an NCO stick leader, a machine-gunner, a trooper, and a combatant-medic. Basic weapons were the 7.62mm FN rifle and belt-fed MAGs.

The RLI Fire Force concept emerged after a few hard lessons in 1974. Using French-built helicopters, some obtained legally and still more bought 'under the counter', as well as antiquated C-47 Dakotas or 'Gooney birds', back-up vehicles and support troops, this was a tactic, though expensive, that worked from the start. Operations in the bush that involved Fire Force always yielded results, some of them inordinately impressive in terms of kills.

What was notable about the RLI was its strength. At best it never numbered more than a few hundred combatants. As long as these men remained active, they were able to counter large numbers of insurgents, with RLI 'troopies' sometimes going out on two consecutive missions a day, three on rare occasions. There were operations when they were dropped virtually onto the heads of those they sought from 200 feet.

Very few counter-insurgency units in any country involved in counter-terrorism operations have managed to achieve such remarkable results. Part of the reason was that this 'organised and extremely lethal bunch of hooligans', as one Salisbury newspaper referred to them, were prepared to take the kind of risks needed. Another is that all the men were well trained, extremely fit and young enough to be bold – and more often than not, impetuous – in the face of the enemy and think nothing of it.

It is notable that many of the tactics instituted by a succession of RLI commanders – as well as by Ron Reid-Daly's Selous Scouts – are today

The Rhodesian Army spread its troops about, even though they were somewhat thin on the ground. This observation post was on a river in the south-east of the country, adjacent to the Mozambique border. (Author's collection)

regularly studied by military institutions abroad, including those in Britain and the United States. Small-unit operations originally evolved during World War II, initiated by David Sterling's Long Range Desert Group, and were later applied in Malaya and by British SAS Colonel Jim Johnson in Yemen while fighting an invading Egyptian Army. Yet, it was RLI tactics that all but perfected this methodology.

The RLI became adept at this type of military operation. An RLI 'troopie' was trained to shoot by double-tapping on semi-automatic: fully automatic fire was almost unheard of. In contrast, the MAG gunner would customarily let rip with short, sharp bursts from the hip that clearly had more stopping power, especially at short range. With time, the gunners would hone this skill to achieve astonishing accuracy. Interestingly, a fair proportion of the RLI complement was composed of foreigners who over the years included many British and American volunteers. They were paid the same as regular Rhodesian soldiers for their efforts.

All these mercenaries saw a good deal of action during the course of the war. Major Nigel Hensen, who commanded the RLI's Support Commando for 30 months, reckoned that his guys were called out hundreds of times in that period, of which only six operations resulted in no contact with the enemy or, as it is militarily phrased, 'lemons'.

When the fighting was done for the day, these off-duty American freebooters would make their way to one of the most exclusive clubs in the country run by American author Robin Moore of *Green Berets* fame. Moore established his Crippled Eagle Club as a kind of unofficial United States Embassy in Salisbury in response to Washington's acquiescence in the face of Soviet encroachment in Africa.

This group of adventurers also managed to ensconce themselves with other American vets who, after service with regular Rhodesian battalions, sometimes ended up guarding farms or were employed by anti-stock-theft units in the country's interior.

The war in Rhodesia started slowly. Having infiltrated the Centenary area in the early 1970s, most guerrilla groups, not eager for direct confrontation, for a long time appeared to be intent on laying mines and attacking the occasional vehicle not in convoy. There were raids on farms, like the one in which Arthur Cumming was murdered, but the biggest effort went towards trying to subvert the locals. This wasn't difficult in the bush where few of the Shona people had any real contact with Europeans anyway.

Significantly, their support in the cities was muted, though obviously, in a bid to portray the war as strictly African against European (even though black troops far outnumbered their white counterparts in the ranks of the regular army), they were bound to have some success. For their part, the Rhodesians reacted by initiating a lesson they'd learnt in Malaya: many rural people were relocated into protected villages, a move designed to cut the insurgents off from supplies of food and the kind of succour they'd formerly enjoyed.

Incredible stories were to emerge from the Rhodesian War, like the one that historian Richard Wood tells of Vic Cook who, with a medic on board, was flying an Alouette helicopter to a local church mission station when a volley of AK rounds slammed into it.

At an insurgent base camp below – as security forces were to discover later – were about 30 enemy soldiers doing their best to bring them down. A quick survey of the damage told Cook that his gunner

Landmines were a problem both to civilians and the security forces throughout the Rhodesian War. Some curious anti-mine hybrid vehicles evolved, such as this 'Pookie', some of which were eventually adapted to serve in South Africa's escalating hostilities along the Angolan border to the west. (Author's collection)

was semi-conscious after being hit by two rounds that had penetrated his body armour. Also, the Alouette's tail rotor shaft was all but severed.

Cook took his craft down to tree-top level, but he was still taking fire because he was almost on top of the enemy.

A lot more rounds hit us and it was fierce. I felt the controls going, there was vibration and I realized that I had to bring the machine down.

More rounds hit us when I lost tail rotor control and the chopper swung violently. Because it would have started to cartwheel if I did nothing, I pulled it up sharply on its tail to knock off forward momentum . . . and while the speed came down, we continued to yaw. It was then that I saw them: there was the equivalent of two rugby teams and they just kept on shooting at us.

At that point Cook saw a group of five or six terrs ahead and decided to aim his helicopter right at them. 'We thumped into the ground nose-first and lost sight of them . . . which was when a piece of the control column came of in my hand.'

The impact jerked Cook forward, knocking his jaw onto the top of the control stick, savagely gashing his chin and stunning him. His foot was also badly cut and in trying to get around, he kept stumbling. Only when he looked down did he see a deep gash with the bone protruding. Worse, his Uzi had taken a hit and was inoperable.

Aware that the engine was still idling – which led the terrs to think they were okay – Cook realized that if the two of them were to survive, he'd need a weapon. Just ahead of him lay a prostrate insurgent who'd been hit by a rotor when the Alouette crash-landed. Alongside him was an AK.

'I knew that if I didn't get to that weapon and fast, we'd all be killed. Though the tech had meantime come to, he said he couldn't move. So essentially, it was up to me.'

Victor Cook then did what he never believed would have been possible. He recovered the Kalashnikov and started firing at the rest of the insurgent group who were about 100 yards away, all the while moving from one bit of cover or clump of rock to the next in what had suddenly become a very personal war. Meanwhile, a Rhodesian Army call sign that had called Cook from Rutenga (in south-east Rhodesia) had heard the crash – as well as the subsequent firing – and summoned help.

That help came almost an hour later in the shape of a Rhodesian Air Force Cessna FTB, which laid down a curtain of fire around the crippled chopper. The RLI dropped its Fire Force into the area not long afterwards and immediately launched a follow-up.

For his efforts, Vic Cook was awarded the Silver Cross. His comment at the time was that he didn't deserve it. 'I only did what was needed to keep us alive', were his words.

At best, the Rhodesians throughout the war were never able to field more than 50 Alouette III's and Augusta-Bell 206s (the latter bought illicitly from the Israelis). In addition, the Rhodesian Air Force had perhaps a dozen Hawker-Hunter fighter-bombers, as well as a handful of Canberras. This wasn't much when it is accepted that the country's entire army, apart from Special Forces, consisted of a single armoured-car regiment, one artillery regiment, a regular infantry regiment (the RLI) which would grow to three over-strength battalions, backed by eight battalions of territorial and reserve troops. All these units were

Though Rhodesian aviation assets were precious, helicopters were often used to ferry casualties to hospital after a contact or a landmine incident. (Author's collection)

multi-racial and included whites, a huge preponderance of blacks, limited numbers of 'coloured' troops (of mixed-blood origin) as well as Asians.

In addition, the paramilitary British South Africa Police or BSAP played a seminal role throughout the war, usually working in close conjunction with the military. Its Special Branch invariably came up trumps with intelligence gathered while working close to the ground in the interior.

The war was restricted not only to Rhodesian soil. Both the Selous Scouts and the Rhodesian SAS (many of whose members ended up serving in Hereford in the UK after the war) took the conflict well beyond the country's borders.

Apart from routine strikes in Botswana (where insurgent leaders became fair game for small Special Forces strike groups), Colonel Reid-Daly would send his men deep into Mozambique to strike at that country's road and rail infrastructure. One such attack involved a clandestine unit successfully destroying a substantial section of

Mozambique's largest oil terminal at Beira, one of the biggest ports along that stretch of the Indian Ocean.

Prior to that, a combined operation involving South African Special Forces – with SAAF Puma choppers, this time in Rhodesian livery – blew up bridges on the main railway line out of Maputo. Because it was the principal insurgent supply line, it set the revolution back about a year.

Then came the cross-border 'Green Leader' strike into Zambia that involved Rhodesian Air Force Canberra jet bombers and choppers, the RLI as well as elements of the SAS and the Selous Scouts. It was launched in an attempt to neutralize ZIPRA's regional command structure near Lusaka. That operation failed, in part because British intelligence agents had infiltrated Milton House where much of the military planning originated. In turn, London tipped-off ZIPRA leader Joshua Nkomo in Zambia and he wasn't home when the Rhodesian Army called.

Another time, the Scouts blew up bridges along the Tanzam Railway in Tanzania more than a thousand miles north of the border. The line ran from Tanzania's Dar es Salaam – the biggest single staging port for supplies needed by the revolutionary armies – to Zambia. Routinely, Selous Scouts 'sticks' would range deep into all these countries, sometimes staying 'external' for a month or two at a time.

Meanwhile, the Rhodesians proved remarkably adept at improvising with their extremely limited resources. They were able to develop the first of many mine-protected vehicles, which saved lives in the war. Subsequent variants of these vehicles eventually saw service in South Africa's border war in Angola and South-West Africa. In the Honde Valley, immediately adjacent to the Mozambique frontier, several times we went operational in the 'Pookie', a mine detector built by a local engineer. It was constructed from Volkswagen parts and used ultra-wide Formula One racing tyres to achieve minimal ground pressure. That was followed by a bicycle-mounted version that, for a while, was deployed to clear bush airstrips in the interior.

For their domestic and external air strikes, the Rhodesians designed and built a wide range of weapons including flechete bombs and napalm-wielding 'Frantans'. At a more mundane level, the country's technicians also developed the 'Road Runner', a transistor radio that emitted a signal only when it was switched off. That allowed the air force to drop their bombs accurately.

This was the same device which, decades later, allowed SAS troops to home in on rebels in Sierra Leone who were holding 11 British soldiers hostage. Calling themselves the West Side Boys, their leader was offered one of these radios as a gesture of goodwill during preliminary meetings to discuss the fate of the hostages.

The gift was accepted with alacrity and two days later the British attacked and managed to rescue all their countrymen.

In the end, it was the distinct paucity of troops on the ground that proved to be the undoing of the Rhodesian military effort. The economy too, was in trouble, as might have been expected when some business, industrial and factory personnel were spending four – and sometimes six months of the year – in the bush.

The RLI's Fire Force could strike at as many targets as it wished. It could notch up incredible numbers of kills, which it did. However, if the country's security forces didn't have the manpower to follow up and maintain a presence in those same disputed areas, the guerrillas would just move right back in again. Which they did . . .

Prime Minister Ian Smith also suffered severely from a UN-imposed arms ban. Whatever sophisticated material his forces needed had to be bought in surreptitiously, usually at much-inflated prices. South Africa's apartheid regime helped where it could of course, but Pretoria had to tread a very careful path. More than once Washington warned the South African government that if it continued to support the 'Rebel Smith regime', the country would face sanctions.

One of the threats included withholding spares for that country's civilian Boeing passenger jet fleet. Another might have been the refusal to allow South Africans entry to the United States. None of this was ignored, which was one of the reasons why, in a bid to force Ian Smith to the negotiating table, Pretoria at one stage threatened to cut off Salisbury's oil supplies.

It was one of several killer ultimatums. Cumulatively, in the end, this sort of pressure had the required effect. It has led to the position Zimbabwe finds itself in today with a psychopath as Head of State and an economy in freefall.

CHAPTER NINETEEN

Zaire: Road to an African War

Covering conflicts in Africa is one thing. However, if you are doing your job and have people firing at you, or are arrested on suspicion of espionage, it is another thing altogether and you tend to take a jaundiced view of the whole situation.

MY EXPERIENCES IN COVERING ZAIRE – today, the Democratic Republic of the Congo – included being accused of espionage, robbed, roughed-up during daily interrogation sessions and locked in a filthy cell. It was done, as one of our jailers commented, 'to await your execution'.

That brush with the Reaper came soon after I left Angola towards the end of 1975. Back on less dangerous turf, I was asked by one of my editors to go into the Sharp End again, which at that stage meant the Angolan War. Since I'd survived numerous encounters there in the past, going back all the way to the Portuguese colonial wars of the 1960s and 1970s, there was no reason to believe that I wouldn't survive again, he argued.

Of course I would, I said. Anyway, those jaunts into the unknown were better than work . . .

The problem just then, however, was that almost overnight every scribe and aspiring cub reporter was eager for a piece of the action. Following British journalist Fred Bridgland's scoop in *The Scotsman* that the South African Defence Force had moved into Angola, the civil war was where everyone wanted to be. However, it wasn't easy to get in there. Suddenly, all sorts of restrictions were imposed on the media by governments bordering on the embattled region. In fact, the acquisition of an Angolan visa at the time was like getting an invite to visit North Korea.

There were clearly other ways of going in. I'd been doing it for years – into Kenya with South African stamps in my passport, into Sudan without the necessary documents, on to Nigeria, whose borders were porous but weren't supposed to be, and then to Lebanon with my second British passport, the one without any Israeli stamps.

We were all aware that Zaire shared common frontiers with half a dozen other states, and, after all, this was Africa! What the bureaucrats of the day had imposed could easily be unravelled by stuffing a few $20 bills into the hands of a prospective obscurantist, or so I thought, though arriving in Liberia once cost me a single $100 bill that I slid into my passport at Robertsfield Airport immigration control.

Essentially, each of the major participants in the Angolan Civil War – the South Africans, Soviets, Cubans, the Americans and obviously the perilously unstable Angolan government itself – all had very good reason for pulling down the shutters, especially as any kind of conflict was likely to deter investors.

For a start, the main Angolan opposition was led by an alcoholic opportunist who called himself Holden Roberto or Roberto Holden, depending on the time of day. He headed the Congo-based *Frente Nacionale de Libertação de Angola* (National Front for the Liberation of Angola) – or FNLA – and for reasons best known to Langley, was backed by the CIA. Whoever made that decision must have been in on some deal because Holden, who died in 2007, was probably the most inept, corrupt and inefficient revolutionary on that side of the pond. The man was also the ultimate blagger and could lie as fluently as one of the old horse traders from the Bronx.

At that time Washington didn't want anybody taking pictures of the weapons then flowing into a region still under their protégé's control, or, for that matter, of the Americans who were assisting this right-wing guerrilla group. The FNLA just then was being portrayed by the media as passionately anti-communist and Roberto and his men were getting all the military hardware they would need to 'fight the commies' in Luanda.

What also emerged afterwards was that South Africa was very much in cahoots with Washington's intelligence services, the CIA included. Much of the weaponry being channelled to the FNLA came from Pretoria, having been flown into South Africa from Europe by USAF transport planes. The last thing the South Africans needed was the kind of international attention – at the United Nations, especially – that was likely to result from exposing these multifarious activities.

Everything was somewhat convoluted and confused, similar to what was happening, or about to happen, in places like Nicaragua, Chile, East

Germany, Chad, North Vietnam, Lebanon and elsewhere. The difference was that Angola was involved another of those intricate Cold War manoeuvres where points were scored in blank spaces on the map and the local inhabitants were of no consequence at all.

Total secrecy was paramount to the success of the venture. As with a later adventure involving Colonel Oliver North – who emerged in another potentially revolutionary situation involving Nicaragua in Central America – there were people in senior positions in Washington who, at all costs, didn't want anybody, the US Congress especially, to become aware that their country was getting cozy with the South Africans. They were the dreaded racists and, for some time already, apartheid had been a dirty word. More to the point, Pretoria's racial intolerance was unacceptable at all levels, irrespective of whether the South Africans were countering Moscow's presence in Angola and, more often than not, doing the CIA's dirty work.

In a way, the scenario resembled an African version of the Bay of Pigs fiasco, because ultimately, that's the way it transpired. The FNLA, for all America's largesse, lost hands down to the Cubans and for the decades that followed, Angola became a strategic Soviet staging post. While that might all be history now, the bottom line was that both Washington and Pretoria shared a common interest in trying to prevent Angola's Marxists from taking over the country's legitimate government. Which was roughly when a second African insurgent group moved into the breach.

Calling itself UNITA– an acronym, in Portuguese, for the Union for the Total Independence of Angola – the movement was run along Chinese communist lines by a big, bluff, Swiss-educated guerrilla who called himself Jonas Savimbi. Originally a member of the Ovimbundu tribe, he had acquired his degree in Lausanne and spouted Mao's dictum at whomever was prepared to listen.

Whatever other criticism might be levelled at the UNITA leader for keeping his irregular forces in the field for more than 30 years, Savimbi was also the last of the great insurgent strategists of the modern period. Before he was killed, he ended up controlling about nine-tenths of Angola. When it came to strategy, this African guerrilla leader made Che Guevara look like a greenhorn.

Always the maverick, Savimbi's single claim to fame was that he hated the Angolan government perhaps fractionally more than he despised Americans. Much of his succour, however – including Stinger

SAMs, then also being handed out to the anti-Soviet Mujahedeen in Afghanistan – originally arrived at Washington's behest.

At the same time, he wasn't alone in his quest to conquer Angola. He had the unqualified support of the British company Lonrho, a comparatively new contact that for more than a decade had been cultivating dubious interests throughout independent Africa. Lonrho's chief executive, Tiny Rowland, made no secret of his intent to include the still-youthful Savimbi among his protégés, to the extent that he even let him use his personal jet.

Though educated by the Swiss, Savimbi was naïve enough at this early stage not to realize that though befriended by Lonrho, Rowland would always put European interests ahead of those of the black people whom the company befriended. London regarded his movement as little more than another player for some of the heftiest political and economic stakes on the continent. He had long been aware that Angola – its huge wealth of diamonds apart – would ultimately emerge as one of the world's major oil producers. Clearly he had a commendably prescient vision about events to come in Africa, though the manner in which he implemented his multifarious ideas, rarely won him any friends.

The final link in this complicated game was Big Brother himself who, at the head of the Popular Movement for the Liberation of Angola – or, more commonly the MPLA – had ensconced himself in Luanda. He was a Luanda-born, Portuguese-educated son of the Methodist pastor who called himself Agostinho Neto, another barrack-room politician who dutifully followed the Marxist line for most of his adult life. What's more, in taking command of the MPLA – and as a consequence, taking over the entire country – he'd achieved power, like the Congo's Mobutu, with a brutality that left most of us 'Old Africa Hands' flummoxed.

If somebody stepped in his way, that poor soul would customarily be found a day or two later gagged, bound and moribund. Other critics of the MPLA were hurled out of military aircraft into the sea about 20 miles offshore. Neto and the pro-American Mobutu had a lot in common, though politically they might have lived on different continents.

The immediate result of all these shenanigans was that Russians, Cubans, East Germans, Poles, Bulgarians, North Koreans and a host of others descended on Angola with a single-minded determination that astonished the West. The country would be theirs, by force if necessary, the objective encapsulated by the watchword: *Angola é Nossa!* ('Angola is ours!'). Interestingly, the exact same battle cry that the Portuguese had espoused when they were still fighting the guerrillas in their 11-year guerrilla war.

To finish the job properly, the Soviets brought with them a lot of trade-goods including weapons, fighter aircraft, helicopters, naval patrol boats and so on. Like Washington, Neto's Soviet masters had no wish to advertise their largesse and, as I was discover for myself, they were arguably the most paranoid of the lot.

As with Lonrho's Tiny Rowland, there was never any question in the minds of the MPLA's communist allies that Angola would not eventually have to pay for all this. Within a couple of years Luanda had hocked all its coffee, half its diamond production and just about its entire offshore fishing rights to Moscow. The same happened not long afterwards in Mozambique and Guiné-Bissau, two more countries that embraced Lenin's credo after Lisbon had unceremoniously ditched Africa.

A lot of fanfare was linked to these developments. Moscow proclaimed that Angola would soon be the 'greatest socialist success story' in all of Africa. At the same time, the Kremlin imposed the usual Eastern Bloc restraints that they had implemented at home: free speech was denied, so was free trade as well as the movement of citizens. In fact, without the right permit, Angolan people were forbidden to travel in their own country.

Step out of line and you couldn't find work either. Finally, journalists were given the kind of attention they'd been getting in Iron Curtain states: you wrote nothing for publication unless you were labelled by the commissar in charge of such matters as 'politically correct'.

There were a number of European left-wing apologists in those days who thought it was all for the good, journalists of the Commitment School, we would call them. These included the likes of Michael Wolfers and Jane Bergerol, as well as the Australian Marxist, Wilfred Burchett. Some were radical enough to be given positions within the Luanda government as propagandists.

The British writer and socialist, Basil Davidson, was also a regular visitor. He even wrote a book on the guerrilla war then being fought against 'reactionary and imperialist forces in Angola' and warned of the antics of dangerous counter-revolutionaries: people like Al J. Venter . . .

That comment stemmed from his reading my first and worst book ever. Titled *The Terror Fighters,* the work followed months spent on operations with the Portuguese Army in Angola.[1] Curiously, while Davidson and I had always been always poles apart politically, I was flattered. In one of his reviews, he even warned his readers to be wary of my 'convoluted political perceptions'. Otherwise, he ventured, it was very well done.

I had recently spent a short time in Angola attached to a shadowy guerrilla group known then to only a few observers as *Chipa Esquadrão* or the Chipa Squadron. Originally part of the FNLA, it was run by a disillusioned former communist by the name of Daniel Chipenda, but we'll leave those exploits – which also almost cost me dearly – for another day.

Having made my way back to South Africa from this visit, part of the way overland, through UNITA lines where several of us were almost shot by some 12-year-olds with Kalashnikovs keen to make their mark, I was eager to get back into Angola, but not through the extremely volatile south. Operation Savannah was in full swing and there were some big stories breaking, including South African Army contingents moving up from the south under the command of Colonel Jan Breytenbach.

Now I was back in South Africa, Angola was very much in the news and my editor was onto me. I had to go back to Angola again, he insisted. Easier said than done, I replied.

My initial thoughts were that I'd try going in the same way I did the first time, by returning to Luanda. However, only a month before a group of MPLA spooks had watched me fly out of Angola into what had since become 'enemy territory' in Nova Lisboa (since renamed Huambo). I'd been warned by a friend working in military intelligence in Pretoria that it would not be a clever move because they might be waiting for me if I tried to return. He said that Cuban and Russian agents were already thick on the ground in the Angolan capital; in fact, I'd met some of them while still there, but at that stage they tended to maintain a rather low profile.

Also, the fact that I'd spent time, gun-in-hand, with Chipenda's force – by now joined by a group of Portuguese mercenaries – hadn't gone altogether unnoticed. For now, I decided, there would be no going back that way.

The alternative option was to try to get in through Zambia. My objective was to try to achieve contact with some of the South African troops who, by now, had invaded the country in their thousands. It was a story literally waiting to break. Which was why I ended up with a group of like-minded scribes camped round the bar at the Ridgeway Hotel in Lusaka. Each one of us was intent on recording history.

A number of issues predicated the next move, including the fact some of our less sedentary colleagues were making remarkable headway and they were doing so from inside Angola. Mike Nicholson of ITN had already achieved a breakthrough by reporting to London that he had spotted South African soldiers in South Angola. Others spoke of mercenaries attached to UNITA forces, but they had no proof. Mike had wandered into a forward South African position at Silva Porto, now Menongue.

Not long afterwards, with Fred Bridgland – the Reuters man in Lusaka – Mike boarded the Lonrho jet on what was to have been a tour of 'UNITAland' – otherwise known as Savimbi country. One of their stops en route to Benguela on the coast was at Rundu, a South African military base and strongpoint near the northern border of South West Africa.

Once the aircraft was stationary on the runway, the two journalists saw rows of Eland armoured cars, stacks of ammunition 20 or 30 feet high, artillery pieces and hundreds of khaki-clad South African soldiers. Parked on the adjacent apron, there were South African Air Force C-130 transport planes being loaded with this stuff and taking off and landing in relays. They didn't need to be told that all this hardware was going into Angola at a heady pace to support the war effort.

Rundu had effectively become the staging-post for the South African invasion of Angola. And there was I, stuck in Lusaka, with all the other inkslingers listening to reports of South African, Russian, American, rebel Portuguese and mercenary doings next door. Worse, I'd been covering the same ground as ITN only weeks before, so I had a pretty good idea of what was going on.

Shortly before flying to Lusaka, I'd even chartered a small plane out of Windhoek, the capital of South West Africa. On arrival in Rundu our plane was directed away from where the activity was taking place.

'If you go in there,' a young officer on the runway warned me as we taxied up, 'I'll order one of my guns to open fire.' He pointed at a heavy machine-gun on a tower overlooking the loading bays and it was clear that he wasn't joking. So who were we to argue?

After we'd been allowed to taxi to a designated area on the far side of the airport and had left the plane, we were told that our presence was illegal. The town was Headquarters, No. 1 Military Area, and the man in charge was Brigadier Dawid Schoeman, who regarded journalists as being a single link in the evolutionary chain above *reptilia*.

In Rundu, separated as it is from Angola by the broad Kavango River – that was soon to have more bodies floating in it than either crocs or hippos – I was about as welcome as an outbreak of cholera.

Yes, said the brigadier, the invasion was on. However, since I had entered a restricted military area without authority, I could be charged with violating national security were I to write anything about the ongoing operation. Furthermore, I'd be prosecuted under the Official Secrets Act. In South Africa in those days you didn't disregard such threats: the old apartheid regime, it has since been demonstrated, killed for much less, and my wife and children were in Johannesburg.

In my mind, the situation was absurd. Also, it was compounded by the fact that the South Africans were very much aware that my politics were hardly radical. I'd always opposed the Russian menace, I told Schoeman, but he didn't believe me. Anyway, he said, he had his orders and journalists, in the Afrikaans terminology of the day, were *kak*.[2] In some respects, I suppose, he might have been right.

There was a delay of several days before the South African Army sent me back to Waterkloof Air Force Base in South Africa in a C-130 transport. On board were six bloodied South African soldiers: all had been caught in a Cuban ambush in the hills above Benguela, hundreds of miles to the west on the Angolan coast, and they were in shocking shape. A team of doctors, including two surgeons and four nurses – were on the hop throughout the three-hour flight back to Waterkloof, the main air force base outside Pretoria.

One of the injured, a youngster of perhaps 18, was also a Venter and I still don't know whether he made it. That was something I would have liked to follow up, but all subsequent enquiries at No. 1 Military Hospital in Pretoria in those rigidly monitored days were logged. You gave your name and your address, together with your telephone number, usually followed by the inevitable: 'Why do you want to know?' That would be preceded by the question: 'Are you a member of the family?' Since I wasn't, end of the story.

In any event, within a few days I was on my way again, this time heading to Zambia. By then it was clear that I would have to try something more radical.

Once in Lusaka, I was told that it might just be feasible to go overland into Angola. However, that meant heading hundreds of miles in the direction of Barotse Province and being stopped at dozens of security checkpoints along the way, each with explicit orders to stop people like me. The Zambian government was very much aware what was going on along their western frontiers and like most African countries, they didn't tolerate journalists.

It seemed crazy, but some of my colleagues were lucky. A former SAS officer and British television cameraman, Nick Downie, afterwards got into Angola to make a film on UNITA as part of a television series I was producing. Then there was Leon Dash, a black correspondent for the *Washington Post*, who hiked more than 2,000 miles with Savimbi's forces – sometimes walking naked through the swamps, clutching his clothes above his head, and sometimes living on insects, as well as frequently coming under fire. His dispaches became a model of reporting on an African bush war. Dash also survived crippling attacks of malaria.

I knew well enough the difficulties linked to going in alone and on foot. In the early stages of the civil war, the notion of a solitary white man (I could not get anyone to accompany me) trudging through some of the most desolate, remote swamp and bush country on the African continent simply wasn't on. In the end the venture was turned down by my editors because Lloyds of London refused insurance cover.

Angola under conventional circumstances, possibly; or Zambia, at hugely inflated premiums, they told the company. On my own and on foot, there was no way. In any event, Republican Press, my employer at the time, was already baulking about money.

Since there was no prospect of my getting into Angola through the Caprivi, because the South Africans had declared the entire Angolan border no-go, or from the east through Zambia, I had to try going north. That meant entering Angola through Zaire, an equally daunting prospect since the country was ruled by Mobuto Sese Seko, one of recent history's tyrants.

The Congo's post-*Uhuru* period, from the 1960s on, remains one of the most confused and violent of any of the 50-odd African countries that achieved independence in the second half of the 20th century. The entire episode was marked by an unconscionable level of violence, coupled to slaughters on an almost apocalyptic scale. It was coincidental perhaps, but it also overlapped with the emergence of the first groups of white mercenaries in the modern period. This vast land of incredible wealth and mind-blowing potential was confronted with a level of avarice and brutality that made most of Zaire ungovernable, a situation, sadly, that still exists today.

Though the Congolese Army had mutinied within days of Belgium granting the country its freedom in 1960, things seemed manageable; at least until a young African army officer took over the government in Leopoldville by force in 1965. One of his first gestures was to rename old Leopoldville – or 'Leo' as we media types called it – to Kinshasa. He went on to establish one of the most violent and oppressive regimes in Africa.

The man responsible was Lieutenant General Joseph-Désiré Mobutu, or as the international community was later to know him, *Monsieur, le President*, whose name ultimately became synonymous with a measure of kleptocracy that even for Africa was remarkable. While the Belgians still ruled, he had been a sergeant, yet among his first gestures to his people was to be become implicated in the murder of one of Africa's great heroes, Patrice Lumumba.

Six years later, Mobutu changed the name of the country to Zaire and his own to Mobutu Sese Seko Bhendu Wa Za Banga, which means 'the all-powerful warrior who, because of his endurance and inflexible will to win, goes from conquest to conquest, leaving fire in his wake', which just about says it all.

His legions of sycophants called him 'The Wise One', or 'Our Guide', and sometimes, 'The Redeemer'. To the amusement of those foreigners living in Zaire at the time, a sequence of this prodigy was shown before the national news each night. He would descend from the heavens in full dress military uniform with a halo perched precariously over his head. Because he was an African leader, no church leaders or diplomats ever protested at this travesty, not even the Pope.

Being Africa, that kind of thing led to even crazier excesses, very much as Zimbabwe's home-grown tyrant Robert Mugabe was tacitly allowed to do almost as he pleased while he ruled from the barrel of a gun. Mobutu killed with impunity during the 32 years that he ran the country. While wielding his baton, he recorded one of the worst human rights records on the planet, executing his opponents by the hundreds – as he did in 1995 when a Durban pilot, Jeff McKay, viewed some of this horror at first-hand.

McKay was flying for the President at the time, a period when there were very few who ever saw or heard of any anti-Zairean protests in the civilized world. Fearful for his own life, McKay sought other work soon afterwards.

Other nations, the United States and Europe included, simply ignored the country which in its first decade of independence had become, as one European newspaper described it, 'Africa's first ring of the Ninth Circle of Hell'. Zaire was blessed with boundless commodities that the West needed, including gold, cobalt, copper and more diamonds that anyone had thought possible to exploit adequately. It was said that prior to Mobuto fleeing to France with his entourage, with billions of dollars, Deutschmarks, British pounds, French Francs and Japanese Yen – as well as hundreds of pounds of diamonds – in the hold, there was a room in his palace that was hip-high in these raw precious stones.

Meantime, it has been estimated that in the years since Belgium so abruptly stepped out of the picture in Central Africa in 1960, between four and five million Congolese have died. The majority perished in wars, civil disturbances, rebellions, or of starvation and disease, but most of all, they died as a result of man's inhumanity towards man.

Mobutu's excesses were the cause of most of it and while he ruled, he was feared. However, that didn't bother him. Always the budding intellectual, he'd sometimes surprise his guests with astonishing little vignettes that he'd probably cleverly prepared beforehand, such as when he told a French journalist, after being asked about the severity of his rule: 'Let them hate as long as they fear.'

The Romans used the expression *oderint dum metuant* and Mobutu applied it with a vigour that shocked us all.

Zaire never really recovered from the *evenements* of the 1960s. Mobutu is long gone, replaced by another revolutionary called Kabila, who in his earlier days had played host to Ché Guevara on one of his rare visit to revolutionary Africa. He, in turn, was murdered by one of his own palace guards under the most mysterious of circumstances and another Kabila, his son, took over.

The organization responsible for keeping the lid on dissent at the time of my visit was Mobutu's original secret police, innocuously titled *Centre National de Documentation* or CND. It was truly a black Gestapo-type organization.

The prospect of traversing this dangerous country to get back into Angola, though not pleasing, offered some stimulating possibilities. After all, Zaire was the passionately pro-American, anti-communist, Western ally in this complicated Central African cat's cradle. And Mobutu was our friend.

The last time I'd passed through Zaire on the way back to South Africa from Nigeria, my travelling partner Tony Cusack was robbed in broad daylight in the local equivalent of Kinshasa's Fifth Avenue by a crowd of youngsters, who roughed us up before we knew what was happening. We should have been more cautious.

Some of the wags in Lusaka expressed doubts about us going ahead. Others told terrible stories about people who had come out of Mobutu's Zaire a short while before. The CND, we were warned, detained and put to death anybody suspected of anti-government or anti-Mobutu activity. They'd been at it for decades and, by now, were well ahead of the Angolans in taking innocent lives, were that possible.

Still, it was agreed, the only other possible way into Angola was from the sea. However, how to achieve that was something else we couldn't even contemplate. Anyway, we said, other journalists we knew had gone in and nothing untoward had happened to them. They'd made contact with the FNLA, which had its headquarters in Kinshasa, but what we hadn't been told was that they'd arrived by air and on direct flights from Europe.

What we in Lusaka did not know was that they – like the rest of us – were kicking their heels in idleness in Kinshasa waiting for something to happen. Nobody in authority in the former Congolese capital would take them anywhere, least of all the FNLA.

The CIA would certainly make sure of that!

CHAPTER TWENTY

Into the Congo's Cauldron

'The country is ruled by a man with the intellect of
an army sergeant.'

Former *Newsweek* and London *Daily Mail* correspondent Peter
Younghusband after almost being put up against a wall and
shot by Congolese soldiers

I T WAS NOT DIFFICULT TO find someone to go into Zaire with me. I had
already struck up an acquaintance with Gilles Hertzog, a young French
journalist freelancing for *Le Monde* and today, very much a part of the
French literary establishment (he's the author of *Le Séjour des Dieux*).
The grandson of Marcel Cachin, co-founder of the French Communist
Party, and related to the French philosopher Bernard-Henri Lévy (with
whom he subsequently co-authored), Gilles had been in Angola at about
the same time as I was. That, unfortunately, was his first trip to Africa
and mistakenly, he believed that I knew what lay ahead. That said, he
was French, which was essential for our exploit because almost nobody
speaks English in Zaire and my own knowledge of the language was
derisory.

When I suggested the prospect of going in, he accepted straight away.
I was only to discover too late that the man was about as radical as they
come on the Left Bank. In his bags he carried several tracts of Marxist
propaganda, some of it from Cuba. There was certainly enough of it to
get us tortured and executed.

It was a stupid move because Zaire at the time was probably the
most anti-communist country on the African continent. Anybody
espousing a radical creed was given short shrift by Mobutu's secret
police. South Africa under the old apartheid regime was similarly
minded, but at least your fate didn't rest on the whims of some obscure
functionary with a pistol tucked into his belt.

However, all that still lay ahead. Meanwhile, bubbly with
enthusiasm, we reported to the local UNITA headquarters in Lusaka the

next morning certain that a remarkable African adventure lay ahead. We wanted to accompany UNITA forces into the field in their war against the Luanda regime, we told a small man dressed in a tight-collared Chinese tunic, which had become accepted as a kind of formal uniform within the movement. It was probably the least practical dress for the tropics, but Savimbi favoured it, which meant that everybody else had to as well.

'Impossible', the little fellow stated in flawless English and totally without malice. 'If you enter Angola without the authority of the Allied Supreme Military Command and you are picked either by UNITA or the FNLA, you will be treated as a spy . . . you will be suspected of working for the MPLA. Worse, you will be executed. The same will happen if you try to enter through Zaire', he warned.

Gilles suggested to the man that he must be joking. He wasn't, he assured us. 'If you want to die, try going into Angola without our blessing.'

He added that neither he nor his superiors had much control over combatants in the field in day-to-day affairs during the hostilities then going on. Since black soldiers were mostly 'ignorant' – his words, not ours – they were hardly likely to respect any press card that we might bandy about. He threw in a rather convincing rider about most of them being illiterate anyway.

'Your media accreditation would mean about as much to the average UNITA soldier as a press release . . . very few have heard of or seen either', which was when he smiled . . .

Then he said something that worried us: 'The same applies to the enemy . . . anyone associated with Western nations will, if they get their hands on you, be treated by the opposition, the people in Luanda and the MPLA as a hostile agent.'

His closing words were forthright: 'Be well aware of the risks my friends . . . Angola is now in a state of total war and as we all know, in wartime, solutions tend to be final.' It sounded like an edict out of the Nazi era.

In view of this, he suggested, why not just be sensible and go home? Forget the whole thing? What was it to us, he asked, that there was war in Angola?

Some foreign correspondents took his advice. After a week or two with too much time on their hands, far too much hooch and too many black girls, the majority went back to Europe, America or South Africa. Others routed their return tickets through Nairobi and Kinshasa. Gilles and I thought about it over a few beers and then headed north by road, later the same day. We'd made up our minds and decided to go in overland.

In spite of warnings, we thought the risks had been exaggerated. In any event, we'd taken the precaution of asking the Zairean Embassy in Lusaka for transit visas and had been told that there would be no problem whatever. 'Just roll up and everything will be fixed up on the border', the official told us enthusiastically.

He was actually quite keen that we should go. I already had an FNLA press card, which meant that politically I was 'acceptable to the cause'. I should simply ask at the point of entry to be taken to the local FNLA commander and all would be arranged, he suggested.

The border between Zambia and Zaire at Kasumbalesa in the extreme north of what, not very long before, had been Northern Rhodesia, was not one of the most impressive of Africa's gateways. Apart from the mines, the region never readily accepted progress.

Outside the copper-producing towns, it was as thickly forested and primeval as it had been when the first white interlopers arrived in the 19th century. What struck us immediately about the area adjacent to the Zairean frontier in which we travelled was the number of roadblocks and troops among a mainly listless civilian community, the majority it seemed, out of work. The place exuded a profound melancholy begotten by an economy in total disarray.

Zambia by the mid 1970s had been independent barely a dozen years, yet the rot caused by Kenneth Kaunda's hare-brained socialist schemes had taken effect. Even so, as we were soon to discover, it was not as bad as Zaire, not remotely so.

The twin border posts – one on either side of the frontier, a few hundred yards apart – were a series of small ramshackle buildings reminiscent of an earlier era. Like the adjacent town of Kasumbalesa, this was a peculiar sort of place in the middle of the bush. The imperial powers a hundred years before had decided exactly how the borders should be drawn on the map of Africa, regardless of whether they cut across tribal or traditional land. On the face of it, someone had walked into the forest at Kasumbalesa and decided that that was where the border post would be.

Thousands of Zaireans and Zambians crossed there every month. Because of shortages of most essentials in Zaire, the traffic – both legal and contraband – was significant. Controls were strict, but you could soon detect that it needed more than just documents to hurry a consignment through. American dollars in the right hands made things work in double quick time. In *Zairois*, the local lingua franca, such a gift was, and still is, called *matabish*.

Gilles and I arrived at Kasumbalesa on foot, after taking a taxi from the bus station. We walked to the border post carrying our luggage but were beaten to it by a busload of Zaireans going the other way. The immigration official on the Zairean side ordered us to the back of the line. In Africa, when a functionary in uniform with a rifle singles you out for attention, you never argue. In fact, it is often good policy to smile and thank him for abusing you. At a roadblock a corporal suddenly becomes a colonel, or possibly even a general, if it suits the purpose.

When, at last, we finally got to this officious little shit and gave him our story, he shook his head, slammed his fist down on the desk and said: '*Pas possible*'. We asked, still smiling, to see *Monsieur le directeur*. That was a mistake! We were proposing to go over his head.

The *directeur* was not there, he declared firmly. He'd gone to lunch, even though it was only ten in the morning. He would not be back before six that evening. It would be better if we came back next week; or preferably, next month. We said we would wait, to which he replied, so graciously that it surprised us both and in English, 'Welcome to the Republic of Zaire'.

Towards dusk the *directeur* himself appeared. He listened courteously to our story and his questions were concise. He later told us that he had spent two years at Louvain University in Belgium. The man was friendly and not consumed by a need to prove anything.

No, he said, with a friendly pat on Gilles' back, there would be no problem. However, we must understand that Zaire was on a war footing. He simply couldn't let anybody through without a visa because that was the law. A visa could be obtained only in Lubumbashi. War dogs of an older generation will remember the town as Elizabethville. From there, he suggested, we would be able to cross the border into Angola at Teixeira de Sousa. There might, of course, be a little delay. 'The war', he smiled grandly, nodding his head.

Gilles and I looked at each other. What was all this rubbish about Zaire being unfriendly? This guy had just disproved all those notions. We were pleased because it all seemed to be coming together . . .

However, he said, still smiling, there was one little problem. We smiled back inquiringly. He declared in his friendliest mién that he simply could not let us go on to Lubumbashi on our own: somebody would have to accompany us, and it would be his personal responsibility. The problem, he added, was that he'd only come off duty at about nine that evening, in about three hours.

In a country as hard-pressed for foreign exchange as Zaire – even though it produces so much wealth in copper, uranium, cobalt, gold and diamonds – it came as a surprise when, promptly at nine, a brand-new French station-wagon arrived to take us to our destination. It was driven by the big man's chauffeur. We'd be accompanied by another member of his staff, an athletic-looking soldier who introduced himself as André.

We had seen André around during the afternoon. The man was clearly military in appearance, and a toughie. Then he had hardly spared us a glance, far less a greeting: no twinkling sense of fun with this guy. André appeared to have no particular function, but he obviously had direct access to the director's office, which indicated rank.

So we set off. I travelled in front with the driver. André and Gilles were in the back. About a mile down the road, André told the driver to stop at a roadside bar: the only one on the two-hour drive to Lubumbashi.

It was a typically African bush joint. A speaker blared out loud local pop music and the only lights were a row of paraffin lamps. Two black whores came over, but André told them to fuck off. They didn't argue, but retreated to a safe distance.

The beers arrived with a selection of dirty tin mugs and our escort promptly ordered two more; for the road, he said. He indicated that we should pay. André moved aside to talk to someone he knew.

I was about to say something about the noise when another man came to our table. He spoke to me in English, his voice hardly audible above the din. 'Listen, my friend,' he said leaning across. 'I am sympathetic towards you because I am Zairean. I was educated in Zambia and I have an English friend . . . a good friend.' He looked around furtively to see what André was doing.

'I am a member of the police here on the border and I saw you at Kasumbalesa today. I must tell you that you are both in very deep trouble. You think you are going to the FNLA, but in fact you have been arrested. Do you understand me?'

Even in that bad light, the colour must have drained from my face for Gilles could see that something was wrong. He tried to interrupt but I raised a hand to let the policeman continue. He obviously knew what he was talking about; how else would he have been privy to our connection with the FNLA?

Gesturing over his shoulder towards André, the man said that we were being taken to a military barracks in Lubumbashi. 'It's the worst in the country. They are taking you to the place of killing. They think you are agents of the MPLA.' André returned at this point and we talked of other things. Our informant's manner warned us not to mention a word. In any event, more beer had arrived and we were again expected to pay. André told us to drink up. I hastily told Gilles to stall him.

Gilles explained that since we had been on the road all day, we were very thirsty. Could he order another round? I produced another ten-dollar bill and the Zairean's eyes lit up. Each round so far had cost ten dollars, three or four times the usual price, our escort pocketing the change each time. When André went off to fetch the drinks, I quickly told Gilles what the policeman had said. I then asked the border guard: 'What the hell can we do?'

'Nothing,' he said. 'Don't try to escape or you will be shot.' André and the driver were armed, he warned. They were professionals. We were in Shit Street, he suggested, big time . . .

On my own, I knew, I could probably have made it to Zambia. I was aware that the road followed the border for some distance before turning inland. I calculated it to lie about a mile south of us, perhaps two. In any event, I was fit and could outrun most others my age. However, Gilles was an innocent in a hostile world and I could hardly leave him.

It was an immediate decision and there was no other way. We were in this together, and anyway, the Frenchman from Paris knew almost nothing about Africa. If I had gone off, he would almost certainly have been killed.

Our options, just then, were limited. Somehow though, I thought, there was hope. There was a Japanese mine nearby – we could see the lights from where we sat. Possibly we might be able to ask permission to stop the car for a piss in the bush and disappear into the heavy forest that hung over the road in clusters. When I mentioned my thoughts to Gilles, I suddenly realized that neither of us knew the area. Worse, for the little we could see of the jungle, it was obvious that much of it was impenetrable. Also, there might be rivers to cross. Besides, Gilles had already told me, he was terrified of snakes.

Then, even if we were to get away, André still had our passports. Lusaka and our embassies were hundreds of miles to the south. If the Zaireans raised the alarm, the Zambians would also be after us once we'd crossed the frontier.

Anyway, we were not yet under close arrest, I said, taking a loftier approach. Then we noticed our driver sitting on the other side of the bar watching our every move. He hadn't touched a drink. Moments later André waved us towards the car.

The 20 minutes or so that we spent at the bar seemed like hours. The two hours on the road to Lubumbashi might have been a whole night. Every mile seemed like ten and every promise of distraction offered relief.

After we had passed through the second roadblock, Gilles leaned forward and, in English, asked what he should do with the set of Ché Guevara's writings that he had in his baggage? 'Christ!' was about all that I could utter just then. I turned my head in his direction.

'You serious?' The revelation was absurd and I was incredulous.

There are about six books, he whispered. I could hear that he was breathless as he whispered and suddenly I was too. It was like asking an airline pilot what you should do with the bomb we had brought on board. Could things get any worse?

To me it was incomprehensible that a Frenchman with a modicum of sense should enter Zaire, one of the most reactionary countries in the world, with a bag full of revolutionary tracts. Had he intended converting the locals? Everybody, everywhere, knew who Guevara was. Ché had actually visited the Congo clandestinely some years before and Gilles Hertzog knew it. He was innocent all right; with the kind of stupid, unthinking naïveté that could get us both killed.

We drove on in silence. I could see no solution. Then Gilles leant over once more and told me that he could reach his baggage with his one hand and that perhaps he could get at the books, one by one, and throw them out of the window.

We were travelling at about 80 miles an hour. In my imagination I could hear the wind ripping open the pages of a half-a-dozen Marxist dissertations as they tore apart in the dark. There was no way that André and his friend would not hear the noise and obviously, they'd investigate. That would be inviting disaster!

In as few words as possible I told the Frenchman not to be a total fucking asshole. 'Don't even think about it!' I spat the words out under my breath. Anything like that would be tantamount to suicide, I quietly inferred. Which was when I asked myself whether this idiot had rocks in his head?

The driver slowed again; another roadblock. Soldiers came forward and one couldn't miss their weapons. For a few seconds we were blinded by headlights. André spoke in Lingala, the Zairean language of the north and I recognized only one word, an aside in French: *mercenaire*. So did Gilles.

We were being represented to the others as a captured pair of mercenaries! My French colleague was in a state of apoplexy, sweat running down his face and I wasn't faring much better.

It didn't help to recall that only a few years before, Hoare's mercenaries had ravaged the old Congo. Those irregulars had sometimes killed more innocents than guilty parties. Consequently, any hired gun in Zaire was a hated breed, especially if the subject happened to be white.

Not long before our visit a dozen Italian airmen, all members of an 'aid' group in Zaire, had been hacked to death in the belief that they were mercenaries. An apology of sorts was offered to their families by Mobutu, but what galled was the fact that at the time, no one had bothered to ask them who or what they were. Or what they were doing there. They were murdered without questions asked.

Now we were in that *galere* and we had Ché Guevara's lucubrations in our baggage to prove it.

It was a time for some quick thinking. André was obviously the man in charge; dour and uncompromising. Yet, I sensed, somehow, he was a man of contradictions: he clearly had authority and hadn't yet abused us in any way, even though his mind was made up about who we were supposed to be. Our only hope lay in trying to win him over. Money was part of the answer. What else? I had a jack of whisky in my bag.

'Could I have a drink?' I asked in my fractured French. 'I have some Scotch in my baggage.'

'Whisky?' the man sounded interested. If I had known then that Scotch was selling for $50 a bottle in Lubumbashi – if you could get your hands on it – I'd have been better prepared. He stopped the car.

The bottle went round, I took a large swig myself because I needed it and then it went round again. The alcohol warmed me, even though the temperature outside was a stifling 35 degrees with humidity to match. It was even hotter inside the vehicle because there was no air-conditioning.

Two more swigs and André had become talkative. By the next roadblock he was garrulous, but by then the bottle was empty. At least I had achieved a small victory because the man guarding us was tipsy.

He spoke of many things, with Gilles translating. His real name, he told us, was Betué Robert. His position at the border was that of military policeman. His rank in the Zairean Army was lieutenant and he'd been trained in military intelligence by the Israelis, spending three months at a camp for airborne forces in the Negev.

Then he said something that knocked us sideways: 'My name among my friends is *l'Assassin*. I am the official assassin for General Mobutu in these parts.' This was a real shock to us because the man was obviously proud of his dubious role as executioner.

Gilles asked him what he got paid for 'eliminating' someone. 'Five hundred Zaire', he answered (then about $1,000). That was for killing an important person, he added. 'Less for someone like you', he smirked, which didn't help. It was his first joke and he enjoyed it. His laughter was like a fury unleashed. God knows, I suddenly felt we'd already been condemned! The assassin was playing with us; a cat with two captive mice. Meanwhile, my palms were sweating. Gilles's eyes, I could see whenever I swivelled round in my seat, stood out like saucers in the half-light.

As we approached Lubumbashi, André turned to Gilles after he had asked where we were being taken and answered with a raucous laugh: 'Don't worry. I'll see you through to the end. Right to the very end', were his words. The driver smiled and I felt like puking. I asked André if we could stay at the Park Hotel in Lubumbashi. I didn't expect him to consent, but I wanted to gauge his mood. He replied blandly that that wouldn't be a problem. 'But first we must report to the barracks.'

I knew then that it was vital to get the man to take us to some place where we could notify our consulates, the most obvious being the hotel or a restaurant. But it was already well after midnight and there was little chance that anybody who mattered would be about. Our only salvation, I decided, was to make contact with another white man; possibly one of the British or Belgian expatriates working in the copper mines.

Speaking English and no longer caring whether the driver could understand or not, I suggested to Gilles that if all else failed he should try to bribe the man, which might have been a mistake. If *l'Assassin* had spent any time in Israel he'd have picked up some English. We talked quietly for a few moments and by now the car was on the outskirts of town. Our driver was being signalled to stop at the last roadblock. While André was busy with the soldiers, I told Gilles to offer him $50 to stop first at the hotel.

André got back into the car. The main road into Lubumbashi stretched ahead, past wrecked cars and derelict buildings that still bore the marks of the civil war a dozen years before. One had taken a direct mortar hit on the roof and, after all this time, there were still broken tiles lying scattered about beside the road.

A sign indicating that we were entering Lubumbashi appeared out of the dark. There were no street lights and for all we knew, there might never have been. Worse, the place seemed deserted because there was no other traffic. There was clearly a curfew in force.

Gilles again spoke hastily to André about the hotel. I could see out of the corner of my eye that money had changed hands. The bribe was working! Thank God.

The car passed down a long avenue of trees and we passed a big barracks, the first of several. I had been to Lubumbashi several times before and I knew that we had a mile or two to go before we reached the centre of the *ville*.

André leaned forward and again spoke to the driver in Lingala. The car slowed. He pointed towards a dirt road on the right and both our spirits sank. Looking back on the events of the previous 12 hours, that specific moment was the most chilling of all: we suddenly realized that we were heading for the unknown. Nobody was even vaguely aware that we were even in Zaire, never mind in the hands of people who could do us harm. Nobody was likely to know either. It was a sensation like nothing else I had ever experienced, not even in Nigeria at its worst, and the darkness didn't help.

From the direction we were travelling, I sensed we were being taken out of town again, on the far side of the city. I turned round to Gilles and voiced my fears but he could only nod. 'Ask him where we're going', I urged. 'This isn't the fucking way to the hotel!' Gilles uttered a few hasty words in French but André stared fixedly ahead. Then he mumbled something about having to report in first. Suddenly the man was sober.

We turned on to a better road, and a row of lights shone ahead. A turret with a heavy-calibre gun loomed out of the darkness. André motioned to the driver to turn left at a big building guarded by a sentry and answered the challenge when called. A set of steel gates opened outwards.

We didn't know it then, but we'd arrived at a Zairean military camp. Our fate was totally in the hands of a man who'd earned his spurs with a select group of Israeli security forces in which he'd been awarded his honorary title: *l'Assassin*!

CHAPTER TWENTY-ONE

Jailed for Espionage in Lubumbashi

An institutionalized custom, together with a Zairean security organization that had been responsible for the deaths of thousands of people, were to play vital roles in our lives during the course of the next few weeks.

THE FIRST WAS *MATABISH*, the greasing of the palms, a tradition in Africa with which all travellers in Central Africa have long been accustomed. In the case of André, the man who clearly held our joint fate in his hands, it was a seller's market.

The second was the *Centre National de Documentation*, with which we would now have an opportunity to become acquainted. To be generous, the CND was something akin to the old KGB, only this was the Zairean version and it was ground roots basic.

We soon found that Europeans who lived and worked in Zaire and who'd been taken into custody were generally treated a good deal better than their African counterparts. However, to Zaireans there were 'whites' and, as we were to discover soon enough, other people with white skins, such as European Portuguese. If we were to judge by the privations to which some of the Portuguese prisoners had been subjected at the hands of this security organization, President Mobutu had already made the distinction long before he came to power.

Angus McDermid, a hugely experienced man who had got to know Central Africa well over several decades, said that Mobutu had once told him that while the Portuguese had been involved with the tribal chiefs of the Congo Basin for five centuries, their record had been tarnished both by history and by blood. 'They fucked our women, they mishandled our men and they constantly deceived us,' were the words, he used during a visit to Lagos.[1]

In short, decreed the Eminent One, all those people who originally came from Lisbon, were oppressors. 'Imperialists', was how he would sometimes refer to them in public pronouncements, to which he would add: 'All of Africa, all black people, have good cause to be rid of them.'

Matabish, by contrast, is a time-honoured part of African tradition. It's much the same as the tip on a restaurant bill in Europe or America. However, a few adjustments needed to be made, and that depended solely on the gravity of a situation. Exactly who you were dealing with also counted. If you gave too little, it reversed its significance, so to speak, and became an insult.

A German was arrested in Lubumbashi before we arrived and was kept in jail for three months while Bonn tried to sort out his problems. The charge was obscure. However, the man had been trying to export the semi-precious stone malachite in bulk to Europe. Ostensibly his papers (which themselves cost a lot in *matabish*) were valid. Evidently somebody in the CND had made the decision that the deal warranted a lot more of the kind of cash that usually came 'under the table'.

While not precisely calculated, such matters have a feel about them. You instinctively know the difference between too little largesse and too much; apparently the German didn't. He should have, because he had been in Zaire for some time and was routinely taking out of the country several tons of the semi-precious stone each year.

His never-made-public 'derisory token' earned him a further charge of bribing a government official, unusual for a country where corruption was so widespread that nothing was achieved without it. By the time the man was released, it had cost him at least $10,000 to win a few friends and influence the powers-that-be. In addition, his stones – already paid for – were forfeited and delivered in a truck to the CND headquarters.

Then there was the case, worse still, of a British pilot who was held in custody by the CND in Kinshasa while we were in Lubumbashi. He'd flown from Luanda and landed at N'djili Airport outside Kinshasa. Technically, he had come from a 'hostile' area and it was assumed that like us, he was an MPLA spy. By the time Gilles and I left the country, he'd been locked up for several months, eventually extended to more than a year. He had his stay extended while Harold Wilson, the then British Prime Minister, had found it necessary to write a cringing letter of appeal to Mobutu, or perhaps it was a series of cringing letters – one never knows with such things.

Our first contact with CND officialdom was hardly encouraging. We'd only vaguely heard of the organization across the bar at the Ridgeway and, frankly, had we known what we were into, both Gilles and I would probably have taken a rain check.

In any event, CND headquarters was our first stop after we had been taken to the barracks on the outskirts of Lubumbashi to register. It was late, and there were few soldiers about, most of them drunk. All were armed. Meanwhile, André told Gilles to stop talking about the hotel. That was out of the question, he told him brusquely at one of the stops. What also became apparent was that this guy was no longer our friend.

Each time the vehicle was stopped at a roadblock, we were suddenly the objects of great interest, almost as if the troops manning them had never seen a white man before. Then, once we arrived at the base, scores of soldiers in their American fatigues surrounded the building we were escorted to, armed guards in front, with more following behind us.

We sat on stools and our surprise was genuine when *l'Assassin* produced three beers. He watched benevolently as our unsmiling black guard demanded another ten American bucks in payment. We were being screwed, but what could we do?

Our guardian spoke on the telephone, again, in Lingala. As before, the only word we could recognize was *mercenaire*. This time it was Gilles' face that flushed. Of deep concern to us both was not so much that we'd been arrested, but that we were isolated from the world outside. There wasn't a soul we could ask to get in touch with someone.

I'd experienced a little of this kind of routine earlier in Angola, though from the other side of the desk, so I had a rough idea of what came next. That was when I said quietly to Gilles, in English: 'Now comes the real test.'

André had spoken to his superiors in Kinshasa and said that we would have to wait and see what happened. I sensed that if more soldiers arrived we were possibly done for. We didn't have long to wait.

Finally the gates to the camp were thrown open. From where we were being held, we had a view of the parade ground outside through a large window in the office. We could also see the portal through which we'd originally entered. Minutes later a car arrived with a single occupant; a good sign, I thought. As we found out later, the newcomer was Mobutu's emissary in the southern Shaba region, an army officer who was clearly not amused at being hauled out of his bed in the middle of the night.

Unlike André, this man tended to remain beyond immediate matters of contention. His job was to issue orders and he barely glanced at us when he walked in. He listened impassively while André spoke and read out the contents of the letter from the Director of Immigration at the border. It was all in Zairois and we understood none of it. Then he strode over, carefully brushing down the front of his jacket as he did so.

He spoke in clipped French: 'Who sent you to Zaire? In whose pay are you? For whom have you been fighting? Have you taken any photographs of Zairean establishments?' Gilles said afterwards that all that was missing was Von Stroheim. The Frenchman answered each question in turn, and afterwards, many more.

Then came the crunch, one that had pretty serious implications: 'When last were you in Luanda?' Before I could warn Gilles to be vague, he'd answered for both of us: 'Only a few weeks ago', were his words.

'Aha!' The man displayed his satisfaction with a smile, though a Gotcha! would have served equally well. 'So you are MPLA!' he barked. He had an intense look on his face and the implications were clear. We had been in Luanda! Therefore we were communists, was his thrust. I tried to explain that it wasn't that way at all, that I'd been with the FNLA.

'Quiet!' ordered *l'Assassin*.

The officer gestured to the soldiers next door and they put our bags in a military transport outside. Gilles could only stare ahead. I tried to remain nonchalant but it was difficult. At that point I raised my hand, almost as if I was in a schoolroom.

'Can I talk?' I asked. André nodded. 'Where are you taking us?' I asked. He avoided eye contact and said nothing. At least they hadn't beaten us. Not yet, anyway. It was also curious that we hadn't been properly searched: Ché's tracts were still intact, for the time being at any rate.

We spent the rest of the night in a cell in one of the western suburbs of Lubumbashi. A fairly big city by African standards and number two in Zaire, it was the country's mining capital. Without copper, it would still have been the tiny village it was when the first white prospectors had arrived from Europe half a century before. During our drive through town there wasn't a white face anywhere. As Gilles ventured, why should there have been at three in the morning?

Our 'cell', we were to discover soon enough, was an old brothel, which formed part of a military barracks near the offices of Union Miniere, then listed as Geocomin in the *Wall Street Journal* and currently operating under some other nomenclature. It was surrounded by a wall, 12 feet high, and guarded at all corners by soldiers in tall towers. We speculated about why they should bring us here since there were plenty of 'proper' jails in Lubumbashi. When we were served with half a chicken between us and more beer it dawned: another step in first separating us from our assets, at $10 a throw with *l'Assassin* as our banker.

Each time we handed over money, André would go out and pay in local currency. He'd pocket the difference and as far as he was concerned, we'd never know. But we did: it was something we'd discussed with the others back in Lusaka. We knew he'd sell our dollars on the black market at many times face value. With a hearty appetite himself, we ended up parting with $50 in less than an hour. André was throwing our cash about like a drunken sailor.

Eventually, at something after four in the morning (they had taken our watches), I said we were tired and needed sleep. A guard led us to our quarters and we were locked up for the night. Before putting our heads down, we spent a while carefully examining the room, which was a bit bigger than I'd expected. It had a small barred window up high, a steel door, concrete walls and a cement floor with no covering.

Gilles said it was strange that no one had searched our bags, which was true: always the unexpected . . .

There was obviously no way that we could escape from Mobutu's hotel. Although there were whores about – we had seen their dark shapes in the shadows as we were escorted in – this was a military establishment, unmistakeably so, even if it didn't rank with your average army barracks.

The beds were filthy, the single mattress caked with dried semen, which was when it dawned: we were being held in the local military bordello, which should have raised our spirits but didn't, in part because cockroaches and bugs crawled all over the wall. Swarms of mosquitoes appeared from nowhere as soon as the guard doused the lights. Gilles, a rather fastidious Parisian, was distinctly distraught.

There was very little sleep that night. We were awake again before dawn trying to work out a scheme that would release us from this hopeless mess. Throughout, I was worried about the Guevara tomes, so at first light I tore a small hole in the mattress and stuffed them in. We could but hope.

Daylight brought a change of guard outside our door as well as *l'Assassin*'s face. He was never happy in the morning, when he would peep through a small hole in the door and order us to get ready. This time he gave a direct order, in French: 'Lay out all your possessions on the bed.' This routine was repeated for several more days, except that on the second morning, surprise! We were taken to a little restaurant in town for breakfast.

White people in African custody sometimes get this privilege, I learnt later, especially if they hadn't yet been charged. The reason is simple: food. Europeans, André explained when we asked him what this was all about, ate differently from black people. We also understood that there was a fee attached to such favours. More dollars, more *matabish*, because André insisted that he pay the bill with our dollar bills.

Then, for the first time, later that morning, we were taken into the headquarters of the CND.

The main security building in Lubumbashi seems small. However, it is multi-layered, with two floors below ground level. The expansive exterior hides a labyrinth of offices that include a reception area, radio rooms, a sleeping area for the guards, dungeons below, torture chambers (we were told) and a number of sparsely furnished cells on the first floor which were used for interrogation.

Radio masts straddled the roof of the building as well as several houses nearby. There were also a number of cells at the back holding black prisoners, all awaiting trial or interrogation. The entire complex was guarded by soldiers armed with American M16s.

Over the course of the following week – without breaks for Saturdays or Sundays – we spent many hours at the CND headquarters in Lubumbashi. Impressions of those events remain vivid.

The first thing I saw when I walked into the room where they initially interrogated us was a large wire wastepaper basket full of discarded rubber stamps. There were hundreds of them. From where had they come? What were they originally intended for? We dared not look too closely, never mind ask: in this building everyone minded his own business.

I also remember clearly the crisp rattle of transmissions in morse, alternating at almost regular intervals with the cries of prisoners in the cells below. In this day and age one might have thought that the morse code had long ago been superseded by short-wave radio. It probably has by now, but not in the Zaire of the 1970s.

It didn't take us long to discover that there were more white prisoners in the complex, including five Portuguese. We weren't allowed to communicate with them, although a glance exchanged is often as effective as a handshake and they seemed to have something of a military bearing. Deserters? We could only speculate. Anybody who is crazy enough to seek sanctuary in Zaire must be mad anyway.

The Portuguese were still there when we left, two of them bloodied, dishevelled and showing signs of having been thrashed. One had a filthy bandage around his head, the other looked away each time we caught his eye. That they were beaten often was obvious and it worried us. Was it to be our turn next?

One morning when we arrived they'd been joined by three other Europeans, one an elderly, white-haired man who spoke only French. The other two might have been Rhodesian or South African, mercenaries perhaps? We never found out what ultimately happened to them.

Another prisoner who had been released two weeks before our arrival was Reinoud von Muhlen, a Dutchman and the regional director for Philips in Zaire's southern Shaba Province. In a search of his offices a month before, soldiers had discovered a radio transmitter which the troops would probably have interpreted in much the same way as having found a code book full of mysterious ciphers in Cyrillic script.

In spite of explanations that the set was about to be installed in the CND offices at Kolwezi – a mining town to the north (and the scene of savage massacres of whites by black soldiers not long afterwards) – von Muhlen was arrested and charged with espionage. This happened even though the CND used Philips equipment throughout the region and von Muhlen was the boss of the local European subsidiary of that massive conglomerate.

From what we could gather, von Muhlen had been badly beaten. While local whites rallied and brought food to his cell, he saw very little of it. The Dutch government managed to get him released, but it took a while.

Moving about Lubumbashi, between our cell and the CND offices, we found it a dirty, depressing town, ineffably so. Garbage was piled up everywhere and never removed. A pall of smoke hung over some districts as people tried to burn their trash, which was difficult because it rained a lot and everything was damp. The people we saw in the streets as we were taken from one place to another looked disconsolate. They walked about as if they had heavy weights around their necks and you rarely saw a smile.

There was little doubt that we were spotted by some of

Lubumbushi's white residents, but they turned the other way if we approached in their direction. This was one place where you didn't crap on your own doorstep: von Muhlen's experiences with Mobutu's security goons had been salutary.

One afternoon, while lingering at the main gate of the CND headquarters waiting for transport back to the barracks, some troops brought in a suspect with his arms bound behind him. His head and face were covered in blood, poor devil. His eyes, dull and sunken, said it all. It was obvious that he already knew his fate. Death and its more brutal preliminaries were inevitable. He looked at me, or rather through me. Part of him was already lifeless. He knew as well as I did that he would never walk out of that place again.

The most striking – and possibly the most frightening – person we encountered in Lubumbashi was known to us only as Zaki. This was a man whose reputation extended far beyond the borders of Zaire and who liked to present a world of silent menace. With good reason. It was heard in the bars of the Copperbelt in Zambia – and in Angola – that Zaki was the original security ogre. He would kill on a whim, though it was rumoured that he had a peculiar predilection for tackling people of Portuguese extraction.

The little bastard was short, stocky and had slits for eyes. He was the sort of man who can turn a pacifist into a potential murderer and from the start we were aware that he took particular interest in our plight. It was his job to find out for whom we were spying. Every day, for hours at a stretch, he would interrogate us, first together, then singly. Having been in Angola only a short while before, I seemed to enjoy his particular attention. There were times when I had to sit upright in a hard-backed chair with my hands on my legs. Zaki always positioned himself behind a large desk while two of his henchmen loomed over me.

Any lapse of discipline on my part would result in a clip on the ear, nothing too brutal, but it hurt. Then, when he discovered that I was living in South Africa, he became the consummate racist: it was payback time. South Africa is a nation of racist thugs, he would shout. My Angolan FNLA connections also puzzled him, though I never admitted to having actually fought for *Chipa Esquadrão*, Daniel Chipenda's guerrilla group, while still in Angola.

The hours spent with Zaki alternated between moderately intelligent conversation and a disconcerting awareness that I was not dealing with anybody rational. Zaki just *knew* that we were spies. He told us so. On dozens of occasions during the days that followed, he repeated the same questions, sometimes latching on to some random fact, such as that my father's first names were the same as mine, and he would worry away at it, like a terrier: he simply couldn't understand the logic. It was hardly a Zairean custom, so, he deduced, I was lying.

Not long afterwards we were led before three FNLA officers who'd been passing through Lubumbashi on their way to Zambia. My FNLA card was produced, which was followed by an interrogation of a totally different sort.

Where had I got the card? By whom was it issued?

The next phase caught me short. Granted, it was just possible that the FNLA card might be genuine, one of the men said. Possibly I had been in Nova Lisboa during the battle for that city, as I had said I was. But on whose authority had I left the front? I was asked. The implications were clear: I was being viewed as a deserter from the Angolan FNLA and that was immediately problematical: in some African countries I could be viewed as having betrayed the cause.

I tried to explain that when I was there, conditions in and about Nova Lisboa were chaotic. In any event, I was a journalist, not a combatant, even if I did have my own FN-FAL rifle. Having got my story and my pictures, I told them, I'd left the country by heading south, departing with a column of refugees, some of whom had been farming in the area not long before. It was all perfectly above-board, I insisted.

To my interrogators, my actions meant one thing: I'd fled in the face of the enemy. I had abandoned my 'brave colleagues' in their moment of crisis. There was only one answer for such crimes the Angolans suggested. The fact that the card that I had been carrying identified me as a non-combatant journalist was irrelevant. Either I was for the FNLA or I was against it. Anything circumstantial counted for nothing. Such is the nature of many of these conflicts, then and now. However, my arguments must have been convincing as the matter was not taken any further, much to my relief, as what they might do to a 'deserter' was too horrible to contemplate.

Another man now entered our lives; *Citoyen* Yambo. In his attempt to break free from the trappings of the former Belgian colonial power, Mobutu had replaced the appellations *Monsieur, Madame* and so on with the words *Citoyen* and *Citoyenne* of the French Revolution. Like the word 'comrade' in other societies, this custom permeated all levels, CND cells included. Since nobody disregarded a presidential edict, I became *Citoyen* Venter.

So it was *Citoyen* Yambo, the head of the CND, who almost studiously wore an expression of bored benevolence, actually rescued two scribes from a fate that was starting to look uncertain,

During the course of one grilling session, I'd produced a number of articles that I'd written for an American magazine on the Angolan war highlighting the danger of a *de facto* Cuban takeover of the Luanda government. Yambo was impressed and showed it with a broad smile right across his face. Journalist or not, I was obviously anti-Angolan and after that initial session, he seemed to take me at my word.

Zaki was overruled when it was suggested that I ought to be tortured to find out the real truth. Poor Gilles: he was on the point of collapse. The Frenchman reacted in curious ways to some of these obstacles. To Gilles Hertzog, our black jailers could do no wrong. He was steadfast in this view no matter what they did, or how many knocks we took. Once we got back to our cell, he would intimate that we, as whites, deserved all that we got. After all, he remonstrated, Africa had been subjected to European domination for centuries. I didn't know until much later that the Hertzog family background was staunchly communist and totally opposed to all that France (or Britain) stood for in colonial Africa.

In one sense, I suppose he was right. In another – with me the butt of vituperation to which I wouldn't subject the guy I liked least – I resented his views of a situation that could possibly cost us our lives. He was consistently naïve and the fact that he'd taken the Ché stuff into Zaire was unconscionable. I said as much, which didn't do a lot for personal relations between the four narrow walls where we were incarcerated. It wasn't cabin fever yet, but it was getting there fast.

I often wondered in later years whether the Guevara books had been found. It could have meant certain death to whoever was being held in the cell at that time, but then the Frenchman never considered that probability. It also mattered little to him, lying there in a dark cell being devoured by mosquitoes, that what was happening to us was simply not right. Our bona fides as journalists were clear. These people, with no evidence to the contrary, had judged us as they would the enemy. Gilles had a ringside view of some of the barbarism taking place around us. Like me, he could hear the screams. However, he remained silent on such issues.

It did not take me many hours to discover that Gilles Hertzog had another habit that was not only unendearing but morbidly stultifying. During the night he'd get up and wash his foreskin in the only basin that we both used, and do so sometimes three or four times in a row. There was a latrine bucket in a corner, which I had to slop out every morning, but that wasn't good enough for this Frenchman. He wouldn't touch it for the purpose of cleaning his dick.

Then, when he awoke, he'd go to the basin, let the water run and pull back his foreskin – right there before me – and do his thing once more. He would do it again after we'd been returned to our cell following the daily 'discussion session' as *Citoyen* Yambo liked to call it.

For a while, at least, I accepted that it was all commendably hygienic, especially under the circumstances of our imprisonment, but not when two people are forced to live together in such close confines. What made it worse was that until I took a real stand on the issue, he simply ignored my protests. I was eventually to wish him a happy *bris* before we parted. I said it would make the life of any woman he married a lot easier if he actually got rid of the damn thing.

André's actions continued to rankle. Barely a day would go without him making some stupid joke about seeing us through, 'right until the very end'. Then he'd laugh and slap one of us on the back, stupid bastard that he was. For all that, we didn't dare insult him because he obviously had enough clout to make things even more wretched. Though it cost us, we were still eating Western food.

Within a short while, as happens to people held in custody without good reason, both Gilles and I began, if not to crack, then to show serious strain. The mind starts to play tricks: rooms become smaller, walls thicker, the underlying rationale, if any, of those with whom you come into contact, becomes ominous. It was the first hint of an all-enveloping paranoia and it worried me,

Under the difficult conditions in which we were being held, our oppressors began to represent everything that was evil. *L'Assassin* was the ultimate monstrosity, some sort of ingrate, and I felt at the time that he should ultimately have to answer for what he was doing. Also, there was his role as a hit man, something he boasted about and which made him even more fearsome. I could only speculate how many 'enemies of the state' he'd iced.

It seemed inconceivable at the time that the Israelis had actually put

A photo taken by Gilles Hertzog outside our prison walls on the morning of our release and shortly before being driven to the Zambian border. Israeli-trained *l'Assassin* – otherwise known as André – is on the right: on the left is the ultimate Congolese *eminence grise*, 'Zaki'. (Author's collection)

this cretin through his paces, but then links between Jerusalem and Mobutu had always been excellent. In fact, they were very much in evidence years later when Neall Ellis was attempting to set up a mercenary flying wing for the dictator. It was undoubtedly Zaire's natural resources that paved the way, diamonds probably, and who knows, perhaps the country's huge uranium deposits.

CHAPTER TWENTY-TWO

Isolated in a Congolese Prison

The experience of being incarcerated in an African prison was horrendous. Yet, looking back, Gilles and I were a lot more fortunate that most in similar predicaments. We were kept apart from the majority of the inmates who, we learnt afterwards, were a violent, dissolute bunch and rape was commonplace.

FOR MOST OF OUR TIME in custody, we were in isolation, and allowed a few minor mercies, such as being able to exercise for an hour a day within the confines of the walled quadrangle.

More important, while our money lasted, we were able to order our single daily meal from a local restaurant run by a Belgian expatriate. Special arrangements were made for our food to be brought to the barracks by the restaurateur himself. Then André's magnanimity would prevail.

One of the soldiers would carry the tray to our cell and dish by dish, everything would be placed on the bed before us. André would haul out his own plate and take half of everything, scooping it off the plates with his fork. With a dismissive gesture, he'd signal that Gilles and I should get on with the rest and we'd split the balance. That routine never wavered, except once, when we opted for prison food . . .

The entire rigmarole was done with a panache that was deceptive. André always made us feel that he was being gracious by allowing us anything at all, and that with food for which we'd paid, which was why Gilles and I liked to suggest to him that it might be better – and easier – to eat in town. At least there we were allowed to get on with our meal without having to share it; André would have his own choices from the menu.

It was those rare occasions that gave us our best hope, a desperate anticipation that we would be seen and perhaps recognized. By now, we believed, the word must have got out that we were missing.

The snag was that nobody in Lubumbashi (as far as we could tell) knew where we were being held, and by which security body. More to the point, in a country where the tyrant Mobutu ruled, it was not the sort of thing you asked questions about.

Having seen us move about town, locals were obviously aware that we'd been arrested. In fact, they admitted afterwards that they'd seen us being taken between the barracks and the CND headquarters under armed guard. We were also spotted those few times when André felt like grandstanding and we were hauled off somewhere 'upmarket' for a meal. For him it was all about 'big eats': for us, not being allowed to talk to a soul, it was a misery from hell.

Looking back, it was clear that our situation was unusual, paradoxical almost. We were prisoners of the regime, yet we were taken out for the occasional meal. Also, we really weren't in total isolation.

André and his bosses must have known that we'd be observed by others. What obviously helped was that *Citoyen* Yambo, Zaki and the rest of the gang weren't yet altogether sure about us, in part because I'd spent time with an FNLA combat unit. I was sure by then that my story had checked out.

Whether I'd been an actual combatant was irrelevant. The bottom line was that the FNLA was composed of a group of guerrillas that enjoyed the patronage of Mobutu. Somebody told me afterwards that it was not impossible that my presence in Shaba might have been construed as a test: Mobutu often devised his own devious, incredibly convoluted little experiments, if only to establish loyalty among those not under his immediate control. As for Gilles, he was a French journalist, plain as day.

The trouble was, we couldn't actually inform anybody of our plight. Even if there was someone around who might have been able to pass on a message, they wouldn't give us a second glance because they didn't want to be taken by the secret police.

We had one opportunity when it might have been possible to get a message out. We'd been taken to the Central Hotel one morning for breakfast. Again we were isolated, but for once our guardian thug was in a communicative mood, probably because we'd bought him beer for breakfast. I asked if I might go to the toilet and he let me go on my own. It was a God-given moment because I knew that the Central Hotel had a callbox. Instead of taking the door to the john I went through the one next to it leading to the lobby. The telephone was on the desk in front of me.

Novelists often hinge their plots on a single crucial event. This was mine. All I needed was a ten makuta coin to talk to the British Consul in Lubumbashi. Ten makutas – about a dime.

I had loose change in my pocket but not a single 10 makuta piece. I handed a 50 makuta coin to the receptionist and asked him for change, but he either had none or didn't want to get involved. A black man staying in the hotel strolled through and he took out a pocket full of money after an agonizing scratch and scrape. Still nothing!

It was unbelievable: my luck failing like that. A single call could have been our salvation. A minute later *l'Assassin* came looking for me. He saw the telephone on the counter and snapped a question at the receptionist.

The negative reply hardly mattered. He was furious. I had betrayed a trust. His trust!

By now Gilles and I were desperate. Long hours of interrogation along with vile living conditions were starting to take effect. Our nerves were shot and we'd started snapping at one another, something that hadn't been missed by our guardians. *Citoyen* Yambo even asked me one morning if there wasn't something that I'd like to 'disclose' about my colleague. It was all nudge-nudge, wink-wink, but I knew what he was after. We were relatively OK as long as Ché Guevara's books remained hidden in the mattress.

Gilles' foreskin was still an issue within our confines and the daily ritual infuriated me. Also, we were plagued by insects. It was only a matter of time before one of us would go down with malaria. André had confiscated all our medication and tablets in the first search, not that there was much, though I always carried a course of antibiotics for general infections and more specifically, the runs.

By now we were also a bit concerned about money. We were spending a lot on small favours, including our daily meal. It was the only food we got and we knew that the alternative was too horrible to contemplate: we'd seen the slop pails being hauled through to the general cells, much of it *sadza*, a maize gruel.

L'Assassin never lost an opportunity to eat with us and as became his daily custom, he devoured half of the food. Gilles and I had to be content with what he deigned to leave behind, pig that he was. However, right then we were worried that we might run out of cash, especially if this nightmare went on long enough. No one enters 'Darkest Africa' with great wads of notes; it just wasn't done anymore.

Then a new complication emerged. Gilles awoke one morning to find that someone had been in the cell during the night. I'd heard movement, which was not unusual because somebody was always banging doors and checking, I'd sort of got used to the guards moving about. There had also been a storm. After he'd dressed he found that all his money had been stolen. He was left with $10 US, which he'd kept in his shoe for an emergency.

We asked *l'Assassin* about it as soon as he came on duty and he denied any knowledge of the theft, even though he was the only man with a key. The next day I lost $160 while in the shower.

It was time to consider our options. We might shout for help at a restaurant; or one of us might try to slip away while going to the toilet. However, we knew that, having raised the alarm, we'd never be allowed out again. After the botched phone call attempt, *l'Assassin* or somebody else in the party always accompanied us.

There might be another option, we believed. One of the Europeans living in Lubumbashi might ultimately come to our assistance if we asked them. It was a chance, but we had to take it. However, first we had to work out how we were to make that contact.

We didn't know it then, but those Europeans living in Lubumbashi were finding life increasingly hard. Even in our brief meetings in the town we could sense that they couldn't be expected to stand up to somebody in authority like André. They knew the CND, what it stood for, as well as its menacing role within Zairean society. Consequently, they kept their distance.

Also, André was always armed: he was clearly no small fish because you needed rank to carry a pistol in Zaire. He'd been flaunting it around as a symbol of authority since we first met.

We were only to discover afterwards that every one of the whites living in Lubumbashi at the time had observed what had happened to friends and neighbours arrested by the CND. A handful had died in detention, too many, they felt. Years later, when I met a man who'd been in Lubumbashi when we were there, he told me that he would probably have turned his back on us, even if I'd come running. 'We were all in the hot box. Your condition was worse than ours, only by degree', was his comment.

Then Gilles had an idea. We would smuggle out a note to someone. The concept was to write an appeal for help on a single sheet of toilet paper, French on one side, English on the other. It was not difficult on a Zairean bog roll since two rolls were never the same. Some were like sandpaper and quite thick.

It was a simple message, starting with the fact that we were journalists. We had entered the country legally to cross over into Angola, been arrested and were being held incommunicado in the military barracks on the west side of Lubumbashi in Shaba Province. Please inform the British and the French consulates in Lubumbashi or our embassies in Kinshasa. We marked it 'Most Urgent' in both languages.

In small print, Gilles also included our full names, passport numbers (I could remember mine because I'd used it often enough) together with the addresses of our respective newspapers. Now all we needed was an opportunity to hand it over. I kept the paper folded under the clasp of my belt, for we were often searched. That complete, we waited for that magic moment when we would encounter another European.

So far we had been held in isolation from them all but, after a few days, *l'Assassin* became a little lax.

Conditions eased a little after about a week. We could now use the CND latrine without André's officious presence. We were even allowed to sit in the sun with other prisoners in the yard at the back of the barracks on some afternoons.

It was while we were taking it easy one day that we had our first real break. We'd kept to ourselves mostly because some of the black prisoners were aggressive and we were sometimes threatened. One or two would make the universal throat-cutting sign as we passed. Others spat in our direction, we could only speculate what would have happened had they shoved us in one of the general cells with that hoi polloi. Not all the scars on the Portuguese prisoners were acquired in the torture block.

That afternoon a dignified old fellow seated himself in the yard within talking distance of where we were. Not at all like the other prisoners, he was neatly dressed, with a friendly smile and Gilles and he soon started to chat. He said, he'd come to see his son, one of the warders. He was taking a break before going home again.

'Home?' asked Gilles, curious now.

Yes, he said, he worked in Lubumbashi. He was cook to one of the managers of Geocomin, the old Belgian mining company. Monsieur Henri someone or another. Gilles turned to me and explained, his eyes sparkling. Then he asked, 'You got that piece of paper?'

Gilles turned towards the old guy again.

'Henri! *mon ami belge!*' he cried. He was, of course, chancing it, though it wasn't unreasonable to assume that this so-called 'Henri' was Belgian. The Congo had been under the control of Brussels for as long as this huge African country had contact with the outside world.

'Please give Henri my best regards,' said Gilles effusively. The old man was clearly flattered at this attention from these two nondescript whites.

'Does he still eat so much?' asked Gilles. It was a reasonable question: most bigwigs heading large industrial enterprises in Third World countries – Africa especially – are overweight. It's their only real pleasure – that and black girls. 'And the wine?' Gilles suggested, trying the familiar touch.

'I'd very much like to see him again,' he told the old factotum.

'Then why don't you come with me now?' replied the cook.

No, Gilles quickly replied, we couldn't leave just then. Perhaps the next time he came to the headquarters. We had something to do before dark, we told him, but said it would be nice if he would give Henri our greetings. The cook got up to go and said he'd be happy to. Before that, I'd gone indoors and retrieved the slip of paper from where I had temporarily hidden it and handed it to the old man.

If the cook had been able to read, he'd probably have showed our note to his son. As it was, without another glance, he put it in his pocket.

We could only surmise that the genial old fellow did not know we were prisoners. There were so many expatriates in Shaba Province that it probably never occurred to him. Anyway, we wore our own clothes, not the drab prison garb issued to Africans and even then, there were white men in the Zairean Army, the civil service and the prison services, so he probably regarded us as legit.

We waited. By the next evening, when nothing happened, we assumed that 'Henri' had not managed to get in touch with the authorities. By the fourth day we'd given up hope.

That was the worst night of all, punctuated by a tropical storm that arrived with an almost cyclonic intent along with blinding flashes of lightning that would brilliantly illuminate our tiny cell for a second or two. To Gilles, nature had gone berserk.

The Frenchman swore that night if he ever emerged from that prison he, the archetypal agnostic, would become a Christian. I could laugh about it afterwards, but the fact is that incarceration does that to some people. Suddenly, I, too, was frightened.

Next morning, thinking that all was lost, we wrote a new message on another piece of toilet paper, this one a bit more detailed than before.

At that point our daily interrogations ended and we were allowed to spend just about every afternoon in the yard. The rains often drove us indoors, but it was better than the cell with its cockroaches, the washbasin and the bucket.

Gradually we came to be accepted by the others, except by one man, the 'chief prisoner', who was in a sense I suppose a 'trustee'. This tough, obstreperous bastard had enough muscle to back any argument and the first time he set eyes on us, he made it clear we were 'not fucking welcome' in his domain.

His name was Ilungi. It was no secret either in the barracks or beyond that he despised whites. He'd killed many, he would boast to his little clique in French and they would roar as they cast disapproving glances in our direction. Gilles translated every word. Later, when we were able to compare notes with the Dutchman, von Muhlen, we learnt that it was Ilungi who had taken all the bribes and had then withheld his food, like a Kapo in a Nazi camp.

Unwittingly Ilungi helped us. It was his privilege as a trustee to be allowed outside from time to time, which in itself was unusual in any CND headquarters, but we didn't question why he had such freedom. He accompanied *l'Assassin* into town with us one morning.

Once again we were taken to the Central Hotel and Ilungi was left to guard us while André went to the bank. We needed to cash a traveller's cheque and he did it for us. As usual he 'charged' us his 'regular' 20 per cent commission.

We settled Ilungi in the most comfortable chair we could find and ordered him a big cigar and three beers. He was delighted. He was also pleased at our servility. About 20 minutes later I excused myself to go to the toilet.

The man at the desk was surprised to see me again. His hand moved over the telephone. He'd obviously been instructed by *l'Assassin* that we were never to use it. In Zaire, it was an unwritten law: when the CND talks, you listen. The next moment a white man entered through the main door: the first I had seen at close quarters for what seemed a year. He was young, slim and well-dressed. He smiled a greeting.

I moved forward. 'Do you speak English?' I asked, my voice cracking.

'Yes', he answered, still smiling. I pressed our bilingual handwritten note into his hand.

'Take this,' I urged, quivering. He stepped back in astonishment and the paper fell to the floor. I picked it up and pushed it back into his hand.

'*For Christ's sake*', I urged, 'read it!' Without acknowledgment, he took the note and walked through the hotel reception area into the yard at the back. As we learnt afterwards, he got busy that same morning.

Within 20 minutes our newfound saviour was at his consulate. Pierre Guth, the French Consul in Lubumbashi, was in a conference, but sensing our messenger's urgency, he read our note immediately. With two of his staff, he set out to find us.

Lubumbashi is not a big place. As we were told later, there were few expatriates who didn't know about our plight, but not having our predicament spelt out, we could be anybody. We'd been labelled a pair of mercenaries by someone and unfortunately that kind of crap usually sticks. In effect, we'd already been written off as a lost cause by most of them.

Guth spoke first to *Citoyen* Yambo, who expressed surprise at the news that two foreign journalists were being held against their will within his jurisdiction. He promised to 'look into the matter'.

At one point the French Consul even spoke to Zaki, who declared flatly that he'd never heard of any such persons. In fact, he told the diplomat, there were no whites in the prison at all. He obviously didn't regard his Portuguese prisoners as whites. However, if he even heard a whisper, he assured the Consul, he'd come to his office personally and tell him, he solemnly lied.

We, of course, knew nothing of this except that Zaki was annoyed when he spoke to us a few hours later. He asked whether we'd spoken to anybody while we'd been in town. Of course, we told him, we certainly hadn't.

A day later an official from the British Embassy in Kinshasa flew into Lubumbashi and demanded to see *Citoyen* Venter. He was allowed ten minutes in our cell, when he carefully checked my passport, which the prison authorities had given to him. In his mind, I could see it all: a South African accent, a kosher British passport with recent Angolan entry and exit stamps, a Zairean prison, all of it very clearly contradictory. As he told me, he first had to make sure that I wasn't doing something irregular before he could take the matter further. He was back in Kinshasa that same night.

It was a year before I learnt that M. Henri's cook, in all innocence, had completely forgotten about our note. He discovered it again while going through a pair of his trousers that he was about to have washed. It had been four days before the message was handed it over to his boss. Henri, whoever he was – bless his heart – immediately informed his superiors in Brussels who, in turn, passed it on to the French and British authorities, but by then they already knew about our plight. My consular visit was a result of that first message . . . and suddenly it all seemed to come together.

While Pierre Guth did his bit, he was hampered by the labyrinthine politics of Shaba Province, blighted as they were by years of insurrection. All this was explained to me by a South African intelligence officer whom I sat alongside on a flight between Johannesburg and Nairobi a long time afterwards. He was travelling incognito because, he said, South Africans of all persuasions were to remain 'undercover' in Black Africa for many years to come. It would be another 16 years before Nelson Mandela was released.

The South Africans certainly knew about me, the man on the flight said, and they'd already liaised with London. Within days of the message getting out, Pretoria had sent an emissary to Kinshasa to argue my case with the Great Panjandrum. Pretoria's relations with Zaire had always been good, but, as it turned out, our release eventually emerged from a most unusual source.

Le Monde, it seems, played a seminal role in achieving our freedom. Using all the influence this newspaper group wielded within the French diplomatic establishment – and it was considerable – an approach was made to Francois Mitterrand, then still in opposition in the French Parliament. He got in touch with the head of a former French colony in Africa, who, in turn, spoke to Mobutu.

I've often speculated about exactly who that head-of-state might have been. Perhaps the President of Congo-Brazza? Brazzaville is just across the river from Kinshasa. Or maybe President Houphouet-Boigny of the Ivory Coast, the great guide, philosopher and friend to many African leaders and, until the end of his illustrious career, on the best of terms with the Elysées Palace. Like Mobutu, President Houphouet-Boigny hated communists.

I don't suppose I'll ever know.

Gilles and I knew it was all over when André opened our cell door several mornings after the British diplomatic visit. Zaki was with him and the two men greeted us enthusiastically with hugs and kisses on both cheeks. We were his brothers, Zaki grandly told us, with an oily, clotted-cream niceness. What a load of bullshit, but Gilles and I played along because this was very unusual indeed. Clearly, something was happening . . .

Zaki said he'd hoped that we'd enjoyed our little sojourn while in his care. We smiled. Then, surprise, surprise, he asked us what we'd like for breakfast? André went off to town to fetch croissants, *confit* and *cafe au laite* and for the first time since we'd arrived in Zaire, we weren't asked to pay.

Later that day the two men accompanied us to the Zambian border in the prison governor's car, escorted by a motorcycle outrider, no less. We weren't stopped at a single road block. The driver parked a discreet distance from the frontier post while André got our passports stamped. More hugs and kisses followed.

'It was good', *l'Assassin* called in French as we walked away. '*N'est-ce pas?*' We didn't look back.

What a difference at the Zambian border post. The officials spoke good English, they conducted themselves like government officials, clad in well-pressed uniforms with starched white shirts and they didn't ask for *matabish*. Most strikingly, they were courteous. 'Welcome to Zambia!' said one of them. We might have been a couple of tourists from Europe on a jaunt. Our Congolese jailors hadn't passed on to the Zambians that until a few hours before, we'd been held in close arrest in one of their detention centres.

Later that day I took a flight from Ndola on the Copperbelt to Blantyre in Malawi and was in Johannesburg before dark.

Only once did I hear from Gilles afterwards. He was both curt and furious, since I'd mentioned his foreskin in one of the articles that I subsequently wrote. I wrote back telling him that he would be much better off if he had it removed!

CHAPTER TWENTY-THREE

'Kill all Infidels – *Allahu Aqbar*!'

> Hizbollah and Hamas [in Israel], Al Qaida, Jaish al Mahdi and
> a range of other militant groups in Iraq. Al Qaida, the Taliban
> and a diversity of associated fighting groups in Afghanistan.
> They are different but they are linked. They are linked by the
> pernicious influence, support and sometimes direction of Iran
> and/or by the international network of Islamist extremism . . .
> Tactics tried and tested on IDF soldiers in Lebanon have killed
> British soldiers in Helmand Province and in Basra. These
> groups are trained and equipped for warfare fought from
> within the civilian population.
>
> Colonel Richard Kemp, formerly both commander of British
> forces in Afghanistan and Intelligence Co-ordinator for the
> British government.

I RETURNED TO LEBANON for an extensive tour in the late 1990s as a
guest of the then Christian chief of the Lebanese Army, General Emile
Lahoud. As a measure of the trust he'd engendered in bringing the
country together – against almost impossible odds – this competent
tactician-turned-politician went on to become the country's President.

Nobody was to anticipate his role – devious and ultimately utterly
destructive – as the principal factotum of Syrian policies along the shores
of the Levant. It took a while, but it gradually became clear to us all that
President Lahoud was taking his orders from Damascus. He danced to
the pipes of former Syrian President Hafez al-Assad and, as we all
feared, Emile Lahoud was instrumental in Syria continuing its
clandestine security role in Lebanon when Bashar al-Assad succeeded his
late father.

For all that, I found in General Emile Lahoud a truly remarkable
individual. He was seminal in rescuing Lebanon from the most
destructive civil war the country had faced in its three millennia of
recorded history. By the time he was able to bring pressure to bear on

the combatants – there were about 100 different armies and militia simultaneously vying for power – the country was locked into an almost permanent state of conflict.

To his credit, he stepped into the breach and created a platform, to which he invited most of the major warrior groups, which would ultimately play a role in bringing a peace of sorts to this embattled nation. Had he not done so, Lebanon might have been permanently ripped apart.

Following lengthy interviews with the man himself, I dealt with some of the issues that faced him in a report subsequently published by Washington's *Middle East Policy*.[1] As he admitted, it was an extremely tough call and his life and those of others involved in the peace process were constantly on the line. What he did not tell me was that Syria's continued subversive role in Lebanon fostered a number of destructive political undercurrents, including, to his discredit, one or more which he led himself.

Meanwhile, following the murder of the Lebanese Prime Minister Rafic Harriri, domestic and international pressure forced Damascus to recall its troops from Lebanon, ostensibly at least. Yet assassinations, car bombings and other acts of terror continue, the majority sponsored by President Bashar al-Assad.

Going back to Lebanon was a thoroughly engrossing assignment. In part, I went in for *Jane's Defence Weekly*, as well as the group's monthly *International Defence Review* for which I'd done occasional work in the Middle East and Africa over three decades. Once I'd made contact with Lahoud's office, a young Shi'ite officer was delegated to escort me.

Captain Hussein Ghaddar and I did a lot in those three weeks together. With this enterprising young army officer – who afterwards went on a course at an American military establishment and by all accounts excelled – I covered great tracts of Lebanon, north and south.

Sharp, erudite and totally fearless, he encapsulated the contemporary image of today's youthful Shi'ite combatant. Ghaddar was focused and well-informed about everything that went on in his own domain and well beyond its borders. From what he told me, he used the web to read all the newspapers in the region, including Israel's *Jerusalem Post* and the more liberal *Ha'artez*. With the Koran in one hand and his AK-47 in the other, this young man cut a striking figure.

On our third day out in Lebanon, Captain Hassan and I went south to Sidon and Tyre and were able to visit the so-called Zionist Front. We were stopped at a roadblock near Nabatiya during a shootout between what was termed 'Hizbollah and insurgent enemies of the people', though exactly who was involved and what took place eluded me. Prior to that, I spent time with the miniscule Lebanese Navy and its new American patrol craft. Finally, there was a stint with a totally integrated Special Forces unit where, only a few years before, its Christian and Muslim components – a group of tough, no-nonsense professionals – had been battling each other.

Throughout this little sojourn in the Levant, it had been my intention all along to try to make contact with Hizbollah, something that *Jane's Defence Weekly* wanted, though they didn't hold out any high hopes because this radical military-politico organization had always been notoriously xenophobic. Contacts with Westerners were few, especially for those working for the non-Islamic media. It happened, of course, but, as Hassan phrased it, you had to have 'connections'.

From the start, I tried to communicate with Hizbollah headquarters in Beirut's southern suburbs, not far from the city's international airport. I did so first by phone, then through one of my Lebanese Army friends, but to no avail. I even sent a fax to a number I was given. Eventually, I

Once General Emile Lahoud was able to stabilize the situation in Lebanon, the Americans came forward and produced naval patrol boats, armour and these US Army surplus helicopters, which were used to patrol the borders. (Author's collection)

took the most obvious route and spoke to one of the bellhops at the hotel at which I was staying: being Muslim, he would know the ropes, I'd been assured. Chances were good that he had somebody within his family circle close to the Party of God.

I wanted to meet with someone senior in Hizbollah, I told him. Two days later the man came back: it might be possible but I should wait for somebody to make contact, he said. It took another week for things to happen and by then I was thinking of returning to London.

One Saturday afternoon, I was collected from my hotel in a limousine and taken first to one office to explain my needs and then to several more. Two more days of delays followed. Meanwhile, I was asked to prepare a list of questions.

Finally, a few days before I was due to leave the country, another car arrived to take me 'somewhere'. I was told not to worry but to trust my new hosts. The idea was that I accompany the driver to a new destination, but there were to be no cameras. Interestingly, no blindfolds either and I wasn't even searched for firearms. On the face of it, it was all straightforward.

Our destination was Harek Horeik, the impoverished, mainly Shi'ite quarter in Beirut's southern suburbs, which was still very much within rifle shot of the city's fleshpots along the Cornice. What gave it away was that there were as many ten-times-life-size posters of the Ayatollah Khomeini as could be squeezed onto a city block without obscuring the view of the residents. These replaced more explicit billboards of the latest Hollywood offerings which can be seen in the main parts of Beirut, and which became fewer the farther south we travelled.

The meeting with Hizbollah secretary, Ibrahim Moussawi, on the first floor of a nondescript office block not far from one of Hizbollah's military encampments, went off without incident. We'd passed the base on the way in, as well as what was obviously a well-guarded communications centre. Then two flights of stairs and a formal salutation followed, at which tea was offered.

In my initial approach to the movement, I'd mentioned that it was my intention to write an article for *Jane's*, my British principals. Consequently, I wasn't surprised when one of the first questions raised was about something that I'd written a short while earlier after a visit to Israel: I'd previously been warned that the organization kept files of everything that anybody wrote on the region. The issue wasn't in any way contentious; instead, I got the impression that mentioning my previous reports on Middle East events had more to do with Hizbollah subtly telling me that they knew exactly who they were dealing with.

Ibrahim Moussawi, Hizbollah's spokesman that day, wasn't entirely the image of the average Party of God functionary that I'd anticipated. Dressed in a dark suit and Iranian-style collarless shirt buttoned at the top, his English was clipped, precise and Middle Eastern. Always the pragmatist, this was no Ivy League or British public school-educated academic. A large Koran sat on his desk at his elbow.

I had my list of questions. These, he said, would need to be translated into Arabic. He would then need time for them to be considered and I'd have his replies, again in Arabic, in a day or two.

We went over a lot of ground involving the role of the Party of God, not only in Lebanon but its links to Iran and Syria, its weapons, their origins and deployment. Moussawi – as might have been expected – was guarded on almost all these issues, the Tehran connection especially.

We talked about the Israeli presence, but he never once wavered from the quiet diplomatic approach that had been notable from the moment he first greeted me. He was a consummate professional throughout. Moussawi didn't mention my request about going to the front with his people and I didn't raise the matter again. If it were to happen, it would almost certainly have been one of the first items on the agenda. I have yet to meet any Westerner who has been on full military operations with Hizbollah, though I'm sure it's happened by now, probably under the auspices of Al Jazeera.

Curiously, nothing more was said about my having been in Israel a short while before which, judging by some of the questions, he was aware of. In fact, he let slip something about my holding a second British passport and that I'd used it to enter Lebanon. Somebody had obviously been doing their homework.

Since the chips were down, I told him that a month earlier I'd spent a short while at one of the IDF front-line positions to the west of Metullah, adjacent to what was once termed 'The Good Fence'. There was no point in being devious: his people could just as easily have gleaned as much from one of several calls that I made to the office of the Military Attaché at the British Legation in Beirut: I took it for granted that my hotel phone was tapped.

The last question Moussawi asked was pointed. Having been on 'the other side', what did I think of the war in South Lebanon? What he was really after was my take on Israel's struggle in the south of the country and in which direction these hostilities might be heading.

I remained candid, replying that I believed Israel would pull back behind its own lines within a year. This surprised him and for first time his smile was genuine, though I suspected that the reaction was more one of incredulity than humour.

As it eventually transpired, I was about a month out in my projection, which I wrote about in one of my *Jane's* reports. The Israelis pulled out of Lebanon altogether 11 months later and for being negatively candid, the Israelis never forgave me.

Having left Moussawi at his South Beirut headquarters (all of which was subsequently totally destroyed by Israeli bombing raids in the summer of 2006) I was back at my hotel in an hour. Three days later I transited Cairo while heading for London, complete with Moussawi's translated text, which appeared in *Jane's Defence Weekly* a week later.

What did rankle was that on my way back to the United States shortly afterwards, I was cleverly 'relieved' of my briefcase on my way in from JFK Airport. The incident couldn't exactly have been construed as a mugging: rather it was a brilliant bit of sleight of hand. One moment my baggage was there and the next, my briefcase was gone. What hurt was that with a lifetime of journalistic experience behind me, I'd always regarded myself as considerably more streetwise than most. The fact is, it shouldn't have happened: I was obviously under surveillance from the moment I stepped off the plane.

Lost in the briefcase, along with several sets of important documents, were all my notes covering the Hizbollah meeting, together with a stack of operational photos from time spent operationally with Hassan.

Though I reported my loss to the local precinct of the New York Police Department, nothing was ever found.

As an extremely successful guerrilla force, Hizbollah has come a long way from the exuberant, oft-times ill-disciplined revolutionaries of the 1970s and early 1980s who waved fists and AK-47s and screamed obscenities whenever Israel or America was mentioned.

According to the United Nations they are few in number, perhaps a couple of thousand hard-core professionals. However, that's deceptive because every man and boy who is able to carry an AK or haul a Katyusha rocket system out of a cellar is a soldier. It also suggests that there are many thousands more. Most support comes from villagers who

With the demise of the SLA in the south of the country, Hizbollah took over the region, for a while using the same equipment and hardware that had originally been supplied to the embattled Christians by the Israelis. (Author's collection)

have been trained, often abroad, and who go about their daily business until they are needed to do a job: 'sleepers'.

As one UN functionary put it: 'The average Hizbollah volunteer will drink tea on his verandah and, given the word, will go down to his basement, assemble a tube and base-plate and then lob off a clutch of mortar bombs or rockets at a given target. He'll then strip his weapon, return it to its hiding place and go back to his tea. That's how the war is waged in these parts.'

The Mullahs with their long frocks, beards and Khomeini turbans – white or black – might seem to be a visible manifestation of Muslim regression to the Middle Ages. Their long term programme is not.

Hizbollah's stated aim – as is Iran's, its mentor and its main source of succour – is to wipe the State of Israel off the map. This is not idle talk. It is a threat that is daily uttered by Al Manaar, the official Hizbollah broadcasting station with its headquarters in Beirut as well as by the Iranian *Majlis* or Parliament.

In a comparatively short time, Hizbollah has become a government within a government with powers of arrest, its own secret police and death squads. Apart from its military wing, there is a well-established and entrenched political structure within the movement that has accumulated a number of seats in the Beirut Parliament, all legally and properly contested within the democratic process. However, when things start to go wrong, Hizbollah tends to resort to threats or intimidation and, more often than not, violence, which some observers fear might ultimately lead to another civil war.

In the old days Hizbollah cadres might only have hinted at action: these days they use force to implement their demands. If warnings are not heeded, the Party of God does what it believes it needs to and if violence is involved, then so be it. During 2007, for instance, nobody could decide on a new President who, according to the constitution had to be a Christian. Hizbollah's Deputy Secretary General, Sheikh Naim Qasim, gave the country's politicians an ultimatum. His words were strident and belligerent, very much in line with the 'new face' of the Party of God.

'After the other side resorts to manipulating the presidency and chooses a person who is not suitable for [that post] we will find ourselves forced to fill the vacuum to prevent the emergence of a constitutional vacuum', said the Sheikh. In other words, the perception in the streets of Beirut suggested that the next President of Lebanon would be from Hizbollah. And if not the next one, then certainly the one thereafter . . .

He went on to say that Hizbollah had been 'patient for a very long time about the repeated violations that the government's group perpetrated'. He suggested that Hizbollah should step in and resolve the matter. In the view of the majority, that was war talk. Coupled as it was to a number of assassinations of prominent Lebanese politicians in recent years, these developments were – and continue to be – profoundly unsettling.

Robert Fisk captured the gist of it in a brilliant article titled 'Dinner in Beirut, and a Lesson in Courage' published in Britain's *Independent* on 29 September 2007. He disclosed that the fear of assassination among Lebanese politicians had become so severe that 46 of the country's MPs were hiding in the Phoenicia Hotel, 'three to a suite . . .'

Apart from Hizbollah's political infrastructure, the movement has a variety of military and paramilitary organizations on which to call. This is a kind of 'Second Lebanese Defence Force-in-Waiting', as one diplomat uniquely referred to it. Essentially Shi'ite, all these groups are regarded by Lebanese opposition groups as a surrogate force with a first loyalty to

Iran. They maintain that the Hizbollah commander-in-chief, Nasrallah, is not averse to taking his instructions from either Tehran or Damascus and it says much that Hizbollah has always worked closely with the leaders of both countries. In fact, as has been demonstrated often enough, Hizbollah as a Shi'ite revolutionary group is an Iranian creation.

More pertinently, there are direct links between Hizbollah and Iran's Islamic Republican Guard Corps (IRGC). This is the same paramilitary group that is responsible for all Iran's clandestine external operations, as well as the country's weapons of mass destruction (WMD) programmes. Significantly perhaps, it was the Guards Corps that was originally responsible for physically creating the Party of God.

Paula A. deSutter, George W. Bush's former Assistant Secretary for Verification and Compliance, made a study of the matter while still at Washington's National Defense University and it is worth reading. She might just as easily have been talking about Hizbollah when she wrote that 'The Iranian government is not easy to understand. There is a gap between its rhetoric and its actions, between its sense of grievance and inflammatory behaviour and between its ideological and its national interests. Nor are its actions consistent.' [2]

Once the Israelis pulled their troops back to behind their own lines, UN forces with UNIFIL continued with their patrols, which were as successful as respective national units allowed them to be. FijiBatt soldiers were as professional as they come, but the Ghanaians soldiers and those from some other third World countries wallowed at the other end of a rather pathetic scale. This patrol, involving Scandanavians, was in a Druze-controlled region in the Shouff Mountains. (Author's collection)

In the past, Hizbollah's Fire Support Unit was responsible for most of the shelling of Israel and even today – though that organization goes under other nomenclatures – much of its training takes place in the Beka'a Valley. There is also what is called the Islamic Resistance, which specializes in infiltration and sabotage. The leadership of all these groups is divided into cells; one rarely has any knowledge of the other.

The actual operational planning by Hizbollah – that which is not fomented in Syria or Iran – takes place in The Dahia, deep in the southern suburbs of Beirut, still a fundamentalist stronghold even though it was almost all destroyed by Israeli Air Force attrition raids in 2006. From there the influence fans out southwards to Tyre or Nabatiya.

It is important to accept, a UN officer at Naqoura explained, that while the Hizbollah political establishment had been formally constituted, its military wing or wings had no fixed address. He went on: 'The Israelis are always searching for them, so they're constantly on the move . . . many of their leaders were assassinated before – though not so often today – but they've learnt some hard lessons. Consequently they take no chances.'

In more recent times, Hizbollah in all its guises, as even its enemies acknowledge, has powerfully emerged from its self-imposed obscurity and can hardly be construed as anything but an extremely well-organized political and military grouping. It is a lot better motivated than the Lebanese government itself: it has its own public relations office that is forthcoming to any person or any government prepared to lend an ear. Nor is this limited to lip service. All attacks on Israeli and SLA positions are routinely recorded by Hizbollah's own travelling film units, which they take into action with them. Such events are afterwards displayed on the Al Manaar and Al Jazeera television networks.

I watched some clips and I was impressed. These people knew what they were doing. Discipline, movement under fire and tactics were professionally executed. Training was thorough; much of it conducted by Iranians and, as I was to discover afterwards, included underwater demolition, Special Forces training (that incorporated airborne jump courses) as well as many of the more obscure tactics linked to evasion and escape.

There are many people in Lebanon who equate the activities of Hizbollah with those of the Palestinians in the country in the early

1980s. They are both right and wrong: while their anti-Zionist objectives might be identical, their styles of implementation are very different indeed.

In their own attempts to incite war against the 'hated Zionists', Palestinian leaders came to regard themselves as above the law. While similar assumptions have become evident in Lebanon more recently about Hizbollah, they're not quite there yet.

Meanwhile, Jerusalem stirs the pot. It is no secret that Israel has always had hopes of generating friction between various Lebanese factions, especially with Hizbollah, now its prime security objective in the Middle East. More often than not, Israeli intelligence agents inside Lebanon – there are many of them – will encourage dissention, suspicion, and sometimes, through third parties, propagate confrontation, often using liberal amounts of disinformation.

It consequently came as no secret in the spring and summer of 2009, that Lebanese security officials arrested several dozen Israeli spies in the country, some of whom had been active for decades. Their numbers included high-ranking government and police officials, a Lebanese Army general or two as well as some agents who were otherwise regarded by their peers as totally committed Sunni and Shi'ite Muslims. In a curious twist in June 2009, Jerusalem admitted that it had been active in Lebanon, and several other Arab states.

More recently, an Israeli spokesman said, the focus had switched to Hizbollah, though he was not prepared to say whether any of those arrested across the border were adherents to the Party of God.

For all that, the main difference between what took place in Lebanon a quarter of a century ago and what is happening today, is that Hizbollah has always had a big brother in Tehran. Nor is it a secret that the influence of Tehran's Mullahs has become more pervasive. The Supreme Spiritual Leader in Iran – powerful and oil rich beyond compare – gives Nasrallah just about all he asks for.

The Palestinians in Lebanon in the old days, by contrast, had only themselves. There were always promises from the Egyptians, the Saudis and the rest, but little ever came of it.

Lebanon, we must remember, is the least devout of the Muslim countries in the Middle East since the integration of Christian, Druze and Islamic fighters after decades of civil war. There are many Muslims – particularly within the country's Sunni community – who regard Hizbollah with great suspicion and who voice fears that the Party of God, if not checked, could lead the nation into another conflict. The majority have had as much as they can handle of extremists, in whatever guise.

Those who were prepared to discuss the matter with a stranger, were of the opinion that if the Party of God had its way tomorrow, it would immediately institute Shariah Law. At its most extreme, as in Saudi Arabia, that requires the cutting off of hands for theft, the prohibition of strong drink and stoning for sexual or commercial offences. They'd put every woman in a chador, as their principals have already tried to do in Iran.

For now, the majority of Lebanese sit back uneasily and observe. They hate the Israelis who occupied much of their country for so many years and any attempt to harm the State of Israel, to cause casualties or dislocation – legal, clandestine or otherwise – gets loud applause. If that were Hizbollah's only motive, then fine. But it is not. Just about everybody in Lebanon fears that Nasrallah has more of what they term 'a hidden agenda' than just 'getting at the Jews'.

For the moment then, Beirut does nothing. They did very little about the Palestinians either, at least until they had to and by then it was nearly too late. It has never been lost on many Lebanese that, like it or not, it was the Jews who pulled those nuts out of the fire when the Israeli Army invaded Lebanon in 1982 and forced Yassir Arafat and his militants to find some other base from which to wage their wars against the Jews

What has also become apparent in the past few years is that nobody in Lebanon underestimates the power of Hizbollah. The extent of their influence and their ability to match needs was well demonstrated during and after the 2006 Israeli attack.

Earlier, in 1982 when the Jewish nation went to war in South Lebanon with aircraft and artillery, and again in 1993 for seven days during 'Operation Accountability', it was the Hizbollah presence in South Lebanon that picked up the pieces and helped those who had been worst affected by hostilities. The homeless were sheltered, given food and, where needed, money. Hizbollah was at the vanguard when it came to repairing much of the damage caused by Israeli artillery barrages and ordinary folk do not easily forget such gestures.

More brutality followed in 2006, when many thousands of Lebanese houses were damaged or destroyed. These were ugly displays of *Schrecklichkeit* that each time left hundreds of innocent people dead. Hundreds of thousands of Lebanese fled northwards to safety – there were more than half-a-million refugees. Around 1,000 Lebanese and 158 Israelis were killed (most of the Israelis being IDF soldiers) including 43 people killed inside Israel by Hizbollah rocket attacks.

One of the consequences of the earlier ceasefire, which again was mediated jointly by the United States and Syria, was what was officially referred to as an 'understanding'. Nothing was signed mind you, but it meant that Israel would no longer shell civilian targets in Lebanon. For its part, Hizbollah would stop hurling its Katyushas into Upper Galilee.

The damage done by Israel in these incursions was enormous. The United Nations immediately went to work to assess how they could help and how much it would cost. At the time, the consensus at UN headquarters in New York was that the problems faced appeared to be insoluble.

Meanwhile, Hizbollah got busy. With its own people and in-house resources, the movement repaired or rebuilt most of the damaged buildings in three weeks. Before the UN inspectors had even completed their assessments, a lot of the work was already done. Hizbollah didn't ask the United Nations for a cent: everything they needed came from Iran. Clearly, the Arab world was impressed.

What emerged from these events, which were both bloody and widespread, was the insuperable vitality of the Party of God. It was perceived – and it is still regarded so today – that the movement's ability is applied with a dedication and exactness that is nothing short of Cartesian. The same applies to Hizbollah's approach to business, whether in the realms of the sacrosanct or with basic commercial or financial matters. The transition has been nothing short of astonishing.

Hizbollah is astute in all its transactions. While they might drive a hard bargain, their word is their bond once a deal is done. Small wonder then that Israel, the United States, Britain and even the Russians take Hizbollah seriously.

In the latter regard, Hizbollah is known to have close links to guerrilla separatists in Chechnya, with Hizbollah combatants known to have been killed in this war too.

On a more visible level, Hizbollah is always most active among the ordinary people. It builds schools and hospitals, pays war pensions to the wounded and the dependants of those killed in action. It cares for orphans and looks after the old, all done quietly, efficiently and without fuss in one of the most mendacious of Middle East states. Within its sphere of influence, corruption is likely to be punished with death.

In turn, Hizbollah makes certain demands. The *sine qua non* is one of unquestioning loyalty to the cause. Everything starts and ends with Allah and his Prophet. You are either for or against Hizbollah; there is no middle way. It also demands a level of obedience and collaboration that is absolute, almost in the historical tradition of Roman Catholic clergy towards their superiors. Most importantly, the Party of God insists on educating the young, with its own Mullahs supervising all instruction.

The most significant consequence of Hizbollah activity is that a whole generation of young people now regard Iran as the centre of their universe and Shi'ite dogma as infallible law. With its rigorous social code (no bad thing in itself in a country where most young people lost their bearings in the civil war) and extreme views, it has become a power.

What most Lebanese (and Syrians, Saudis, Egyptians, Jordanians and, of course, Europeans and the Americans) fear most is that Iran might use these people to carry out its own programme of regional domination, even though nobody wants to be dragged into another war. And then, one needs to ask, what will happen when Iran acquires its own nuclear bomb? Even if it is a primitive 'atomic' device, Iran's cadres speak about it often enough.[3]

There is also a genuine fear that since much of Hizbollah propaganda is directed at that part of the population with the least to lose and the most to gain, that the Mullahs might ultimately end up with a good share of political power in their quadrant of the Levant. We're also aware that such things tend to lead to conflict, which, going back a bit was one of the original causes of war between Iran and Iraq in the 1980s.

Many people suggest that it could happen again, but this time, under a totally different guise and, once more, in Lebanon.[4]

CHAPTER TWENTY-FOUR

Tete Convoy in Mozambique

'For twelve wearisome years, the Portuguese and the *mesticos,*
those of mixed European descent and the six million Africans
have been learning to live with their grim little war. On every
street in every town and village there are soldiers, white and
black, swaggering and conspicuous in their jungle camouflage
uniforms. The original 3,000 has become 60,000.'

Al Venter's *Africa at War,* 1973[1]

WHILE PORTUGAL FOUGHT ITS MILITARY campaigns in Africa, the town
of Tete – a strategic African settlement dominated by a huge
suspension bridge across the Zambezi River – came to represent one of
the last of the embattled outposts of an imperial tradition that had lasted
half a millennium. When I visited the place in the early 1970s, what was
going on in this vast land on the east coast of Africa was a chapter of
recent history about to close.

I'd gone through Tete with Michael Knipe – the London *Times'* man
in southern Africa at the time – and we were to discover an archetypal
Portuguese-style settlement similar to those that could be found in many
parts of the southern half of the continent. These were critical times in
what European pundits would term 'Africa's Liberation Wars'.

But for the great Zambezi, Tete could have been mistaken for Luso
in Angola or Cacheu in Portuguese Guinea, where the first of Prince
Henry's navigators made landfall on African soil looking for fresh water
during their bid to discover a sea route to the spice islands of the East.

By the time we arrived, it was clear that the ongoing conflict in the
adjoining region had been tough, especially for the hardscrabble black
population for whom, apart from the military, opportunities to earn
those few extra escudos were sparse. Almost all of the town's Portuguese
civilians had left a year or two before, in part because normal
commercial activity had ended. More likely though, they had been
intimidated by the war as more often than not, hostilities would start at

415

the edge of town, almost as soon as the sun disappeared over the jungles to the west.

With all the soldiers and military vehicles about, there was no mistaking that armed rebellion was on Tete's doorstep. As hostilities gradually became more intense, mines began to take a bigger toll. There wasn't a day that we didn't spot vehicles towed in from the bush or hauled back to town on low-loaders after they'd been blown up or ambushed. Many more trucks were destroyed by landmines than in enemy ambushes, their cargoes either removed or, when oversized – like mining equipment or industrial plant – abandoned, hopefully to be recovered another day. The rebels would see to it that they rarely were.

Such was the nature of insurgency in this remote corner of tropical Africa that fringed the Indian Ocean, a very different kind of war compared to what was going on just then in South-East Asia.

Moving through Mozambique in the late 1960s and early 1970s was always an experience. The region was remote and, because of the isolation, there were few independent observers either willing or able to chance their luck in this unforgiving corner of Africa. Communications were invariably a consideration, especially in the interior: most of the time they simply did not exist. There were phones, but they didn't always work. Faxes and cell phones were not yet on the market. You considered yourself lucky to get a call through to Europe or America once you'd left the comfort of Mozambique's big cities of Beira or Lourenco Marques, though a fat bribe helped if you were prepared to use military equipment.

Getting about was problematic. You either travelled in convoy or you didn't go anywhere. Between the towns of the central regions and the north, convoys happened about twice a week. However, if the guerrillas had been active, delays were commonplace, sometimes as long as a week. Much depended on the competence of the local garrison commander.

Our road to Tete, overland from South Africa, was circuitous. After crossing the Limpopo River, Knipe and I spent a week in Rhodesia – then also at war. The intention was that he would return to Johannesburg from Mozambique while I would keep on going north. I would travel the length of the Tete Panhandle – first to Malawi and then on to Lusaka in Zambia (then another black African country technically at war with the 'White South'), my final destination being Mobutu Sese Seko's Zaire, which had formerly been called the Congo.

However, like others on the road, we had to wait for the next convoy and for three or four days, Tete became home. It was a distasteful sojourn in the town's only hotel, the Zambezi, where the plumbing didn't work and meals, such as they were, were an unappetizing and often unsanitary affair.

There was little to do in a heat that was both soporific and enervating and if you hadn't packed a reasonable supply of books, you were left staring at the walls of your hotel room. There was no air conditioning either. A film or two might have helped, but the only movie house had been shuttered and even if it hadn't been, whatever might have been on offer would have been in Portuguese, without subtitles.

Most of the time when we did hit the town – always after dark when a light breeze came off the river – we were left to make our way past a succession of people who seemed to do little more than drink cheap wine, or thugs who would offer us a local girl for the price of a cocktail. The Portuguese military presence was everywhere, the majority in their battledress, and they made the best of their off-hours in the torpid, dust-choked streets. Army trucks trailed endless little sandstorms in their wakes as they trundled through town and that didn't help either.

Wrapped around a dirty crossroads on the banks of the third biggest river on the African continent, Tete could easily have passed for a film set depicting the early years of the great American trek to the west. The only difference was an occasional, modern-looking building and a communications aerial on the tallest hill that overlooked the town. There was nothing to remind us that the settlement was one of the first inland trading posts built by Portuguese mariners who first sailed up this great waterway in their shallow-hulled galliots in the 15th century.

While fighting against the Portuguese, the Mozambique liberation movement, Frelimo, received a lot of assistance from radical groups abroad. One of their regular publications was this one, produced in Scandinavia, which shows a guerrilla patrol moving through an abandoned village.

Much of what happened in Tete centred on the couple of thousand men of the 17th Battalion, as well as the three or four helicopters and ground support squadrons that made up the bulk of the town's defences. Essentially, it was a captive market, for the troops had nowhere else to spend what little they earned. The colonial gloss and glitter of Lourenco Marques – Maputo today – lay more than 600 miles to the south.

For those who took that extended overland leg southwards, there were still more military convoys for the first leg of the journey, at least until you reached Beira – Mozambique's second city – as I was able to do on my way back home more than a month later.

There were big plans afoot for Tete, we were told in the first in-house briefing with Tete's military commanders. One of the biggest hydro-electric dams in Africa was being built across a gorge on the Zambezi River, more than 100 miles upstream. That construction, we were assured, promised long-term dividends, but as we now know, it was only completed after the war ended. By then the majority of the Portuguese had decamped back to the *metrópole*.

At that stage, getting the dam finished on schedule had become a formidable task, especially since it was to be the biggest man-made body of water in Africa, second only to Egypt's Aswan. For their part, the insurgents hurled everything they could muster at both Portuguese civilian and military interests in efforts to halt construction. Along the way, many lives were lost.

Twice each day, starting at dawn, lurching open trucks that carried two platoons left Tete to guard the shipments of supplies, men and equipment heading towards the gorge. This was the easy part, because the road was tarred and the threat of mines was minimal. However, that did not stop the ambushes, which seemed to keep an intermittent pace with the convoys and would take an almost inevitable daily toll.

Tete's Barracks Square was where all military activities were coordinated. Writing about the place, British writer James McManus recalled that it looked 'absurdly Beau Geste'. From there, too, patrols around town would set out before dawn each day and check routes leading in and out for booby traps and mines which, we were to discover, were sometimes responsible for the first casualties of the day.

Security in and around Tete was tight and strangers were invariably regarded with suspicion. We fell into this category and it came as no surprise that journalists like Knipe, James McManus and me, though tacitly accepted because we'd made the long haul north, were not made overly welcome. In any conflict, we were already aware, the Fourth Estate is routinely regarded with suspicion and the Portuguese military establishment was no exception.

In my case, I was fortunate because I'd previously covered the war in Angola. Also, I'd been given an informal letter of introduction to the local commander and that opened some doors. Having experienced combat on the west coast, and then transferred my allegiance temporarily to Mozambique, it didn't take long for me to be accepted as 'one of them'. The trouble was that it invariably happened after the metal cap of the first bottle of aguardiente had landed in the bin.

In spite of the booze and bonhomie, talk about the guerrilla role in the conflict remained guarded, especially in the presence of us scribes. Reports of actions and casualties were a given, but there was never any serious talk about the adversary: it was almost as if the guerrillas didn't exist. Casualty figures were always 'secret' and when there was an 'incident', discussions in the officers' mess were usually conducted in whispers.

The general approach to the war was different from that which you'd find in other conflicts, such as in the Congo, Algeria or neighbouring Rhodesia. One got the idea that many Portuguese officers liked to think – and some actually believed – that it was all a rather temporary affair, a bit of trouble with local savages that would soon be over, we were told often enough. I found this to be a patronizing attitude that was annoying. We'd all done time at the sharp end and this conflict, and Mozambique, were very different from what I – and others – had already seen in Angola and Portuguese Guinea. There, at least, the Portuguese Army didn't ignore the threat. Rather, they got to grips with it.

My convoy left Tete at dawn. In a straggling line astern, the trucks rumbled across the river and were halted briefly at what passed for a tollgate at the far end of the bridge. There were machine-gun emplacements at several points along the structure, some illuminated by a string of searchlights that continually swept across the water below during the dark hours.

One by one, the sleepy-eyed drivers paid the fee and moved the last 10 or 20 miles of metalled road to Moatize. There, under military supervision, we would assemble for the remainder of the trek to the Malawi boarder, more than 100 miles to the north.

Some of the trucks in our column were bound for Blantyre, the commercial capital of Malawi, a tiny country that straddles the north-western border with Mozambique. Others were heading further north, where they would again cross into Mozambique territory and where hostilities were at their most intense.

The majority of vehicles travelling with us were ten- or 12-wheelers, including a number of low-loaders from Johannesburg factories which hauled freight bound for the Zambian Copperbelt. The drivers were a motley bunch, mostly professional haulers, some white, the majority African.

There were few among them who were indifferent to what lay ahead. Their guffaws and uneasy, conscious swaggering as they gathered in groups prior to our setting out were typical of travelling groups under strain. They'd all survive, they confidently told each other and they'd smile and nod their heads. What a way to earn a living, one of them chuckled.

There were many opinions about what lay ahead, as might have been expected in an area where there were landmines buried in the soft, gravel-topped laterite shoulders along the route and where Portuguese and insurgent forces had been making almost daily contact for almost a decade of war. The enemy was out there, waiting, the drivers would tell each other. Then the banter would start again: who would drive behind whom, which drivers were considered lucky or had experienced this kind of thing before and had come out unscathed. Anybody who had done six or eight trips across this narrow strip of no-man's land without being hurt automatically earned great respect from his colleagues; he was the man to watch, they'd say quietly among themselves.

Somebody pulled out a bottle of South African brandy and everybody took a swig. A few Portuguese soldiers nearby barely noticed, and if they did, they said nothing. There would be no policing on this stretch of road.

There were many views about what lay ahead. Quite a few of the drivers had been shot at or mortared and just about everybody knew somebody who'd been hurt. Not too many killed, it seemed.

'One man he die last week . . . Mulatto . . . his truck he go . . . boom . . . very big mine!'

That came from a swarthy trucker from Madeira. His observation was lost on many because of his poor English and nobody made any comment. Most of the drivers continued doing what they'd been busy with or looked deep into their cups or tin mugs. Other drivers kept drinking, even though the sun had barely clipped the thorn and baobab trees clustered to the east beyond the railway station and coal dump at Moatize.

The man who spoke had a lot to say during the three-day convoy run. He'd done the trip often enough he told us, and made the point that he preferred to travel somewhere towards the rear of the column.

'Better others hit the *minas*', he'd quietly comment, going colloquial when nobody else was listening. All we knew about him was that he was bound for a settlement in the interior which had been attacked often in the past. His cargo was his own business and he said so; that security thing again.

Apart from two buses packed with Africans on their way home from South African gold mines, there were about 35 trucks assembled at Moatize. Some were taking cargoes through to Zaire and sported Rhodesian plates. These would be replaced by Zambian tags for the final leg of the journey.

There were two private vehicles on the road with them; our Land

Landmines were always a problem while hostilities continued in all three of Lisbon's African outposts – Angola, Mozambique and Portuguese Guinea (today Guiné-Bissau). Here Portuguese soldiers are handling two versions of anti-personnel mines. (Author's collection)

Rover, which had Dutch registration, and a medium-sized English car on its way to Zambia. The driver, a youngster from York, was under contract to one of the copper mines and had returned from a long leave in Britain with his vehicle. He'd been forced to head east and cross at Tete after waiting for six days at the Kasangula Ferry in Botswana; he said he'd risk landmines and ambushes 600 miles to the east rather than take his chances with President Kaunda's undisciplined Zambian Army in an unstable hinterland where South African forces regularly intruded.

He'd made that choice after reports had come across the river of drunken soldiers having fired on another civilian car which had tried to cross southwards. A female passenger had been wounded . . .

Portuguese bureaucracy and a tendentiously aggressive enemy eroded our schedules from the start. We were told the journey would take eight hours. It lasted three days. On that first morning, we were all left standing in the sapping heat of the Zambezi Valley for four hours before we eventually pulled out.

An hour before leaving, a group of civilian officials – they were in khaki and displayed rank – approached the convoy. The bureaucracy that followed quickly became tiresome. Names were checked against lists, vehicles against registration plates, passports perused, cargoes vetted, instructions issued and questions asked. Weapons, tape recorders or radio equipment? 'Anybody with binoculars?' somebody queried. There was no reaction, even though one of the drivers sported a 400mm tele-lens for his Nikon camera.

Finally, the civilians were required to sign a document, in triplicate, which exonerated the Lisbon government against claims in the event of any kind of military action. The final paragraph, in good English, indemnified Lisbon against losses that might be inflicted on us by the Portuguese Army and Air Force.

We signed, anything to avoid delay.

At this stage Erico Chagas, a young Portuguese army lieutenant introduced himself. He'd been watching us from a distance and only then did we understand why. He needed to get to Munacama, he told us. He would travel with us, admitting that the Land Rover offered the most comfort. There was no question of his asking permission: it was already a fait accompli.

Young Chagas was to join his unit, about 30 minutes by road from Zobue, one of our destinations in the north. Born in the Mozambique capital and educated in South Africa, he spoke good English. We gathered that he'd been fighting for two years and, on the face of it, was clearly professional in his approach to all things military; the young man was tough and seasoned both by Africa and by conflict. As we were to discover later, Chagas liked to say that he'd seen and done it all.

We were happy to have him on board; with a Portuguese Army lieutenant in our vehicle, we'd be spared further inspection.

The young officer was casual about most things, including the prospect of combat. It helped that he was as familiar with the bush as his native trackers. As to being ambushed while travelling in convoy, he was dismissive. Of course we'll be ambushed, he declared impassively, 'but the bastards never come very close . . . much of it is just noise'.

'Mines, yes! But ambushes . . . ha!'

His comments were derisory, and sometimes contentious. The *terroristas,* as he called them, rarely caused any real damage, he said. 'They don't aim, so the shots are almost always high. And anyway,' he suggested, 'it is old law. Unless someone is firing specifically at you, chances are that somebody else will be hit . . .'

He was explicit that we travel towards the rear of the column. He pointed at the truck belonging to the Maderian. 'We stay behind him. He knows the tricks.' The man from Maderia had already spaced himself well down the line. It was his contention, we learned, that the more wheels that passed over the track before us, the better. 'Let others take chances', he reckoned.

More instructions were issued by our escorts, who had called us all together. Chagas translated. We were to stay between 50 and 100 metres behind the next vehicle. If the truck ahead of you was hit, the explosion shouldn't affect the truck immediately behind, though sometimes a rear and not front wheel detonated a mine, which often enough caused casualties among those in the cab behind. The military spokesman stressed that each vehicle should follow exactly in the tracks directly ahead; as he said, slowly and distinctly, 'not to the right of it and not to the left, but *on* the tracks of those who have gone before'.

Because of the dust, this might sometimes be difficult, one of the other officers conceded.

Should one of the vehicles be blown up, it then became the responsibility of the troops escorting the column to search for more landmines, because they were rarely laid singly. When that happened, he declared, nobody was to exit his vehicle and move about.

'There are landmines for trucks,' the officer declared, with Chagas keeping pace with a good translation, 'and there are landmines for people. Consequently when the terrorists lay a bomb for a vehicle, they hope that some inquisitive person might get out and walk about to find out what was causing the hold-up.' That had happened often enough before and there had been casualties, he disclosed.

By now some of the Rhodesian drivers had edged closer to better hear Chagas' translation: few had more than a basic understanding of the language.

The officer continued: 'Remember all of you, and this is important. With landmines, all casualties are serious.' He added that a wounded man often meant calling for a helicopter to evacuate the victim, 'but there are times when there are no helicopters available . . . so the man can die.'

He told us that while there would be several officers travelling as passengers to re-join their units up-country, the convoy would be in the charge of a sergeant, a wiry, intense little man whom he brought forward and introduced to the gathering.

His name is Viera. Officially it is Sergeant Viera and he knows this business very well. When he tells you to do something, you listen. You do not argue, even if you think he might be wrong. Follow his instructions carefully and without delay because there are sometimes very good reasons for doing things in a hurry. This is a war, people, not a tourist jaunt and this man will lead you all through to the other side . . . *Boa sorte*!

The most impassive of the drivers gathered around in Moatize that morning were the black Rhodesians. They'd heard the same story often enough, both prior to hostilities and now that conflict had enveloped much of the region.

We got to know some of them in the days that followed and they were a resolute group. 'Riding shotgun' – which, they reckoned was preferable to saying they were being guarded by Portuguese colonial troops – was their way of putting bread on the table and though they weren't happy with the risk, they didn't complain. We were to discover that there were moments when they possibly knew the ropes a little better than their youthful Portuguese Army escorts. Some had lost colleagues on this road and each one was out to ensure that mistakes of

The great bridge straddling the Zambezi at Tete, two days travel by road north of Lourenco Marques, today Maputo. From here on northwards, all movement was by convoy. (Author's collection)

the past wouldn't be repeated. Their heavy vehicles, many with their company names painted on them – Swifts, Watson's Transport, United Transport, Heinz and others – stood at the vanguard of the procession.

A 10-ton Albion truck from United Transport's Malawi office headed the civilian column. The driver said he was carrying Caterpillar spares and was headed for Zaire. He'd travelled the route for almost two years, he disclosed, and for reasons of his own he preferred to travel right up front.

By 10:00 that morning, the first army truck that would provide our escort rumbled past. It was a hefty Berliet, heavily sandbagged around the driver's cab. Because the hood had been removed, we could see more sandbags fitted around the wheel cavities. We only learnt later that Portuguese convoys rarely moved about with their hoods intact. Too many troops had been decapitated by these steel sheets, which were sometimes blown sideways by detonations.

A short while afterwards, another squad of troops arrived, all in regulation camouflage uniforms. Each was armed with Heckler & Koch G-3s, standard issue in Lisbon's African war zones, most times casually slung over their shoulders. There were also some MG-42 LMGs around. A few more troops had mortar tubes, a bazooka or two and, here and there, bundles of shells neatly slotted into canvas carrying bags that they humped over their shoulders like back-packs. Just about everybody had additional belts strapped onto their webbing with grenades and extra ammunition.

The newcomers seemed lively and animated, though there were those among them who were clearly nervous; they stayed that way until they got into the swing of things. One or two looked as if they still had a couple of years to go to make 18, never mind the ripe old age of 20.

The unit sergeant-in-charge – he was also to take his orders from Viera – was 22 and had already been in Africa for two years. Over a couple of drinks on the second night out he told us that in a stupid patriotic moment he'd voluntarily cut short his university studies to fight, but now couldn't wait to get home.

A short while later more army trucks roared past and pulled up nearby. An officer disembarked and, barking into a walkie-talkie, gave somebody at the other end a string of orders. We were ready to move, said Chagas.

The column rolled forward, a sandbagged Berliet as the vanguard. One of the Unimog troop carriers moved into position towards the middle of the convoy, about five vehicles ahead of us. Its soldiers were clustered around a heavy machine-gun mounted on a fixed tripod on the back. An imposing width of steel plating swung about as the weapon rotated on its pivot. Moments later there was a clicking of bolts down the line as soldiers tested their weapons.

With another Berliet bringing up the rear, we were relieved to be on the move, but it was a tedious process, covering perhaps 12 miles that first day. Almost from the start, there was evidence of conflict in the area to the north of Moatize.

Barely five minutes from the railhead, our cherished tarred road ended abruptly, making for a smooth transition from a relatively level surface to rattling corrugations and potholes that might have swallowed a goat. Once on the dirt, huge swathes of dust enveloped just about everything – trucks, soldiers, civilian cars and their passengers, up our noses, into our ears and across the windscreen, which needed to be swiped every ten minutes or so.

The 'brown-out' seemed to be suspended above ground for the duration and in that heat, thirst became our most constant companion.

Minutes later we passed an abandoned, broken-down villa, its faded, off-white walls pock-marked by shell holes and splinters of many actions. It was a scene symptomatic of all of Portugal's wars in Africa and is still the kind of scenario you're likely to see these days on CNN the BBC in news reports about rural Afghanistan.

The bush around us was a riot of tropical overgrowth that sometimes hung over the road for miles at a stretch. It was so thick that the guerrillas might easily have taken up their positions within touching distance of our vehicles and we probably would never have known.

Minutes later, another building came into view, also partly blown apart. Chagas pointed at a window-sized gap that yawned across one of the front walls, probably caused by a mortar shell or an RPG-2. The building might have been used for training by the Portuguese Army, he suggested.

Suddenly more such derelict buildings came into view and quite a few displayed evidence of hasty evacuation. There were broken beds and burnt roof timbers spread untidily about outside and, occasionally, a burnt-out pick-up or tractor abandoned around the back. This was no training ground, I retorted, and Chagas didn't reply.

Minutes later the truck immediately ahead of us, still dutifully following the convoy track, skirted a large round hole in the middle of the road. Strips of crumpled metal lay scattered along the verge. We spotted the buckled front suspension of a truck that lay discarded in the nearby bush. The rest of the vehicle had apparently been removed by an army recovery unit. Chagas offered no further comment: he had no need to for the crater in the middle of the road said it all.

The further north we travelled there were more holes along the tracks, more of the detritus of war. Twice the convoy stopped and we sat and waited as the sun beat down from a brassy sky. Even a light breeze might have eased the discomfort, but for the majority, it was sauna time. Sweat rolled off our foreheads in translucent droplets.

'They're checking for mines', said Chagas after talking to one of his colleagues who, contrary to orders, was making his way down the column on foot. And that was when he told us that he'd lost three members of his unit from mines in the past eight months, all of them while on patrols in open bush country. The tally included a close buddy with whom he'd gone through training.

The convoy started to roll again, but our progress was even more laboured than before. Delays, we were aware, were to be expected, but this was ridiculous. In the final two-hour leg that first afternoon, we were never able to gather enough speed to shift into third gear.

Finally, we slowed to a crawl and it got so bad that somebody on foot might easily have outpaced the convoy. We futilely tried to catch a glimpse of the countryside through the tall elephant grass on both sides of the road and there was little conversation.

At one stage we passed an abandoned corrugated-iron tsetse fly control station – it, too, pitted with holes. 'More training?' I asked. All Chagas could do was smile.

Small wonder then that tsetse bothered us. Each time one of these insects entered the cab, there was a furious session of flapping round. Anything that came to hand became an improvised fly-swatter and for good reason, as the tsetse's bite is as painful as that of a horse fly.

Chagas would view our antics with amusement. To him this was just another convoy and in any event, he said, there were more tsetse flies at his base in the interior than anybody had cared to count. For the rest of the time, Lieutenant Chagas would bury his nose in the English-language papers and periodicals we'd brought with us from the Cape.

As we progressed, the rigmarole became stultifying. It was a constant round of stop and start again. We'd go a few hundred feet and the column would again slow to a crawl. In the initial leg, we might have covered perhaps three miles in the first three hours. Then the pace slowed still further.

It could have been worse, someone said, at least we were on the move. Once the sun reached its apex the heat became intense. There was no other way we could go, because we were still in the Zambezi Valley.

Finally, a man in uniform guided the trucks into a clearing alongside the road. The heavier vehicles were pulled into an oblong laager, completely surrounded by bush, some so close to the jungle that there were branches pushed hard against their cabs. Buses and passenger cars were pointed to a position towards the centre, but we found a spot to park the Land Rover on the perimeter under some shade.

Meanwhile, our escort troops spilled out in groups and disappeared into a low building where only three of the original walls still stood. It had probably been someone's home in the long and distant past.

The structure was rickety, its roof about to collapse. In normal circumstances nobody would have gone near the place. However, what was left of it offered a modicum of cover in an otherwise primeval terrain.

The following day started early. Even before the Portuguese soldier nearest us had been able to dismantle his mortar, the Rhodesian drivers were running their engines. We'd been warned the night before that it would be another long haul.

There had been activity elsewhere during the night. We'd heard a few blasts in the distance and then, several times, bursts of automatic fire. It was nothing definitive, or anything to which the lieutenant might venture an opinion. It happened all the time, he shrugged, the war . . .

Barely five minutes out of our bivouac, the convoy stalled to a halt. Unlike previous hold-ups, this was a lengthy delay, culminating in a heavy blast up ahead. 'Another land mine', said Chagas. 'They must have blown it'. For the first time while with us, the officer displayed a little enthusiasm. 'You will see later when we hit a real minefield how they do it', he said, his eyes burning with anticipation.

We travelled into the morning for several more hours and all the while the possibility of the column encountering more landmines remained the principal preoccupation for everybody. Every few miles the column would stop while the soldiers scratched the dirt with their *picas*, or dug small holes in the road in the perennial search for bombs.

Towards noon, another explosion followed, much bigger than before and Chagas said something about it probably being an anti-tank mine.

Air assets in Lisbon's three African colonies that were battling insurgency were minimal. Ground support roles in Angola, Mozambique and Portuguese Guinea were sometimes provided by these World War II vintage T6 Harvards, which dropped either napalm or 'dumb' bombs on real or suspected 'terrorist' positions, usually with little real effect. (Author's collection)

Possibly a TM-46, he said, the Russian version of the wartime German Tellermine 42. Word came down the line that it had been detonated by the troops in the lead Berliet.

So it went on, the stops and starts that centred not so much on the people who laid these bombs – though they were around, of course – but on the mines themselves. We'd come upon holes in the road, some huge and perhaps three feet deep. Others were barely larger than potholes. Or perhaps they were potholes, somebody would quip.

Occasionally we'd spot scraps of steel and rubber scattered about the road; tell-tale evidence of some previous carnage. There was never talk about casualties, though obviously they happened.

In one area, near a bridge that had been partly demolished by Frelimo guerrillas, the remains of a burnt-out truck lay on its side alongside the road, its cab ripped apart by what must have been an awesome blast. Alongside the dusty track – yards away – lay the wrappings of army field dressings, empty plastic plasma bottles and wadding. Some of it was tinged black with coagulated blood. There were flies everywhere.

It was clear that the dressings were relatively fresh, which suggested that it might all have happened a day or two before, probably on the southbound convoy and certainly before the last rains, which would have washed away all this evidence.

The next time we stopped, one of the troops told us what had happened. He'd been on that southbound convoy and had joined us on the way north again; it was his job to search for mines. He explained that a black Rhodesian driver working for a transport company out of Salisbury had been caught in the blast. His legs were badly mutilated and he had large gashes in the head and arms. Because he was losing blood, they had radioed to base for instructions. Fortunately, the air force had one of its gunships deployed in the area and they pulled him back to Tete. The driver lived, we heard later, but he went on to lose a leg.

What was noteworthy, the soldier said, was that within a couple of hundred yards of the incident, several dozen more landmines were uncovered in an operation that involved many soldiers and took more than a day. The bombs were mostly anti-personnel types, but there were no more casualties. 'Not that time', he smiled. The truck had toppled over onto its side after two more TM-46s had been detonated *in situ* during that operation.

Then for us, on this hot February morning, the inevitable happened. Quite suddenly, we were involved in an event that might have had serious consequences for one or more of the vehicles if a Portuguese Army scout, perched precariously on the roof of the lead French Berliet, hadn't spotted something on the road ahead.

There were human tracks that had caught his attention, we heard afterwards, as we were in an area where there hadn't been anybody living for who knows how long.

Having stopped the column and dismounted, the soldier moved slowly ahead, as close to the edge of the road as the bush would allow in case anti-personnel bombs or booby traps had been laid. That was when he spotted wires. Moments later, a volley of shots rang out from a gully on the far side of the convoy: it was automatic fire and it came in bursts.

For three of us in the Land Rover, squeezed as low onto the floorboards as our bulk would allow, the conflict had suddenly become interesting. None of us had any idea where the shooting was coming from or who might have been the target. Seconds later the rattle of more shots rang out from another position towards the rear. This was what the Portuguese drivers had earlier referred to as *Flagelacau*, a whipping burst of gunfire and a quick getaway.

As the firing continued, our military escort retaliated with enthusiasm. From both ends of the convoy they ripped off a stream of tracers in a broad arc across the bush. The heavy machine-gun on the Unimog followed, together with several dull mortar plops. Then, every few minutes, three or four more . . .

Though we'd been ordered to stay put, it didn't take us long to emerge from our cramped vehicle and we found ourselves close enough to watch a clutch of detonations a few hundred yards away in some heavily foliaged jungle country. By then our tracers had already ignited several fires in the dry brush and within minutes the entire area was enveloped in smoke.

Viera, our youthful sergeant, meanwhile moved through the periphery shouting instructions. He ordered a squad of black soldiers to take up positions along the length of the column; they were to lie prone in the bush, he told them, and face the direction from which the first shots had been fired, Lieutenant Chagas explained.

'*Terroristas*', he muttered dismissively.

Several of the troops took their chances and opted to cross stretches of gravel that hadn't been cleared in search of better vantage points. Because of the problems ahead and the uncertainty of the strength of the guerrilla force, the next hour or two saw a lot of movement up and down the length of the column. There was so much movement along the road that some of the troops barely bothered with following in each others' tracks. The mine threat had become secondary, though Chagas reckoned that some had almost certainly been laid in the area.

One of the officers from the lead Berliet came down the line and indicated to our lieutenant that the insurgents had laid an as-yet undetermined minefield ahead, which was when we were ordered to get back in our vehicle and stay put. The entire area first had to be cleared, he explained. Worse, it could take the rest of the morning.

There were several more bursts of automatic fire from the insurgents. Then they fired several clutches of mortars, which landed way off target behind us. It had taken us almost half a day just to get this far.

The army eventually cleared the minefield, though it took hours longer than anticipated. A total of 14 mines, two round metal TM-46s and a dozen anti-personal bombs, were detected and detonated. There were no casualties – on either side in all probability – because by now I'd set no great store in the ability of the troops guarding us. It was a job they had to do, but they displayed little relish.

For our part, we gambled on the notoriously bad marksmanship of the enemy.

While Lieutenant Chagas viewed most of what was going on around with what appeared to be an amused detachment, his approach was very different when we moved a few paces from the vehicle. It didn't matter that that was our only option in heat that had become crippling. When we found the shade of a large fever tree preferable to the Land Rover, he marched briskly across to where we had taken up station.

'You are taking chances,' he said sternly. 'unnecessary chances . . . this area hasn't been cleared . . . and we don't know where *they* are.' We had no option but to return to the truck.

Then he surprised us all by going off towards the head of the column, in a huff, we thought. He returned with a smile on his face, telling us that he'd asked permission for me to come forward so that I could watch the demolition process. I was the only news-gatherer in the group, so the request made sense, he reckoned. Moreover, I'd watch the goings-on from the gun platform of the lead Berliet, he stated. Apparently, he'd explained to the lead commander that I'd covered the Angolan War and that I wanted to 'compare notes'. I grabbed my Nikons.

The system that the Portuguese Army employed to clear mines was basic, though clearly not without risk. A number of trained soldiers – black and white – would spend several minutes assessing the situation on the road ahead. If they felt that the surface might conceal mines, a stick of four would disembark and walk slowly ahead, using their steel-tipped wooden lances, about the length of a golf club, to probe the soil. Soft, recently disturbed soil would customarily indicate mines.

The lances were named *picas*, after the Portuguese bullfight probe, a curious anomaly at a time when there were any number of electronic mine-detecting devices available. Yet I was to see that throughout all of Lisbon's conflicts in Africa, these primitive handheld staffs were always regarded as the most reliable means of detecting those insidious weapons that remain as much of a threat in the new millennium in some parts of the globe as they were 30 or 40 years ago.

It was interesting that the convoy had on board a variety of electronic gear for the purpose, all with NATO designations. However, this equipment was rarely unpacked from its bulky, suitcase-sized containers, one of the officers explained, because it was all but useless along roads where huge amounts of metal debris lay about. That included cans, tin foil, spent cartridge cases, spare parts and the rest – all discarded over the years by minor armies of transients like us.

It took our group about 90 minutes to find seven mines: a large anti-tank bomb surrounded by six anti-personnel mines. All the latter were PMD-6 mines; rudimentary pressure-activated blast devices, each in its own little wooden box.

We were aware that the PMD-6 had already been widely used in Cambodia, but because of Mozambique's vast distances, the insurgents had taken to manufacturing some of these devices themselves. The forest provided the wood, while explosives and detonators were brought into the war zones from Tanzania on peoples' backs.

Not all landmines deployed by the guerrillas were primitive. The insurgents soon imposed significant losses among government troops by using larger TM-57 anti-tank mines. Also deployed were PMN 'Black Widow' mines and the deadly POM-Z, both anti-personnel devices already well blooded in Vietnam.

In the final stages of these heady African colonial conflicts – as in Rhodesia and South-West Africa afterwards – RPG-7s had begun to supersede the more ubiquitous RPG-2s.

Midday brought us the short distance to the Portuguese Army para-commando camp at Muxoxo. For at least an hour before we reached the base, the unit's pair of helicopters provided air cover against further insurgent forays. Camouflaged Alouette gunships would move at a fair pace above the bush, sweeping low and often doubling back to previous sites, their heavy machine-guns strafing suspect positions. The pilots would sometimes wave as they passed.

Muxoxo offered few surprises. The dilapidated building at its centre had once been a farmhouse and was surrounded by neat rows of army tents that housed the garrison. We welcomed the opportunity to buy warm Manica beer at five times the going rate in Lourenco Marques. In the milieu of the Portuguese shopkeeper in Africa, passing trade has always been lucrative.

The men at the camp had a fairly large area to patrol, at least by today's counter-insurgency standards. They were backed by their handful of helicopters, which air-lifted small units to wherever intelligence reports indicated the guerrillas might be working, or possibly concentrating assets. The unit averaged about four operations a week, mostly when road convoys were expected.

Muxoxo was strategically placed and responsible for security on that section of the rail link between Moatize and Caldas Xavier and these activities often took heli-borne sorties long distances towards the southeast. These were short, swift 'search and destroy' hits which sometimes offered unexpected surprises.

During our brief stay, two captured Frelimo insurgents were brought

It was a dirty, dusty, sometimes dangerous experience travelling in much of Mozambique during wartime. Generally though, the convoys got through without too many problems, though they were constantly sniped at. (Author's collection)

in. One was an old man hardly able to walk, obviously malnourished and definitely no belligerent. Yet both admitted they'd been linked to a rebel sabotage unit that had been operating near the rail town of Goa. They had been taken while preparing food for their compatriots in the bush, men, whom they admitted, had been responsible for a spate of attacks on the railroad that winds its way to Beira at the coast.

Ultimately, it had been a squad of Portugal's crack *Commandos Africanos* who had scored and subsequently dealt with a larger group of insurgents who had been spreading mines about in the region. Several hundred anti-personnel mines were seized, but curiously not a single anti-tank mine.

The two captives were first interrogated, then fed. More interrogation followed before they were flown to Tete for a more professional session, after which they would probably be transferred to one of the prison camps in the south, Chagas reckoned. After doing some independent news-gathering of his own, the lieutenant told us that the men would probably be of some use to the security forces.

'They claim they were shanghaied. Had they offered any resistance they said they would have been shot' he explained. 'Trouble is' he added, 'they all claim that . . . but the truth is they probably would have been killed had they not cooperated . . .'

It was late afternoon when we finally made contact with the southbound convoy at the road junction to Caldas Xavier. The crossroads were marked by a primitive wooden signpost on which none of the directions were discernible.

We were again warned that the area had not been cleared of mines and that we should be circumspect. Spent cartridge cases littered the area and its approaches.

While approaching the intersection, we'd crossed a small river that had been prominently signposted in both languages: *Zona Armadilhada*: *Minefield*. This deterrent was Portuguese and had been laid in a bid to prevent the guerrillas from setting charges at the base of the bridge and possibly destroying it. As somebody mentioned, the measure was decidedly two edged since it also prevented anybody travelling in our convoy from getting water at a time when stocks were getting low. Water shortages on board the buses, we knew, were already critical, especially among the children.

The oppressive heat which had followed us across Africa from the

Zambezi Valley hardly made matters any easier. Even so, a handful of passengers did make an effort. In a small column, some of the men and boys traipsed single file down a path towards the river, each one stepping carefully in the imprint of the man directly ahead.

One of the older soldiers later told us that the week before, a civilian had tripped a mine. He hadn't been killed, but it did underscore some of the privations that those who had few resources faced when moving across this corner of East Africa.

'He needed water very badly – not only for himself, but also for his family. So he set out on his own in spite of warnings from the troops. As he stepped near the water his foot triggered something that shot a small mine about six feet into the air.' It was later determined that the device was similar to the notorious South-East Asian 'S mine', or what the Americans liked to call the 'Bouncing Betty'. Lisbon used these munitions to good effect throughout their colonial conflicts.

Apparently, the man who had tripped the mine while going for water was lucky that eventful day. The mine detonated almost within touching distance of where he stood, but it was apparently facing the wrong way. The victim was concussed by the blast, but not a single shard of shrapnel penetrated his skin.

We waited an hour for the oncoming convoy to arrive. From the start we could see that conditions were much harder in their sector than in ours and a number of times we heard detonations.

Chagas came back not long afterwards to tell us that the approaching column had taken a casualty. He wasn't specific, but said something about a mine. Moments later an evacuation helicopter veered over our heads and prepared to land in open ground near the crossroads. Ours was the first convoy the pilot reached and he had no way of knowing which of the two columns had triggered the bomb.

Having established that much, the chopper lifted off again, leaving a dense cloud of dust whipped up by its rotors. We watched as the helicopter sped northwards barely a yard above the tree-tops. A minute or two later he was on his way back to base, this time at a higher altitude and making directly for Tete Military Hospital.

When the oncoming convoy eventually did reach us, the word went out that a man had been killed. He'd been second in the line in the unit's main *pica* squad, his point man having apparently stepped over an anti-personnel mine. The soldier behind was not so lucky and he took the full impact of the blast.

Three other members of the *pica* squad were lightly wounded, but they were able to continue with their duties even though their leader was limping badly from a large cut on his thigh. In Vietnam, a wound like that would have meant immediate evacuation to the base hospital. With the Portuguese Army in Africa, such matters were accepted in the line of duty.

Portuguese troops weren't awarded Lisbon's version of the Purple Heart because there wasn't one.

We travelled halfway through the night to reach Mussacuana. The road had been cleared by the oncoming convoy and it was essential to cover the prodded ground as quickly as possible before the insurgents laid more mines. The same held for the convoy that passed us and was heading in the opposite direction. They'd want to cover as much of the ground that we'd cleared.

However, we weren't quite fast enough. A heavy monsoon-like downpour provided the drivers with the almost impossible task of following exactly in the tracks of the vehicles ahead and, within an hour, two more vehicles were blasted. These were heavy trucks, one from Johannesburg, the other from Salisbury, and both carried cargoes destined for the mines in Zambia. What made it ironic was that the insurgent groups who'd laid the mines were actually using Zambia as a base. The mines that had destroyed the trucks had actually originated from there. Now these same guerrillas were helping to disrupt the economy of one of their allies . . .

There were no more incidents that night. The mines had been detonated by the back wheels of both trucks, giving credence to reports that the insurgents where using a more sophisticated type of landmine that had recently been brought in from South-East Asia following the de-escalation of American military involvement there. Only much later were we to learn that these were ratchet mines.

A curious name, ratchet mines used by the Viet Cong were usually set to detonate after a pre-determined number of wheels had passed; sometimes 10 or 12, often double that. The fact that the trucks involved were well down the column when they were blasted, underscored this development. It could have been us.

One of the vehicles was travelling in our column barely 100 yards ahead of us. The blast happened about a mile out of the village of

Capirizanje, our next stop on the long road north. A heavy downpour was pelting down when the blast ripped through one of the open windows of the Land Rover and the column halted.

For a long time we sat in silence, accepting that it would have been foolish to get out and see what was happening. Only when the convoy started to move again and we carefully followed neat rows of new tracks created through the bush around the stranded vehicle, could we see that a set of back wheels on one of the low-loaders from South Africa had been shredded.

Not long afterwards we passed a quarry alongside the road, illuminated by lightning as we passed. We were experiencing one of those African thunderstorms for which the Zambezi Valley is known, the water sometimes coming down in spurts big enough to fill a bucket overnight. Three or four flashes of lightning told us that the area had long ago been abandoned. Some of the trolleys that had probably been part of the facility lay on their sides. A few yards away, a wheelbarrow without its wheel rested upside down in the mud, more reminders of a conflict that had already spanned half a generation.

Mussacuana arrived unheralded. We'd climbed steadily in the mud and muck and suddenly, just before midnight, there were lights ahead. The rain had lifted minutes before and as happens so often in a region only a few hundred miles from the Indian Ocean, the settlement in the mountains above Capirizanje lay swathed in mist. The ground was sodden, for it had poured here as well.

A soldier on guard in an improvised machine-gun turret shouted a greeting. We replied in English and he turned his back on us.

At least the beer would be cold . . .

CHAPTER TWENTY-FIVE

Serengeti Must Not Die

Serengeti is one of the great natural treasures of our time. Yet it is threatened by poachers. One of Africa's great national parks is menaced by groups of well-armed paramilitary groups who murder game guards, as well as the occasional tourist found in the wrong place at the wrong time. Each night they target large numbers of animals. The so-called 'cullings' are ongoing because there are simply not enough rangers to counter what some have already termed 'a mini-invasion of illegals'.

SADLY, IF THIS SITUATION IS allowed to go on, the unthinkable might happen; this wonderful animal reserve, one of the best-known game parks in the world, will die.

The scenario is fraught with imponderables. Involved are poachers, bandits, a bankrupt government, corrupt politicians as well as an inept and badly trained army. There is no air support to speak of and the legal system is not beyond coercion whenever 'incentives' are offered. The bribes come in heavy manila envelopes stuffed with American banknotes.

The situation is linked to a level of bureaucratic obfuscation that, to the average Western mind, simply defies description. As one expatriate observer tartly commented, 'that's unfortunately the way it goes in these parts'. This imbroglio not only involves Serengeti. Other Tanzanian game parks – like the Selous National Reserve – are similarly affected.

A generation ago it was Kenya where poachers – many of them Simba rebels from Somalia armed with automatic weapons – killed all the rhinos. They had already set about destroying large herds of elephants, a considerable task and it is sobering that they almost succeeded.

For those parts of Africa that still have rhino, killing them for their horns is largely a cyclical process. The authorities take action, the poachers back off, somebody imports more rhino from South Africa and the process starts all over again. By mid 2009, the number of rhinoceros in East and Southern Africa was the highest for almost two decades. A year later their numbers were decreasing again at an alarming rate.

Yet it was not always so. In the mid 1960s I would regularly travel between Nairobi and Malindi by car, often taking the shorter route through parts of the beautiful Tsavo National Park. Along the way, we'd often encounter elephant herds, so vast that we'd have to stop at the side of the road until they'd crossed, an exercise that could sometimes take five or ten minutes.

These days, only small herds of elephant remain, the ivory of their predecessors long ago shipped to India or China. In both Kenya and Tanzania, the smoke and mirror swindles of 'allowing' poachers access to herds of elephant so that they can be shot for their ivory tusks stretches all the way back to their respective capitals and the crooked politicians who control them.

Dar es Salaam, the beautiful and ancient tropical city on the fringe of the Indian Ocean, first mentioned by Pliny the Elder, lies at the heart of much of it. As in most countries in Africa, Tanzania's leaders have proved to be corrupt, which is also why it has followed the same route as Kenya: almost all of its rhinos have been poached. The majority were slaughtered for their horns, which were bought by Chinese parties, ground-up into a powder and used as a primitive form of Viagra.

Caught between these vagaries in the country's national reserves is a tiny, but resolute, band of conservationists and game guards who regularly match their wits against the poachers. They are a dedicated, ill-equipped and chronically underpaid band of veterans, but they are willing to put everything on the line, including their lives, in their often futile attempts to stop the killings.

Justin Hando, head of the Tanzanian paramilitary Anti-Poaching Unit in the Serengeti National Park, was the man in charge the last time I visited East Africa. Responsible for some of the most spectacular concentrations of wildlife in the world, he was emphatic: 'Our animals are being killed in great numbers and if these people are not halted, then it won't be long before the process becomes irreversible.'

He encapsulated his argument with a simple analogy. If poaching were allowed to go on, the word gets around. Soon everyone and his uncle comes running to get a share of the booty. The perception among many of these illegal hunters, he stressed, was that an almost unlimited supply of fresh meat was available. It was there for the taking, and if a game guards got in the way, they did the necessary . . .

Security arrangements within Serengeti remain primitive, largely due to budget constraints. While the poachers are armed with Kalashnikov AK-47s, the Tanzanian game guards 'make do' with leftovers from earlier wars. This scene shows morning parade at one of the camps. (Author's collection)

Moreover, if successful, the illegal hunter would then be able to add another firearm to his already-substantial illegal armoury.

According to Hando, criminals poached between 150,000 and 200,000 wildebeest each year in Serengeti. 'Never mind what they end up killing in the rest of the country . . . Serengeti is the worst, because there is such an exceptional multiplicity of wildlife to be found here . . . we count our losses in the millions', he declared.

That is only part of the story. Apart from wildebeest, poachers kill tens of thousands of other animals in the park. That tally includes elephant, zebra, antelope, gazelle, buffalo and just about every other form of wildlife in this East African region.

'If it's edible,' he says, 'they kill it. Or the poorer people who come across into the park will trap it . . . and they're not concerned about how this business goes down.'

Hando reckoned that because Tanzania was one of the most impoverished countries in the world, a lot of what these people butcher is used for barter. It was all pretty traditional, he explained: a wildebeest haunch will bring in a few kilos of sadza or corn. A complete carcass might fetch a half-tank of fuel. Or they exchange the skin of a Grant's gazelle for a second-hand pair of shoes, though a fully processed zebra hide (which will eventually reach the tourist market) often commands as much as $100. That's a minor fortune in a country where a man with just a fraction of that amount in his pocket is king.

It was Justin Hando's job to stop this activity, and he admitted that it was never easy, in part, because the people are hungry. His department operates on the tiniest of budgets, which anywhere else would be regarded as negligible. There are vehicles, but almost all are old. For those they do have, there is little fuel. With almost no exceptions, the game department can offer only primitive living conditions for Hando's crews. Still, it says much that he has achieved a measure of success.

Of the 14 vehicles at the disposal of the Anti-Poaching Unit in Serengeti when we spent time with him, only nine were in running order. Significantly, even smaller European, Asian and American game parks are better equipped. Some of his Land Rovers (which averaged about 2,000 miles a month) were way past their 'expiry date'. That some were mobile was remarkable, but somehow it seems the crews managed.

Hando was blessed with a reasonably efficient technical staff and they did what they could to keep the vehicles on the road, though a shortage of spare parts was a perennial issue with headquarters. He admitted that a consistent problem was that spares sent to him from Dar es Salaam often disappeared along the way.

There were more serious problems. By the time we got to Serengeti, five of his staff had been murdered and several more wounded. These events didn't always make the the headlines for fear of alarming the tourist trade and even when some of it became public, the more macabre details were routinely kept out of the press.

For Hando and his men, survival in this hardy African outpost is a struggle that is unrelenting. Brushes with nature must also be taken into account; two of his men were bitten by snakes shortly before we arrived and one of his drivers savaged by a lion. Two more were almost drowned when they tried to cross a stream that had become a torrent following rains that Nairobi described as 'unseasonable'.

He'd lost crew from other causes. Two of his men were taken by crocodiles, though they were off-duty. Historically, he said, many more people were killed by buffalo than any other animal in this vast African region, though in Sub-Saharan Africa as a whole, the hippo takes the most human lives.

Another problem is the size of the park: even by African standards it is immense. At 8,500 square miles, the reserve is bigger than Connecticut, and while the great African plain does have links with the outside world, these are tenuous. Radio communication with headquarters, for instance, is fine, but that's on the coast at Dar es Salaam, 500 miles away.

More serious, the park is not fenced and one of the roads through it links several towns in the west of the country around Lake Victoria with Arusha and the Kilimanjaro area, towards the east.

Serengeti is also affected by several African wars in the region. Rwanda and Burundi are only a hard day's drive away and some of the automatic weapons used by poachers come in from there. Additionally, the civil war in the Congo to the immediate east goes on, which further complicates matters.

Settled in a string of modest pre-fabricated offices in the grounds of the park headquarters at Seronera (the park's vet is next door), there was a constant stream of visitors to see Justin Hando when we visited the place.

Some asked for protection to work in remote areas of the park, like that adjacent to the Soit Ololol Escarpment, which is sporadically declared a no-go area because of bandits. Others, like us, wanted to talk about future projects, including the possibility of building a 'fort' with American money to counter illegal hunting.

Hando explained that while poaching remained endemic in all of Africa, it was especially widespread in Serengeti. The reason, he suggested, was obvious: few of the natives in the adjoining regions had jobs and there were almost no industries. Come what may, people simply had to put bread on the table and clothe and educate their children. Consequently, much of the illegal activity is centred on Serengeti's proliferation of wildlife and like it or not, it is all irrevocably linked to Africa's burgeoning population.

There are also those, he suggested, who regard access to Africa's wild animals as a right, with the argument running along the lines that before the white man came to East Africa, these people always hunted there. It is difficult to counter such logic on a continent that starves.

Justin Hando's Anti-Poaching Unit during our visit had a staff of 156 rangers. About a third were on patrol at any one time. Others worked in administration, manned radios or had days off. Still more were in training, which was also conducted in-house.

We were shown the figures. A party of 22 of his men had gone off to a funeral. Being Africa, distances are often vast and it would sometimes be a week before they returned. Also, because of AIDs, a disease of epidemic proportions in all of East Africa, funerals were becoming more frequent. Increasingly, this blight affected his staff, which meant that he could rarely count on more than 50 rangers on call at any one time. There were 46 rangers out on patrol when we were with him and it sometimes dipped as low as 30.

An average four-man patrol, he told us, lasted anything from seven to ten days. Moreover, in order to be even moderately effective, the unit had to be self-sufficient. As he said: 'They sleep in the wild with lions and hyenas for company . . . with the antelope and the occasional jumbo these were often the only creatures they see.' Apart from illegal humans, he added.

Contact with wildlife is fine, he said. You accept the rules. When there were big cats about, you stayed in your vehicle or in your tent, unless you were all gathered around a big fire in what locals refer to as the 'boma' – a secure, semi-enclosed area - which was where the last meal of the day was served.

'When the men are out there and settling down after a hard day in the bush, they sometimes turn their lights towards the nearby bush and invariably pick up the reflection of more than one large set of eyes . . . there are always lions about. Beyond them, there are hyenas', he added.

Two-legged intruders, by contrast, were a totally different proposition. They operated in gangs ranging from a handful to as many as 20 at a time and were often better armed than the rangers. Interestingly, intruder weapons sometimes included bows and arrows and the poison with which the arrows were tipped could paralyze a man in seconds. Moreover, if not immediately treated with anti-venom – and then only if the antidote was available – the victim could die. Some park rangers had been murdered with these primitive weapons.

Hando stressed that it had become so bad in recent years that poachers were the most persistent threat to the rangers.

A recent development involved some ranger posts coming under fire from intruders using Kalashnikovs, which was one of the reasons why the camps we visited were guarded by armed scouts. The routine when we moved across the park was to radio ahead to tell a camp we were on our way. They would then keep an eye open for us and sometimes send out an escort to greet us.

'So far, we've been spared the heavy stuff,' said the head of the Anti-Poaching Unit, 'but who knows what can happen tomorrow?'

A significant part of the problem was that not all units in the field had radios. As Hando explained, a short-wave radio in Tanzania is expensive; a transmitter/receiver with import taxes and other duties can easily cost $8,000, even if they were available. The Anti-Poaching Unit, Hando confided, needed four more of these radio sets immediately, but both his and the coffers of his department were empty, he explained.

He admitted that without good communications, things sometimes went awry, especially when a unit ran into gangs of poachers.

'No radio means no back-up and frankly, the poachers know it', he added.

A couple of days before we got to Serengeti, Hando's game rangers had intercepted a group of bandits attempting to haul 150 used vehicle tyres into a remote area of the park. All were of old manufacture and incorporated steel wire banding around their central core. They were going to be cut-up and the wire used to make snares to trap wildlife. While this method of trapping is unconscionable anywhere else in the world, it is an everyday thing in Africa. It sometimes took animals days to die and some of larger beasts, snagged around the neck, slowly strangled themselves to death in their struggles to escape the wire nooses.

What became obvious after spending even a short while with Serengeti field units, was that Justin Hando had a difficult job on his hands. Considering all the obstacles, he somehow seemed to manage.

He disclosed too that apart from keeping pace with illegal elements in vehicles, fixed-wing aircraft are also used by the Anti-Poaching Unit when park budgets permit. During the early 1980s, the Tanzanian government tried using helicopters against illegals. Dar es Salaam had been offered several five-seater choppers that might have been ideal for the job, but costs of crews, fuel and spares were prohibitive.

'There just wasn't enough money around to keep a single helicopter airborne, never mind several', one of those who had been involved told us. Then someone suggested they bring in a couple of two-seaters, but in practical terms these proved useless for the envisaged tasks.

Altogether, the Anti-Poaching Unit has 18 stations, each under the command of a local commander, of which eight are at gate stations leading into the park and the rest spread about intermittently in the interior of the reserve.

The most difficult time, Hando believed, was after the first monsoon rains, which usually start around May. It is then that great herds of animals – hundreds of thousands of animals simultaneously – get on the hoof and start their annual migration northwards towards Kenya. By July and August there are millions of animals bunched up in columns that are sometimes a hundred miles long or more.

'It's difficult to maintain static locations when that kind of phenomenon happens', Hando suggested. 'Also, my rangers need to move along with the animals to keep track of developments . . . and that is when they are most exposed to danger. The poachers sometimes lie in wait for them, in a conventional ambush.' So far, he admitted, this criminal activity had been fairly low-key, but it was getting worse, especially since there were now homeless Congolese refugees entering the area from the west who wouldn't think twice about murdering somebody for whatever money he had in his pocket.

Fortunately, most insurgents tended to abandon everything and make a run for it when challenged. However, he acknowledged, that might change were they to acquire heavier weapons. Also, he reckoned, his men were dedicated to protecting wild animals, not fighting a war. 'They're game rangers and they do outstanding work. But they're not soldiers.'

An additional dimension to the problem is an unobtrusive but aggressive banditry within Tanzania's northern reserves. In recent years it has become endemic. Much of it results from a dissident Somali presence, which has meant trouble wherever these people appear.

In some areas it had become volatile enough for places to have been declared no-go areas by the authorities, largely because the Somalis are regarded as both aggressive and ruthless. The manner in which they 'run' their own country is instructive of this trend: Somalia is currently the most lawless place on the globe!

Though attacks have been few, the rebels have recently turned their attention to ambushing the occasional tourist group, usually those visiting remote areas. Pickings are easy because, obviously, visitors to Tanzania are not allowed to carry weapons. Consequently, when the occupants of a vehicle are stopped (usually after being shot at) everything is stolen, by force if necessary, which is one of the reasons why only a fool travels along Tanzanian (and Kenyan) national park roads at night. Hando disclosed that it was especially bad along the approaches to Lake Natron, beyond the eastern boundaries of the park.

A party of four French tourists was attacked the week before we got there: they were hit by an armed gang shortly before sunset. Travelling in a two-vehicle convoy in the Naabi Hill Gate area just before dusk, shots rang out in the half-light. The radiator and windscreen of the lead vehicle were shattered, injuring the driver. He lost control and inadvertently ran his Land Rover into a truck parked alongside the road, which probably belonged to the attackers. Moments later the party was surrounded by six or seven men, identified by one of the game scouts afterwards as a renegade group of Somalis.

The visitors were forced to hand over all their valuables – including shoes. One of them complained that there were lions about and demanded to know how they were expected to survive the night without them. 'We have no water left either', she told the bandits.

'Just be glad that you are European', one of them retorted in fairly good English. Drawing his hand across his throat, he said that things would have been very different had they been American.

This was no idle threat. An American woman was murdered by Somali poachers in Serengeti a short while before. Even today, the authorities are reticent to comment about the incident, possibly because so many visitors to East Africa's game parks are from the United States, though the event did get some coverage in the media.

The attack on the French group before we arrived was followed by another on our last day in Serengeti. We had been gradually moving towards the east and the Ngorongoro Crater, which we'd intending visiting the following day.

At the time, we were sitting with our Dutch hostess around an open fire in the grounds of the Lake Ndutu tented camp before dinner. Cocktails in hand, we'd also made a game of picking out the eyes of a pride of six or eight young lions with her flashlight: some of these fine creatures weren't more than 30 yards away.

Just then, a report came through on the radio that Venance Kong'oa, the Ngorongoro District Police Commander, had been murdered by Somali terrorists earlier that evening. Like the others, he had been ambushed at dusk. We learnt later that five other policemen had been shot after being taken captive. We had crossed that same route twice while in the region, both times towards dark. It might easily have been us.

Wildlife conservation consultant Jaco Ackerman has spent years trying to help counter some of the threats facing one of the finest game parks in the world. A hidebound bureaucracy hundreds of miles away in Dar es Salaam thwarts most efforts, as does corruption, which takes place on a regional scale throughout East Africa, more often than not with expatriate Chinese behind much of it. Jaco is shown speaking to a Serengeti National Park game guard at one of the armed camps in the interior. (Author's collection)

While not yet serious enough to prompt a general alert, the Tanzanian government immediately dispatched a military Field Force Unit to the region to launch a follow-up. However, again they lacked the resources to be effective because their radios were faulty, or perhaps it was the operators who hadn't learnt to use them properly. Consequently the reaction force came up empty-handed. In retrospect, a single helicopter might have done the trick.

Once back in Dar es Salaam, a source in the Tanzanian Ministry of Defence told us that groups of Somalis had been terrorizing the area for more than two years. Until then, he said, the government didn't like to act because the problems were mostly seasonal. Also, they were concerned about the effect such action might have on the tourist trade.

According to a police officer who spoke off the record, the poachers brought textiles and consumer items across the Kenyan and Ugandan borders and exchanged them for poached wildlife or cattle. It also emerged that earlier operations to net bandits had been unsuccessful because the Somalis often forced groups of Maasai tribesmen to shelter them. They would be warned that their wives or children would be slaughtered if they didn't cooperate.

'It's difficult for folks to argue with people who will kill with impunity because they know there is hardly any chance of them being caught', the policeman said.

A well-known East African authority on African wildlife was outspoken about the inability of the Tanzanian government to counter what he referred to as 'a situation tantamount to a limited guerrilla war'. If things continued in this way, he reckoned, Serengeti would eventually be stripped of much of its resources. It was a 'spreading, suppurating cancer that gets worse the longer it is allowed to go on', he declared. 'Eventually, others get to see how easy it is and they start the cycle as well.' Tourists, obviously, were the softest of targets.

We were asked not to mention the man's name. As he explained, 'I'm doing good work here and being Africa, it doesn't pay for *wazungus* [the Swahili word for foreigners] to be outspoken about anything that might be regarded politically incorrect.'

Once before, he'd caused problems in Dar es Salaam, including an incident that eventually made its way to the Office of the President. He'd commented on filth around main camps on the long haul up the slopes of Kilimanjaro. There was no running water, he'd pointed out to those in charge of tourist facilities, and the toilets, such as they were, hardly rated a mention.

Following that incident, he'd been warned: keep quiet or leave the country.

Serengeti, for all its problems, somehow manages to cope and even with all the poaching, the range of wildlife is awesome.

While there are fewer elephants than there were 30 years ago and the rhinos are all gone, other animals abound. Even the lodges are overrun by families of hyrax and baboons that had become accustomed to tourists feeding them. However, some had become aggressive and visitors were warned about getting too close.

To the casual visitor, it seemed difficult to understand that this minor paradise might be threatened by outside elements, groups of thugs who did not regard wild creatures in the same light as they did.

Within a day of arriving, for instance, we'd spotted a herd of about a

East Africa has been targeted by poachers for more than half a century and terrible damage has been done to all wildlife in the region. Compared to the pre-independence period, there are only a fraction of these beautiful creatures left. Now they are being indiscriminately slaughtered in the Selous Game Reserve in Tanzania. This photo of Somali-based poachers in Kenya's Tsavo park was taken by Mohammed Amin a few years ago.

hundred elephant, which was when a female – with calf – trumpeting and ears billowing, rushed our Land Rover. We moved on and within a few miles there were scores of mating lions. It was the season and the ritual customarily goes on for days, with coupling taking place dozens of times.

There was also a pride of five cheetah stalking Grants gazelle almost within walking distance of the main camp and then we found a single leopard in a tree just outside the main camp at Seronera. This was unusual, since there are only a few hundred left in Serengeti.

While travelling along the north-eastern limits of the park we encountered migrating herds of wildebeest and there were thousands of them. By October, they will have turned around again and headed south. The cycle is eternal and has been going on forever.

Yet it's not only wildebeest that migrate. A couple of hundred thousand zebra and Grants gazelle also move north on nature's greatest natural trek. Most other animals stop short of Maasai country, where they are likely to be hunted, but these go on, into some of the Kenyan reserves.

Almost a million-and-a-half wildebeest set out on the annual trek each year and by the time its over, they might have lost a fifth of their number to predators and poachers.

Getting to Serengeti is always an experience. We moved overland from Arusha in northern Tanzania and it took a day in a four-wheel drive vehicle to reach our destination of Seronera Lodge.

Once off the tar, it was a tough, dusty slog across the mountains. The roads were bad and there were times when it seemed they hadn't been graded for years. During the rainy season it was worse, Hando said: these great African plains often turned into quagmires which could cripple four-wheel-drive vehicles. Nor can you use aircraft; some of the strips would have become like shallow lakes.

Interestingly, the reserve also caters for the backpacking community. Those who cannot afford the lodge, can camp at specific locations, though these are generally not fenced and at night seem to attract their share of wildlife.

What to do, stuck out in the open, if you need the toilet? Simple, explained one of the visitors: it had happened to him three nights before.

He'd had a sudden attack of diarrhoea some time after two in the morning. Worse, his entire group of campers had earlier been made very much aware of the presence of a pride of lions. One of the beasts had actually roared while passing his modest one-man pup tent. As he recalled, a tent without a bathroom attached suddenly became an issue.

In such circumstances, he told us, you did what was needed: you very quietly unzipped your tent flap, inch-by-inch, until there was a hole, just big enough to shove your butt through. Then you let go, possibly with a roar. While you might wake your neighbours and possibly startle some of the lions, the deed will have been done. As he recalled, there was much relief all round.

The clever move then, he reckoned, was to pull the zipper up as quickly as possible and wait for morning. 'Just make sure you're up before daybreak to clear away the mess', he warned.

On our fourth and last day with the Serengeti game guard unit, we headed north-east from Seronera. The intention was to visit one of the park's most isolated camps that lay beyond the old German Fort Ikoma.

An historic installation that pre-dated Kaiser Wilhelm's war, it was magnificently placed on the edge of Rift Valley escarpment. We'd already been made aware that there had been some heavy fighting there between the South Africans under General Jan Smuts and the Germans, all of which had taken place early in the previous century.

Fort Ikoma's turreted fortifications, though impressive, were

Fort Ikoma was built by imperial Germany's colonial administration more than a century ago when Berlin ruled this part of East Africa. Perched on the edge of the Rift Valley escarpment and with wildlife everywhere, it should be the ultimate African tourist destination. Instead, Tanzanian bureaucracy has intervened and the place is falling to ruin. (Author's collection)

crumbling. A tourist company, hoping to make some money had spruced the place up during the 1970s and had even added a swimming pool. However, the development didn't work and there wasn't a soul around when we visited the place.

The old fortification had a certain allure about it because of its location. From the balustrades it was possible to observe just about every species of game in East Africa, but that was about all. There was no restaurant, no accommodation, no anything. Even the water had to be filtered if we wished to drink it.

After independence, the place was turned into a military barracks by Julius Nyerere's socialist government and the old fort damaged by neglect. In some places the walls that were once a yard thick had collapsed. If you intend to visit the place, watch out for cobras between the cracks, Hando told us. There seemed to be an awful lot of snakes about.

The Tanzanian government erected these billboards at all the entrances to Serengeti
National Park. (Author's collection)

Our ultimate destination – one of the camps off the Muguma Road – was a couple of hours drive further north, in the direction of Lake Victoria. Not marked on any tourist map, the ranger fort lies in a region that is crossed by the migratory path. Along the way, we encountered tens of thousands of wildebeest as well as countless zebra. Small clusters of predators operated independently along the fringes of this vital, milling mass.

Hyena seemed to be everywhere. Indeed, one of the immediate impressions of Serengeti was that there are probably too many of these ugly beasts. In the old days, their numbers were culled, like vermin, to control their influence within the ambit of the predators, but no more. In some areas they appear to be dominant, robbing cheetah and other cats of their kills.

Our destination was a camp that consisted largely of a square the size of two or three football fields. The entire complex was surrounded by a 12-foot concrete wall with strongpoints at each corner manned by rangers with automatic weapons. Their job was to keep those inside safe from attack.

Hando told us earlier that most of these strongpoints usually housed several dozen people. Rangers rarely travelled to a permanent posting in the bush without their families and contact with the world outside was limited to a single-sideband radio.

A couple of hours before dark, we called into headquarters by radio and said we were heading out. We'd seen what we'd wanted and were eager to move on. Hando came on the line: he was about to call us anyway he said. He didn't want us travelling in that part of the reserve on our own and without an adequate escort, which just about said it all.

One of Africa's finest game parks is under serious threat and the problem is that just about nobody outside Dar es Salaam seems to be aware of it. . .

CHAPTER TWENTY-SIX

The Balkan Beast: Landmines in Croatia

There's an aphorism about landmines in the Balkans. The
Good Lord, say the Croats, created Hell. The Serbs reciprocated and devised the PROM-1, the worst in bounding anti-
personnel mines. Not much bigger than a beer can, this is an
inordinately vicious weapon. Its shrapnel can penetrate almost
any body armour and can cut through the average Kevlar
helmet like cardboard, as it has done often enough for those
who have tried to clear these deadly bombs. Kosovo at one
stage was full of them . . .

B Y THE TIME THAT RICHARD Davis and I got to Croatia at the end of
Balkan War, there weren't many mine-clearing specialists working
there who didn't have something to say about the PROM-1.

The war that preceded these clearing operations had been a bitter
struggle that had left behind a legacy of hundreds of thousands of
casualties. Many were as a consequence of having triggered mines. We
were aware, too, that by the time the Allies eventually clear all of
Kosovo's landmines, there will still be more in other regions where the
fighting had been fierce, Bosnia and Croatia included.

Since it is official that all mines must be cleared – and ultimately,
they will be – it is how this is done that focuses the mind because where
landmines are in the offing, the PROM-1 is among the deadliest.

Mine-clearing teams working those areas are often fortunate to spot
them before they are accidentally detonated. They also need to cope with
the reality that they were originally laid in clusters. When that becomes
apparent, the word is usually whispered down the line and those involved
stop what they're doing to establish the next best course of action.

By the time the Dayton Peace Settlement was signed at Wright
Patterson Air Force Base in November 1995, much thought had already
been given to the best possible way to accomplish some kind of peace
accord between the warring factions in the Balkans. What was certain
was that whoever was involved would be faced with an extremely

Croatian mine-clearer operates a remote bomb-detecting robot that is covering
ground adjacent to a rail track near Gospic in search of mines. (Author's collection)

difficult task and that more casualties would follow. In the words of one
American specialist, 'The problem is that these mines are a bitch to get
at.'

Other issues soon became apparent, including the fact that some
PROM-1s were unstable. The only way to handle them was to destroy
them *in situ*. 'We like to blow 'em where we find 'em', he added

The officer admitted that once buried, the devices were difficult to
spot, especially when the ground was thick with grass and shrubs, which
is how it gets in the Balkans in summer time. You only need to brush
against one of the PROM-1's minuscule protrusions to cause a reaction.
When that happens, the bounding mine is hurled a couple of feet into the
air and the blast that follows will kill just about everything, and
everybody, nearby. It wasn't surprising that one of the hallmarks of Balkan
minefields was the number of dead domestic animals found in them.

Trouble was, the man added, 'the business part that protrudes above
the ground isn't much bigger than a matchbox.'

According to Colonel Richard Todd, then still a youthful American
Special Forces veteran with much experience in both mines and
ordnance that dated back to Vietnam, you have about a 60 per cent

chance of being killed if you are within 30 yards of the explosion. 'It happens so fast', he added, 'that most of those involved usually aren't even aware of what is happening', he reckoned over dinner on our last evening in Zagreb, the Croatian capital.

By then, Todd had been working with mines in the Balkans for several years. He explained why the PROM-1 was deadly.

'Unlike the "popular" Yugoslav PMA-2, the blast mine that you find everywhere in Bosnia, Croatia and Kosovo, the PROM-1 is what is termed in the trade, a group fragmentation mine.' It was designed, he explained, around the original German 'S' mine, which caused such terrible damage in World War II and which the Allies notoriously dubbed 'Bouncing Betty'. That language was carried over into the Vietnam era, but it's in little use today among mine-clearing specialists.

'The trouble with the PROM-1 is that it has a devastating effect when it blows . . . a bit like a proximity fuse on a mortar or artillery shell going off right alongside you', he commented. 'And because it can be laid with multiple trip wires, as the war progressed, it became the obvious weapon of choice among the Serbs. They liked using it because a single PROM-1 could take out a group of people, or even a squad of soldiers on patrol.' Not everybody might have been have killed, he maintained, but the casualties were horrific.

Towards the end of the war, reckoned Todd, the device was increasingly deployed in urban areas. 'They'd been laying them in Kosovo, Bosnia and here in Croatia, almost as if they had a license to do so', he said.

'Some mean weapon, and not to be trifled with', Colonel Todd warned.

When Richard and I met the colonel for the first time, he was at the head of a UN Mine Action Team in Zagreb and he had files full of PROM-1 incidents, some of which made for disturbing reading.

In spite of multiple warnings, PROM-1 casualties continued unabated. A member of his team was killed shortly before we arrived. Operating with dogs in an area-reduction programme, the operator obviously did not spot the mine that either he or the pooch tripped. Two shards of shrapnel penetrated his brain and he was dead in an instant. It was a most unusual phenomenon that his dog, working only yards away, was unharmed. As someone said afterwards, 'Miracles happen . . . even in the Balkans.'

There was nothing whimsical about me and Richard Davis setting out for the Balkans to accompany a mine-clearing team during the

Without dogs, many of the minefields would have been extremely difficult to clear. The hounds would be sent into suspect areas ahead of their handlers and quickly pinpoint explosives. (Author's collection)

course of their duties. Indeed, Richard had been involved with related disciplines for many years. It was he who, several decades before, had invented concealable body amour – otherwise known as 'bullet-proof vests'.

Originally composed of ballistic nylon and, later, of a space-age material called Kevlar, invented by DuPont specifically to provide the motor vehicle industry with safer tyres, these vests had already saved several thousand American lives by the time we got together to go to Croatia, part of what had previously been called Yugoslavia,. Today, there is not a single law enforcement agency in the United States that does not insist on the wearing of body amour during the normal course of duties.

In going to Croatia, we would link up with a group of friends who had previously worked Angolan minefields. In doing so, Richard had a two-fold purpose. First, he believed he might be closer to solving the single biggest problem currently faced by mine-clearers when trying to destroy or lift these bombs: that of injuries to the head caused by close-quarter explosions. Second, he wanted to make a study of issues linked to the industry.

We had no idea of the immensity of the problem. It was only later revealed that something like three million mines were laid in Croatia, the majority along former battle lines. Both sides made liberal use of the bombs, which were quite often laid to protect specific defensive positions. They also had a role in areas of strategic and economic importance like railways, utility stations, pipelines and, for some obscure reason, even within the Plitvice National Park, which somebody explained was an infiltration route.

More importantly, most minefields were unmarked. Even where maps did exist, these were almost always inaccurate. Additionally, as a result of years of fighting, there was a huge amount of unexploded ordnance – UXO. There was more than 300 tons of the stuff in the one area around Dubrovnik alone.

Some idea of what was involved can be gained from the fact that at least 5,200 miles of Croatian territory was littered with mines. In addition there were 3,000 more miles that had to be cleared in Eastern Slavonia, the last Serb-held territory. Nothing about these problems could be regarded as small scale: for instance, more than 15,000 mines were laid in the area behind Sibenik, close to a popular tourist spot, the Krka waterfalls.

The mines took a terrible toll. In the decade after 1990, in excess of 1,000 people were permanently disabled, many with amputations. Other statistics state that more than 300 children were killed, with 1,000-plus injured by mines. A decade on, there have been many more casualties.

Through all this, Richard Davis hadn't been inactive. Indeed, he'd already produced something of an adequate counter to some of the anti-personnel mines that American, British and other coalition forces were encountering in Afghanistan.

What he'd done was to design a reasonably effective way to prevent soldiers having their feet blown off if they triggered an anti-personnel mine. I was fortunate to be involved in first-stage testing processes where explosives were used to establish parameters, all of which took place in the back yard of his home base in Central Lake, Michigan. My job was to take photos of what happened when he detonated a 4-ounce charge to try to destroy a simulated foot.

Richard's thinking on this issue was basic. He created a series of pads that consisted of 40 sheets of Kevlar and which were carefully cut to a relevant boot shape; these would be inserted into the boot. Since the material is quite thin, it is not in any way uncomfortable. In fact, he made a pair of the pads for himself and he'd been wearing them for four months by the time I joined him. They were comfortable enough to be used permanently, he declared.

While 4-ounce charges totally destroyed the pad and the boot, the infantryman's foot, battered, bruised and possibly broken, was saved. As he pointed out, the average former Soviet PMN anti-personnel mine contained roughly 1.3 ounces (0.216 kilograms) of explosives. The Italian

Milelba 'Type A' mine was of a similar weight. And since the pads were able to withstand blasts of double that amount of explosives, he reckoned it would be comforting to the average grunt out on patrol to know that he might not lose a limb, or even part of one if he triggered an anti-personnel mine. Since then, the family company, Armor Express, also of Central Lake, Michigan, has gone into full production of these revolutionary little pads and Davis has patented his invention in 70 countries.[1] Also, scores were passed on to the Department of Defense for testing both in the United States and under combat conditions abroad. A Special Forces group at Fort Bragg received several sets for on-site evaluation.

This is no one-off fad: in 2009 Armor Express was awarded a five-year contract by the Pentagon to supply the United States Marines with combat jackets for use in hot spots like Iraq, Afghanistan and elsewhere. That is in addition to concealable body armour contracts from a host of law enforcement agencies throughout North America.

I put the idea to Richard, at very short notice, of the two of us travelling to Croatia to do a survey of what landmine clearing entailed and he met up with me in London.

Being the more enterprising member of this two-man expedition, he flew in from Detroit with 800 pounds of excess baggage, almost all of it large sheets of Kevlar. These, he explained, would be used to fashion a 'robe' which, though not fully protective against a limited landmine blast, might increase the odds of the victim surviving more or less intact.

With bags, baggage and enough Kevlar to make hundreds of 'vests', we were finally ensconced in two of the finest suites in one of London's best hotels. Meanwhile, I prepared travel plans for the next leg.

Obviously, with Croatia having just emerged from years of conflict, it wouldn't have been wise to fly into Zagreb on a scheduled flight. All that Kevlar in our baggage – six or seven bales of it – would almost certainly have triggered questions. We could only imagine what kind of reaction our luggage might have generated among local customs officials: 'Kevlar? Landmines? Clearing bombs . . . ?'

This sort of thing was still very much restricted where we were heading, the domain of the sanctioned few whose job it was to deal with those problems. Ostensibly, because we didn't have official permission for the task ahead, we intended to declare ourselves as tourists. Kevlar or not, we'd come to see the sights . . .

Finally we managed to work out something feasible. We'd go all the way across Europe by train, first by EuroStar to Brussels where we'd link up with the overnight express to Vienna. From there we'd take one of the smaller lines, across the mountains, through Slovenia and into Croatia. Our friends would be waiting for us at Zagreb.

It was one of the great journeys of my life, which says something because I've travelled a lot. We never skimped on porters and from London's Victoria Station we were safely ensconced in a first-class compartment only minutes after a couple of black cabs had dropped us off.

It was the same in Brussels. The only difference then was that we had our own personal railway carriage for the duration, complete with mahogany-panelled deluxe suites and Fritz, a uniformed butler-type factotum, to attend to all our needs. He stowed the Kevlar, made up our beds, served drinks before dinner and then prepared a five-star meal which, when we eventually arrived at Vienna the following day, earned him a five-star gratuity.

One of the memorable occasions was throwing open the shades of my suite the following morning on the final leg east of Salzburg. We were high in the mountains and, it being summer, everything was lush and green. I was still in bed, drinking coffee that Fritz had served from a silver tray when I was suddenly greeted by a herd of deer pulling away from the train while racing up a fairly steep incline. What a magnificent sight: both unexpected and inspiring.

The tiny rail link across the mountains from Vienna to Slovenia's Ljubljana was even more spectacular. It's a beautiful part of the world, barely

Many of the towns and villages were totally destroyed, like this one near Gospic. The trouble was that some of the ruins had been booby-trapped, or mines had been laid in the vicinity. (Author's collection)

accessed by tourists even in high season. In places the incline was so steep that we might have stepped off the train and walked alongside our coach.

The next stop was Zagreb and, as promised, the guys from the South African mine-clearing company Mechem were waiting for us at the station.

We started early the next day with a briefing on landmines and it was instructive.

There is simply no magic bullet for clearing these things, we were told. In order to do the job effectively, those involved needed to draw from a 'toolbox' of three fundamental disciplines. These were human and mechanical de-miners, as well as dogs that had been trained to find the bombs.

The instructor went on: 'None of these assets on their own can do the job properly. You need one to check the efficacy of the other.' Nor are these disciplines either free or cheap. 'It is expensive to run and maintain a de-mining operation. So too with the specialists who are doing the job: they are paid good money to do a good, if dangerous job.

'So is insurance to cover them in case of accident. Similarly, you constantly need to train more people because nobody stays long in this kind of business. That too, costs money', he stated.

There were then a number of countries clearing mines in the Balkans, all of them involved in seven-figure dollar contracts linked to foreign aid. In Croatia, the Russians were followed by Italy, Germany, Israel, the Netherlands, the United States (Ronco) and Mechem of South Africa. That mix varied with time, but it set the scene. There were also a dozen or so Croatian firms, though their numbers increased with time and gradually took over the bulk of the work, not because they were eager to experience risk, but because of the kind of cash involved. By Croatian standards, these were big bucks. One of the firms involved was Mungos, one of the largest Balkan companies specializing in this sort of work.

Mechem, to whom we were attached – following contracts in Angola and Mozambique – operated with a project leader plus seven others: two team leaders, two dog handlers, a driver/mechanic and a couple of demolition specialists. A former member of the Koevoet counterinsurgency group active in the Border War ran the show. He explained that all his men had good Special Forces military experience and, not to make too fine a point of it, all were trained medics in trauma medicine. 'There have been moments when these attributes have come in pretty handy', he reckoned.

The men worked seven days a week until the contract was complete, in this case, a 60-day signing. To save money, everybody lived rough, usually starting at six and working through to seven or eight at night. They had a meal in the morning before they started and the next time the crew saw food was when they'd finished for the day. Time lost to rain was made up afterwards.

Operating under contract with this foreign mine-clearing team were 40 Croat de-miners headed by four team leaders. Additional crew (according to Croatian law) included two each of doctors, medics, drivers, dog handlers and ambulances plus an interpreter, all of whom had to be paid for by the contract company. Other companies were similarly bound by red tape, which most foreign contractors reckoned was a legacy of the old political system. It didn't take any of us long to see that the majority of ancillary personnel were superfluous and, therefore, a total waste of resources.

Foreign mine-clearing specialists with whom we spoke said that while the quality of Croatian mine-clearing was good, their clearance rate was mediocre. Their lethargic approach to the issue reflected a typical communist attitude to hard work, he suggested. Almost all the expatriates maintained that if they'd been able to bring their own people into the country to do the work, they'd have been able to cut operating crews by half. Others believed that were that to happen, the job would have been done in half the time.

There were several categories of mine-clearing in the Balkans. The first was humanitarian. Because almost everybody was broke, there was precious little money available for mine-clearing areas immediately adjacent to residential areas, often with consequential disastrous results, especially for the younger generation. Most effort was invested in commercial projects, with economic goals such as the one around Gospic, about 100 miles south of Zagreb. This involved the clearing of anti-tank and anti-personnel mines around the only rail link running from the capital to the southern coastal cities of Split and Dubrovnik.

Contractually, the problem at that stage was that landmine clearance only extended to 15 yards or so on either side of the line. It meant that minefields that fringed the line – some of them several acres in extent – remained hazardous because there was no money to penetrate further. By the time we got there, the World Bank had given Zagreb a $7m loan for clearing the bombs, but because the money eventually had to be repaid, the Croats weren't falling over themselves to get the job done.

Thus, while mine-clearing teams had a good handle on what was needed, the civilians who lived and worked in these areas didn't. Their casualties were significant, and after a while, some of the incidents didn't even make the news. In other parts of the country mine detonations occurred just about every week and the consequences were rarely anything less than horrific.

A few days before we arrived in Gospic, one of the local residents was killed after tripping a PROM-1 about 100 yards from the railway station: he'd been walking home from work. A huge hole gouged from the turf was still visible when we got there and we were still able to watch mine-clearers working around the spot.

While driving on isolated country roads around Gospic, we were told that another problem facing mine-clearing teams was a rather obvious lack of patience among local residents to get the job done. Pointing to fresh tractor tracks on both sides of the road, our guide explained: 'Quite often the farmers don't even wait for us to finish. They just ride around and occasionally they'll trip a TMRP-6 (anti-tank mine) which can reduce a three-ton truck to a heap of scrap.'

Or, he reckoned, farm animals would do it for them. The Gospic countryside was littered with the bones of dead cattle and horses. Apparently, it was the same in Kosovo, where locals were anxious to get their lives together again.

One of the more difficult problems in the central Balkan regions was coping with heavy undergrowth or bush, especially in summer. After five years of waiting for mines to be cleared, some parts of what had once been farmland had all but reverted to forest. Before clearance work could be attempted, trees, stumps and other detritus had to be removed so that teams could bring in heavy equipment.

Also, it was dangerous. Everybody involved in this business was aware that mines laid a decade before didn't simply disappear with time. Nor did they become inert because they simply weren't manufactured that way. There are cases on record where landmines laid during the Vietnam War are still being accidentally detonated by civilians.

One of the Mechem technicians considered hiring a Caterpillar, though he wasn't sure what the authorities would say, or, as he admitted over a couple of pints, exactly how its owner might react.

One of the more telling observations during our visit was that because the town of Gospic lies on a main road heading towards the

Dalmatian Coast on the Adriatic Sea, it was often crowded with German and Scandinavian cars heading south for the summer. Very few of these transients were aware that there were mines in the surrounding countryside, or even right alongside the same roads where they'd sometimes stop for a break or to let the kids run around.

The reason for this ignorance was simple: Zagreb did not allow signs to be displayed that might have warned the many thousands of visitors who passed along these roads that the area had once been a war zone, and that there could be landmines. Such signs might affect the tourist industry, the bean-counters argued back at headquarters.

Consequently, said a UN official, most people passing through the country had no idea that they might have stopped on the verge of a minefield. 'Sometimes I see cars parked with children playing in nearby fields. It's only a question of time before there is a disaster', he intimated.

Richard Davis spent several days trying to devise some system that would protect mine-lifting personnel from injury. It wasn't something new. Others had tried and failed, the most common impediment being that crews worked unprotected, out in the open and almost always in the final stages of clearing an area, on their feet. If a mine was tripped, there were no barricades of steel or vehicles to hide behind.

Mines, we discovered soon enough, were there in abundance. But too many of them lay beyond the 15-yard cordon that this and other companies were being paid to make safe.

On an afternoon stroll along a mile or so of rail lines to the south of Gospic, Richard and I – carefully choosing to walk *on* the rail ties, rather than beside or between them – came to a field where, over several years, dozens of anti-tank mines had been exposed by rain.

There was simply no ignoring these perfectly round, bulky cheese-shaped steel bombs with their screw-pin detonators sticking out on top, all clear as day and lying randomly out in the open. The only problem for the Mechem team was that they lay beyond their designated contract area. Somebody else would eventually have to be brought in to dispose of them.

For the personal protection of individual mine-clearers, Richard initially believed that he might have something of a solution by designing a 'wrap-around' Kevlar robe that would protect the technician, literally, from the ground up. It was a huge sheet of the material that completely surrounded the man. Also, it opened out on top, above his head, the idea being to deflect the blast upwards. Amour-plated glass would have to be sewn into the front area to allow for visibility.

Possibly the single biggest problem facing the modern-day mine-clearer is that while there is good quality padded protection available for the job, none of it is perfect. Also, it can be bulky or unwieldy. In summer, anything constricting quickly becomes intolerable.

In any blast – where temperatures of about 3,000° Centigrade might be generated – the head of the individual involved is the most exposed and, obviously, the most vulnerable part of the body. Also, helmets normally worn by mine-clearers when out in the field (and which resemble the kind of gear used by welders) are open along the bottom where this protection sits on the chest. Obviously, that would mean that any kind of blast from below would totally envelop the head. Even worse, such high temperatures usually result in the victim's eyes being vaporized.

Richard believed that by making a single-piece garment that the clearer slipped on over his head and reached all the way down to the ground would eliminate that threat. Obviously the arms would have to be accommodated, a simple matter to somebody who was already making a huge range of body amour in his Central Lake factories.

While in Gospic, Richard made a number of sketches. He even got one of the local women to stitch something together for him. While it was light and pliable enough even if it did look like something out of *Star Wars*, the new development didn't fit the bill. In fact, a single garment, for all its other advantages, impeded the kind of sensitive touch needed for detecting and uncovering landmines.

There were several other computations considered, usually in consultation with some of the mine-clearers, but nothing feasible emerged. In any event, after a week, it was time to go.

Richard intended returning to Croatia a couple of months later with one or two more prototypes, but before we knew it, Mechem had completed their contract and were out of there. Some of the men who had hosted us were heading either for Angola or Cambodia.

As for the body armour project for mine-clearers that Richard David had initially been focused on, he tried to get something going but there were no takers either in Zagreb, the Croatian capital, or anywhere else in the Balkans. We'd taken half a ton of Kevlar to the region as baggage, in itself worth a small fortune, but in the end, nothing happened.

CHAPTER TWENTY-SEVEN

Balkan War Joint-STARS Offensive

The Joint-STARS, or more correctly, the Joint-Surveillance
Target Attack Radar System concept, has been described by an
American pundit as having the potential for doing for modern
warfare what the Internet achieved for communications. He
reckoned that real-time display of movement on computer
consoles on board aircraft would ultimately change the way
that wars are fought . . .

GOING INTO A CONFLICT WITH the US Air Force must be one of the
great experiences in any war buff's life. My turn came in the
Balkans in the summer of 1996 when Operation Joint Endeavour was
drawing to a close. It involved sorties in Joint-STARS – an airborne
battle management, command and control, intelligence, surveillance and
reconnaissance platform – as well as a series of in-flight refuelling
operations in regions adjacent to where the war was being fought.

The primary mission of Joint-STARS has been described as the
ability to provide theatre ground and air commanders with ground surveillance to support attack operations, and targeting that contributes to
the delay, disruption and destruction of enemy forces.

As explained by one of the officers on board our modified 707-300
series former commercial jet, which had once been used to haul cattle in the
Mid-West (the other in Frankfurt at the time had ended its commercial
career with Qantas), the aircraft had, in a sense, not only been modified, but
'remanufactured'. With the requisite radar, communications, operations and
control sub-systems required to perform its operational mission, it allowed
field commanders to see, as he succinctly put it, 'well beyond the other side
of the hill'.

As might have been expected, Joint-STARS operations have since
been seen as a feature of other conflicts, including all of those currently
taking place east of Suez. This activity has also been very substantially
upgraded, and was sensitive and secret enough, at the time, to be
guarded by armed personnel who were posted alongside these aircraft

whenever they were parked on the apron at Frankfurt. Their orders, we were told at our first briefing, were explicit: 'If any unauthorized individual approaches Joint-STARS aircraft, shoot to kill . . .'

As my informant explained, 'given the acknowledged dependence of armies on wheels [or tracks] for much of their mobility, heavy firepower, armoured protection, supplies and engineering support, the ability of the Joint-STARS system to detect, locate and target these assets in any sort of weather or cloud cover must be a huge advantage that today's armed forces must still fully exploit.' Ultimately, he added, it would involve a totally different approach to warfare itself. It would affect how armies and air forces are eventually deployed in combat and even how they might be equipped.

I applied to go in with the USAF to cover this aspect of the Kosovo war on a whim. I was living in Chinook, Washington, and the great McChord Air Force base was kind of 'up the road' – though still four or five hours drive away, depending on the weather – so I used my Jane's cachet to gain entry. A week later the trip was on.

I was told that I'd be going in with Japan-based *Newsweek* lensman Charlie Cole, an adventurous news-gatherer who, among other exploits, regularly made his name by being in the right place at the right time. He was at Beijing's Tiananmen Square when Chinese troops and tanks dispersed dissidents and the photo he took at the time made history: a lonely student protestor who challenged supreme authority by standing in front of one of the tanks. The young man was taken away by the police and never seen again. Charlie's picture of the event appeared later that week on the cover of *Newsweek*, taken in spite of the presence of a group of security guards with cattle prods who tried to keep the media at bay.

Back in the United States, prior to leaving for the Balkans – and with our appropriate security clearances in place – we were told to report to McChord the day before we were due to leave. On

Charlie Cole standing in front of a US jet fighter. (Charlie Cole)

arrival, Charlie and I were given our own quarters in the wing normally reserved for generals, complete with well-stocked mini-bars that were operated on the 'honour' basis. While a lot was taken for granted, not everything came free.

What we were told shortly after we arrived at the base was that we were to fly to Europe in a C-141 StarLifter, that beautiful old workhorse of Air Mobility Command that has since been superseded by the even more expansive C-17. A four-engine jet, the C-141 (it was finally retired from active service early in the new millennium) had an overall length of 168 feet and a payload approaching 50 tons.

It was interesting that one of the first publications I inadvertently paged through while sitting in the cockpit after take-off, was a booklet with the words 'Top Secret' printed in large letters on its cover. A most interesting document, it provided complete instructions on stowing thermonuclear bombs on board. I was obviously spotted and later, when I wanted to reacquaint myself with some of the details, it had mysteriously disappeared. Somebody onboard obviously decided that this scribe had no business going through such sensitive material.

The Balkans conflict was one of the last big operations involving C-141s. Late in 1995, the Pentagon ordered the deployment of 20,000 US troops to the former Yugoslav Republic of Bosnia as part of a multinational peacekeeping force. Eighteen crews and six aircraft from McChord were in place at Rhein-Main Air Base, Germany, by mid December that year, ready to play their part. In spite of severe weather conditions, McChord crews and aircraft were soon flying troops and equipment into Tazsar, Hungary, for Operation Joint Endeavour.

The flight to Frankfurt was a delight. There were two stops, the first at McGuire Air Force Base in New Jersey and from there on to the Portuguese-held Azores in the middle of the Atlantic Ocean. It was dinner time when we got there, and we had time on hand while freight on board was offloaded and the plane refuelled to enjoy a few rounds at the local bowling rink on the periphery of the island's civilian/military air base.

Once airborne again, it was time for bed. There are enough bunks onboard the StarLifter to allow every member of the crew at least a few hours of prostrate shut-eye. I asked to be woken about an hour out of Frankfurt and slept in total comfort throughout.

Having flown between Europe and America more than 100 times in a professional career that spans decades, this trip, I discovered, was the most

USAF strategic bomber and transporter – now phased out of service – that took us to Europe and back again from the McChord Air Force Base in Washington. (Author's Collection)

pleasant crossing ever. What's more, the trip on board the C-141 was courtesy of the US government, which underscores my most basic personal premise about journalism: it is better than working . . .

Having been ensconced in Frankfurt, Charlie and I became integral members of the crew after we'd all been billeted in one of the local hotels. Daily, depending on the nature of the mission, we'd be taken through security to whichever area we'd be flying sorties from.

One of our first tasks was viewing air-to-air refuelling from one of several USAF KC-10 and KC-135 'flying tankers', which returned to Germany after a good day's work. Though pretty mundane to those doing this sort of thing each day, each sortie had its moments, especially since we were usually operating almost within sight of what was then still the Yugoslavian coast.

It was a massive operation and in the final weeks there were almost 4,500 personnel from a dozen NATO countries including Canada, France, Germany, Italy, Spain, Turkey, the United Kingdom and the United States. At any one time there were more than 100 NATO aircraft in the air around us, the majority heading in from air bases in France, Germany, Greece, Italy and the United Kingdom or from aircraft carriers in the Adriatic.

Sometimes, it would be only half a minute between one of the fighter jets having topped up and another arriving under our port or starboard wings to do the same. Since we were linked to the cockpit, we could listen to all transmissions taking place, including some fighters heading in to us with almost-empty fuel tanks and perhaps a minute of flying time left.

It sometimes needed a pretty deft hand at the controls to manoeuvre these fighters into position under the boom so that the receiving receptacle atop the fighter's fuselage could marry with the fuel line.

Apart from the usual range of USAF F-15s, F-16s, and F-18s, and US Navy EA-6Bs, there were also French-built Mirage 2000 fighter and ground-attack aircraft, Super Etendard and Jaguar fighter-bombers as well as Tornados operating from a variety of air bases in Italy, including Istrana, Gioia de Colle, Practica di Mare and a host of others. Add to those tallies Dutch F-16s, British GR-7 Harriers as well as Sea Harriers, Spanish EF-18s, German Jaguars, Turkish F-16s and many others. All had their specific requirements and some were thirstier than others.

It was, as one British journalist described it after seeing this operation from up close, 'a veritable air armada'. As he declared, it involved the most modern planes available from many like-minded nations and was something that modern-day Europe had never before experienced on this scale.

To us supernumeraries, it was interesting that the KC-10 from which we took many of our pictures is a military version of the McDonnell Douglas DC-10 and can carry an average payload of 40 tons. The KC-135, used for in-flight refuelling, is a military version of the Boeing 707.

We were to discover afterwards that in an effort to improve the capabilities of the Air Mobility Command (AMC) tanker fleet, and to provide support to carrier-based aircraft, wing-mounted drogue refuelling pods were installed on a number of both KC-10s and KC-135s. This was done largely to provide the extra margin of receiver safety necessary for over-water operations.

Everything linked to fuel delivery took place at the rear of the plane, where we would sit in comfortable seats and view the process from up close. We could wave at the pilots if we caught their eye, though most of the time they were preoccupied with monitoring a situation that could rapidly become critical if not properly handled.

Since some of this work took place over enemy territory, combat jets that came in never switched off their weapons systems during the refuelling process. Several times we'd watch a pilot break off contact and swerve away, sometimes violently. Their onboard radar had picked up hostile emissions from the ground.

As it was explained afterwards at a pre-flight briefing back at base, the Serbs needed to activate their ground control stations in order to

View from refueller of an F-16 being refuelled during the Balkan War. (Charlie Cole)

'lock onto' NATO aircraft flying above if they were to have any hope of firing their SAMs, of which they had an inordinate number. Almost all the missiles were of Soviet origin and quite a few were very sophisticated indeed. Occasionally, Coalition aircraft were fired at, but the moment the enemy activated its missile radar systems, all fighter planes in the vicinity would be alerted. Within moments, several clutches of missiles would be heading in towards the target on the ground.

Quite a few Serbian anti-aircraft crews died in such strikes. To us, flying at a moderate height in an unarmed, converted passenger jet, the support was comforting. It was good to learn afterwards that NATO forces never lost a single airborne tanker as a result of enemy activity.

The refuelling system was basic. In the KC-135, the boom operator worked in a prone position. In the KC-10, by contrast, there was a small chamber at the rear with three seats and a large reinforced window, almost two by six feet in size, which the operator used to observe everything going on below. The boom would be lowered and he'd watch the receiving aircraft coming in, directing him by radio if necessary to make small adjustments in speed or altitude.

We'd observe the entire process carefully while a system of mirrors allowed the 'boomer' to monitor other aircraft in formation off the KC-10 wing tips. The boom was ten feet longer than the KC-135's and featured 'fly by wire' flight controls and an increased fuel transfer rate of up to 1,500 gallons per minute.

Then followed our sortie on board one of the Joint-STARS Boeings, which almost didn't happen for me because my security clearance hadn't come through from Washington by the time that crew call was sounded. Five minutes later, one of the officers poked his head through a door and gave a shout. I was on my way, the first non-American civilian to have this experience.

But first, some background to what it's all about.

One of the concepts that originally brought the Joint-STARS project to fruition was the fundamental truth about conflict: in war, he who achieves better movement on the battlefield invariably dictates its outcome. That little maxim is as apposite today as it was in the time of Napoleon's swift attack at Austerlitz. It was equally valid in Vietnam and in Operation Desert Storm, which is one of the reasons why the system is referred to as 'The Window to the Battlefield'.

The difference today is that Joint-STARS is designed to give those involved in a ground war – whether it be Kosovo, Iraq, the Philippines or Afghanistan (or Syria or Iran in the future) – the living dynamics of the battlefield. Most significant, it comes in real time.

In the same way that the E3 Sentry (AWACS) provides all-weather surveillance, command, control and communications in the air, the Joint-STARS concept is land-fixated. Operational procedures allow it to act in concert with ground-hugging AH-64 Longbow Apaches by digitally passing along targeting information. Co-ordinated with a good mix of manned and unmanned assets, it has the potential for a truly seamless data transition, either in peacekeeping or in the sort of debacle that the Allies faced in Kosovo.

When we were aloft over Kosovo there were four or five of these machines in full operation, several of them based in Okinawa to monitor developments in North Korea and, obviously, offshore China. The tally of converted Boeing 707-300 series aircraft for this work is ultimately likely to number more than two dozen, with a fair proportion designated for the Far East.

As explained by Lieutenant Colonel Kevin C. Peterson and Major Phillip G. Basinger in a post-Kosovo report, the Joint-STARS is an Army-Air Force system designed to provide immediate surveillance intelligence, targeting, and battle management to the land component commander:

> The system is made to support a corps-size unit and consists of a USAF and Army aircrew, and what we like to call the 'business end of the system', the Ground Station Module (GSM), operated by the Army.
>
> The E-8, using its chin-mounted multimode radar, collects moving target indicators (MTIs), fixed target indicators (FTIs) as well as synthetic aperture radar (SAR) imagery. It downlinks all this information to the GSM.
>
> GSMs not in the footprint of the aircraft data-link might task another GSM to relay the data through a satellite at a reduced data rate using built-in satellite communications radio.
>
> Once fielded to military intelligence (MI), aviation, and artillery units, the GSM will be the most numerous MI end-item in the Army, located from maneuver brigade up through echelons above corps (EAC).

Our crew on take-off from Frankfurt numbered 23. Two were US Army specialists, one of whom was the deputy mission crew commander (DMCC), and this pair operated at the rear of the plane in conjunction with the air force specialists onboard. It was their job, together with those manning the other 16 work stations, to provide intelligence and targeting information to the Combined Air Operations Centre (CAOC) at its Southern European headquarters in Italy.

Information requests such as area searches, SAR images, and a good deal else besides, were relayed through workstations on board. There were a number of variations: more requests for data that came in from the Joint Analysis Centre at Molesworth in England (one of the primary downlink points for Joint-STARS data) or an asset on the ground that needed clarification about something that was visual.

There was also a direct link with our aircraft's airborne adjunct, the

EC-130 Airborne Battlefield Command, Control and Communications (ABCCC) and with the Army's Ground Station Module through a secure Surveillance Control Data Link. I was told that up to 15 ground stations could simultaneously pass text messages back to the Joint-STARS and our three VHF radios were primarily used to communicate with them.

Once 'in orbit' adjacent to Kosovo, the aircraft flew tight figure-of-eight circuits of classified length. If anything on the ground moved, the aircraft, in theory, would detect, locate and support attacks against it. Because visibility was not a factor, no matter what the weather, such operations could go on around the clock, though most missions are a bit more than half a day. Ours lasted 14 hours and included an in-flight refuelling session from a KC-125 tanker.

Long hours aloft should be truly boring. However, in reality it stayed interesting from the start because there was always something happening. On one of the earliest flights over Kosovo, before we got there, one plane hadn't been on-station for an hour when it was thrown into an almost vertical dive. That left some crew members who hadn't been strapped in clinging to the roof of the aircraft.

No reason for evasive action was given. However, the crew was aware that such things only happened if threatened by hostile missile or aircraft action. What was clear was that there were either enemy fighters scrambling or there had been a missile alert.

The threat factor stayed sobering while we were aloft. Crews have refused to remain on-station without a combat air patrol (CAP), though numbers and types of fighter escorts were secret. The crew was emphatic: 'No CAP and we're out of here', they would state.

The Joint-STARS defensive strategy is simple. Should enemy aircraft suddenly become a threat, the crew wouldn't waste time before heading in the opposite direction.

The issue of Yugoslavian ground-to-air missiles remained uppermost in all our minds while we were up there. From what I was able to observe on the consoles, mobile SAM-6 batteries were thick on the ground in Kosovo. There were also long-range SAM-3 batteries, some of which had been targeted by the time we arrived, according to a Pentagon briefing a month earlier.

Certainly, that destructive potential was raised often enough during the course of hostilities. Missile (and Triple-A) threats, while not taken lightly, were invariably balanced against intelligence reports from ground observers and the fact that any Joint-STARS orbit was always beyond the maximum missile target range of the latest version of ground-to-air missiles that Belgrade acquired over the years from Moscow. Almost everything in the Serbian armoury, we were aware, was former Soviet Union in origin.

It was interesting that during our flight there were some active concentrations of ground forces radar-tracked near the southern and eastern borders of Kosovo. There were also indications of a lot of activity along the Albanian and Macedonian frontiers and it quickly became clear that the Yugoslav Army was preparing for a major ground action.

No US spokesmen would comment on this aspect, even though in places the ground was cluttered with hardware. That included armour, which indicated a substantial military presence.

Meanwhile, the US Air Force has lifted some security restrictions surrounding the ability of its long-range, air-to-ground surveillance system to locate, classify and track in virtually any weather, on-line and in near real-time, a variety of enemy ground targets.

Although the concept is old hat – a prototype Joint-STARS test-bed was originally used to track, locate and target Iraqi divisions in Operation Desert Storm (especially during the Battle of Al-Khafji) and Airborne Reconaissance Low (ARL) and the Mohawk systems are also active – very little about this long-range detection weapon has been made public.

Tactically, the Joint-STARS system operates from the safety of friendly airspace. Our aircraft, for instance, was able to peer about 150 miles across borders and do a stand-off analysis of enemy ground assets. Each aircraft carried a phased-array, mechanically operated radar antenna housed in a 25-foot dome or 'canoe' under the forward fuselage area. It weighed tons and we could feel it thudding as it alternated its scanning role from port to starboard. That equipment provided the necessary data for pinpoint strikes by aircraft, missiles or artillery for fire support.

We were also told that Joint-STARS ground-tracking radar, in a single eight-hour sortie, could search an estimated 200,000 square miles of terrain, though the officer warned that the aircraft was unable to identify targets. Other assets such as Unmanned Aerial Vehicles (UAVs) or Human Intelligence (Humint) might have been used to clarify the information still further.

Most details regarding operational and acquisition procedures on board Joint-STARS aircraft remained classified. However, information made available in a briefing by the unit commander at the Rhein-Main Air Force Base, indicated that its fundamental operating modes included Wide Area Moving Target Indicator (MTI) surveillance and Synthetic Aperture Radar (SAR).

Covering a 60-square-mile block, the images brought up on the aircraft's monitors could be split into eight grid areas. These were electronically scanned in azimuth with a rapid revisit rate of seconds. Or it could be narrowed down to search an area of a bit more than a square mile.

Depending on earlier intel reports – or something spotted on the screen – potential targets might have been subjected to intensive repetitive sector searches. Movement detection involved a Doppler shift system coupled to phased array radar.

For example, the system was sensitive enough to differentiate (but not specifically identify) between wheeled and tracked vehicles, picking up a reading bounced off the tracks of a moving tank or APC. This appeared on the monitor as a yellow dot: in the area over which we were orbiting there were stacks of them. What happened was that the MTI displayed moving vehicles or amour as moving imagery (dots) and SAR as still photos. Also, as we could see, MTI could be displayed on a variety of backgrounds from SARs to military maps to slope-shaded maps.

Much of the technology was space-age stuff. For instance, rudimentary analysis was provided by Joint-STARS' Synthetic Aperture Radar/Fixed Target Indicator (SAR/FTI), which produced area images almost comparable to the negative of a photo, complete with shadows off surrounding mountains. In some areas the effect was almost 3-D.

By pushing out energy bursts in a succession of small grids (which, in turn, sent back images) it was able to identify clearly features such as runways, buildings, and aircraft on the ground, or even rail tracks. In turn, the system sounded out reflective energy, or, in the argot, 'fine imagery'.

Another revolutionary development, and one more pointer to the future, was that each set of images could be automatically stored in electronic target folders and immediately downloaded into the aircraft's database. Ground activity on a particular day might be called up on the aircraft's computers an hour or a month later to examine before-and-after anomalies. Thus, our Joint-STARS platform had the ability to indicate immediately whether there had been any new troop arrivals, or, possibly, fresh construction sites in the area of operations.

In another area it might pinpoint repairs surreptitiously being made to a bridge that had been bombed a day or three months before. SAR data maps of Kosovo contained the precise locations of critical non-moving targets such as bridges, secreted motor pools, harbours, factories, airports, buildings or camouflaged vehicles as well as armour.

Obviously, anything new-fangled always has detractors. From my own observations, the system appeared to be cumbersome. Following some serious tactical blunders that left innocents dead, follow-through instructions for any attack were always very carefully assessed (and sometimes re-assessed). Any strike needed to be filtered through half a dozen or more commands, having first been cleared from above. It could be a time-consuming process. Also, targets needed to be cleared by all NATO member nations, of which there were 19 at the time. That implied very specifically that this was the first war fought by 'committee'. Even the original Korean War of the 1950s, a UN campaign from beginning to end, wasn't hampered by anywhere near as much bureaucracy or obfuscation.

There are also those who reckon that the Joint-STARS system might have been too complex for the job, though this would be ignoring the basics of a quite remarkable system that was regarded as impractical a couple of decades ago. From personal observation, it was clear that there were time-delays in acquiring information and processing detail for a strike, which sometimes took a while. The sighting, for instance, of a tank or an enemy convoy on the ground, followed by a command to a fighter strike element nearby, might involve a ten-minute time lapse, sometimes longer. Independent verification, often from intelligence elements on the ground (an essential adjunct), involved still more time. By then the target might have disappeared into a mountain hideaway.

In an article titled 'Too Much Data, Too Little Intelligence?' the role of Joint-STARS in peacekeeping operations in Bosnia was analyzed by Lieutenant Colonel Colin Agee, deputy commander of an Airborne Military Intelligence Brigade out of Fort Bragg.

While conceding that Joint-STARS was lauded as a 'star performer' in Desert Storm, he wrote in Jane's *IDR Extra* (May 1997) that as the IFOR mission proceeded, 'the use of Joint-STARS to track military movement became harder', in particular because of the difficult terrain. He went on:

> Perhaps the biggest challenge to effective use of the system was data overload: the inability to distinguish significant MTIs from

the voluminous data stream . . . The screen would quickly fill with MTIs, making it difficult to determine those of military significance.' From personal observation (last May), it appeared to this observer that the system still needed some fine-tuning and on the face of it, still worked best with a good pair of eyes on the ground.

As he pointed out, during the first month of operations over the Balkans, the aircraft seemed to be hampered by a variety of technological problems, particularly in a flying electronic platform with so much potential for glitches. Any operational Joint-STARS flight has two electronics technicians onboard, but even then things happen.

In an early flight, one of the workstations had to be shut down because of smoke fumes detected by a crew member. Another report in *Aviation Week* (3 May 1999) said that their aircraft operated with a poor satellite communications antenna and a faulty vapour-cycle cooling system, which made for a cold working environment.

Also, trying to keep the aircraft in the air needs about 60 ground maintenance personnel and they seem to have done well. In the first month of Kosovo operations, the unit missed only one flight, significant because both planes were deployed over the Balkans every day. It was accepted logic that to be truly effective, three such aircraft were needed to provide NATO with around-the-clock surveillance.

The role of the Joint-STARS unit in southern Europe, we were initially briefed, was threefold.

In the Balkans war, Joint-STARS provided indications and warnings of friendly and enemy movement on the ground.

Its surveillance system allowed for intelligence assessment and, as a consequence, intensive preparation for future battlefield activities.

The system is totally uninhibited by cloud cover. A well-defined and powerful line-of-sight communications system, once on-station (and in conjunction with E-3 Sentry AWACS elements) becomes a factor in the further deployment of other airborne elements of the Theater Air Control Systems (AETACS). These can include assets such as the Air Force RC-135V/W River Joint (Sigint), an occasional U2, the Navy's EP3, the Royal Navy's Nimrod Electronic Intelligence Gathering aircraft, France's RC12 surveillance system, Airborne Forward Air Control

(ABFAC) as well as ABCCC along with ground TACS units.

Operating in a region as rugged and mountainous as the Balkans presents its own peculiar set of problems. Since the system is line-of-sight, the high, broken Balkan terrain tended to influence surveillance coverage through screening and disrupting communications. I was to observe that shadows caused by the mountainous terrain could be seen clearly on the SARs. Also, the shadow effect tended to assist the adversary in concealing assets.

Clearly, this affected radar images as much as it did contact with clandestine units on the ground – London sources indicated to this writer that 'some' British SBS (Special Boat Service) personnel were active inside Kosovo at the time and that American SEALS might have infiltrated Kosovo in small groups and were liaising with KLA forces active inside the disputed territory.

The SAR and FTI capability used in conjunction with MTI and MTI-history displays allowed a limited post-attack assessment to be made by operators following a strike on hostile targets. Significantly, major advanced elements of the programme included software-intensive radar with several operating modes; the unique antenna with three receive ports; four high-speed processors capable of performing more than 600 million operations per second, as well as associated software.

In effect, though, while Joint-STARS is the magic bullet of the future and tends to reduce the need for visual armed reconnaissance sorties to locate targets, keeping friendly casualties to a minimum, it could never dispense with the human element altogether. The system works as follows.

While possibly monitoring a number of frequencies simultaneously, Joint-STARS – in conjunction with Combined Air Operations Centre – spots a convoy of vehicles moving somewhere within the target area of the future. First the specific area is electronically isolated. It is analyzed and assessed by ground staff at CAOC as well as by Joint-STARS personnel. Finally, the potential target is referenced to previous electronic imagery in the onboard database and graded according to priority. If the subject is confirmed hostile by other theatre assets, ABCCC might then order in a strike wing.

Prior to leaving Frankfurt, the pilot would receive pre-flight briefings that included details of up to 20 priority targets. All would have been pre-located by a combination of UAVs or the activity of infiltrated agents or something spotted on the ground by previous Joint-STARS flights.

Once in orbit I was shown the day's target list that had been numbered according to priority. Meanwhile, the Mission Crew Commander (MCC) would start at the top and try to work his way down – in conjunction with a variety of strike assets that would do the actual hits – though the system was flexible. If something else of significance came up in the interim, it would have been targeted. Ultimately, the objective was that the Joint-STARS MCC would be working indirectly with AH-64 Apaches, though that concept still needed a measure of streamlining.

The choice of using sixties-vintage Boeing 707s as vehicles for the E-8C Joint-STARS programme – many of them acquired abroad from a variety of commercial airlines – was unusual. Most of the pilots complained about these Boeing 707s being underpowered. Others would have preferred more altitude.

Several factors for the choice prevailed, including budget constraints. Another was safety; the 707 passenger jet still holds the best commercial safety record. One of the officers involved disclosed that once the decision to proceed had been made, they scoured the world for them.

Size was of paramount importance. The 707 has the advantage of holding more of the operator workstations that are essential for onboard battle management. The need for more additional workstations has been seen in AWACS, simply because they influence the span of both intelligence and control, which, in the words of a spokesman for the manufacturers of the system, 'are key factors in J-STARS' ability to target large numbers of dynamic [moving] targets'.

The contract to deliver – initially at a cost of about $225m per machine, but these days, a good deal more – was awarded to the Northrop Grumman Corporation. The first four systems had an 11-hour endurance (22-hour flights with in-flight refuelling were routine).

The electronics on board any one of these aircraft were formidable and, since those early sorties in the Balkans, have been supplemented by a good deal more. Even then it was stressed that a single Joint-STARS Boeing 707 platform had a greater computer capacity than all the combined assets of America's E-3 Sentry (AWACS) together: the USAF had 33 AWACS in its inventory at the time.

The main computers on board at that stage were 6 Mil Vax 866 mainframe computers. Two were systems monitoring, one was a hot spare. Three more were general-purpose computers, one of which handled local area network (LAN), another radar and the last was also a spare. Each of the 18 operational workstations on board was a Digital Equipment Corporation machine with a 133 Mhz processor, 512 MBs of RAM and two multi-GB hard drives (obviously this would be much advanced at the end of the first decade of the new millennium).

A point made by a technician on board was that they are prohibited from switching on the system over developed areas. The power activates every electronic garage door below the aircraft track.

Operating in the crowded air lanes over Southern Europe presented other problems. Balkan airspace was sometimes so crowded that it could be harrowing. Our own flight had a narrow miss with a fighter while on-station. A day later a Joint-STARS Boeing 707 en route to the Adriatic avoided a head-on collision with a passenger jet by going into a dive, pulling four or five Gs. Wrong data had apparently been given to the oncoming plane. Later the same day, there was another near miss in cloudy conditions when two of the escort fighters had to take evasive action within a couple of hundred yards of the Joint-STARS aircraft.

Several observers were of the opinion that allied aircraft proved to be a greater threat than any fighters that the Yugoslav Air Force might have been able to muster. Also, there was a lot of adverse comment about the ability of military ATC personnel to control the air movement associated with the campaign, which is possibly a lesson for the future about working over densely populated areas. Air traffic control was so bad sometimes that Joint-STARS aircrews were frequently ordered to operate under the 'see and avoid' rule.

As for the threat of enemy fighters, which anywhere else might have caused problems, the US Air Force had not yet funded a self-protection suite for Joint-STARS. NATO intelligence was only too well aware that a number of Yugoslav Air Force MiG-21s were stationed at Pristina, only minutes' flying time from where we were airborne. They apparently resisted attack because all were secreted in deep mountainside hangers that made conventional attack impossible for the duration of the war.

It was interesting that the one time that Belgrade attempted to put Yugoslav Air Force MiGs in the air – possibly in a bid to stymie Joint-STARS activity – it took a handful of Coalition planes only 39 seconds to shoot down three of them.

CHAPTER TWENTY-EIGHT

Helicopter Drug Raids in Zululand

One of the interesting asides made in Parliament in Cape Town recently was that marijuana is still the biggest cash crop in South Africa's KwaZulu/Natal.

T HE HELICOPTER-ORIENTATED OPERATION along the Tugela River in the KwaZulu/Natal Midlands in the winter of 2006 lasted three weeks. Though conditions were tough, we ended up destroying the equivalent of about 20 tons of what some people like to call 'wacky backy'. Others know it as marijuana, pot, cannabis, grass, widow, ganga, weed or, more colloquially to Amsterdam's coffee shop imbibers, Durban Gold.

On this trip to KwaZulu/Natal (still called Zululand by the majority of people who live there), I joined a group of cops searching for the drug in a huge inland part of the country that adjoins the Indian Ocean.

Because of the season, it wasn't the plants that we targeted. There were many of them, of course, sprouting early in just about every little valley, cranny and secluded canyon, but it was the seeds we were after.

Backed by a combined paramilitary police and army contingent, armed elements were dropped at short notice by chopper into some of the most remote corners of the region. The men would go in and without formality, knock down doors and, on several occasions, walls. The search was basic: a hunt to find the secreted little kernels that were perhaps a quarter the size of the average match-head. In places they were found bundled together in tins, 44-gallon fuel containers and plastic bottles, sometimes millions of seeds in a single hideaway.

Most were hidden in drums, sometimes a hundredweight of seeds at a time. Others were wrapped in plastic and covered in sack-cloth to keep the damp out. Still more were stashed under beds, in cupboards or buried in the ground. One batch that must have weighed 50 pounds was discovered under an old bath that had been turned upside down in the back yard of a school.

There was a lot of money invested in the business, especially when you consider that a lone marijuana seed can fetch anything between $2

Drums of seed were recovered, worth millions of dollars on the open market. A single seed sells for several dollars on the British market and there are millions of seeds in this can alone. (Louis de Waal)

and $8 dollars on the clandestine London market. Much depends on supply and demand and, obviously, when the time is right, a bagful might easily be worth a fortune. One South African visitor who smuggled the dried, seed-rich bud of a single marijuana plant to London recently and boasted about it afterwards, said that he sold his little pile – that probably wouldn't have filled a matchbox – for almost $300.

At one stage while working with the police out of Winterton, a small town in the foothills of the Drakensberg Mountains, I had a drum of the stuff in my hotel room and it stayed there for a week. Under appropriate conditions and with the right contacts, the pile (that could have weighed about 60 pounds) might easily have bought me a comfortable home somewhere outside London.

Finding the stuff wasn't easy. Marijuana seeds are an extremely valuable commodity in societies where money is scarce. The narcotic is composed largely of a dry, shredded, green-brown mix of flowers, stems, leaves and seeds and is more commonly called dagga in South Africa. It is said to be regularly used by about four per cent of the world's population and, according to the UN Office on Drugs and Crime, about 0.6 per cent daily. While it is not the most potent mind-altering substance, its major biologically active chemical compound is tetrahydrocannabinol (delta-9-tetrahydrocannabinol), commonly referred to as THC,[1] and today it is acknowledged by the experts to be about a dozen times stronger than the same weed passed around by some parents and grandparents during the 1960s and 1970s.

What is immediately obvious to those involved, on both sides of the law, is that like cocaine and heroin, the sale and export of marijuana has become a hugely lucrative business. Also, the ramifications are thoroughly international. One of the chief suppliers of pot – specifically to the European market – is Southern Africa.

Intrinsically, our role was to remove – by force, if necessary and invariably backed by firepower – what was sometimes the only source of income for a community. In some places it was the sole means of support for entire groups of families. It was tough work, hard on the body and on emotions in an environment where many people hardly have enough cash to put bread on the table for their kids.

However, whether in KwaZulu/Natal in South Africa, in British Columbia or Peru, or along the length of the Rogue River in Oregon where some of America's finest dope is produced, it is against the law to possess the stuff, never mind grow it commercially for an always expanding export market. In all these countries, national or parliamentary edicts dictate the law.

One of the immediate consequences of what we were doing was that while we remained active in the eradication process, we were under constant threat. While our choppers weren't fired on from the ground in that operation, they had been at other times. Also, quite a few of those arrested in this pursuit were armed.

More worrying, this was 'high octane work' as it was phrased by a journalist who accompanied us, accentuated by the fact that almost all of the cops with whom we operated had been wounded at least once before, because such is the nature of crime in South Africa these days.

Zwoyo Ntoshabala was a member of our group. A 28-year-old constable with South Africa's crack National Intervention Unit (NIU), his list of wounds in action included blast trauma in an explosion in a house that had been booby-trapped by a drug lord.

Sterre Wandrag, a 37-year-old captain with the NIU had been shot in his buttocks before he joined us in Winterton. Even more serious were wounds sustained by Captain Craig Benn, a 42 year-old NIU Captain. Apart from being hit on the head with a hammer – a powerful blow that was intended to kill him – he had previously been shot twice in the chest, once more in the thigh and another time in his foot. Craig has since left the force in disgust.

The man running ground operations in Zululand was 48-year-old Captain Bazil Da Silva, who'd been shot twice by the time we worked together. He'd taken a bullet in his torso and another in the arm, as well as machete blows to his trunk.

Overall, the routine that faced these cops wasn't as difficult as it was demanding. The air component was headed by René Coulon, a fifty-something South African Police Services (SAPS) Senior Superintendent in command of Durban's Air Wing, KwaZulu/Natal. Married with five children, René originally flew choppers in the South African Air Force in Angola and in his 'new' job; he'd been chasing criminals for more than a decade.

Louis De Waal, another Senior Superintendent in command of the Cape Town SAPS Air Wing, flew up specially to lend a hand with one of his unit's Hughes 500s. Together with the balance of the air component, almost everybody was billeted at the Bridge Hotel in Winterton in the Natal Midlands. The rest of us stayed at what was probably the best little bed and breakfast joint in the region.

Susan le Grange took very good care of us at Lilac Lodge where her dinners were always home-cooked and exquisite, which was unusual for a low-key countryside tourist establishment. Her food was good enough for the SAPS guys to eschew most of what was on offer at their hotel and, instead, eat with us.

Then, before first light each morning, we'd head out towards the east in the choppers, the trucks having set out from base two hours before. At a predetermined RV – we tended to use different ones most days – the operation would start almost immediately.

The Hughes 500s that we used were all fitted with American spraying machines developed by an Oregon company. Compact, practical and light, they are used world-wide in drug operations – including those in Afghanistan to counter the annual poppy harvest. The systems are also used in more conventional agricultural pursuits, for which they were originally designed.

It was rare that we didn't spot fields of dagga along the way as soon as we got away from the settlements. Sometimes there were scores of them, mostly secreted alongside the occasional river that we'd cross while

A police helicopter in a marijuana field in KwaZulu/Natal: there are thousands such marijuana growth points in Southern Africa, much of the produce going to a burgeoning European drug market. (Will Henshaw)

heading east towards the coast. The pilots would arrive at their temporary base where the rest of gang was waiting, then fuel up and get started.

The chemicals they used were potent. Any marijuana plant sprayed was dead in minutes. Once contaminated, the plants couldn't be harvested: they were tainted and consequently 'out of the chain' as it was phrased by René Coulon.

The Police Wing handling this side of things in South Africa has expanded exponentially with demand. From a handful of helicopters a few years ago (which included the ultra-rigid and now-outdated Eurocopter BK-105s) the number of six-seater AS-350 Squirrels in SAPS livery are currently into double-figures. There are also Eurocopter BK-117s that can uplift ten passengers. Their presence stems from a joint project involving Eurocopter and the Kawasaki group.

The BK-117s have been remarkably successful, Eurocopter having built more than 400 machines since the late 1970s, with quite a few of them finding their way to Africa. With its maximum range of more than 300 nautical miles and capacity of two crew-plus-four, this helicopter has seen use in a lot of anti-drug operations.

Additionally, there were the Hughes-500s deployed. These were

During a three-week operation in Northern KwaZulu/Natal – or what the history books tell us was formerly Zululand – about 20-tons of marijuana was either destroyed by aerial spraying or recovered from caches. Partly financed by the American DEA programme, the South African Police do not have either the manpower or the helicopters to keep pace with the volume of drugs being produced. (Louis de Waal)

small, versatile machines that date back to when they were first employed in combat spotting in the Vietnam War. Thereafter, the 500 saw service in a variety of guerrilla wars that included El Salvador, Colombia, the Middle East and elsewhere.

Many of the choppers in service with the SAPS Air Wing were originally acquired with subsidies from the UN Drug Agency, as well as with cash outlays from the US Food and Drug Administration (FDA), which for quite a few years has been involved in training South African drug eradication teams.

Current anti-drug operations south of the Limpopo – which sometimes also include operations in the neighbouring states of Swaziland and Lesotho – have come a long way from efforts at eradication even a decade ago. Rural operations in those days often involved both the SAAF and the Police Air Wing.

In one programme, a few years ago, Pretoria set aside R3 million for an eight-day operation in northern KwaZulu/Natal. It included scores of police and military vehicles as well as Oryx (the upgraded, locally produced Super-Puma variant) and police helicopters. However, because finance was critical, nothing was scheduled for eradicating the numerous dagga plantations in the area.

'There simply wasn't the money to do any more', said a senior security officer. 'In any event,' he added, 'you have to recognize that there are those in authority who are not happy that a sector of the community might be deprived of a traditional means of earning a living . . . it's often their rural relatives growing it . . .'

We found dagga in abundance throughout the region, but almost all of those plantations were ignored. In a raid near the convergence of the KwaZulu, Swazi and Mpumalanga borders in the vicinity of Pongola, a single BO-105 detected four major dagga plantations with the combined value of the crops estimated to be excess of $3m on the European market. At the ruling exchange rates of the day, that was almost six times more than the cost of that particular law enforcement operation. Of the five or six major growth points uncovered (two were more than three-acres in extent) only one patch was ripped out and burnt.

Then – and today – uncovering such harvests can be dangerous work. Most of these plantations are huge and secreted in inaccessible hilly country. Their owners, aware that the authorities are on the lookout, go to a lot of effort to camouflage their approach paths.

One plantation was uncovered by chance when a mounted SAPS anti-stock-theft unit ventured into a heavily foliated krantz in search of stolen cattle. Having discovered several fields of verdant six- or eight-foot high crops that were on the verge of being harvested, the four-man patrol came under fire. The SAAF was called to the rescue and the patrol was extricated, but only after one of the men was wounded.

What has become clear – following recent security incursions into the region – is the emergence of a powerful anti-establishment mindset that underlies sentiment throughout the region. Local residents simply don't appreciate having their principal source of wealth 'eliminated'. In recent years, there have been firefights involving dagga growers and the police, as well as with some military units.

In another attack on a squad in the process of destroying a marijuana plantation near Mkuze, the police came under Kalashnikov fire for more than an hour. The matter wasn't resolved and an SAAF

Oryx with a back-up force was brought in, again to extricate the group. None of this activity ever made the news.

In a bid to disguise large-scale illicit activities, there are many KwaZulu villages – even as far south as the outskirts of Durban and parts of the South Coast – that grow their own patches of the drug. Some are quite extensive, as any private pilot who regularly traverses the area will confirm.

These little plots – usually between 50ft and 100ft square – can often be clearly seen, the dagga usually planted between regular crops. Though the majority of these mini-marijuana plantations are in full view of circling helicopters or small aircraft, the inadequately manned police force most times ignores them if it is clear that it is for 'own use'. Obviously, even a modest crop grown on 5,000 square feet will deliver a sizeable amount of the drug: so, one must ask, who's kidding whom?

While cultivating the plant, officially, is a crime, a member of SAPS media relations in Durban told me that 'we don't exactly turn a blind eye, but if we aren't circumspect, we'd have to arrest just about every other Zulu farmer in the province. Examine it for yourselves – just about every other plot in the interior has its dagga plants.' It was a tradition that went back centuries, he stated. Also, he conceded that it was impossible to stem the flow, adding that smaller patches of the drug offered poor returns compared to some of the more expansive, well-irrigated and cultivated stands in remoter parts. Some are said to be financed from abroad, but he wasn't prepared to elaborate on that point.

Another type of operation involving the Police Air Wing in KwaZulu/Natal is the ongoing search for stolen cattle. Some of these operations extend over areas of about 10,000 square miles. The one hunt on which I accompanied police units started near the town of Vryheid in the north of the province and steadily spread out northwards towards the Mozambique frontier. As it matured, its focus shifted towards the border of the neighboring country of Swaziland.

Most search activity took place in remote areas where the bush and undergrowth were dense. Being a semi-tropical region didn't help either. Also, the region was remote in places. Aircraft had gone down there in the past and it had sometimes taken weeks to recover them. A four-seater which crashed in bush terrain more than a decade ago was never found.

We left the Police Air Wing base adjacent to Durban's international airport before dawn on a clear Monday morning and headed directly north. For much of the journey we covered good agricultural lands straddled by the occasional surfaced highway.

However, then the infrastructure started to deteriorate. Good thoroughfares north of Ngoma gradually gave way to dusty side roads in the bush. Finally, we were left with a succession of obscure tracks that snaked through the hills.

Most of the Zulu villages that came into view were modest and consisted of a few grass huts and a kraal for cattle. This is still a part of Africa where a man's wealth is dictated by the number of cows he owns. That and the number of wives he can afford to maintain. Both are traditional touchstones of status within this largely tribal society.

The region between Zululand's great Tugela River and the Pongola seems to have always been beset with security problems in the past. In places such as Tugela Ferry, strangers – and people in uniform, especially – are at risk if they go in there at night.

These are communities that are subdivided into more clans, fiefdoms and dynasties than anybody has bothered to list. It is also a society that has an unusually long memory: an innocuous, off-hand insult made long ago might, for the moment, be put aside, but it is never forgotten. As a consequence, inter-tribal factional killings are commonplace.

The Task Force plan was for SAPS elements – operational in Northern Natal with the South African National Defence Force (SANDF) for the duration – to link up with a combined force of about 250 army, police, air force and civil defence 'volunteers', some of whom were deployed adjacent to the Swazi border. Also involved was the Swaziland Police Force who, for the first time, was operational on South African soil; from past experience, some of the cattle likely to be recovered had been stolen in Swaziland. It was to be a ten-day operation against what were termed 'lawless elements' from both countries.

While the job of the main section was to recover livestock, security elements used the opportunity to search for criminals as well as gangs, escaped prisoners, illegal weapons, firearms 'factories' and, finally, gunrunners. The region remains a conduit for weapons smuggled into South Africa from neighbouring territories.

If time allowed, we were told, the force would destroy whatever marijuana plantations were spotted from the air. However, it was suggested that this was low on the priority list.

Apart from our own 105s, a single air force Oryx was dispatched as back-up from Waterkloof Air Force base near Pretoria. The main ground force was transported by the Air Wing, together with an assortment of about a dozen army vehicles, including Buffel troop carriers which, interestingly, are making a comeback on some Natal estates. Farmers are buying this surplus military equipment privately, largely for home protection, as well as for use against stock theft gangs.

In order to stay within budget, most of the men – air crews included – brought their own food. The total cost of the ten-day entire operation to the security forces was roughly R3m, or about US$300,000 at the 2010 rates of exchange.

By comparison, a similar-sized operation in Europe or America would easily have cost that per day, never mind the cost of additional logistical components.

Law is enforced a little differently in Africa, to which former Colonel Craig Mackrory can testify. Mackrory was a veteran of a succession of South Africa's battles in Namibia and cross-border raids into Angola, and thereafter, the SAPS Air Wing. Since superseded by Senior Superintend René Colon, he is no longer with the Air Wing, having moved on to the more tranquil waters of one of the Indian Ocean islands.

A few years ago, flying a police helicopter around the Tugela Ferry area, he spotted a number of burning huts below. That was hardly unusual since there is often somebody burning somebody else's home somewhere in the region. On going closer, he was suddenly greeted by the spectacle of a heavily armed Zulu Impi or battalion, of about 600 men. Mackrory had been working the area long enough to recognize them as members of the Sijozeni Zulu clan, one of the most bellicose in the Kingdom

You don't often see a traditional Zulu regiment in South Africa any more. Impis are a legacy of centuries past and the great Zulu king Chaka and others before and after him. However, violence in the 'New' South Africa has tended to harden and to coalesce in tribal sentiments. The fact that this great African tribe has been reverting to its old ways, says much for the kind of brutality which has almost become a South African way of life.

This Impi, Mackrory noted – with their distinctive mottled brown and black shields and assegais glinting in the morning sun – were interspersed by some warriors carrying firearms. The group moved across a low knoll at the double, clearly expecting trouble.

As his chopper's glide path took him over the next hill, another Impi came into view. In-between there was all that was left of about a dozen burning huts. Bodies lay where they had been struck down. All of this destruction, he was to learn later, belonged to a second Zulu faction, the equally belligerent Ngcengeni clan.

There was nothing new about any of this, Mackrory suggested afterwards. Intelligence reports had been circulating back in Durban all week that the clans were itching for war. It seems that there were differences that needed to 'sorted out', which meant there would be killings.

As he pointed out, these might have included something as mundane as not honouring a *lobola* – the requisite bride price paid when a man takes a woman – or it could have been revenge killings for deeds that might have been committed half a century ago. 'Zulus have phenomenal memories', the colonel stated.

In South Africa's brief history of conflict it has always been an unwritten law that when the Zulus are on the march, they are best left alone. It is in the interests of the authorities to look elsewhere when Impis clash. Ignore that fundamental precept and it might be your brains that end up splattered across the countryside.

Tugela Ferry enjoys another special notoriety, because many of the criminals operating out of there are sometimes armed with automatic weapons. Many are Soviet AK-47s, smuggled across the border from Mozambique. Others might be regular South African Army carbines stolen during armed robberies in the country's big cities.

These weapons slot in well as crime continues to escalate in present-day South Africa. The age of the knobkerrie has been superseded – as any crook in Zululand will tell you, it's easier to shoot someone than beat him to death. Also, life is cheap, especially in a region where the daily wage is often as low as $5 a day, and sometimes half that, and that's if the labourer involved can get work.

Consequently, there are a lot of desperate men in this remote area a couple of hundred miles north-east of Durban.

So it was that Mackrory was suddenly faced with a potential crisis, involving almost a thousand Zulu warriors, who had already left a number of tribesmen dead. Also, he was very much aware that the two groups had deadly intent and if something wasn't done, there could be a lot more of them killed, women and children, too. His job, as a police officer, was to try to put a stop to it.

He flew low over the next hill. Moments later he banked and headed back towards the two Zulu regiments. First some of the Ngcengeni scattered. Then a few of the Sijozeni militants gave way. By the time he had gained enough height to try to make an assessment, both groups had started to regroup. Because the local police station was only a few minutes away by vehicle, Mackrory made a last pass over the Impis. Meanwhile, he radioed base. Time was short, he stressed and while this wasn't exactly war, it was close.

The South African Police Services BO-105 helicopter, while ideal for police 'search and spot' work, was never intended to be employed as a trooper. Normally this chopper carries a crew of two, heat and height permitting.

'So I had to act pretty smartly,' Mackrory recalls. 'By now, I'd been speaking to the ground commander. We decided even before I'd landed that we needed to get some of our guys between the two groups. Obviously that was a tricky option but it was worth a try', he reckoned.

As soon as I touched down, two of our guys were waiting to board. Each was armed with R4 rifles, standard SADF issue in .223 caliber. That was all very well, but we were aware that the two groups probably had quite a few AKs of their own. The more immediate problem, once these first two men had been dropped, was that they'd be isolated in the middle of two groups of fighting men. Worse, the majority were tanked up and the rest high as kites on pot.

It was clear that they'd been partying all night in anticipation of the battle. It was imminent, he radioed base.

'While there was a slim chance that nothing would happen until I was able to bring in more troops, we faced the prospect of the two groups moving in on them,' Mackrory explained.

Finally, after he flown 20 more police across from the station, it was all over bar the shouting. Observing small squads of well-equipped para-military police being dropped along several high points that surrounded the potential killing grounds caused the warriors to think twice. That was when the two groups started to disperse.

The colonel believes that his initially buzzing the two groups possibly helped to disorientate them. 'Also, many Zulus had served in the army in Angola . . . they probably weren't certain whether the BO-105 was armed like a helicopter gunship. Of course we weren't. But it helped to have a few gun-barrels protruding out of the open door while we circled . . .'

South African security services have been fighting a low-intensity struggle in the lush farmlands of KwaZulu/Natal for quite a few years. As in Northern Ireland, issues are intense enough to sometimes involve the army and the South African Air Force. Arriving at the scene of some of the battles afterwards, the authorities might find eight dead in one village, 20 in another. Then, a week or six months later, another attack: payback time.

Those not hacked to death in these vendettas are shot with a variety of firearms, many of them homemade. Some are so basic that any firearms specialist might regard them as hazardous to fire. However, since these guns can be made in any backyard and are being used in domestic crimes, personal attacks and robberies, it's important to take a close look at them.

As one ballistics specialist declared: all are lethal. Many are adaptations of the ubiquitous American 'Saturday Night Special'.[2] Others are cheeky adaptations of 12-bore shotguns, which have been the most popular weapon of choice in less-developed regions because of the spread of fire. Used at close range they are almost always deadly as, in close quarters, it is difficult to miss whether you are high or not. More significant to the perpetrators, the rationale among those using shot-shell is that there are few tell-tale ballistic 'fingerprints' for the police to work on afterwards. About half the weapons brought in while I worked with the police were shotguns. Ammunition was plentiful: just about every farmhouse has a box or two of shells.

Quite a few members of the police with whom I was associated during several tours of operation in South Africa had taken fire from improvised weapons. One police officer had a Remington 870, 12-bore shotgun fired at his chest at a range of a few feet. Even though he was wearing body armour, it knocked him out cold. Apart from a bruise the size of a plate that stayed with him for months, he wasn't badly hurt. A foot higher, he reckoned, and he would have taken it in the face.

There is no question that, despite an increased security presence in KwaZulu/Natal, dissident groups are active in the territory and as long as the SAPS hunt them, they are obliged to turn to their own resources to acquire more weapons, which has resulted in many remarkable adaptations.

Technical expertise, while basic, is largely Heath-Robinson. It rarely involves machines. In the mountains, where most of the workshops are situated, there is often no electricity and tools can be as basic as a hammer, a hacksaw and a file, together with an *umfaan* to provide the muscle to drive a set of cowhide bellows over a primitive charcoal fire.

One starting pistol I was allowed to handle had been made into an effective single-shot weapon. It was .22 long-rifle calibre and had been used in a political assassination that was big news at the time. A prominent member of the largely Zulu Inkatha political establishment had been shot behind the ear from point blank range. The man died instantly.

Using some of the weapons was nothing short of perilous. One or two had fairly large gaps between the receiver and the barrel. In some, the cartridges were so loose-fitting that the gun emitted a sheet of flame from the breech.

'Often, if the piping is too big for the cartridge, a short length of wire is wound around the base of the brass to keep it in position' my source, Mike P., a veteran police ballistic expert, stated. This was often the case with 9mm Parabellum pistols.

The most basic system employed by these improvisers was to have two lengths of piping, one that fitted neatly into the other. A small, sharp piece of metal – the firing pin – would be soldered to one end and with the cartridge in place, you literally banged one end against the other. Obviously, you needed to be sure where the barrel was pointing just then.

'Tricky, but it works, though not always if you've been drinking, which is often the case', said Mike P. Also, you had to know how to hold it. Fingers had been severed in the past by not paying enough attention at that critical moment.

A new development, he said, had been to take toy pistols or revolvers, drill out the barrels to make them look authentic and use them in bank hold-ups, for which South Africa is now the acknowledged world leader. If, for instance, an AK is not available, the 9mm Para is still the preferred calibre. Another armourer reckoned that such basic devices would work for five or six rounds, after which the barrel tended to split.

The best homemade weapons, it was generally accepted in Natal were made by a fugitive known to the police as 'Dum-Dum' Dumisane. He was appropriately named. Having eluded the police for years, he taught his associates how to nip off the tip of a bullet to create more serious wounds.

Dumisane was also a shotgun boffin. One of his creations was recovered while I was still around. It was 12-guage and was fired as a handgun. Those who have tried it have said that you needed strong wrists!

Curiously, there are an astonishing number of military carbines about – AKs, South African Army R4s in 5.56mm calibre (the South African hybrid of the Israeli Galil), an occasional FN 7.62mm, often left-over from Rhodesia's guerrilla war, or a former Portuguese Army G3 – also in 7.62mm calibre – that might have been brought across the border from Mozambique. As army-backed police operations start to take effect, this illegal arsenal is thinning, but as long as supply doesn't keep pace with demand, more guns will arrive from somewhere.

Most of the people living in South Africa's embattled zones agree. Barely a week goes by when farmers and, increasingly, their families, aren't killed or wounded in road ambushes or attacks on isolated homesteads. Many of those involved maintain that as the attacks increase – with scores of rural people killed each year – it's little more than a concerted effort to drive them off their properties. They point to the fact that along the foothills of the Drakensberg Mountains, Mpumalanga (formerly Eastern Transvaal), Limpopo to the north and elsewhere, some farms have already been abandoned by their former owners, especially those with young families.

What is certain is that the hyperbole associated with the killings has been heightened by the death toll. It's difficult to police a situation barely a step removed from anarchy.

Over the years the SAPS Air Wing has had many experiences involving shoot-outs with criminals, such as the time, shortly before the Tugela Ferry incident, when the Air Wing was called upon to react to a fire-fight on the coastal road north of Durban. Because it was election time, political tempers were frazzled.

Then, while trying to arrest the occupants of a stolen car, a police unit in the Umzinto area, to the south of Durban came under sustained AK-47 fire. Barely 30 minutes before that, an armed gang had robbed a store, which is why the alert had gone out in the first place.

Shortly afterwards, explained one of the officers:

we were told that the group had originally been linked to *Inkonto we Zizwe* – the military wing of the African National Congress – a grouping not always favourably regarded by people of Zulu extraction. If that were the case, one of the offices confided, these people were dangerous. They would possibly have received military training abroad.

About 20 minutes later, a police helicopter arrived over the scene. The pilot spotted three men armed with AKs in a sugar-cane field below, almost surrounded by a squad of security personnel. Circling, he ventured lower. Suddenly the helicopter shuddered. Then it happened again, almost as if somebody were banging on the fuselage with a hammer. There was no mistaking the impact of bullets, some of which had struck his rotor.

'The 105 started to vibrate and I knew that we'd been hit. But when a round struck my joy stick, I looked for a clearing to put down.'

The fire-fight ended after two of the robbers had been killed and the third wounded. There were seven guns between them, including three AKs together with almost a thousand rounds of ammunition. The police officer said he was lucky to be alive because of the volume of fire had been intense. Only later were they able to establish that the bullet that hit his joystick had exited the cockpit within a whisker's-breadth of his face.

While flying police choppers in South Africa might not be everybody's idea of fun, it has its moments.

In one of the several occasions that I was with the Police Air Wing operating out of Durban, we were involved in car chases. There was also a body search along a remote river valley off the Tugela River after a flash flood, where we found a cadaver and airlifted it out. That was followed by a couple of robberies that left criminals dead and, ultimately, the recovery of three men killed on a mountaintop. These were all black Eastern Cape farmers who had been gunned down in an ambush by soldiers of the Lesotho Armed Forces.

The three men were part of a 26-strong group of local 'vigilantes' who had been frustrated by government inaction following earlier stock raids out of the neighboring country and decided to do something about it themselves. They'd been following stock thieves who, with the stolen herd, had moved over the mountains into Lesotho.

Although the bodies lay across an international divide, it was left to one of the 105s to haul them out. That too was touch and go because Lesotho at the time was still smarting from a South African military invasion that had left 60 Basotho nationals and eight South African troops dead.

As for the future of the South African Police Air Wing, nobody is certain where it is heading. The respective squadrons are still up and kind of running in all the major urban centres, but African politics has played a significant hand in thinning the numbers of professional aviators.

Senior Police Superintendent René Coulon arrived back at the Air Wing to find that a former desk sergeant with no experience either in flying helicopters or in aviation generally had been appointed over his head. He queried the issue with Police Headquarters in Pretoria and was peremptorily told that the woman was effectively 'running the show'. No explanation was given and nor did René ask for one. He submitted his resignation from the force the same day. Then, just before the 2010 World Cup, he was reinstated. Things seem to happen that way in Africa. Other officers to whom I spoke mentioned similar problems. The government wants more black pilots and whether they are professionally qualified or not, they will hire these individuals. Already there have been some serious accidents and as a consequence, lives have been lost.

Postscript

Clay lies still, but blood's a rover,
Breath's aware that will not keep,
Up, lad, when the journey's over,
There'll be time enough to sleep.
A. E. Housman

Endnotes

Prologue

1. After leaving the Rhodesian Army, Nicholas Della Casa spent some time travelling around South Africa. One journey took him into Botswana where he left a locked trunk with a friend. He didn't disclose that it contained military items, including explosives, at a time when security in Southern Africa was at an almost paranoiac level. Once Nick had left Botswana, his friend's house was one of several raided by the Botswanan Police. The baggage was opened, the stuff found and the man charged. As a consequence, he was to spend time in a Botswanan prison. Yet, a simple letter from Nicholas to the Botswanan public prosecutor – Nicholas was abroad at the time, so they wouldn't have been able to touch him – could have circumvented this disaster. Instead, without good reason, he chose to do nothing.

2. Al J. Venter, *War Dog: Fighting Other People's Wars*, Casemate Publishers, US and UK 2006, pp 445–460

3. Chris Munnion, *Banana Sunday*, Ashanti Publishers, Sandton, 1992. This is a marvelous book that encompasses a wealth of stories collected by the author from journalists who worked the African beat, as well as other Third World outposts of the former Empire.

4. Peter Younghusband, *Every Meal a Banquet, Every Night a Honeymoon*: Jonathan Ball Publishers, Cape Town, 2003

5. Arkady Babchenko, *One Soldier's War in Chechnya*, Portobello Books, London, 2007. This book, though harsh and uncompromising, is a brilliant exposition of this kind of experience. It should be required reading for everybody going to war.

6. Jennifer Crwys-Williams, *Despatches – The Best of Two Centuries of South African Journalism*, Ashanti Publishing, Johannesburg, 1990

Chapter One: Getting to a Lebanon at War

1. Robert Fisk, *Pity the Nation: Lebanon at War*, Oxford University Press, Oxford, 2001

2. I deal with the revolutionary role of the Pasdaran, which became the forerunner of present-day Hizbollah, as well as its role of fostering terror both in the Middle East and the West, in great detail in my book *Iran's Nuclear Option*, Casemate Publishers, Philadelphia, 2005, cht 12, pp 253 *et seq*

Chapter Two: Levantine Woes

1. Al J. Venter, 'General Lahoud's Rise to Power', *Middle East Policy*, Washington DC, Volume VI, Number 2, October 1998

2. As the civil war progressed and car-bombs became commonplace, that situation changed radically. Although there are few cities as clogged as Beirut (parking had always been impossible, anyway) all Christian hotels started using security

barriers for protection and we often had to look elsewhere. When that happened, you needed a permit to get anywhere close to the main structure: that meant more questions, more controls. The cycle was eternal, with one means of destruction supplanting another as soon as solutions were devised to counter them.

Chapter four: Lagos and an Army Mutiny
1   Only after the Biafran War was the Nigerian capital moved to Abuja, a totally artificial city erected in the jungle that emulated what had taken place years before with Brasilia.

Chapter five: Biafra: The Build-Up
1.   Other countries involved in boundary disputes that led to conflict in the post-independence years included Uganda and Kenya, who had differences over the Mount Elgon area of East Africa; Chad and Libya; both Congos (involving differences about who owned the oil-rich enclave of Angolan Cabinda); Botswana and Zimbabwe, who were involved in shooting matches over territory along the Upper Zambezi; Morocco and Algeria (Polisario claimed stretches of former Spanish Sahara); and, perhaps the bloodiest feud of all, which took place quite recently between Ethiopia and Eritrea, and which claimed tens of thousands of lives. The Bakassi issue continues to fester and both Nigeria and the Cameroon have moved troops close to their respective frontiers.

Chapter six: Survival in a West African Conflict
1.   Al J. Venter, *War Dog: Fighting Other People's Wars*, Casemate Publishers, US and UK, 2006
2.   *Qat* or *Khat* is a DEA-classified drug that contains the alkaloid cathinone, an amphetamine-like stimulant which causes excitement and euphoria. About 70 per cent of the population of Africa's Horn and many people in the Yemen are addicted to it.

Chapter nine: A Central American Conflagration
1.   Al J. Venter, *The Chopper Boys: Helicopter Warfare in Africa*, Stackpole Books (US), Greenhill Books (UK) and Southern Books (South Africa), 1994

Chapter ten: Somalia: Wars of No Consequence
1.   Introduction to Chapter 29, Al J. Venter, *The Chopper Boys: Helicopter Warfare in Africa* Stackpole Books (US), Greenhill Books (UK) 1994

Chapter fourteen: Israel's Border Wars
1.   Robin Wright, *Sacred Rage: The Wrath of Militant Islam*, Andre Deutsch, London, 1986

Chapter seventeen: Bounty Hunt in Rhodesia
1.   Al J. Venter, *The Zambezi Salient*, Robert Hale, London, 1974
2.   Al J. Venter, *War Dog: Fighting Other People's Wars*, Casemate Publishers, US and UK, 2006, pp 217–222
3.   During the Rhodesian War, the colloquial term for guerrilla or insurgent

fighter was 'terr', an abbreviation of the word terrorist.

4.   Jerky made from the African kudu, which after the Eland was the second-largest antelope on the continent

5.   Government-controlled 'Protected Village' or strongpoint, similar to the *Aldeamentos* system in Portugal's wars in Africa.

Chapter nineteen: Zaire: Road to an African War

1.   Al J. Venter, *The Terror Fighters*, Purnell, Cape Town, 1969

2.   For those not familiar with Afrikaans, the English translation of 'kak' is shit.

Chapter twenty-one: Jailed for Espionage

1.   An aside made to the author in Lagos in the 1970s by Angus McDermid who covered East, Central, South and West Africa for the BBC World Service from 1959 to 1972.

Chapter twenty-three: Kill all Infidels – *Allahu Aqbar*!

1   Al J. Venter, 'President Lahoud's Rise to Power', *Middle East Policy*, Washington DC: Volume VI, Number 2, October 98

2   Paula A. deSutter, 'Denial and Jeopardy: Deterring Iranian Use of NBC Weapons; National Defense University, Washington DC, 1997

3   Like al-Qaeda, Hizbollah has long maintained that since Israel is a nuclear power, only the ability to retaliate with nuclear weapons would achieve the desired objective of 'wiping the Zionists off the map' as it is so often phrased in both the Iranian *Majlis* (Parliament) and on Hizbollah's radio and al-Maneer TV networks.

4   The author deals with the Iran-Iraq War in detail in *Iran's Nuclear Option*, Casemate Publishers, Philadelphia, 2005, cht 2, pp 45–66

Chapter 24: Tete Convoy in Mozambique

1   Al J. Venter, *Africa at War*, Devin Adair, Greenwich, Connecticut, 1973

Chapter 26: The Balkan Beast: Landmines in Croatia

1   Armor Express, 1554 East Torchlake Drive, Central Lake, MI 04966; Phone (231) 544-6090

Chapter 28: Helicopter Drug Raids in Zululand

1   The membranes of certain nerve cells in the brain contain protein receptors that bind to THC. Once securely in place, THC kicks off a series of cellular reactions that ultimately lead to the high that users experience when they smoke marijuana.

2   'Saturday Night Special' is American law enforcement terminology for an inexpensive and usually badly made firearm, often produced in bulk with ill-fitting parts, but still able to kill somebody. While a quality pistol or revolver might cost $600 or more if legally acquired from a registered gun dealer, gangs in the United States are able to buy 'Saturday Night Specials' on the street, sometimes for as little as $100.

Acknowledgments

T HE FULFILMENT OF A BOOK of this magnitude involves the pulling together of many minds. It started with Madelon, long before I laid the almost-complete manuscript before David Farnsworth, my publisher in Philadelphia. She followed the progress of the book from early on and, while rarely effusive about my scribblings, she declared after her first read that this was the one that would work. She reckoned it was my best book yet and I suspect she might be right. Farnsworth passed the manuscript to Stephen Smith, his chief copy-taster, and he loved it. After putting the project in the hands of my agent, Curtis Russell, in Toronto, Casemate was ready to go.

A lot of things still had to come together before we reached the stage at which we actually had something tangible. These included the illustrations and Bruce Gonneau in Durban played a critical role in scanning hundreds of slides and negatives and sending them abroad. More photos arrived from people like Charlie Cole of *Newsweek*; Dave McGrady who organised the bounty hunt in Rhodesia; Harry Claflin, with whom I shared a bunkhouse at the Ilopango air base in San Salvador; Louis de Waal and René Coulon, both of whom head Police Air Wings in South Africa; my old friend Richard Davis, with whom I went into the Balkans on that crazy adventure involving landmines; and the indomitable Jaco Ackerman who, with my old friend Brian Gaisford in New York, organised the Serengeti safari.

Without Walter Volker and Manie Troskie taking care of some of the groundwork for me from South Africa, I might have floundered.

One individual above all others stands out. That is Anita Baker, my editor, who took this work in hand and produced what you have before you. With a huge amount of detail, it was never an easy job, but Anita completed the job in half the time that it normally takes to cobble together 500 pages.

My lovely Marilyn put up with me through a good deal of it in Sault Sainte Marie in Canada and, certainly, that needed a lot of patience. Finally, I would be remiss if I didn't thank Susan Sizemore of Seaside, Oregon, for her efforts involving research when I most needed them.